The Countryside

*Ten Rural Walks Through Britain and
Its Hidden History of Empire*

CORINNE FOWLER

SCRIBNER

New York   London   Toronto   Sydney   New Delhi

Scribner

An Imprint of Simon & Schuster, LLC

1230 Avenue of the Americas

New York, NY 10020

Originally published in Great Britain in 2024 by Allen Lane as
Our Island Stories: Country Walks Through Colonial Britain

First Scribner hardcover edition June 2024

SCRIBNER and design are trademarks of Simon & Schuster, LLC

Simon & Schuster: Celebrating 100 Years of Publishing in 2024

For information about special discounts for bulk purchases, please contact Simon &
Schuster Special Sales at 1-866-506-1949 or business@simonandschuster.com.

The Simon & Schuster Speakers Bureau can bring authors to your live event. For
more information, or to book an event, contact the Simon & Schuster Speakers
Bureau at 1-866-248-3049 or visit our website at www.simonspeakers.com.

Maps designed by Neil Gower

Manufactured in the United States of America

1 3 5 7 9 10 8 6 4 2

Library of Congress Cataloging-in-Publication Data has been applied for.

ISBN 978-1-6680-0397-8
ISBN 978-1-6680-0399-2 (ebook)

To my fellow walkers: Sathnam Sanghera, Graham Campbell, Ingrid Pollard, Peter Kalu, Bharti Parmar, Charlotte Williams, Raj Pal, Zakia Sewell, Ibrahima Seck and Louisa Adjoa Parker.

'Did you not hear me ask him about the slave-trade last night?'

'I did – and was in hopes the question would be followed up by others. It would have pleased your uncle to be enquired of farther.'

'And I longed to do it – but there was such a dead silence!'

Jane Austen, Mansfield Park, 1814

Contents

1. Jura and Jamaica

3. Whitehaven
and Virginia

2. Grasmere
and Canton

4. Darwen, Mississippi
and Surat

5. Dolgellau and
the Americas

6. The Cotswolds
and Bengal

7. Norfolk
and Grenada

Pangbourne
and India

8. Hampshire
and Louisiana

10. Cornwall and
the Americas

9. Tolpuddle, Australia
and Barbados

Preface

The British countryside occupies a special place in the national imagination. Long seen as a place of idyllic seclusion and retreat from urban life, the countryside symbolizes the soul of Britain. Well over a century ago the poet A. E. Housman, while working in London, saw the Shropshire hills as a 'land of lost content', a place of almost prelapsarian innocence. For many today, the countryside – its fields, its picturesque villages, its stately homes surrounded by their beautifully landscaped grounds – represents something steadfast and reassuring, something that has existed since time immemorial. Indeed, it is hard to exaggerate the depth of feeling about the British countryside, which is attached to ideas of nationhood as though by an umbilical cord.

Given this, it can come as a surprise to find that the nation's uplands, shorelines, valleys, lakes, villages and fields were profoundly shaped by the colonial world: British[1] trade, conquest, economic activity and direct rule from the turn of the seventeenth century to the decline of empire in the early twentieth. But during these four centuries, the British countryside underwent profound change. Just as cities like Liverpool, Manchester and Birmingham grew into great, smoking, industrial conurbations, so colonialism also affected the remotest corners of the land: from small Cumbrian ports and Scottish islands to rural Norfolk and the depths of Cornwall.

We tend to think of rural Britain as detached from the history of empire but, if we look closely, our countryside speaks volumes about colonialism's distinctive phases, dimensions and impacts. It is easy to forget this, because each generation lives at an ever-greater historical remove from those times. Our education system supplied most of us with only a thin knowledge of British colonialism, especially its many historical and geographical variations. Now that we are being refamiliarized with this history, the topic has provoked unnecessary alarm in some quarters. These feelings are strong and personal. Yet we are faced with a choice: we can either embrace a full history of the British Isles or we can choose a partial, comforting version.

In this book of walks through the British countryside, I set out to discover the unique colonial connections of rural places. Embarking on such a journey requires some ground-clearing. For some, a book which connects the British countryside to colonialism may baffle and even offend.

British colonial history requires emotionally intelligent approaches. It triggers everything from ancestral trauma to actual denial. Depending on where you stand, learning about the British Empire can be disorientating, painful or revelatory, sometimes a combination of all three. For this reason, knowledge is not something to be weaponized but to be shared. To explore how colonial activity transformed the countryside is to understand that rural places reflect Britain's imperial past and diverse present more than we realize.

As a professor of colonialism and heritage, I have a longstanding interest in the way empire intersects with country houses in particular, and rural history more broadly. Despite having presented the evidence in calm and respectful ways, the hostile response from British politicians and journalists makes me all too aware how sensitive a topic colonial history is. This opposition to public discussions about colonial history intensified when, in 2020, the statue of the seventeenth-century merchant and politician Edward Colston was toppled by Black Lives Matter demonstrators. He was a deputy governor of the Royal African Company, and some 84,000 enslaved Africans were transported across the Atlantic under his watch. When – soon afterwards – the national focus on slavery history moved far inland from our old slave-ports to British country houses, some felt that our rural past itself was in jeopardy. Yet, in expanding and resourcing public understandings of the countryside's colonial past, we can tell our islands' stories and address colonial legacies from a position of knowledge rather than fear.

This book combines historical research with my love of the countryside. I had weekly childhood country walks with my parents and, as a student, I even did the thousand-mile walk from Scotland's northern-eastern tip, at John O'Groats, to England's south-western headland, Land's End. Then, as now, I found there are some amazing stories to tell about the earth beneath our feet. Consequently, I've designed walking routes for this book which pass through places which were changed by British colonial activity. Each walk is easily accessible and, should you be so inclined, you can do the walks yourself. Along each route, I explore the links between these local landscapes and the far-flung former colonies that did so much to shape them.

Colonial history is not just a collection of facts; we need to talk about the evidence so that we can process its meanings. Our current reassessment of Britain's colonial past is defined by our conversations about it. Wanting to convey some in-depth conversations about our colonial countryside, I chose ten walking companions who have ancestral connections to empire, and who enabled me to see the villages, hills and fields through which we walked in a new light: they have long explored the geographical and historical contours of these places.

For if we know where, and how, to look, these local histories of colonialism are frequently hidden in plain sight. From the Hebridean Isle of Jura, whose past intertwines with that of Jamaica, to the lanes of rural Dorset, resonant with their associations with Barbados and Australia, my walks take in the full range of colonialism's impacts on the British countryside. Along the way, they reveal the business ventures of William Wordsworth, his family and literary circle; the links between Welsh wool and African enslavement; and the connections between a Hampshire banking family and plantations worked by enslaved people in America's Southern states. Nothing, indeed, is more revealing than the names of rural regions and villages which proliferate wherever Britain's colonial activities spread. Jamaica alone bears witness to this history: from the plantations of Aberdeen and Culloden, to Kintyre District and Newport, Kendal, Devon, Islington,

Highgate, Richmond, Falmouth, Warwick, Windsor Castle, Cornwall, Cambridge and Middlesex. Just as colonized countries had new place names and identities thrust upon them, so were enslaved people's identities obscured when they were renamed after British places like 'Isle of Wight' and 'Whitehaven.'[2]

It's perhaps no surprise that many of the routes walked here are to be found on or within reach of Britain's western, Atlantic, coastline. Slaving ships sailed from Britain's Atlantic-facing ports to West Africa. They transported enslaved people to the West Indies and returned to Britain laden with plantation goods. Britain's ports played unique roles in this triangular trade, vastly enriching them in the process. Ships from Liverpool sailed to the Bight of Biafra and the coasts of Central West Africa to embark enslaved people for transportation to the West Indies and North America. Bristolian vessels, meanwhile, journeyed mainly to modern-day Angola and south-east Nigeria before undertaking their onward slaving voyages to the West Indies. Atlantic vessels from Northern England and western Scotland, en route to tobacco plantations in Maryland and Virginia, sailed around the Northern Irish coast to avoid attacks from enemy ships from European nations at war with Britain. The channel ports of Poole, Weymouth, Bridport and Lyme Regis along England's southern coast were all connected to slavery through exports like wool, for which there was unstinting demand in the colonies, and imports of commodities produced by slave labour.

Yet slavery was not just about the triangular trade between Britain, West Africa and the West Indies. It was a vast system which revolved around commodities like sugar, tobacco and cotton. The British slavery system involved banks, finance and insurance. It relied on transport, logistics, warehouses and industrial invention. Slavery brought wealth and inheritance to some. This money was reinvested in land and factories. It paid for political power, buildings, art, institutions, railways and much more. Infused into Britain's economic system, slavery – though largely geographically remote – was omnipresent and part of everyday life.

Some of these locations in which I walked still have a sense of true remoteness. Jura, an island in the Inner Hebrides off the west coast of Scotland, takes plenty of getting to. But, like many of the places here, it's sustained today by tourism: walkers and nature-lovers come to see its rich wildlife – stags, puffins and seals abound – and its Scotch: Jura is a site of whisky pilgrimage. Colonial history is everywhere to be found, from windswept Cumbrian coastal towns to the English Lakes, from Lancashire's classic cotton landscapes to Snowdonia's sheep-fields. I found that limestone Cotswold villages – packed with boutique hotels, delicatessens and ye olde pubs – have surprisingly strong links to the East India Company, whilst East Anglia is just one part of England to turn up links between Caribbean slavery and the long and inglorious history of enclosure, the legalized annexing of common land where people once grew crops, grazed animals and gathered firewood. So, too, did I trace the intercontinental journeys of agricultural labourers in south-western England, transported to British penal colonies in Australia and modern-day Tasmania because they tried to obtain better working conditions. Ending in Cornwall, as I once did as a student decades ago, I discovered the forgotten significance of Cornish copper mines to West Africa and to sugar plantations in the West Indies.

History, above all, is about people. Before I set off, it's worth reflecting on some uncomfortable truths about the British countryside and the values it represents. Consciously or not, a proprietorial sense of White, rural belonging is common. Even though, as I'll show in these pages, Black people have lived and worked in the British countryside for centuries, their presence today triggers negative reactions.[3] In 2021, when an episode of the BBC's *Countryfile* was devoted to a walking group called Black Girls Hike, there was a public outcry, with people saying that they didn't belong, that they didn't deserve a special programme being devoted to them or else that their feelings of unease when in the countryside were unfounded. The volume of complaints prompted the producer to defend the programme by explaining that minority groups are half as likely as White people to spend time in rural places.[4] On the same programme the Black adventurer and presenter Dwayne Fields said that Black people are sometimes unwelcome in the countryside, an observation that prompted another 575 complaints.[5] Trying to open up new perspectives on green spaces is similarly considered threatening: the television gardener James Wong came under media fire for explaining the links between botany and empire. Following this adverse coverage, Wong received death threats and was heavily trolled on social media.[6]

Yet, as it did then, British colonial history still touches us all. Inevitably, many people living in Britain today have ancestral connections to empire. My mother's family is French. Some of my ancestors were slave-owners on the Caribbean island of Haiti as well as East India Company sailors from Lorient in the northern French region of Brittany. My son is descended from Africans who were transported from Benin and the Congo by European slave-traders to Venezuela in South America.

My French ancestors built and profited from slavery. My son's African ancestors endured and resisted it. Europe's colonial story has not ended. It makes its effects known in the nations of former colonizers and colonized alike. Like almost everyone else growing up in twentieth-century Britain, the education system provided me with the faintest outline of colonial history, and it has taken me years to learn what I know now. These local country walks combine historical evidence and personal reflection to further illuminate how vast and varied the British Empire really was.

Finally, this book is offered as an antidote to brash posturing and the mutual incomprehension of people with different relationships to British colonial history. Through these companionable walks and conversations, I hope to shine new light on our past, by looking closely at the landscapes themselves. Exploring the history of Britain's countryside is not incompatible with a love for it. This new knowledge may be disturbing, shocking at times, but, rather than alienating us from the landscapes we all love, it can deepen our relationship with them.

We need to look at rural Britain differently. Its local histories reveal the cumulative effects of myriad colonial activities, whether that involved Virginian tobacco, maritime trade, slaving along the Gold Coast or South African gold mines. Whether it was battling in the tropics, owning plantations, opium-trading or plant-hunting, colonial engagements reshaped shires and counties across Britain. This book, and these walks, follow where the history leads. Readers familiar with the histories of British ports know that Glasgow thrived on sugar and tobacco and that Lancaster and Liverpool profited from sugar then cotton; they know that Manchester was dubbed 'Cottonopolis' and that Bristol was a slaving port. But the impacts of these port cities reached deep into the countryside. *The Countryside* explores ten such places to demonstrate how colonialism truly reshaped rural Britain.

The Countryside

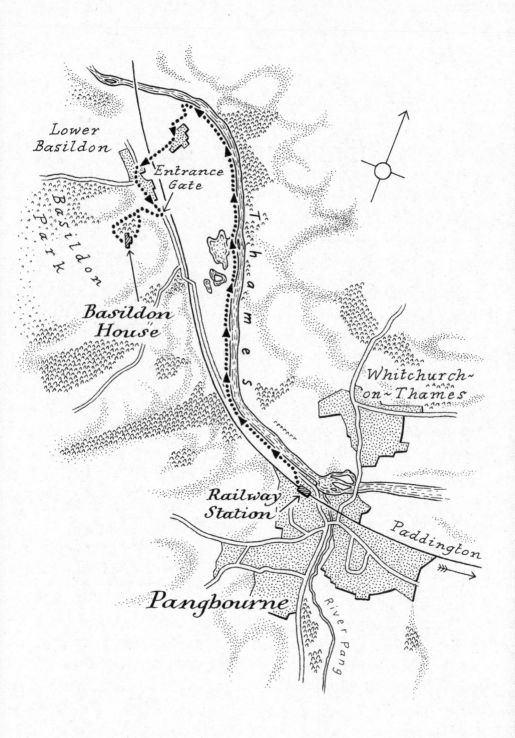

Lower
Basildon

Basildon Park

Entrance
Gate

Basildon
House

Thames

Whitchurch-
on-Thames

Railway
Station

Pangbourne

Paddington

River Pang

Introduction:
A Colonial History of the British Countryside

The southern English county of Berkshire is a pleasant land of water meadows, tranquil pastures and rolling hills. It's a landscape that puts me in mind of pastoral poems – frequently written from the perspective of country house proprietors or visitors – evoking the rural idyll, of countryside as paradise, and of the shepherd's life as the ideal career choice. Yet, secluded though its villages seem, Berkshire has always been within easy travelling distance of London. The River Thames, which flows right through it, brought people into the middle of the capital, and from there to the sea. For centuries, Berkshire was the perfect location for politicians and wealthy businesspeople and, though motorways and commuter trains have replaced boats and horses, so it remains today. Among the county's longstanding inhabitants are the royal family: Windsor Castle, with its expansive parks and forest, sits high above a bend in the Thames.

I took the train to Pangbourne, some 20 miles west of Windsor. Perched at the confluence of the Thames and the River Pang, the settlement is ancient: its name was first recorded in 844 CE. The Pang, which gives the village its name, is a tributary of the Thames, a chalk-stream which remains full of life despite the farm fertilizers, pesticides and sewage which pollute the local rivers. Voles still swim in its water meadows, just as they did when Kenneth Grahame used to go boating thereabouts in the early twentieth century. Along with other riverine creatures, the water vole appears as Ratty in Grahame's much-loved children's classic *The Wind in the Willows*, a book which re-enchanted generations of readers with the English countryside: its financial success enabled Grahame to retire to a gable-ended cottage in Pangbourne, where he lived until his death in 1932.

Crammed with listed buildings and expensive real estate, Pang-bourne has long attracted people with money: people in search of this bucolic idyll. In the eighteenth century, wealth flooded into Pangbourne, much of it linked to the East India Company. Founded in 1600 by English merchants to trade between Europe, South Asia and the Far East, it became far more than a trading company. Acquiring its own army, it fought rival East India Companies from the European powers such as France and Holland, competing for the lion's share of trade in spices, cotton, silk, indigo and saltpetre. The English – later British – East India Company established and defended warehouses, forts and trading posts all over India, including Bombay, Calcutta, Madras and Surat. Over time, it conquered territory, col-lected taxes and eventually colonized India. When East India Company employees had made their pile and returned home, many headed for the Thames valley – so many, in fact, that it became known as 'England's Hindoostan'.[1] A former governor of Madras lived 3 miles south of Pangbourne, at Englefield; the former gov-ernor of Bengal, Warren Hastings, had a residence at Purley Hall, a mile or so from the village.[2]

I had come to Pangbourne in search of one of these figures, Sir Francis Sykes. I planned to walk the riverside path along the Thames valley to Basildon Park, a landscaped and wooded estate surrounded by a handsome brick and flint wall and, within it, the house that Sykes built: a grand Palladian pile, constructed with the proceeds of his Indian adventures, and now owned by the National Trust. With me would come the historian Sathnam Sanghera, author of the influential *Empireland*, a personal journey into British colonial his-tory.[3] As we walked, we'd talk about Britain, India and the culture war into which our work had plunged us both.

It was a bright spring day after a winter of Covid lockdowns. I stood on the platform of Pangbourne station feeling like Mole in *Wind in the Willows*, emerging from his underground home and blinking in the sunlight. The station was empty and, waiting for Sathnam's train, I sat on a bench, warmed by the sun. Above the platform, white fascia boards reminded me of cricket pavilions. They were peeling and needed a lick of paint.

Sathnam was the only passenger to get off the train at Pangbourne. He made his way along the platform towards me, his rucksack on his back. He seemed lost in thought, so I waited for him to reach the station exit, where I stood. We'd met before at Powis Castle during the filming of his Channel 4 documentary *Empire State of Mind* about the legacies of colonialism and I later interviewed him in front of a literary festival audience in London. Though his expression was serious, as it often is, his accent immediately made me feel at home; we are both from the Midlands. 'I'm looking forward to this walk,' he said. I appreciated his enthusiasm and was little surprised that he turned out to be a good-natured walking companion, even lugging his heavy laptop around in the heat because there were no lockers at the station. He didn't complain once.

His book *Empireland* voices some uncomfortable truths about Britain's relationship with its imperial past. It met with both praise and, from some quarters, loud opposition. This opposition was sometimes couched in racial terms. Sathnam received letters and messages telling him to go back to where he came from if he didn't like British history: not, of course, to his home town of Wolverhampton, but to India. He was also dismissed by some as a figure on the extreme far left – which came as news to Sathnam, who writes for *The Times* newspaper, has voted for all three political parties and considers himself to be squarely in the centre of British politics. Even so, some of his more persistent detractors who would repeatedly turn up to his book events confronted him with hostile questions, following up with irascible correspondence. I personally witnessed this in action. During the London festival event that we did together, a man in the audience put his hand up and commented at length about how bad an author he thought Sathnam was. It turned out that this man was one of the people who lightly stalked Sathnam. 'Just wait for his letter,' Sathnam said. A letter duly arrived some days later, addressed to Professor Fowler and Mr Sanghera. I was a terrible interviewer, the letter complained, and Sathnam was lying about India. This happened at almost every event, and it was tiring and predictable, Sathnam said, 'Every. Single. Time.'

'Ready to set off?' I asked Sathnam as we exited the station. 'Let's go,' he replied. Then, following Mole, we set off for the riverbank and the Swan Inn, a pub with literary connections: it features in Jerome K. Jerome's classic travelogue *Three Men in a Boat*. Back in the late nineteenth century, Jerome described the surrounding countryside as 'glorious' and the pub as 'quaint'. Today, the scene is quainter still: its antique roof topped with mismatched tiles of amber and fox-red, the Thames running right past it. The inn was inviting, and we were tempted to stop and laze about with a drink, but, sticking to our walk, we set out on the riverside path towards Basildon Park estate, some 2 miles distant. It was Sathnam's first visit to Basildon Park. As we walked, I told him about the house's builder, Sir Francis Sykes. A West Yorkshireman, Sykes was not born into wealth. The East India Company offered unparalleled financial opportunities, and in 1751, like many at the time, he headed to Bengal to take up a job with the company. In India, Sykes' rise – like Hastings' – was meteoric. He became joint chief minister to the Nawab of Bengal, then an exceptionally powerful sovereign ruler. But Sykes' loyalties lay with the company rather than the Nawab, whose allegiance lay with the French, then competing with the East India Company for influence in Bengal. However, he sold this Nawab down the river by participating in secret negotiations with his enemy and successor. Sykes' actions allowed the company to beat the Nawab and his French allies in the 1757 Battle of Plassey, or Palashi. It was a decisive moment in Britain's relationship with India: the company gained tax-collecting powers over millions of people and took control of the Bengal treasury, which it depleted in the years that followed.[4] Sykes was richly rewarded for his role in Plassey.

Already well connected with the upwardly mobile Warren Hastings, with whom he traded privately in diamonds and other valuable commodities, Sykes was spotted by Robert Clive, commander-in-chief of the East India Company armies, who appointed him as Resident at the Court in Murshidabad and Chief at nearby Cossimbazar and also declared that Sykes 'might be thoroughly relied on'.[5]

Now Sykes oversaw tax collection in Bengal and Orissa, a lucrative and influential position. Continuing to trade extensively in tobacco, saltpetre, silk and timber, Sykes made his own fortune before returning to England to spend it.[6]

'The experience of Sykes matches the stories of many other wealthy East India Company officials,' Sathnam said as we continued along the Thames path, watching flickers of sunlight as the river rushed past us. To our left, straggles of pink Himalayan balsam smelled like ripe peaches and the heavy white heads of cow parsley bobbed in the breeze. 'I'm not surprised that people called Sir Francis the "nabob",' said Sathnam. We discussed the pejorative term, an English corruption of the Indian title *nawab*, given to Mughal rulers: it was used in Britain to express contempt for company returnees. Such contempt was public and widespread, and often deserved. In the late eighteenth century, the *Town and Country Magazine*, a popular periodical devoted to society scandal, defined a *nabob* as someone who had 'by art, fraud, cruelty, and imposition, obtained the fortune of an Asiatic prince and returned to England to display his folly and vanity and ambition'.[7] Men with Asian wealth, like Sir Francis Sykes, were figures of opprobrium – people suspected that they were corrupt – and they did their best to whitewash the dubious origins of their newly acquired wealth.

Sykes returned to England in 1769, aged thirty-nine, having amassed the breathtaking sum of around £700,000.[8] His East India wealth granted him entry into elite society, gaining him a coat of arms and a baronetcy. He cultivated the life of an aristocrat, acquiring three country estates, one in his native West Yorkshire, another in Dorset, and his third property was Basildon Park.[9] Ordering the old house there to be demolished, he commissioned a residence to reflect his status and ambition. The result was an imposing neoclassical mansion with a recessed Greek-style portico and an octagonal drawing room which overlooked wide terraces at the rear. Sykes also commissioned a kitchen garden designed by the fashionable landscape architect Lancelot 'Capability' Brown.

It was nearing lunchtime, the day was warm, and we were making good progress. Hawthorn bushes were in flower, and the meadows awash with buttercups: we half expected to stumble across Ratty. As we chatted about Basildon Park, our conversation gravitated naturally to the National Trust and its uphill struggle to tell the fuller histories of the properties in its care, like the one we were about to visit. Sathnam said, 'What happened with the National Trust report?' I told him the whole story. In 2020, I found myself in the middle of a major news story after co-authoring an audit of published academic research about the colonial histories of properties belonging to the Trust. Almost as soon as the report was released, I, my co-authors and the Trust itself were plunged into a culture war, with influential media figures and even politicians portraying us as public enemies and haters of British history: we were 'at war with the past', shouted one among many similar headlines.[10] 'Fury as National Trust vows to press on with "woke" review into colonial past,' read one headline, in an article quoting the politician Nigel Farage, who accused the National Trust of 'trashing' Britain's past.[11] 'It seems,' said a commentator for *Spiked* magazine, 'that while the National Trust is prepared to go to great lengths to guilt-trip visitors into feeling ashamed of British history and to push its volunteers into supporting woke causes, it is failing to do the task it was set up to do – to conserve historic buildings.'[12] 'These sorts of articles came out every few hours at the height of the coverage,' I told Sathnam. Inflammatory coverage of this nature sent an avalanche of hate mail my way. The question was, why?

Sathnam and I had previously talked about what prompted such extreme responses. Now, as we headed towards Basildon Park, an old couple passed us and doubtless caught snatches of our conversation: 'the status of British country houses . . . the pleasures of visiting them.' This, we agreed, was a major factor. As a nation, we love visiting these sumptuous properties: iconic heritage symbols in which fact blends with fiction, which are woven into our culture and consciousness. 'But we've also got plentiful evidence about the realities of how they were built,' Sathnam said, 'and how they worked.' This was true. We also have a vast body of literature, from Jane Austen's *Mansfield Park* and Charlotte Brontë's *Jane Eyre* to Evelyn Waugh's *Brideshead*

Revisited and Kazuo Ishiguro's *Remains of the Day*, that conveys the complexity and sophistication of country-house life and that, itself popular, has gone on to inspire heritage film and costume dramas which have gained international followings, from *Downton Abbey* to *Bridgerton*. Many visitors beat a path to Basildon Park because of its role in, among others, a film adaptation of Jane Austen's *Pride and Prejudice*[13] (and, perhaps bringing a different demographic, *Pride and Prejudice and Zombies*). Aside from their popularity as settings for film and TV, such houses are potent heritage symbols, their architecture, furnishings, libraries, galleries and landscaped grounds customarily praised for the cultural values they project: all designed to celebrate and radiate beauty.

Yet country estates like Basildon Park were once – and still are – about so much more than heritage. As status symbols, these massive houses solidified ideas of class and social hierarchies. Regional power hubs that were intimately linked to parliament, government and empire, these houses also dominated local lives. The vast estates that they oversaw transformed the landscape, establishing the patterns of British hedgerows, fields and roads.[14] The enclosed parklands that surrounded these magnificent houses were often gained through parliamentary Acts of Enclosure, which removed lands from common use by local people, destroying communities in the process. At Houghton Hall in Norfolk, a whole village was relocated to provide the house's occupants with uninterrupted pastoral vistas.

And, in very many cases – whether passed down through generations or newly acquired – these great houses also belonged to people of the world: politicians and legislators, colonial merchants and slave-owners, East India Company officials and administrators of empire. They used their newfound colonial wealth to create these lavish interiors, decorated with Chinese wallpaper, Indian silks and dazzling objects from all corners of the British Empire. Among the classical works in their libraries could be found books on Jamaican plantations or brightly illustrated descriptions of fauna and flora in far-off, now colonized, lands.

But, as Sathnam and I now remembered, simply making these

connections was to invite a wave of hostility. A few weeks after the 2020 National Trust report was released, a group of fifty-nine Conservative MPs and peers calling themselves the Common Sense Group declared a 'Battle for Britain' against 'subversives fuelled by ignorance and an arrogant determination to erase the past and dictate the future'.[15] The group's leader, Sir John Hayes, condemned the report as 'unpatriotic'. After the Conservative MP Jacob Rees-Mogg had denounced the report for 'denigrating British history', two parliamentary debates were held about the National Trust.[16]

As a named co-author of the Trust report, I felt the full force of this backlash. Angered by the report, the Common Sense Group homed in on my Colonial Countryside project, a child-led history and writing project steered by historians. Run in partnership with the Trust, it enabled 100 pupils to study country houses' colonial histories, write essays, give talks and tours, curate exhibitions and attend a children's history conference. Now, the Common Sense Group demanded that my funders – the Arts Council and Heritage Lottery Fund – not pay for any future project of mine because it was illegal to spend public money on what they called 'political projects'. This, in their view, fell into that category.[17]

All of which prompted what felt like fairly kneejerk responses. After the Charity Commission had investigated the National Trust for having brought the charity sector into disrepute – the Trust was vindicated – a Freedom of Information request later discovered that the Commission had opened its investigation on the basis of just three complaints.[18] And when, in 2022, the Conservative MP Andrew Murrison set up an all-party parliamentary group to scrutinize the National Trust's plans to incorporate colonial history into accounts of its properties, the Trust itself was not invited to participate.

One of the report's most powerful opponents was the journalist and author Baron Charles Moore of Etchingham, who protested: 'Why should I pay a hundred quid [subscription] a year [to the National Trust] to be told what a shit I am?'[19] But, in the view of many historians, such responses were rather missing the point – not just of the report, but of history more generally. In the words of

Cambridge academic Priyamvada Gopal, 'history is not a comfort blanket'.[20] And, as the historian David Olusoga pithily points out, 'history doesn't care very much about our feelings ... country houses are not a soft play area.'[21] Ultimately, most people agree that more knowledge is preferable to less. Looking at country houses through the lens of British colonial history simply adds more to the picture, another layer to that which we already know. Furthermore, avoiding discussion of colonial history is itself a legacy of colonialism. Silence is no neutral position: it aids and abets selective views of our national past. Even though colonialism is integral to the history of the British country house, generations of country house visitors rarely heard mention of it. And, as Sathnam and I had each discovered, breaking that silence was in itself an act of disruption.

What was more, notwithstanding the various attacks on the National Trust report, there was widespread public support for our approach. While some media claimed that in the wake of the report, droves of National Trust members were resigning their membership in disgust, the contrary proved to be true. Following the report's publication, Trust membership rose by 400,000, from 5.6 million before the start of the Covid pandemic in February 2020 to almost 6 million by 2022. Meanwhile, Colonial Countryside and the Trust report were publicly defended by Britain's Museums Association, the Royal Historical Society and other historical societies, who argued that researchers should be free to investigate sensitive histories without threat or intimidation.

Standing in the path of this media juggernaut, I was rarely given any right of reply. While I received daily support from complete strangers, the comment sections below hostile newspaper articles cheerfully offered suggestions about how I should be killed. My safety was threatened, I was unable to go out unaccompanied and had to call the police to inform them and ask their advice on many occasions. I took the decision to answer my hate mail. I'd respond by asking people what had upset or angered them – it was usually clear to me which articles they had read – and would discuss my own research and the historical evidence. Almost always, the exchange would conclude with my correspondent wishing me well. Dialogue and openness, it seems to me, is the antidote to culture war. It's an approach that goes to the heart of the Colonial Countryside project, the National Trust report and this book.

We turned inland, leaving the river behind; the meadows gave way to farmland. Dragonflies flitted through the long grass; a peacock butterfly opened and closed its clownish wings. It felt good to be outdoors. Geese honked and flapped overhead, forming a V-shaped skein above our heads.

It was hot now, and we paused to drink water in a field neatly combed with plough-lines. A rust-red chaffinch fluttered by with its blue cap; a curious robin watched us from a nearby hawthorn hedge. The open sky was cloudless and full of promise.

'Part of the responsibility lies with school education,' I said, and Sathnam nodded. 'What did you learn in your school history lessons?' I asked him. We compared notes: Birmingham classes for me; Wolverhampton classes for Sathnam. 'The Norman Conquest,' he said. 'The Tudors, the English Civil War!' I replied. 'The Great Plague and the Great Fire of London?' he asked. I nodded. Our teachers all skipped the British Empire and focused on the Industrial Revolution. 'With its colonial dimensions removed,' I added. For both of us, World War history followed on from there. Today, the history curriculum is changing, with pupils studying British immigration history and much more, but the fact remains that most Britons received a very different education. What's more, history teachers' own education affects their capacity to inform future generations about colonial history. 'I recently spoke to a group of trainee teachers,' I told Sathnam, 'and gave them a quiz on the basics of the British Empire.' 'What happened?' he asked. 'They got every single question wrong,' I said.

Our mutual memories of school history, then, are standard fare. Even today, you'd struggle to find much mention at school of, for instance, the English colonization of America. Few pupils learn about the Virginia Company – a trading company licensed to establish colonial outposts and claim territory for the English crown – which was formed by a group of investors in 1606, in anticipation of handsome profits. (Fewer still know that the playwright William Shakespeare was one of those investors.)[22] When the Virginia Company presented potential investors with the case for colonization, it did so arguing that England could become a global dominion to rival that of the Mediterranean powers, especially Spain. The company even flagged the side benefit that England's undesirables could be shipped to Virginia and put to work there – such undesirables including debtors, the irreligious and the poor.

'Popular culture plays a role, too,' Sathnam added, 'especially romanticized films and novels about British India.' Such depictions of the British Raj, he went on, helped familiarize us with the latter part of British rule in India. Even so, we both agreed, most of us are far hazier about the East India Company's establishment in 1600, its European rivalries, its private armies and its territorial conquests. Neither do many of us appreciate the degree of cultural ransacking: the Victoria and Albert Museum's South Asian collection, for instance, came from the old East India Company Museum. 'What about the Indian experiences of famous figures like the Duke of Wellington?' I asked. Wellington is remembered mainly as the general who won the 1815 Battle of Waterloo, when an army comprised of English, German and Dutch contingents defeated Napoleon's forces in a victory that brought the Napoleonic wars to an end. 'But Wellington learned much of his military strategy fighting for the East India Company,' I said. He fought in wars that extended British dominance in the subcontinent: strategy that he later implemented against Napoleon.[23]

Our conversation drifted back to British schools. In 2022, pushing back against calls for curriculum reform, the British government issued history teachers with guidance on giving lessons about the British Empire. It warned teachers to follow their legal duty to be impartial by ensuring that lessons about colonialism focused on positive, as well as negative, aspects of empire. Historians of empire disparage this as 'the balance sheet approach to empire'. In response,

Sathnam wrote an opinion piece posing the question: who gets to judge what was good or bad?[24]

Sathnam's point was that such judgements depend on our relationship to that history. Jawaharlal Nehru, India's first prime minister following Indian independence, had long opposed British rule over his nation. Waving the British goodbye, he wrote that in their eyes, the good of empire outweighed the bad, while Indians thought precisely the opposite. Nehru's conclusion was that any relationship based on coercion or force – something that undoubtedly applied to Britain's relationship with India – was destined to turn sour.

Yet successive governments have failed to provide generations of British schoolchildren with the tools to ask these questions for themselves, that is to say, with a good working knowledge of the history of the British Empire. Arguments in favour of changing the curriculum have been made time and again. (The historian Miranda Kaufmann, author of *Black Tudors*, even recommends that we need history lessons about the long campaign to include colonial history in the curriculum.)[25] In the meantime, people have been left to educate themselves.

Continuing on our path, we spotted the diminutive red-brick tower of St Bartholomew's church beyond the meadow, its grey-white flint walls matching Basildon Park's elegant boundary, just a quarter of a mile away. The church, Sir Francis Sykes' last resting place, was closed: inside, I knew, was a fine marble memorial to Sykes by his widow, recording 'the affection which had ever subsisted' between the couple. 'He possessed many of the virtues of public,' it reads, 'all of the virtues of private and domestic life.'

We pressed on, across a humpbacked railway bridge near the village of Lower Basildon. Commuter trains rushed by. Returning to the subject of culture wars, Sathnam recollected a conversation he'd had with the distinguished historian of the Indian subcontinent William Dalrymple, who told him ruefully that he'd written books on the same topic for years without receiving a single hostile letter. Sathnam and I compared notes on our experiences and how we dealt with them. For me, such aggression was a relatively new phenomenon. Sathnam was, he shrugged, used to it: having experienced racism all his life, he had long since learned how to process others' prejudices against him; now, he drew on his reserves. Besides which, he added, twenty years of professional experience also came into play: 'I'm a journalist,' he told me, 'I'm used to it.'

We paused on the bridge. 'I wasn't good at school history,' Sathnam acknowledged. But the history he was taught held little interest: there was nothing to engage him. Then he remembered, one history lesson made him sit up: about the Irish potato famine and Bloody Sunday. 'That Irish history rang a distant bell in my head,' said Sathnam. It made him think of India, British India. He began to read up on it. Astonished and disturbed by his ignorance of a history which was part of his own inheritance, he felt compelled to research it properly. How could he have gone through an entire education system, he asked himself, and been kept in ignorance of it? This lesson was a kind of slow-acting catalyst for *Empireland* and this was how he, a literature graduate and journalist, became an informed and influential writer about the topic.

Understanding current affairs, he continued as we walked on, demands a good working knowledge of colonial history. I recalled news coverage about a visit to the Caribbean by the now Prince and Princess of Wales. Demonstrators against their visit drew the attention of the world's media to the royal family's historical involvement in slavery. This was something the royals could embrace, I suggested to Sathnam. Given their platform, 'they could use it to educate the British public about the Crown's role in slavery. Reparative history'.[26] Sathnam nodded in agreement. For the first time, we agreed, Caribbean debates about reparation for slavery were beginning to interest the British public. Various conversations had started: from proposals that the royals make a formal apology for the monarchy's role in historic slavery or that European nations should fund Caribbean slavery museums to suggestions that higher-than-average levels of illiteracy among present-day Caribbean populations be understood as a long-term consequence of slavery.

The lane doglegged. We joined Reading Road, the fast road skirting Basildon Park's flint wall, and the footpath petered out. We tramped along the verge, Sathnam leading, as traffic shot by. As he walked ahead, I reflected on everything he'd told me. We had discussed colonialism's ideological legacy. Above all, that legacy was racism. 'Have you read that Salman Rushdie essay about racism as a legacy of empire?' I'd asked Sathnam. He had. Rushdie argued that British racism would remain unaddressed until its colonial origins were accepted and understood. 'What stood out for me,' I'd said, was the idea that 'for 400 years, White Britons were told that they were superior to colonized people. It was a staggering length of time when put like that.' Rushdie had argued that this collective indoctrination 'was hard to unlearn', Sathnam had said, finishing my sentence for me.[27] I followed Sathnam along the verge and thought that Rushdie's essay, written in the 1980s, could have been written yesterday. What Rushdie meant was that British colonial rule rested on the principle that supposedly inferior races should be naturally subordinate to superior races. From Australia to South Africa, this ideology of a natural hierarchy based on assumptions of racial difference did not merely exist in people's minds: it was enshrined in colonial law.

Finally, we got relief from the traffic, as the Basildon Park wall gave way to a pair of imposing wrought iron gates flanked by a pair of octagonal stone gatehouses. We had arrived.

Ignoring a clattering of raucous jackdaws that glared down from the gateway, we walked through the open gates and followed a curved path which snaked upwards through low trees. The enclosed parklands extended in all directions, a reminder that this land, claimed by Sir Francis Sykes, was once a place where local people could wander freely. We don't much associate parliamentary Acts of Enclosure with colonialism, but there are strong links between the two. I felt strongly that colonial historians should not have to choose between writing *either* about empire *or* about rural poverty. As these examples illustrate, British colonial history and British labour history are part of the same story.

Finally, Sykes' house came into view. A spectacular sight in honey-coloured Bath stone, it was designed by the eighteenth-century starchitect John Carr in the fashionable Palladian style – named after the Italian Renaissance architect, whose clean lines were then all the rage. Situated at the end of a plateau, Sykes' residence, with its temple-like portico and pillars, would have commanded views of pleasure grounds from the front and the distant Thames from the rear, where formal gardens were surrounded by elegant balustrades.

Sathnam stood beneath the Palladian pillars by the main entrance. We looked out across the extensive grounds and remarked that the lawns were clipped to perfection. Ahead of us a vast pine tree cast an inviting shade across the grass. We lingered by the house and continued our conversation as some wood pigeons flew by. I remarked that some country house owners have embraced their colonial past, by researching it and talking about their findings. Sir John Sykes, a present-day descendant of Sir Francis, spent years exploring his ancestor's life in India before contributing a chapter to a book called *The East India Company at Home*.[28] Another example of such openness is the owner of Harewood House in West Yorkshire, built shortly before Basildon Park. The 8th Earl of Harewood, David Lascelles, has spent two decades looking into his family's historic connection to Barbados, the source of so much of their wealth. Today, visitors to Harewood House learn about its connection to the British slavery system, and how the 8th Earl's ancestor, Henry Lascelles, began as a customs collector at the Barbadian port of Bridgetown, a lucrative profession that led him to become a banker to plantation-owners. He bought plantations, sugar distribution warehouses and slaving ships; his son, Edwin, came to control twenty-four plantations. With their enormous combined profits, Lascelles and his son bought Harewood estate in 1738, and Edwin Lascelles appointed John Carr – later employed by Sykes – to build a vast new neoclassical house.[29] In 2021, David Lascelles sat down with the actor David Harewood – whose enslaved ancestors worked on Barbados plantations owned by the Lascelles family – to have a conversation about slavery. The two men discussed their shared history: a history in which one family profited from the suffering of the other. For me, their conversation brought to mind Martin Luther King Jr's much-quoted dream that, one day, the descendants of enslavers would sit down with those whose ancestors were enslaved.[30]

We walked into Sykes' house and stood in the opulent, pillared entrance hall with ceilings so high that we craned our necks to look up. There were two plaster griffins in a frieze above a doorway: a typical neoclassical feature, and a knowing one. I said to Sathnam, 'griffins were the mythical beasts which guarded Indian gold.' 'An appropriate reference to the origins of this wealth,' replied Sathnam. Climbing the elegant staircase, we entered the pale-green dining room which has lost nothing of its eighteenth-century grandeur, with its stylish dining table and speckled marble pillars. On the day we were there, with some of the rooms closed for renovation, much of the furniture was covered in dust sheets, but I knew that inside one of the cabinets stood a Chinese porcelain tureen belonging to Sykes, and a dinner service made in India complete with the image of an Indian princess. According to family legend, the princess promised to release Sir Francis when the Nawab of Bengal held the British under siege before Robert Clive defeated the Nawab during the 1757 Battle of Plassey.[31] The long dining table was covered up and the dinnerware placed in temporary storage. 'But, normally,' I said, 'the dinnerware bears the Sykes coat of arms and you can just make out a veiled princess bearing a rose.' We passed through an imposing Palladian drawing room, octagonal in shape with an Italianate ceiling and Regency chandelier. The whole room was painted fierce red with golden plasterwork. 'Very gothic,' said Sathnam. 'It really is,' I said.

We descended by narrow stone servants' steps – inelegant by comparison with the main staircase – and admired the Garden Room with its imitation Indian wallpaper and its doors opening onto the garden terrace. 'We did an exhibition here,' I said. It was called 'India and Me', featuring stories of the local Indian community in Reading with an animation which brought the woodblock-printed wallpaper to life with its elephants, temples, camels and palm trees.

Wandering back through the house, we emerged into the sun, and to the crowds that, enticed out by the weather, had begun to arrive. Sathnam went to find a table in the courtyard which was close to the entrance hall, while I wandered into the café to buy lunch. At the till, an older volunteer was scowling. I asked him how his day was as I paid for the sandwiches. He'd just been in 'some sort of diversity training', he replied, 'what a waste of time', and rolled his eyes. With a long queue behind me, I just had time to mention that Basildon Park had a significant Indian history and that broadening its visitor base made a lot of sense for a place within reach of cities like London and Reading. He didn't seem to know about the history, and I moved on, conscious of the queue behind me. Rejoining Sathnam in the courtyard, I kept the volunteer's comments to myself. The fact was, the history of Basildon Park's house was probably more closely connected to Sathnam's heritage than to mine – and the volunteer's.

Not all propertied families are comfortable talking about their ancestors' colonial histories. After the National Trust report was published, I received emails from the owner of one such house, who objected to it featuring in the report and tried to persuade me to remove the relevant entry. Her family, she admitted, had indeed invested in a company which traded in enslaved people – her ancestors bought South Sea shares – but the family lost their money and so did not profit from it. Aside from the fact that this hardly explained away the family's attempt to profit from slavery, the owner's explanation missed the point. For the report's aim was not to inflict reputational damage, but to deepen public knowledge of colonial history's importance to British country houses. If indeed the owner's ancestors had to leave their country house as a result of the South Sea Company's collapse in 1720, this was a significant family event, and surely ought to be included in accounts of the house concerned. Such objections to opening up country houses' colonial histories illustrate the problem of viewing history through a prism of guilt and fear.

Slavery is always the most sensitive aspect of British colonial history. For, while the National Trust report details country houses' Indian connections far more than slavery links, it was invariably referred to as 'the slavery report'. This label itself indicates an emotional response: the idea that the National Trust produced a 'list of shame', a phrase adopted by newspaper reporters at the time. It ignores the report's actual focus on all aspects of the British Empire, from sea battles and colonial governance to abolitionist and anti-colonial activity.[32] The aim was not to name and shame, but to identify Trust houses' various colonial connections and learn more about them.

Sathnam smiled when I told him about my South Sea Company letter. 'Thinking like that just reduces history to the question of whether one event or another was good or bad,' he said. As Sathnam rightly insists, a sound knowledge of the workings of British colonialism gives us so much more. It allows us to understand why, and how, our nation became what it is today. Whether adults or children, without such understanding we all miss out, unable to make historical sense of the multicultural society in which we, our children and our grandchildren live.[33]

Lunch over, Sathnam bought us ice-creams, and we sat on the lawn admiring the parkland that stretched out before us. We had fallen naturally into country-house-as-leisurely-pursuit mode, the pleasurable aspect of stately home touring. This was our Good Day Out – a former National Trust slogan: unhurried conversation in beautiful surroundings, away from the hustle of everyday life, traffic jams and ringtones. I thought of the man behind the till, wishing he could envisage a more inclusive rural idyll, a democratized version where no one batted an eyelid at anybody else.

We walked past 'Capability' Brown's kitchen garden. Very little remains of this kitchen garden – and nothing of Brown's plans – but shadows on the garden walls mark where glasshouses once stood.[34] As the shadows started to lengthen, we reluctantly started to retrace our steps. Weaving our way back through the grounds, we came across a field of daffodils. Sathnam snapped them for a post on Instagram.

As we walked through the gates, I noticed two stone pineapples carved into the pillars: a recurring motif throughout country houses of the period, when exotic fruits were often grown in heated orangeries, something only the wealthy could afford. Architectural references to landowners' colonial wealth, like the pineapples, tended to be subtle, oblique. Men like Sir Francis used their colonial wealth to buy their way into powerful society, to establish themselves among aristocratic families, essentially by living and behaving like them. Some even implied their own noble ancestry by mimicking the medieval houses of old landed families, like the neo-Gothic Penrhyn Castle in north Wales, rebuilt in the early nineteenth century by George Hay Dawkins Pennant, the second cousin of the slave-owner Richard Pennant (like Sykes, Pennant got himself an MP's constituency and a baronetcy), and Dorset's Fonthill Abbey. Built in the Gothic Revival style that vied with and eventually displaced the neoclassicism of houses like Basildon Park, Fonthill was the brainchild of William Beckford, whose wealth – you've guessed it – was derived from the Jamaican plantations on which well over a thousand African slaves worked and suffered. Just as the already wealthy sons of aristocratic families filled their houses with goods acquired on their Grand Tours through countries like France and Italy, so those with colonial wealth similarly filled their houses with European luxury goods.[35]

Sykes' Asian wealth bought him more than land, splendid architecture and fine soft furnishings.[36] His daughter married into the aristocracy, and Sykes himself became an MP, first for Shaftesbury and then for Wallingford, both constituencies within easy reach of his estates. Providing new routes to power and wealth, East India Company careers allowed men like Sykes to overleap the old propertied establishment and disrupt the existing social order. Another such was Thomas Pitt, the governor of Madras, whose Indian fortune paid for a country estate in Dorset: his grandchild and great-grandchild both became British prime ministers.[37] Newly rich men like Sykes and Pitt, then, put down a whole new layer of dynastic wealth, one that continues to this day.

Such wealth could only be gained with the help of Indians who knew their trade. Sir Francis had business ties with an influential Indian merchant named 'Cantoo Baboo'. This wealthy and skilled intermediary became his trusted agent, accountant and estate manager. He had the Englishman's absolute trust. As a close ally of Robert Clive, Sir Francis was accused of corruption, reminding us that the business affairs of colonial figures were often fraught and complicated. Despite the allegations of corruption, Sykes' bond with Cantoo Baboo held firm. Sir Francis wrote three times to the governor general of Bengal to ask that Cantoo Baboo might 'enjoy what he has, in Peace and Quietness', so that he was not dragged into the corruption scandal through association. That same year, Cantoo Baboo sent barrels of mango chutney to Basildon Park at great expense.[38] The East India Company was exploitative in the extreme, but personal relationships sometimes prevailed. As Sykes' descendant John Sykes recounted in an essay about the history, the two families have remained in contact to this day.

On his return from India, Sir Francis was accompanied by an Indian servant named Thomas Radakissan. In his will, he left Radakissan a mourning ring and 7 shillings a week, then the equivalent of two days' wages, for the rest of his life. A National Trust volunteer discovered that Radakissan stayed in the area, marrying a local woman, and their descendants are still living in Britain and far beyond.[39]

Over time, then, those who got rich from the colonizing activities of the East India Company, or from plantation slavery, converted their fortunes into land, status and political power.[40] These were reassuringly domestic and socially elevating enterprises which ensured their 'natural' place at the top of the social order. Even investment in stocks and shares seemed respectable: to many, the Royal African and South Sea Companies, with their ponderous names and royal charters, sounded harmless enough.[41] In Britain, the popular perception of many of these figures at the time was as benevolent philanthropists, founders of hospitals and orphanages, creators of jobs, upholders of the established order.

It was by no means obvious that such wealth was rooted in colonial violence.

The spring air was warm. As we retraced our steps and the Thames flowed lazily in the sun, I was half tempted to plunge in. Laughing voices carried from the opposite bank. But the light was fading, and we had a train to catch.

My first walk had begun in a country house setting. But even before the train had pulled out of Pangbourne station I felt that local history was leading me in a new direction. It was not just that British landscapes were transformed by newly wealthy landowners, though they were; it was that the actions of colonial figures like Sir Francis Sykes impacted on labouring and landless Britons. The men who worked for the East India Company or who owned plantations were often the very same people who enclosed common land, became MPs and denied ordinary people the vote; who ran cotton factories and copper mines. Above all, then, I wanted to address a question that was repeatedly levelled at me during the culture war: what about Britain's oppressive labour history? It is true that such questions sometimes close down conversations about the British Empire, but I wanted to know what would happen if I separated these questions from their imputed intent and made a serious attempt to answer them.[42]

In fact, labour history and colonial history are deeply intertwined. Back in 1963, the social historian E. P. Thompson published his seminal *The Making of the English Working Class*. A ground-breaking 'history from below', it explores working-class culture in the late eighteenth and nineteenth centuries, the age in which landowners were investing their profits from plantations, slavery and various colonial companies in fine houses and sweeping estates. Thompson wanted to offer a corrective to the kind of history that habitually depicted working-class people as dim-witted, ignorant or primitive. Although his book largely overlooked female labour history, it painstakingly detailed the trials of agricultural labourers, wage suppression, food riots, machine-breaking, disenfranchisement and unionization. It looked at how the labouring classes organized themselves in opposition to landowners, magistrates and parliamentarians.[43] Rural poverty was an unpleasant reality for generations, and it endured until well into the twentieth century. Ronald Blythe's 1969 *Akenfield*, a vivid depiction of life in a Suffolk village from the turn of the 1900s to the 1960s, documented quite how hard that life was. In one story, a teenage boy clears a field of dock leaves for a shilling an acre, money he gives to his mother. The boy's family lived in a tied cottage: should his parents leave their agricultural jobs or fall foul of their employers, they would lose their home. Such families were often at the mercy of the local squire and farmers who determine the wages they received (the same boy, in a new job, received half a crown – enough to buy a few pieces of candy – for sixty hours' work). As late as the 1960s, tied cottages in rural England remained attached to low wages and long labouring hours. Accommodation was scarce, and agricultural labourers had little choice than to accept the pittance they were paid.[44]

The experiences of British labourers and of colonized people are intertwined. Britons who mistreated colonized and enslaved people were often one and the same as those landowners who opposed parliamentary reform, suppressed wages, evicted tenants or enclosed fields. Those who owned plantations and enslaved people also turn up in British history as politicians who sent British convicts, sex workers and vagrants to work as indentured servants in the West Indies or transported political prisoners to hard labour in the colonies.

Though the intertwined nature of empire and British labour history is still coming to light, parallels between oppression at home and abroad were not lost on people at the time. The nineteenth-century Tory abolitionist and campaigner against child labour Richard Oastler compared mill-owners to tyrannical slave-owners.[45] William Cobbett's *Rural Rides* of 1822 was a pioneering work of investigative journalism in which the author journeyed through the south-east and Midlands of England, compared the conditions of England's rural factory workers with enslaved people on cotton plantations, suggesting that the former suffered more.[46] Such a comparison was of course inaccurate: tied labour, oppressive labour conditions and rural poverty are not the same as the intense cruelty of chattel slavery.

Cobbett, however, was not alone in comparing oppression at home and in the British colonies. In the course of this book, I try to distinguish different kinds, contexts and degrees of oppression while highlighting the historical relationship between colonization overseas and working conditions history at home. In nineteenth-century Britain, for instance, opiate abuse was rife, the trade in opium and laudanum not just legalized but actively encouraged by the British government, owing to the immense profits to be made. The tragedies of opiate addiction were played out in Indian processing factories and Chinese dens. But laudanum was also used in Britain, notably by mill-working mothers required to return to work three weeks after giving birth, and who needed to keep their babies quiet.[47]

The customary opposition between colonialism, on the one hand, and British poverty, on the other, has present-day parallels. Working-class Britain is largely presented and imagined as White, as though race and poverty had little to do with one another. Yet poverty disproportionately affects people of colour, and Sathnam himself grew up in a tiny terraced house in Wolverhampton.

Back on the train to Paddington, it wasn't long before the rhythms of daily life imposed themselves. Laptops perched on knees, Sathnam and I worked through our respective email backlogs. But the memory of wild meadows and sitting on the lawn at Basildon stayed with me, as did the stories we had encountered and Sathnam's conversation. I was struck above all by his tendency to underplay the difficulties that his book had caused him. Sathnam felt, he said, that my experience of the culture war, the relentless abuse provoked by the publication of the National Trust report, was worse than the hostility he had encountered when *Empireland* was published. But I knew this wasn't true. Having witnessed it, I saw that opposition to his work focused relentlessly on his racial identity. Sathnam's philosophical attitude expresses the triumph of courage and openness over fear and intimidation.

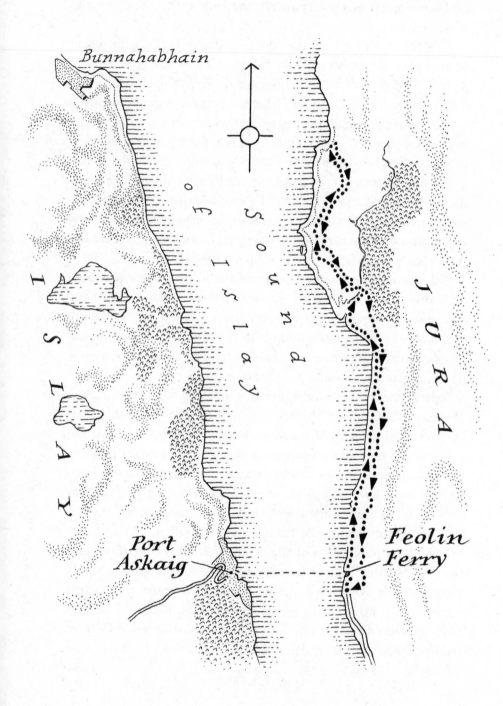

The Sugar Walk: Jura and Islay

They say there are more Jamaicans than Scots with the surname Campbell. In 1700, a Scot named Colonel John Campbell established a plantation at Black River in south-west Jamaica. Originally a soldier from Inveraray in Argyll, he enslaved 460 people and had many descendants. As the eighteenth century wore on, more Campbells – and, generally, more Scots – arrived to take advantage of Jamaica's expanding slavery economy. Many became plantation-owners, overseers and estate managers. Today, there are Campbells from Kingston to Montego Bay – but there are Campbells of Jamaican heritage in Scotland too.

Graham Campbell, the Scottish National Party's first Caribbean-heritage councillor, is fascinated by this Jamaican connection. Together, we planned to visit the Isle of Jura in western Scotland's Inner Hebrides. When I told people we were going to Jura, they immediately assumed our intention was to visit its famous whisky distilleries. Friends would jokingly offer to go in my suitcase and ask whether Graham was a whisky connoisseur. The real purpose of our journey, though, was to explore his family history and the region's historic links with Jamaica.

The Campbells ruled the Inner Hebrides for centuries. They succeeded the MacDonald clan, which had dominated the entire region as Lords of the Isles until the 1600s, when they opposed the right of King James IV of Scotland to the Lordship. James promptly handed over Jura – and the neighbouring island of Islay – to the Campbells of Argyllshire. This historic county encompassed vast tracts of western Scotland, and its Campbell family branches are myriad. When we first discussed our walk, Graham told me that his great-great-grandfather was an Argyllshire Campbell, but he did not know whether there were family links to Jura. Either way, he knew that Jura's Jamaican connections ran deep. The island's craggy southern side was bought in 1726 by Daniel Campbell, a wealthy Glasgow merchant who traded enslaved people and tobacco in Boston and the West Indies before finally settling on the neighbouring island of Islay (which he also bought).[1] Whereas Islay flourished under the Campbells of Shawfield, who invested in the local flax industry, the islanders of Jura had a very different experience under the Campbells of Craignish, the branch who sold their Jura lands to Daniel Campbell. As the new landowner on Jura, Daniel Campbell did little to arrest the population decline caused by his predecessors, who had evicted crofters from their small farms and given the land over to sheep grazing and deer forest. Though he in turn sold the island before his death in 1753, less than a decade later, impoverished islanders were emigrating from Jura to British colonies in the New World.[2] The legacy of these years is still perceptible; Jura's forested eastern side is criss-crossed with deer fences and the island has more red deer than people to this day.

Jura's sugar connections continued. In the 1830s, Colin Campbell became the sixth of eleven Campbell lairds to rule over the island. He was a partner in the sugar trading company Campbell, Rivers & Co. alongside the trustee of his Jura estate, complete with grazing land and hunting grounds, lands which were by then worth a staggering £49,609. These sugar-trading business circles were close-knit, and Colin Campbell's sister Ann married a co-founder of the Glasgow West India Association, which opposed the abolition of slavery, while his sister Barbara married a sugar baron named Alexander Campbell of Hallyards.[3] For these reasons, Graham and I referred to our Jura trek as the sugar walk.

I'd first met Graham two decades ago in a public meeting organized by Glasgow Welcomes Refugees, about child asylum seekers who were being held in a local deportation centre. Chatting to Graham after the meeting, he had mentioned the Campbell clan's slaving past. It was a fleeting conversation, but his words stayed with me. I wanted to know more, and Graham was keen to explore the Campbell link to his Jamaican roots while his ageing father still lived. Sketchy though the family history is in the mind of Graham's father, Lawrence, time is running out to discover more. Neither are Graham and his father alone in this experience. In trying to trace their ancestry, people of Caribbean heritage across Britain, Europe and North America often find that their research yields little or nothing. The slavery system robbed people of their names and gave them new ones. Enslaved people were initially given numbers, then a single forename like Betty, classical names such as Nero or sexualized names like Venus as well as the names of the enslavers themselves. African family ties were severed because it was these new names which were recorded on plantation inventories which listed the enslaved.[4] For their descendants, this renaming often represents a definitive rupture with their past, a phenomenon little understood by those of us without this historical wound. (When I discussed this once during a talk in Bristol, an audience member told me afterwards that it was the first time he'd heard his own lost Caribbean ancestry publicly acknowledged.)

On rare occasions when families do make research breakthroughs, their discoveries are bittersweet. This was the case for a US citizen, Shonda Brookes, who discovered that one of her ancestors was sold for $1,000 and another was valued at $400. Though, she said, her own flesh and blood were treated like 'a dining room set', this disturbing discovery was preferable to nothing.[5] However painful, Shonda was relieved that part of her family history had at least been restored.

Graham found that his Jamaican family line quickly ran into the sand. He is, of course, descended from people whose original names were taken from them, and the sheer number of Jamaican Campbells make his family hard to trace. When I asked a Jamaican archivist and expert in plantation records to look into Graham's family history, she said right away that the surname would pose a challenge. The best chance of tracing the right Campbells, she advised, would be to trace the female line using maiden names. The researcher already had the details of Graham's main female relatives, but Graham contacted more family members and drew up a longer list of female names. Armed with this information, the researcher headed into the archives.[6] My hope was that, after some months, something might be discovered. Meanwhile, off we went to Jura.

I didn't plan to write about the getting there: the car journey from Glasgow to the mainland port of Kennacraig and the ferry crossing from western Scotland to Islay and from Islay to Jura. In the end, though, the travelling assumed an importance all of its own because the history of sugar and the Campbells confronted us wherever we went. It started with our rendezvous at a carpark in central Glasgow. This seemed mundane enough, but the carpark was on Jamaica Street, in the heart of the eighteenth-century Glaswegian heritage quarter, known as Merchant City.

From the early seventeenth century onwards, Atlantic trade placed the western coastal city of Glasgow on a global stage. Glasgow merchants were heavily involved in transatlantic slaving voyages, which were part of an integrated economic and trading system. Finance was provided by Glasgow-based bankers and insurers, while the city's merchants employed agents in the West Indies and Virginia who imported to Britain sugar, tobacco and other goods produced by enslaved people. Meanwhile, manufactured goods were exported to the slave-owning societies of North America, South America and the West Indies. Unsurprisingly, given the money to be made, Glaswegian businesspeople supported the slavery system politically and militarily, upholding pro-slavery legislation and fighting colonial wars.[7]

The profits of enslavement flooded into the city, underpinning Glasgow's rapid expansion, industrialization and agricultural development.[8] Today, the splendid architecture of Merchant City serves as a reminder of this wealth.[9] As a local politician in Glasgow, Graham has successfully led efforts to make Scotland's slavery links better known. Until recently, denying Scotland's involvement in slavery was a default position, though reminders of this involvement run through the city's fabric: sixty-four street names have slavery associations, including the memorialization of sugar and tobacco barons.[10] Two of them – Buchanan Street and Cochrane Street (after the tobacco merchants Andrew Buchanan and Andrew Cochrane) – were relabelled George Floyd Street and Sheku Bayoh Street by local campaigners. A man in his thirties, Sheku Bayoh, died in Kirkcaldy under police restraint, on 3 May 2015. Six policemen knelt on his body whilst his hands and feet were bound. Bayoh died on the pavement. This use of restraint was so reminiscent of George Floyd's murder in Minneapolis that campaigners put up new street names to connect present-day Scottish racism with the country's slaving past.

Graham was waiting for me at Jamaica Street carpark with an 'I LOVE SCOTLAND' bag slung over his shoulder. He was slightly out of breath, having hotfooted it from the Scottish National Party's political conference so as not to miss our ferry to Islay, from where we would travel to Jura the following morning. As we drove through Glasgow's city streets, Graham watched the first minister's speech on his phone. He glanced up when we passed Nelson Mandela Square: it was once called St George's Place, he said. He laughed because nobody minded renaming it, since St George wasn't Scottish, but the patron saint of England: Glaswegians were perfectly happy to do away with reminders of anything English.

We drove out of the city along dual carriageways and through corrugated concrete tunnels towards Argyll. It was a blustery September day. About an hour later, we paused by the shores of Loch Lomond, where bracken rusted on the hills and the woodlands were golden. The loch was choppy and sent slivers of mountain and forest dancing across its surface. I was busy telling Graham about a 1990s novel I had just read by Dirk Robertson, a London author. This crime caper was all about the Highlands' slavery connection.[11] With a cover depicting grouse country through the crosshairs of a gun, its title is picked out in tartan with the colours of the Jamaican flag (reminiscent of Graham's email signature with its crossed flags of Jamaica and Scotland). I told Graham about the plot: a Black Londoner flees a Glaswegian police chief who tries to prevent him discovering his Scots-Jamaican ancestry. Initially out of place in rural Scotland, the protagonist comes to realize that the Highlands are his true inheritance. This light-hearted forerunner of change was published a decade before Scotland began to address its slavery connections in earnest. Graham had never heard of the book, but he laughed out loud at its title: *Highland T'ing.*[12]

As we left Loch Lomond behind us, Graham shared scraps of information that he'd gleaned from his father about his Campbell ancestry. He reiterated that his father did not know much. Graham's Scottish great-grandfather, Captain Percival Campbell, was associated with the Port Maria area – known as 'Santa Maria' to the Spanish, who had preceded the British colonists – in north-eastern Jamaica. Captain Percival owned old plantations on an estate between Free Hill village and the coastal town of Oracabessa. The family knowledge of Captain Percival stopped there, though Graham mentioned that this land was near a site where Christopher Columbus was once marooned after a storm called Oracabessa.[13] *Oracabeza* is Spanish for 'golden head', describing its illumination in the sun.

It was not just Scots, like Percival Campbell, who owned land in this area. Free Villages were created after the 1833 abolition of slavery, as places where free people of colour could live. A block purchase of land near Oracabessa was made by a Baptist minister called James Phillippo, using donations from abolitionists. This block was then divided up into smaller plots for free people of colour to buy and build houses on. Through these purchases, Baptists like Phillippo aimed to address slavery's legacy of landlessness and poverty. One minister reported that a single block purchase of land would build houses for seventy families. These Baptist ministers offered their assistance in throwing off the oppressive planter class, but held a narrow view of life beyond the plantation system, wanting Black men to resemble White abolitionists and Black women to become housewives, keeping clean houses and neat gardens.[14] Nonetheless, Free Villages offered sanctuary to many Black families during this period.

Graham had read academic papers which showed how formerly enslaved people and their descendants gathered enough resources to buy land near Free Hill village using money they had worked to save through selling food they'd grown. Some Jamaicans bought plots for themselves whilst others bought plots from the Baptists. This much he knew. But, without proper documentation or family records, his family trail ran cold.

Forty miles from the ferry port of Kennacraig, Graham asked to make an unscheduled stop at Inveraray Castle, the Argyll Campbells' family seat. 'Percival Campbell was from round hereabouts,' he said, 'but we don't know exactly where.' The wind had dropped, and Inveraray's white town buildings made peerless reflections in Loch Fyne. The surrounding hills were garnished with copper trees. Driving over Aray Bridge on the approach to Inveraray, we got a clear view of the castle. I gasped. It was seriously imposing, like a French château in the Loire Valley. This opulent castle has been the seat of the Argyll Campbells for over three centuries. It was completed in the 1780s and is still home to the current duke, the 13th chief of Clan Campbell.[15]

As I told Graham later, a link labelled 'Slavery Statement' appeared at the foot of the castle website in 2023. The statement described new research into the castle's colonial history and detailed the discovery of a receipt – for boots, shoes and 'two blacks' – belonging to the 1st Duke of Argyll in the early 1700s together with a 1754 baptismal record for a family servant and 'native of the East Indies' called William Campbell. This detail alone perfectly illustrated Inveraray's mixed colonial histories, looking west to the United States and West Indies, but also east, to India. In addition, the statement read, a son of the 4th Duke became the British governor of South Carolina while other family members married into famous plantation-owning dynasties, the Izards and the Glassells.[16]

It was the kind of dreary day that the Scots call *dreich*, and I huddled into my coat as we walked along the drive and through the castle parkland. Graham didn't seem to notice the cold. The gloom set off the castle's gleaming turrets; its windows glittered like eye-balls. We circled the castle and passed manicured paths and trimmed lawns. The rose garden was bare, all thorns and no petals. The castle itself was closed to visitors.

Nonetheless, we tramped on. As we rounded the building and approached the front door, Graham smiled and said, 'the Campbells have an annual clan gathering. They never invite me!' We stared at the oversized entrance. 'We should knock and announce you,' I said. Graham nodded in agreement, but our courage failed us. We retreated to an ornate stone bridge nearby. The drizzle had eased, and so we sat and admired some nineteenth-century graffiti carved into the stone. From the bridge we could see forests across the salt-waters of Loch Fyne, the view dominated by a wooded hill crowned with an extravagant folly.

For generations, the Campbells of Inveraray Castle have had the comfort of knowing their lineage. But, as the Campbell clan's Jamaican counterparts know all too well, plantation violence took many forms: estate records were meticulously kept but served the plantation manager, not his inventoried human beings. For people like Graham, this lost family history presents slavery's tragic personal legacy.

Rainclouds darkened the sky. As we walked back towards the castle, its whole edifice was illuminated from behind as though stage-lit for the unacknowledged Campbell who wandered beside the beech hedge, lost in thought.

From Inveraray we drove along a finger of land towards the Mull of Kintyre beside the sea loch, past cottages and rough fields. Along the road to Kennacraig port, saltwater lapped the land on either side, the tide advancing and retreating across wrinkled sand beaches. You felt it almost possible to leap from one seashore to another. The entire area has many lochs which almost touch, but never do: an apt metaphor for Scotland and Jamaica, perhaps, whose histories were long seen as separate. Yet Graham's ancestral homeland of Jamaica is full of Scottish names. There are Jamaican estates named

Aberdeen, Alva, Arboll, Ardoch, Ardsheal, Ayr and of course Argyll – and the list carries on, right through the alphabet.

Family names are, of course, central to this history because Scotland's slavery business was a 'clannish' affair.[17] The Campbell clan formed business networks across the Americas, with Campbell fathers, uncles, brothers and cousins stationed at strategic locations in South Carolina, Virginia, Grenada and Bermuda.[18] They held the fort for each other, watching one another's plantations and allying themselves in business and colonial administration.

As we neared Kennacraig, we swapped notes on the long history of Jamaican Campbells. The first Campbell in Jamaica, Inveraray-born Colonel John Campbell, settled at St Elizabeth in the south-west of the island in 1700, where he bought and enslaved many people. He was born at Inveraray but eventually became a Member of the Jamaican Assembly. His Jamaican memorial conveys him as a benevolent man who bestowed riches on the island.[19] Another notorious Campbell, Duncan, took full advantage of empire's lucrative business opportunities. He owned Jamaica Hanover estate, known as Saltspring, and sold sugar and rum. He also shipped tobacco to sell from colonial America.[20] When these ventures faltered, Campbell won a contract to repurpose his old vessels to take advantage of the new Hulks Act of 1776, the British government paying him handsomely for incarcerating felons in brutal and insanitary prison ships. Many prisoners were locked up and later transported to Australia for offences ranging from theft to joining a union or campaigning for greater representation of ordinary people in Britain's parliament.[21]

The many Campbells from this era whose ancestors settled in the West Indies include Farquhar Campbell, whose family received compensation for 197 enslaved people in Demerara, and who bought the Isle of Rùm. He was descended from Farquhard Campbell, whose 'coloured natural son' was schooled in Lanarkshire: just one example of the Campbell clan's Jamaican demographic legacy in Scotland.[22]

Some 30 miles from Kennacraig port, we passed a sign to Campbeltown. This prompted us to talk about the Campbell clan's Indian connections, rediscovered recently, in which Campbeltown features quite prominently. The economic historian Andrew MacKillop has unearthed significant East India Company links with the Scottish Highlands and Islands. For Campbells at all levels of society, the East India Company provided a range of opportunities to get rich – or at least find paid work – from clerical and military positions to tax collection, official governance and private trade. For landless labourers and tenants, the company offered potential routes out of poverty.[23] There was a strong military dimension to this. Highlanders from places like Campbeltown fought in many Indian campaigns, particularly late eighteenth-century battles to secure East India Company influence over southern India. During these battles, Highland troops fought in monsoons and waded through rice fields.[24] The Campbells rank high in the recruitment data among Highlanders and Islanders, a phenomenon which reflects clan and regional relationships and loyalties. In 1777, six Scotch Companies were recruited to the Madras and Bombay armies. The officers were all Campbells.[25]

Campbeltown is a deep seaport near Kintyre with whitewashed houses. It got its name when James IV gave the town to the Argyll Campbells after the MacDonald clan contested his right to be Lord of the Isles.[26] It is the most westerly harbour on the British mainland, and ships could sail from Campbeltown along sea routes to either the West Indies or India. In 1774, two locals returned to this seaport from East India Company service: Lieutenant Colonel Samuel Kilpatrick and John Clark set about spending their East India Company profits on bettering their local town, each donating a substantial £39 to help 160 impoverished locals, sums that would then have made a material difference to the town's economy.[27]

Some former company employees came back with levels of wealth only to be seen among the local gentry.[28] But for many Highlanders returning from India, colonial profits were modest: enough to transform a life or two – especially given the low cost of living. Highlanders and Islanders could do a lot more with their East India money than Londoners.[29] Nonetheless, land purchases with company wealth did buy political influence. Between 1754 and 1790, a third of Scottish constituencies were represented by MPs with company links. Perthshire, Inverness-shire and Ross-shire were held by multiple East India Company men for decades.[30]

Agriculture was also part of the story. Company profits bought and developed land. In a single year, 1790, Asian money was lent out at twice the rate of average bank loans. This money funded agricultural schemes all over the Highlands. It paid for ditch-digging, field enclosure, tree-planting, fishery creation and landscape design. In this way, owned and borrowed Asian wealth altered the landscape. These local impacts of company profits would then have been clear for all to see.[31]

All of which goes to show, Graham and I reasoned as we neared the ferry port, that it pays to combine discussions of Atlantic slavery and East India Company activity when thinking about the colonial history of the Highlands and Islands. Whether you were a Duke of Argyll or a Campbeltown resident, it was clear that wildly different kinds of imperial activity had a cumulative impact on the countryside and local villages: the tentacles of empire extended into small places like Campbeltown, Islay and Jura. Significant tracts of local land passed into the hands of people who made their money at opposite ends of the British Empire, including parts of Mull, Islay, Lewis and Jura.[32]

Graham was pleased when he spotted the ferry's name, *Finlaggan*, his favourite place on Islay: it was, he said, an eerie loch with a tiny island, where the Lords of the Isles once held council. The funnel belched thick smoke, obscuring Kintyre's pink evening hue. The departing shoreline was blue, streaked with silver.

This passage, from the Mull of Kintyre to Islay, reaches across the Irish Sea to Ireland and, from there, to the Atlantic Ocean. These same shores would have been where Daniel Campbell and his family departed for Jura in the early eighteenth century. When he relocated to Islay, he would have likely taken this same sea route, watching the wide western coastline recede from the heaving deck of a sailing ship.

The ferry was surprisingly swift, propelled along by the notoriously strong currents. Within minutes we had cleared the long headlands on either side of us. We climbed onto the deck. Graham began singing Paul McCartney and Denny Laine's 'Mull of Kintyre'. The breeze was brisk, but, from across the deck, I caught the line about dark distant mountains with valleys of green. Funny. Like many English people, I knew the tune but not the words. Graham carried on singing as the coastline sank into the sea.

Since the notorious Daniel Campbell was one of our chief reasons for coming to Jura, we mused that Graham might even have been distantly related to this branch of the Campbell family, so drawn was he to the place. We recapped on what we knew about the history. Born in 1672 into an old Argyllshire family, Daniel Campbell first got involved in colonial trade when he served as an apprentice to a merchant called Robert Campbell – possibly a relative – accompanying ships to Boston in 1692. Graham and I had both read that Daniel Campbell spent two years in Boston and the West Indies, trading enslaved people and tobacco. On his return to Glasgow he developed a major interest in the colonial trade. As his wealth grew, he lent money to cash-strapped Highland chiefs, becoming private banker to the first Campbell Duke of Argyll. Daniel Campbell had aristocratic pretensions of his own: he bought Shawfield estate to the north of the city and commissioned a mansion of the same name in Glasgow itself.[33]

Shawfield Mansion was a large, three-storey residence, topped with an imposing balustrade. An elegant stone staircase led from street level to the front door, which was topped by a Doric cornice; on the garden gateposts were sphinxes, guarders of secrets. The bedrooms were on the upper floor, where roof windows allowed the light to pour in. The private garden was decorated with sculptures.[34] As well as property, Daniel Campbell's wealth bought him political power and influence: in 1716, he became Member of Parliament for Glasgow, a seat he would hold for eighteen years. Campbell was widely known for his role as collector of customs and excise, and with his own trading past he would have known all the tricks. After the 1707 Act of Union between England and Scotland, Scotland was obliged to pay revenues to the British Treasury: Daniel Campbell oversaw import duties on goods like molasses and tobacco. He ran a tight ship, becoming unpopular with Glasgow tobacco merchants for cracking down on their habit of deliberately under-weighing it to pay less tax, a practice that had long given Glaswegian merchants a competitive advantage over English rivals in ports like Whitehaven.[35]

Daniel Campbell may have been vigilant over other people's imports; he was less so with his own, and his reputation for dishonesty preceded him. For a full seven years, the British Treasury demanded his customs accounts, until he relented and finally sent them. He was reprimanded for abusing his customs position by importing his own brandy tax-free, but the reprimand carried little weight. Campbell was also the commissioner for Inveraray, enforcing the post-Union customs law in local seaports – and, in the process, appointing his favoured tax collectors, surveyors, supervisors and customs officers.[36]

While Daniel Campbell evaded taxes on his own brandy, he made sure his fellow Scots paid theirs. In 1716 he helped enforce a tax on every pint of ale and beer sold in Glasgow, and nine years later was widely believed to have been instrumental in extending the Malt Tax across Scotland, which raised beer prices.[37] Scots were literally up in arms: widespread rebellion was threatened.[38] In 1725, late at night, Campbell's Shawfield Mansion was attacked by a large crowd. Fortunately for Campbell, he and his family were out of town at his Woodall residence. The crowd had come prepared with clubs, hammers and other implements. After looting the house, they set the floorboards alight and smashed the garden statues. By the time they had finished, only the burned-out walls and roof were left.

Such was Campbell's unpopularity that, it was rumoured, Glasgow's provost and magistrates were complicit in the attack. Campbell perhaps thought so too, later calling in a town council loan out of resentment.[39] (If this was the case, it didn't stop government troops firing on unarmed protesters the following day, killing nine bystanders and wounding nineteen others.)[40]

So outraged was Daniel Campbell's brother at this turn of events that he wrote to the prime minister to complain about his brother's 'barbarous treatment' by Glaswegians. Campbell, he argued, should be compensated because he had simply been doing his job in enforcing the Malt Tax.[41] Parliament approved a compensation award of £6,080, which, as punishment to Glasgow, was to be paid from the city's Malt Tax revenues.[42] Deciding he'd had enough of Glasgow, Daniel Campbell put the money towards his purchase of the islands of Islay and Jura, which set him back £12,000.[43]

Islay had long been the seat of Hebridean political and economic power. Settling with his family in a house near Islay's commercial centre, the village of Kilarrow, Campbell cut a very different figure from that of his Atlantic trading days.[44] He extended Islay House – then Kilarrow House – a neat, elegant white building which is now an upmarket hotel. Dabbling in historical and scientific knowledge, he funded the production of various books, including a maritime atlas and a history of empire, a *History of Scotland* and a record of commerce. He also contributed money to four books about Sir Isaac Newton's scientific discoveries by the renowned mathematician Colin Maclaurin, a professor at Edinburgh University whom Newton held in high esteem.[45] So did Daniel Campbell: Maclaurin had produced a mathematical calculation which allowed customs officials to use dipsticks to measure the amount of molasses in a barrel, a process with which Campbell was more than familiar.[46]

Daniel Campbell's house on Islay would have commanded a fine view of Jura which, today, is described as Britain's last wilderness. Thirty miles long and only 7 miles wide, Jura has few waymarks for walkers. Its northern tip is hoof-marked by goats. The island is dominated by twin mountains of basalt and quartzite known as the Paps.

From Islay, Graham and I took the ferry to Feolin, Jura's tiny landing stage. Graham was talking about the layers of history: about how Daniel Campbell, politician and merchant, placed himself at a remove from Atlantic world slavery and, in doing so, established Islay's flax industry. Such are the historical ironies of colonial profiteering, which so often transferred this wealth – as it passed through the generations – to local investments like these. I looked into this detail afterwards and found that Campbell achieved this partly by lengthening tenants' leases. His grandson later used his inherited wealth to develop the island's fishing and agricultural industries.[47] Commonly, secondary investments like these were the offspring of colonial wealth.

It was sunny and almost warm as the small car ferry puttered towards Feolin from Port Askaig. The journey took less than ten minutes, and we got perfect views of Jura's rugged shores. The sea was completely calm, though clouds boiled around the Paps. I had half-wanted Hebridean gales to conjure up Caribbean hurricanes, a symbolic merging of weather systems, but we couldn't have asked for better weather.[48] The ferry docked with an emphatic clang, and we disembarked.

On Jura, the grass was like rust, and a blue road cut through the dying heather. Now we would go on foot, so I peered at the curved beachline, hoping Graham wouldn't discover my deficient wayfaring skills. I needn't have worried. Even I couldn't get lost: there were no footpaths, and all we had to do was follow the shoreline. From the landing point at Feolin we would take a 5-mile walk across pebble beaches until a handful of houses would signal the approach to a white sandy bay known as the turquoise beach. From there we would leave the shore and return to Feolin along a rough track.

From Jura we could see Islay's undulating green hills clearly, so close it seemed we could reach out and touch them. Graham pointed across the strait to an old distillery crowning a rolling hill. Though it never came out of his bag, Graham had brought a set of full whisky sample bottles for a little light sampling of the famed Jura whisky distilled on the island. Restricted by the ferry crossing timetable, we had decided to give ourselves enough time to visit Jura Distillery at Craighouse after our walk, 8 miles away across the island.

Waves lapped over pebbles and we crunched the shingle underfoot. The beach petered out in a tumble of rocks, covered with cormorants. I wondered if we'd see seals. We continued along the shore until we reached some impassable rocks and went in single file along some sheep tracks and over cliffs to reach the next walkable beach. Above the shoreline the ground was spongy and uneven, making us high-step over matted grasses. This was the pathless terrain a friend had warned me about. Once, he and his wife had got lost on Jura. After several hours his wife stopped, exhausted, and let out a primal scream. He'd only once heard her make that sound before, he said: when she was giving birth.

Glancing inland, we noticed that the Paps had disappeared behind some mist. Our conversation had returned to Graham's Scottish family history. His father Lawrence was attracted to Scotland but had never been: Graham moved to Glasgow from London twenty years previously, unaware at the time of his Scottish ancestry. As a Rastafarian, Graham told me, he could have followed Rasta tradition by dropping his Campbell surname, a mark of enslavement. But he felt attached to the name and was glad that he retained it because this kept him focused on the Scottish–Jamaican connection. All he knew of his Scottish great-great-grandfather was that he cherished three books: the Bible, the works of Shakespeare and the poems of Robbie Burns, who was born in 1759, shortly after Daniel Campbell died. Burns is considered Scotland's national poet, and his Scots dialect poems are still so celebrated across the world that people sing his 'Auld Lang Syne' each New Year and, on 25 January, celebrate his birthday with haggis and whisky on Burns Night. There are statues of Burns all over Scotland: in stone or iron, standing and seated, arms folded and unfolded, with and without a dog, with a cloak, quill or plough. So popular was he that statues of him were frequently funded by public subscription.[49] Over 700 streets are named in his honour.

But Graham also knew that Robbie Burns became interested in

Jamaica, intended to move there and even wrote a poem about his impending journey there. As a farmworker, Burns needed an income to pursue his writing career and had turned to the plantation business for an answer. During this period, thousands of Scots went to the Caribbean as plantation-owners, overseers, bookkeepers, joiners and blacksmiths (just as others had gone out to India). Burns found a job at the Springbank plantation, 50 miles east of Oracabessa, where he was due to work for a man called Charles Douglas as a bookkeeper. (Burns himself described his future employment as that of a 'poor negro driver', or overseer.) The problem was that he could not afford his fare to Jamaica. Though he eventually booked a passage to Jamaica twice, in 1786, he didn't board the boat either time. Then, meeting with unexpected literary success, his plans changed: when his *Poems, Chiefly in the Scottish Dialect* achieved widespread acclaim, he moved to Edinburgh instead.[50]

Behind every good poet is a love story, and Burns was no exception: a love song he wrote to one of his muses, Mary Campbell, of Campbeltown in Argyll, reveals his Jamaican plans: 'Will ye go to the Indies, my Mary?' urges her to come with him to the Caribbean. The song glosses over the brutality of his intended role and concentrates on 'the charms o' the Indies', tempting the poet's love-object with images of Eden: 'O sweet grows the lime and the orange', the song goes, 'And the apple on the pine'.[51] In any case, Mary died of an illness in the year of the planned voyage but was immortalized by the poem. The would-be connection of Burns to Jamaica still inspires poets today. After our Jura walk, I came across a poetry collection by Shara McCallum called *No Ruined Stone*, which imagines what would have happened had Burns worked on the plantation and fathered a child with an African woman.[52]

We picked our way along the coastline, discovering a succession of beaches. Occasionally, Graham stopped to collect the colourful shells. Here, the strait was so narrow that you could almost swim it. Rutting stags sometimes do, so desperate are they to reach a possible mate on the facing shore. September was the rutting season, and we listened for the tell-tale throaty bellows but heard nothing; eventually, we came across a drowned stag, its stinking corpse swollen like a pufferfish.

We crossed an old bridge over a creek and encountered a lone farmhouse called Inver Cottage with a garden of mossy rhododendrons. The only route was right across the garden. I hesitated. 'It's fine!' Graham said. Heading for a gate, we found a farm track and followed it. We didn't see a soul over a mile of tufty ground which forced us into a tiring high-step. Approaching the shoulder of a hill, we saw the ominous sight of a Highland cow with horns like upturned spears, guarding a new-born calf. Graham was rightly wary of cattle and had recounted ominous tales of people who had been injured by, in his words, 'angry *coos*'. I'd been brought up not to fear cattle and would walk past any herd. (As I'd told Graham, this was almost my undoing. I'd once crossed a field and ignored a bull, which bellowed repeatedly then lowered its horns and gave chase, forcing me through a hedge.) And now, this Highland cow stood facing us with her new calf: she was not to be trifled with. But Graham knew how keen I was to see Jura's best turquoise beach. He was too. All the beaches we'd crossed were beautiful, but this one was reputed to have whiter sand and bluer water than all the rest. We sidled past the cow, backs to the fence, telling her how lovely her calf was. She stared, chewed, then stopped. Her glare was intimidating, but she let us pass.

A pebbled beach soon gave way to bleached sand: we had arrived at the turquoise beach. I could see why Graham loved this place. It was true: the white sand really did turn the sea turquoise. The sea was as still as a painting.

As we sat and ate our sandwich lunch, a small red boat growled along the strait. I took photographs, trying and failing to capture the red boat's contrast with the turquoise sea and Islay's green hills beyond. Lunch over, I took off my boots and socks and went for a paddle. The sea was ice-cold. 'It *looks* like Jamaica,' Graham observed, 'but it doesn't feel like it!'

It was early afternoon, and we checked our watches. If we walked back to Feolin, we could squeeze in a visit to Jura Distillery. Tempted though we were to retrace our steps along the beaches, we didn't want to push our luck with the Highland cow, and so stuck to the original plan of walking the last 2 miles along the one-track road a little inland from the coast. The road allowed us to talk without turning our heads while walking in single file, as we had done along the cliffs.

It was three-thirty in the afternoon when we arrived back at Feolin. As we got there, a ferry docked. In the distance we could see Port Askaig with its white houses and dark band of trees on the hill. It was still daylight, and we had a couple of hours to spare, giving us enough time to visit the distillery. Feolin was demarcated by a rusty old sign and a pebble-dashed toilet block: *port* felt like too grand a word for it. But we could not help lingering: we knew that this little landing point once saw deeply unhappy scenes of departure.

Jura was one of the ominous settings for the infamous Highland Clearances, which lasted around a century from the 1750s until, in 1886, the Crofters Holdings Act was passed by parliament to protect land tenants' rights. During these bleak decades, landowners wanted to yield better profits by creating large pastoral farms and game-hunting reserves. Deer forests, like the ones on Jura, loomed large in their plans. They evicted thousands of tenants who grew food and grazed animals on their land. Many evicted tenants were farmers whose families had subsisted in those places for generations. In the later phase of the Clearances, famine and poverty befell the evicted families, exacerbated by punishing rent rises.[53] Largely in desperation, many set sail for the British colonies, actively encouraged by landowners and their estate managers. For many, the hope was that they might become landowners in the colonies. A regional newspaper called the *John O'Groat Journal* described how landlords swept tenants from their lands like litter.[54] In 1767, fifty islanders migrated from Jura to Canada. Setting off from this very spot at Feolin, they must have made a miserable group, huddled by the shore.

Scotland's depopulated Highlands and Islands have been lamented by generations of writers, who commonly depicted dispossessed tenants as the rightful inheritors of local glens, pastures and fishing grounds.[55] The old landlords had been Highland chiefs, but their estates were bought by a new breed of landowners with fewer kinship ties. These men saw that deer hunting and sheep farming were more profitable than tenants who struggled to pay their rent. Game hunting attracted rich visitors, inspired by influential depictions of the Highlands and Islands' Romantic landscapes. This hunting cult was especially inspired by Sir Walter Scott's novels, featuring untamed Romantic landscapes that were blissfully remote from industrial bellows and factory smoke. These drastic changes of 'improved' land use ruined the livelihoods of existing tenants and small-scale farmers, causing intense struggles over land use.

Estate managers in the Highlands and Islands found cunning ways to drive out unwanted tenants. They raised rents and created bigger, more expensive plots of land. The most brutal of them resorted to destroying cottages. Some Highlanders starved. Some died of exposure. Others eked out an existence on crofts at the edge of the old estates. Thousands fled to towns and cities or sought work in quarries, factories or fisheries.

In the second phase of the Clearances, landowners and their agents saw emigration to the British colonies of Australia, Canada and New Zealand as a solution to poverty and hunger among their stricken tenants. In this, they were influenced by Thomas Malthus, a professor who trained young men to work as civil servants for the East India Company in Hertfordshire. Malthus' 1778 essay about population growth expressed the view that no amount of agricultural development could feed everyone. The impoverished should go elsewhere.[56]

The Highland potato famine added to the woes of farmers and crofters. This South American vegetable was first introduced to replace expensive grain with cheap potatoes, but when blight struck in the 1840s and 50s, Highlander and Islanders' reliance on potatoes made everything worse.[57] During the Highland potato famine, newspapers reported the stink of rotting potatoes. Mild and wet conditions created the ideal environment for fungal disease. The potato crop failed in three-quarters of crofters' parishes. *The Witness* paper called it the worst disaster for generations. Death rates went up. Surviving burial registers show marked increases in the deaths of children and older people. Officials reported three times the usual death rate in Mull in 1846 and 1847.[58] Of those who survived, yet more had to abandon their birthplace. Yet more migrated to the colonies.

The most influential historical account of the Clearances was Donald MacLeod's *Gloomy Memories*, published in 1857. MacLeod was evicted from Rossal village on the Sutherland estate, in the north-eastern Highlands, where some of the cruellest evictions took place. MacLeod and his neighbours were turned out of their homes, and his family was reduced to crofting at the foot of the Strath.[59] MacLeod conveyed his anger at this degradation. He published his collected letters to expose the callous actions of landowners and complicit authorities. Caledonia's valleys, he wrote, were being turned into sheep walks and hunting grounds. Hungry tenants watched sheep eating their corn or walked through deep snow, shouldering their possessions.[60]

Sutherland estate's manager was Elvander McIver, notorious for his ruthlessness towards tenants. He was formerly employed by the owner of Tulloch Castle, who inherited the castle – together with £30,000 from Jamaican plantations – but bankrupted the estate.[61] When the herring industry failed, Elvander McIver reduced the population on Sutherland estates by enlarging plots of land, knowing the tenants could ill-afford the increased rent. In Elphin he confiscated grazing land from tenants and added it to a sheep farm. McIver's eviction list included widows, a blind person, a drover, a teacher and a weaver.[62]

McIver subscribed to the Malthusian view of poverty and population growth. He firmly believed that the land was unable to support everyone that lived on it. When the potato crop failed, he disapproved of proposed poor laws which obliged landowners to provide rent relief during the famine. He said it would create unhealthy dependencies. After the 1836 potato famine, he considered emigration to

Canada and Australia the only option. He assisted this process, on one occasion drawing from his own family funds to pay for the tickets of evicted tenants. As he watched Highlanders departing Scottish shores, he comforted himself that it was for their own good.[63]

Domestic dramas like these have made it difficult for historians to focus on the colonial dimensions of such events.[64] But a new generation of historians has begun to explore who the new landowners were. Iain MacKinnon and Andrew MacKillop discovered that slavery profits played a crucial, overlooked role in the Highland Clearances.[65] Land purchases in the Highlands and Islands doubled in the 1830s, when slave-owners were compensated for lost slave labour following the 1833 Slavery Abolition Act. Forty per cent of these lands were bought after compensation money was claimed by those who owned or inherited plantations. All in all, when the direct and indirect beneficiaries of slavery wealth were combined in the analysis, over half of the Highlands – 1,834,708 acres – was bought by people in the slavery business, or who received plantation profits through inheritance or marriage. West Indies plantation wealth allowed landowners to buy, or retain, land.[66]

Well over half of this land changed hands as the Highland Clearances peaked. Those who made money through the slavery business removed thousands of people.[67] One such was James Evan Baillie, who shared compensation for over 450 enslaved people.[68] He personally received over £100,000, roughly the same amount he used to buy land in Glenelg and Glenshiel.[69] His estate manager recorded in his diary that the land was bought using 'compensation for freeing Colonel Baillie's slaves in Jamaica'.[70] Following these compensation awards Evan Baillie bought land in Badenoch, the western Highlands, Glenshiel and Letter Finlay.[71] He then built Glenshirra Lodge and the Duke of Gordon Hotel to put up hunting guests.[72] Evan Baillie was no model landlord. A journalist who visited his Glen Shiel estate was shocked by his tenants' squalor.[73] By the 1840s, Evan Baillie owned vast swathes of the Highlands. He also sent many Scots to labour on his plantations, providing employment in a region of the world that he had never visited.[74] When pressed, he contributed £2 to the local Poor Fund, but this miserly contribution was doubly ironic: half the impoverished people listed were his own tenants.[75]

In 1883, the Napier Commission was set up to investigate the causes of depopulation. Recipients of slavery wealth cropped up regularly in the commission report.[76] One prominent example was the slave-owning Cluny family, which owned the islands of Barra and Uist in the Outer Hebrides. A Member of Parliament, Colonel John Gordon of Cluny, evicted nearly 3,000 tenants so that his land could be given over to grazing sheep. The Clearances from his large estate, which extended across Benbecula, South Uist and Barra, are considered to have been particularly ruthless. There was social unrest on his estates and mass emigration to Canada.[77] John Gordon of Cluny was unsympathetic to social protest. As an MP he opposed workers' unions, saying they threatened the British constitution. Despite being one of Scotland's richest men, John Gordon was a notorious miser, obsessed with saving money. He hated spending it, going miles out of his way to avoid toll roads. One critic even joked that John Gordon refused to leave his bed because he thought he couldn't afford to get up.[78] Another example is the slave-owner Nicol Martin, on the Isle of Skye. The Glendale Risings happened after Martin forbade people from collecting driftwood for their fires or rushes for their thatched roofs. Martin's tenants also complained to the Napier Commission that they had to give Martin ten days' free labour each year. He made them 'work like slaves', they said.[79] These practices were condemned by the Napier Commission. Its findings led to the 1886 Crofters Act, which brought the Clearances to an end. Today, on islands like Jura, the Clearances are a distant memory.

It was late afternoon when we reached Craighouse, Jura's biggest settlement: a cluster of cottages with a tiny shop and a curved stone pier. We'd driven east along the island's only metalled road in a state of expectation, but Jura Distillery had already closed. Looking for consolation inside a village shop, Graham discovered a bottle of

Jura-made rum and wondered if this was the island's alcoholic nod to the Caribbean connection, made just across the road at the distillery. The bottle's label made no mention of any historical link to Jamaica. Rum secured – how apposite, we thought, to be bringing rum rather than whisky back from Jura – we drove back towards Feolin past the deer forests created by the Campbell family. The wire fences went on and on. A stag leaped off the sandy track, and I thought that the landscape really did seem scoured of people and filled with deer. We reached Feolin, boarded the ferry and – as we crossed the sound between the two islands – commented that the distant cars at Islay's port made it seem like a comparative metropolis after Jura.

The air smelled of seaweed. On the ferry Graham told me about the more inaccessible sights that he wants to see for himself on his next visit to Jura: Corryvreckan whirlpool, off the island's north coast. Corryvreckan's angry roar can be heard for miles. Caused by Atlantic currents, the whirlpool struck us as a geographically apt symbol of the ancestral vortex caused by Scotland's violent encounter with the West Indies. The idea of Corryvreckan returned to me when, months after our walk, the Jamaican researcher got back in touch. She'd pursued every possible avenue of enquiry but, sadly, had to admit defeat.

It would, of course, have brought satisfying narrative closure to announce that Graham's lost family history was found, that the researcher solved the mystery and came up trumps, that we recovered Graham's lineage and drew his entire family tree. But Graham's story remained elusive. Encountering this emptiness is the experience of people with Caribbean heritage everywhere. The historian Kris Manjapra has compared it to staring down a blue hole in the Atlantic.[80] Rather like the Corryvreckan whirlpool, we thought. Hundreds of years after slavery's abolition, the impact of its denial of humanity, even identity, to enslaved people lingers on. Slavery's giant, intergenerational whirlpool still turns.

Back on Islay, Graham said we should drive to his favourite location of Finlaggan, just 3 miles inland from Port Askaig. We reached it at sunset, and the place was deserted. Graham explained to me that it was from here that MacDonald chiefs ruled as Lords of the Isles between the fourteenth and sixteenth centuries. We walked towards some ruined stone buildings, and he pointed to an islet just off Finlaggan's shore. It was perfectly round like a grassy coin. This was the council chamber where the MacDonalds sat and deliberated. Here they met the kings of England, Scotland and France on equal terms.

When a man was initiated into this lordship, he would place his feet in carved stone footprints and take his rightful place as a leader who might follow his predecessors. That was the principle, anyway. Ultimately his rule was supposed to be noble, never self-interested.[81] That was when I realized why Graham was so drawn to Finlaggan. This was a place of deliberation by councillors: here, then, his political ancestors met. Of course, Graham's political world bears no resemblance to that of the ancient MacDonalds – people from other times entirely. For Graham, political power truly is about service: tenancy rights and community empowerment, a far cry from Daniel Campbell's priorities.

The sun was like Midas, turning the loch to liquid gold. Long grasses shimmered on the surrounding hills. Even the stones glittered. We walked to a wooden bridge which led to the round isle. A sign warned: 'Deteriorating Bridge. Do Not Cross.' Graham ignored the sign. 'It would be rude not to,' he said, 'and if I go first, I'll be the one to fall in!' I followed him across the bridge to the old council chamber. On either side, brown reeds sighed like the souls of bygone chiefs. Here, in this place, Graham was in his element. Finlaggan was the true seat of this Scottish-Jamaican Campbell.

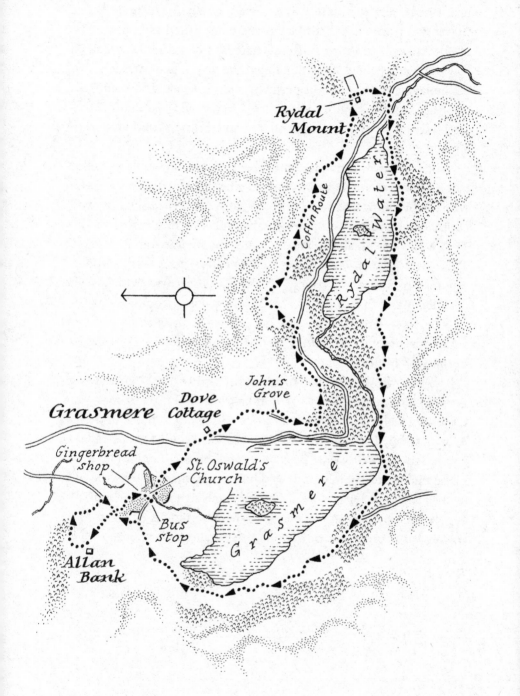

Rydal Mount

Rydal Water

Coffin Route

John's Grove

Grasmere

Dove Cottage

Gingerbread shop

St. Oswald's Church

Bus stop

Allan Bank

Grasmere

2.

The East India Company Walk:
Wordsworth and the Lake District

The Lake District is the largest National Park in England, now a UNESCO World Heritage Site. Situated in Cumbria, this vast park consists of plunging mountains or 'fells' and over thirty lakes – or 'waters', 'tarns' or 'meres', as they're known. Tourists and holiday-makers flock here, heading to do water sports or take boating cruises at Lake Windermere, or seeking out the peace of Rydal Water, which reflects bracken, mountain and cloud in its mirrored surface. There are no motorboats or water-skiers on Rydal Water, just hardy swimmers and the splash of oars.

People have found inspiration in this extraordinary landscape for centuries. In the late eighteenth and nineteenth centuries it became associated with Romanticism, whose characteristic emotional sensitivity to the natural world found cultural expression in art, music and above all poetry.[1] Three miles north-west of Rydal, nestling beneath the great fell of Fairfield, is Grasmere village. This unassuming cluster of cottages and an Anglican church is perhaps the epicentre of English Romanticism, for it was home to William Wordsworth, the movement's founding poet. Grasmere, and Dove Cottage – once home to William and his sister Dorothy, now a museum dedicated to the Wordsworths – remain a place of pilgrimage for poetry lovers. Ten miles south of Grasmere is a seventeenth-century farm called Hill Top, where Beatrix Potter, the natural scientist, conservationist and creator of *Peter Rabbit*, settled in the early twentieth century. The global fame of these two very different figures – Wordsworth and Potter – make the Lakes an essential stop on any English literary tour.

My walking companion was the Guyanese-born British photographer Ingrid Pollard. As the commissioned photographer of Colonial Countryside (my child-led history and writing project with the National Trust), Ingrid had accompanied pupils on country house visits. The night before our walk, over dinner in Ambleside, we swapped memories of those outings to National Trust properties: the giggling schoolgirls trying on costumes; the group that burst across the country house lawn like racehorses out of their starting gates. Most striking was our vivid memory of pupils kneeling beside a seventeenth-century carved figure of an enchained African. Later I realized that I had not actually witnessed this scene in real life, having been in another room at the time: I was in fact recalling the striking photograph Ingrid had taken of the scene.

That night, Ingrid was staying in Ambleside, but I had to get back to the Youth Hostel at Grasmere a few miles distant. Belatedly, I remembered it was a bank holiday and, after saying goodnight, wandered out to check the bus times. There were none. I looked up taxis: the drivers were all on holiday. I would have to walk. My options were the main road, or the more scenic footpath alongside Rydal Water. Deciding on the latter, I struck out, watching the setting sun turn Rydal Water coral pink then continuing along the path in the failing light. Soon, every woodland shadow seemed like a crouching figure. Reprimanding myself for choosing an isolated route which I had never walked before (and without a map), I retraced my steps to the old road, itself now barely visible in the growing darkness. At the crown of the hill, I passed a man with a head torch, hurried past a fir grove then pressed on as though navigating a dark sea, aiming towards some twinkling cottage lights: Grasmere. I was relieved to reach it. *Never do that again*, I told myself.

Yet my hair-raising night walk had part-traced the route I'd planned for the following day. I would walk with Ingrid from Grasmere village to Dove Cottage, the Wordsworth home and museum. From there we would take a woodland footpath to Rydal, a village which lies halfway between Grasmere and Ambleside, on whose edge stands Rydal Mount. This was the favourite home of William Wordsworth, who lived for much of his life there until his death in 1850. A pretty white house which still belongs to the Wordsworth family, it stands on rising ground at the edge of a five-acre garden and has good views of Rydal Water. From there, we'd take the lakeside path skirting Rydal Water, and follow its descent to Grasmere Water. Then, we would take the winding lane back towards Allan Bank, where Wordsworth also lived for two years with family and friends, including his poetic collaborator Samuel Taylor Coleridge.

The next day I stood at Grasmere's bus stop awaiting Ingrid's arrival from Ambleside. It was late spring, but the air was chilly, and rain threatened. When the bus drew in, Ingrid emerged wearing a mustard-yellow hat, grey-rimmed glasses and a blood-red fleece – an experienced walker prepared for all weathers. We retreated to a nearby café for pre-walk mugs of tea, sitting next to a window misted up with condensation. Ingrid explained that she knows the Lakes well. As a young woman she would drive up from London in a van with friends, and they'd rent a big house near Grasmere Water. 'I've kept coming back ever since,' she said. These Lakeland experiences led her to pioneer photographic explorations of race and the countryside. Back in the 1980s, she became increasingly frustrated by the absence of Black faces like hers in the postcards and images of the region, so she created *Pastoral Interlude*, a photographic sequence featuring Black people in the countryside. It's a work that challenges the idea that Black people who live, or venture into, rural England should be considered as some kind of trespassers. One image in the sequence is captioned: 'The owners of these fields; these trees and sheep want me off this GREEN AND PLEASANT LAND.' Another caption plays on Wordworth's 'Daffodils' poem, with the words: 'I thought I liked the Lake District, where I wandered lonely as a Black face in a sea of white. A visit to the countryside is always filled with a feeling of unease; dread.'[2] As the first prominent study of Black people's exclusion from the countryside, *Pastoral Interlude* inspired many Black Britons. Despite alluding to rural racism, it does not communicate fear so much as assert the right to be in the countryside and to enjoy it, as Ingrid has done all her life. The work remains both deeply influential and relevant today, especially given that walking groups such as Black Girls Hike and Muslim Hikers now bear the brunt of considerable hostility: responses suggesting that, to many, the countryside remains persistently associated with Whiteness.

Ingrid's fascination with Wordsworth country, and her fruitless search for Black faces in tourist images of it, found expression in her *Wordsworth's Heritage* of 1992, a sequence of photographs designed as an age-tinted souvenir postcard. In it, a sketch of Wordsworth is surrounded by four photographs of Black walkers – friends of Ingrid's – examining maps, staring at the camera and sitting by a waterfall. Mimicking old world tourist-speak, the caption reads, 'Ms. Pollard's party stops to ponder on matters of History and Heritage.'[3] This image was pasted onto billboards throughout towns and cities, bringing conversations about rural representation to Britain's urban centres. 'Every time I visited the Lake District,' Ingrid said, 'I was tempted to sneak my postcards into tourist shops.' She never did, though.

As Ingrid knew, William Wordsworth's brother John was deeply involved with the East India Company, not based in India like Sykes of Basildon Park, but as a sea captain. John lost his life in a shipwreck as a result. The wider Wordsworth family was drawn into John's misadventure, and William himself was gravely and permanently affected by it. 'You'd never know it,' Ingrid said. She was right: the customary tourist portrayal of the Wordsworths rarely highlights the family's associations with India, or, as we were to explore, China, Barbados and Mississippi. On that cold, rainy spring morning, Ingrid and I set off through Wordsworth country to explore this overlooked history.

As we set out on the first leg of our ten-mile walk, cars tore along the busy road to the market town of Keswick, which skirts the eastern side of Grasmere Water, and it was a relief to turn onto the old road up to Dove Cottage with its lime-washed walls, double chimneys and slate roof.

It was too late for daffodils, but now bluebells covered the hillsides and grassy banks. A blackbird sang on the garden wall, which Ingrid, a keen gardener, inspected for unusual moss species – and soon found one. 'I wish I could nick that,' she laughed. 'Imagine having Wordsworth moss growing in your garden.' Ingrid also shared the Romantics' obsession with rare ferns, which she also spotted around the cottage. Wordsworth's friend Samuel Taylor Coleridge, she explained, admired ferns and wrote about them, while Dorothy Wordsworth collected specimens and grew them in this same garden.[4]

We entered the cottage, and, as our eyes adjusted to the interior darkness, Ingrid wondered that anyone could write a poem in it. We leafed through some reproductions of Wordsworth's handwritten verse, and the nearby guide smiled in agreement when Ingrid laughingly observed that Wordsworth was surrounded by adoring women who tended to his every need. Dorothy gardened, cleaned, sewed, scrubbed and baked – as well as copying out his poems multiple times. A gifted writer herself, Dorothy's own influence on his poetry went unacknowledged for over 200 years until academics started to realize the significance of her journals and poems to her brother's work.[5]

But Ingrid and I were interested in William Wordsworth's finances as much as his poems. Poetry's precarious relationship to money is often overlooked. Then as now, writers funded their literary endeavours by undertaking clerical work, relying on subscribers or seeking wealthy patrons.[6] Often unable to rely on earnings from their poetry, they tried to make a living in other ways too. Given Britain's extensive colonies in the late eighteenth and early nineteenth centuries – from Australia and Canada to India and the West African Gold Coast – much available work was linked to colonial trade and investment. Like many writers of his era, Wordsworth understood that colonial ventures provided a potential revenue stream and investment opportunity – and thereby offered a compelling route to balancing his artistic needs with providing for his family.

★

Ingrid and I climbed the hillside from Dove Cottage for a view of the plunging fells which have attracted and inspired so many. Despite overcast skies, we were not disappointed. The hills were a bright, almost lurid green, girdled by stone walls; the fields were lined with trees in full leaf, waving at the auburn fells beyond.

We gazed out across Grasmere Water beneath us. Near its western shore, set apart from the village, we could see Allan Bank, a house that Wordsworth disliked because it spoilt his view – though he eventually moved his growing family into it. Now, the house belongs to the National Trust, which listed Allan Bank in its 2020 report on colonialism. Here is the listing, in full:

> *Allan Bank, Cumbria*
>
> The poet William Wordsworth (1770–1850) lived for a time at Allan Bank. He and his sister, writer Dorothy Wordsworth (1771–1855), are both known for expressing views in opposition to slavery. Their brother, John Wordsworth (1772–1805), became Commander of the East India Company ship *Earl of Abergavenny* in 1801. He captained two successful voyages to China, in which the family invested.
>
> Wordsworth's third voyage would have made the family a considerable sum, but the ship sank a few days into the journey, causing the death of John and many others.[7]

Though the listing seems innocuous enough, the media response to it was furious, and highly misleading. An article in *The Times* was headed: 'Wordsworth's home linked to slavery? It's nuts, says descendent.' Above was an image of the poet Wordsworth with his head in his hands. Although the Allan Bank entry identified the Wordsworths' colonial connection as being with the East India Company, rather than slavery (in fact, you'll note, the listing went out of its way to mention William and Dorothy's opposition to slavery), the poet's living descendent was quoted as being upset, stating that John Wordsworth 'wasn't trading slaves' but 'buying and selling spices' and that William Wordsworth 'didn't have a colonial bone in his body'.[8] In the *Daily Mail*, a historian of post-war Britain wrote an article entitled: 'How Dare the National Trust Link Wordsworth to Slavery Because His Brother Sailed a Ship to China?'[9] Here, again, the headline mischaracterized the Allan Bank report entry as connecting William Wordsworth with slavery. But the historian's main objection was that the business activities of John Wordsworth were tangential, as he saw it, and had little to do with the celebrated poet. But, in fact, the stories of Wordsworth the poet and Wordsworth the family provider were inextricably linked.

The 1805 shipwreck of the *Earl of Abergavenny* was a national tragedy, with one of the highest death tolls in British maritime history. It was a commercial disaster too: the custom-built vessel went down with one of the East India Company's largest-ever investments.[10] For the Wordsworth family, John's death was both a personal tragedy and a financial disaster – and it would leave its mark in William's poetry.

By John, William and Dorothy's time, the Wordsworths had been involved in colonial business for three generations. Along the way they discovered that the British Empire did not always make people money. Richard Wordsworth, grandfather to the poet, had been a legal agent and steward to the Cumbrian landowner Henry Lowther, 3rd Viscount Lonsdale. In 1720, the Viscount, like many others, lost vast sums of money in the notorious financial crash known as the South Sea Bubble. After Britain won the right to transport and sell enslaved people to Spanish America, the South Sea Company had bought the contract from the British government for some £9.5 million, which represented a large portion of the national debt. It had been assumed that the company would make a fortune from trading in enslaved people, and in Britain, the excitement over expected profits reached fever pitch. Many people invested and, desperate to get their hands on South Sea shares, paid vastly inflated sums for the opportunity. Instead, there was a crash, and in the resulting economic turmoil, thousands of families were ruined.[11] Among them was the Viscount, whose financial affairs were consequently in disarray when Richard Wordsworth came to work for him.

With Wordsworth's help, the Viscount managed to salvage the

Westmorland portion of the family estate by selling off family lands in Yorkshire and Durham but still died in debt.[12] The true beneficiary of this retained Westmorland estate was the Viscount's heir, Sir James Lowther, who through marriage and inheritance accrued vast tracts of land in Britain's north-west – Westmorland and Cumberland with its port of Whitehaven – and Christ Church plantation in Barbados.[13] Sir James' wealth came from coal; it also came from slavery.[14] An estate inventory for Christ Church plantation lists 'Negro Men', with the names bestowed upon them by slave-owners: a 'driver' called Adam, a 'Boyler' named Yorkshire and a groom called Meaburn, the name of the Westmorland village where Lowther's father was brought up. Listed female field workers include Madam Lucy, Phillida, three 'house negroes' and 'Cubbah', with a note saying that she is 'past labour'. These names, eighty-six of them, are followed by lists of 'Negro Boys' and then livestock, including a bull named Butcher, an ox named Spring and a calf called Lovely. The document hints at the brutalities which bordered daily existence. A half-century later, people on the Lowthers' Barbadian estate would attempt to resist their enslavement, rising up in the failed bid for freedom known as the Bussa Rebellion.[15]

Sir James Lowther's wealth brought him political power. He became the Conservative Member of Parliament for Cumberland. His base was Cockermouth, an ancient town on the edge of the Lake District then undergoing rapid growth, in part due to the burgeoning colonial trade coming through ports like Whitehaven, on the nearby Atlantic coast. And, like his father before him, he hired a Wordsworth to look after his business and legal affairs: John Wordsworth, son of Richard, and father to John and William the poet. In 1765, John Wordsworth moved into Sir James' newly acquired Cockermouth mansion, now known as Wordsworth House, where he lived rent-free. The following year he married Ann. It was in Wordsworth House that their children were born: William in 1770, Dorothy a year later, and John in 1772.

In 1768, Sir James was convicted of political corruption and sent to Newgate Gaol. John Wordsworth, who had provided legal services to the disgraced baronet, suffered by association:[16] many years later, his daughter Dorothy recalled that 'amongst those who visited my father's house he had not one real friend'.[17] Sir James inflicted more than just reputational damage on the Wordsworth family. The baronet owed John thousands of pounds in expenses. This sum, which was never repaid, would have left the Wordsworth children a comfortable legacy and given William Wordsworth some freedom to write. (Sir James was prepared to spend money when it suited him. The year before John Wordsworth's death, the baronet offered the British government a fitted, fully-manned warship with seventy-four guns for use during the American Revolutionary War, a lavish gesture which burnished his public image.[18])

The Wordsworth siblings had a happy childhood in Cockermouth until, in 1778, their mother died, leaving them and their father bereft. When their father died five years later, the Cockermouth house was shut up, and the children dispatched to be raised by relatives. As the children grew up, separated from each other, it was John – less studious but more practical than his siblings – who turned his hand to repairing the hole that Sir James Lowther had left in the family finances. Aged sixteen, he trained for a maritime career and joined the British navy. After sailing to Barbados, he left the navy and joined the East India Company, working his way up through the ranks on voyages to Jamaica, the United States, the Azores, India and China.[19] His ultimate aim was to gain sufficient experience to be awarded command of a company ship on the lucrative trade route from Britain to India and China.

In the meantime, he concentrated on climbing the ranks and learning how to profit from private trade. He and his uncle, a sea captain, sailed twice to China. John also sought to include his family in these schemes. The siblings' eldest brother Richard was a London-based lawyer, and William had modest funds because his friend Raisley Calvert died and left him a £900 legacy around this time. John asked for £100 from Dorothy's savings account in Carlisle Bank. Implying by his wording – 'that hundred pound' – that this was the sum total of her savings, he planned to invest Dorothy's money in private trade. Their brother Richard promised to guarantee her money should it be lost in the investment.[20] In fact, though John did not make a profit on these early voyages, he came to understand where big profits were to be made: in opium.

John learned that, having opened up the poppy-producing regions of Bengal and Bihar, the East India Company had a monopoly on its trade. This had happened some years before, in the 1770s. Opium imports to China, where there was huge demand, had doubled in the last half of the eighteenth century.[21] The company's opium trade was strategic and circumstantial. Its ultimate goal was not to trade opium for its own sake so much as find a way of buying Chinese commodities like silk, porcelain and tea for British consumers. Silver was needed to pay for these goods, but – apart from opium – the Chinese were uninterested in anything which the company could supply. Chinese traders paid for the opium in silver, which the company then used to buy Chinese goods. This is how John Wordsworth became acquainted with the narcotics trade. In 1797, he brought marijuana for the poet and family friend Samuel Taylor Coleridge, who would later live with William Wordsworth's family at Allan Bank.[22]

Initially, John Wordsworth's opium-trading efforts were small-scale. He did, however, see that enormous sums could be made through opium for captains and crews who were allocated the right trade routes – between India and China – and who had sufficient money to invest. This focused his mind on securing command of a company vessel which would sail between India and China. He knew that being a ship's commander would vastly increase his private trading allowance. The following year, as John sailed to Canton with his uncle on the *Osterly*, the Chinese Emperor banned opium smoking in China, and a ban on opium imports soon followed. Undeterred, East India Company employees relied on corrupt customs officers to smuggle opium into China.[23] It was during this Canton voyage that John made £100 on opium sales: far more profitable than the legal trade in tea, he informed his uncle.[24]

John was painfully aware that his brother William was short of money. The two were close – William sent poems to accompany his brother on his voyages[25] – and John wanted to provide material help, which William was ready to accept. William had, he wrote, been living on parsley, vegetables and air.[26] This was something of an exaggeration, but it was nonetheless true that a better income would allow William to meet his household expenses whilst finding time to write poems.

The year of John's voyage on the *Osterly*, Wordsworth published *Lyrical Ballads* with Samuel Taylor Coleridge. The following year, William and Dorothy moved to Dove Cottage in the Lake District, a move he had suggested to his sister following a two-year stay in Dorset, which had given them a taste for living together. Above all, the move was also designed to embrace William's vocation as a poet by living in a renowned natural setting.[27] The siblings arrived at Dove Cottage on Christmas Eve in the final days of the eighteenth century. William wrote to Coleridge four days after their arrival, mentioning that Dorothy had a toothache and they both had colds.[28]

That year, in January 1800, John came to stay in Grasmere. Dorothy managed her excitement at his impending visit by going outdoors to pick wild thyme and columbine. When John and William finally arrived, the siblings stayed up talking until 4 a.m.[29] The visit – which extended from January to September – rekindled the relationship among three people who had been separated as children: they walked, fished, swam in the lakes, collected plants and seeds,[30] and bottled rum, the by-product of West Indian sugar.[31] They received visitors, including Coleridge, who developed an instant fondness for John.[32]

On one of Coleridge's visits during these months Dorothy felt unwell and took laudanum, a tincture of opium in alcohol.[33] This was freely available over the pharmacy counter. Actual opiate addiction, now globally widespread, had even reached the rural isolation of the surrounding Lakeland villages; Coleridge himself was an opium addict. So too was a future tenant of Dove Cottage, the writer Thomas De Quincey. A disciple of Coleridge and Wordsworth, De Quincey first encountered opium during his studies at

Oxford in the early 1800s and had initially used it as pain relief for neuralgia. Opium, which would plague his life, was the subject of his most well-known work, *Confessions of an English Opium Eater*.[34]

On 29 September 1800, John left the Lake District to continue his mission to persuade the East India Company to give him command of a ship.[35] Dorothy and William accompanied him on foot for the first part of his journey to London. The three said goodbye at Ullswater. Dorothy, who was protective of her younger brother, wrote fondly of John, calling him a 'poor fellow' and 'poor John'.[36] A year later, William recalled John's visit in a poem called 'The Fir Grove', where he contrasted his own poetic vocation with John's worldly affairs. For William, the fir grove was a place for 'studious leisure'. By contrast, the poem conveys the idea that John's maritime experiences informed his relationship with nature, giving him both a 'watchful heart' and a sailor's 'restlessness of foot', pacing beneath the trees. In the poem, William imagines his brother walking a ship's deck until he could return to Grasmere.[37]

An ironic tension underlay the poem, for although William Wordsworth came to associate the grove with John, he disliked fir plantations in the Lake District. This was particularly the case with Scots pine, which he considered foreign, as it was not native to the Lakes.[38] The fact was that so many mature oaks – trees native to the region – had been felled for naval shipbuilding that they were now growing scarce: nobody, complained one commentator,[39] had any motivation to wait eighty to 100 years for an oak to reach maturity when they could make more immediate profits from younger, faster-growing trees.[40] With ships getting larger, huge quantities of oak timber were needed. John Wordsworth's future command, the *Earl of Abergavenny*, supposedly used the timber of 1,400 oak trees.[41]

Here we were, Ingrid and I, walking through landscapes which meant so much to the Wordsworth siblings. After a short walk alongside the long mossy wall on the hill above Dove Cottage, we reached the wood immortalized in 'The Fir Grove', which Dorothy and William took to calling John's Grove, in their brother's memory.

We had no trouble understanding why the spot meant so much to them. The new leaves were luminous. Grasmere Water glittered beyond the pine trees in a play of light which Dorothy once compared to a shoal of herrings in the lake.[42] Like Dorothy, Ingrid was quick to identify different shades of bluebells and was delighted to discover half-hidden violets in the verges. I wandered over and parted the long grass to see the faded blue petals for myself. I wouldn't have spotted them in a million years. 'Have you ever walked with a photographer before?' Ingrid asked laughingly. She rarely confined herself to the footpath and her detailed observations were educating my eye. We wondered whether the thick pine-trunks were the same trees mentioned by Dorothy in her journal, under which she would write, and she and William used to lie listening to birdsong and the sound of running water.[43]

Ingrid told me she was intrigued by the people whom the Wordsworths associated with in the Lakes. One family friend was William Wilberforce, the MP and anti-slavery campaigner, who liked to holiday there.[44] Wordsworth's uncle, meanwhile, had forged a friendship with Thomas Clarkson, who in 1795 built a house in Ullswater, where Dorothy and William had parted with their brother John. Clarkson was profoundly committed to the anti-slavery cause and rode tens of thousands of miles on horseback to advance it, as did many abolitionists of his day who were Black. Some years before, in the single year of 1787, he had ridden over 3,000 miles, organized more than 200 anti-slavery committees and sent over 100 petitions to parliament.[45] There were, Ingrid recalled, some interesting visitors to Dove Cottage too. Dorothy's journal mentions a series of beggars who came to the door, many of whom had been involved in war and colonial activities. One woman told how her husband was wounded serving in the West Indies; another, a sailor, had spent years aboard a Royal Navy battleship but now had no pension to live on. One old man explained that his close family had died in Jamaica. One day a sailmaker sat with Dorothy and William in the cottage for two hours and told them about his Guinea voyage on board a slave-ship, an experience he never wanted to repeat. The stranger, Dorothy wrote, reminded her of their brother John.[46]

In London, John had succeeded in his aim. He was overjoyed at his promotion to commander, in 1801, and now wore its blue uniform with yellow buttons and a cocked hat. He wrote excitedly, calling his new command a 'very noble' ship. The vessel was indeed handsome, with a black hull and thick gold stripes around the gun ports. It belonged to a fleet of forty ships designed with increased capacity for holding tea, following a parliamentary cut in tea duties which made it more profitable to trade.[47] John wrote to William's future wife, Mary Hutchinson, in triumph: 'what a rich dog they say I am to be', his letter said. Financial success, it seemed, was assured.[48]

In June that year, John's siblings finally received their own glad tidings. Sir James had died, and his relative, Sir William Lowther, was apparently willing to honour the unpaid debt.[49] There was no immediate relief, but the Wordsworths made a formal claim of £10,388, 6 shillings and 8 pence – a fortune, in those days – and waited hopefully for the money to arrive.[50] The money would allow William to marry Mary Hutchinson, whom he'd known since he was a child, which he did the following year, on 4 October 1802. Dorothy would live with them in Dove Cottage until they all moved to Allan Bank in May 1808.

In 1801, John Wordsworth had set sail for China on his first voyage as commander. He appears to have been liked by his crew, earning the soubriquet John the Philosopher, owing to his even-tempered disposition.[51] In May that year, he sailed to various ports for supplies, including Penang – to buy pepper, tin and betel nut – and eventually arriving in the Pearl River Delta in January 1802, sailing twice to Canton from Macao.[52] Dorothy also invested some money in this voyage, but John lost money rather than profiting from it, though rising tea prices reduced his debts.[53] While John was away, William continued to write, his poems inflected by thoughts of his brother – 'To the Daisy', in praise of the flower's year-round gift to nature, recalled a letter John had written him while staying on the Isle of Wight, describing the flowers as: 'white stars upon the dark green fields'.[54] These words inspired three daisy poems of the same title, all written in 1802 but subsequently revised after John's death.

That June, William's attention was caught by the great uprising of enslaved people on the island of Haiti, led by the charismatic Toussaint L'Ouverture, himself the educated son of an enslaved man. Against the odds, the movement had seized power. When the French reinvaded, L'Ouverture laid down his weapons in exchange for an amnesty and a French commitment not to restore slavery. The French did not keep their promise, and L'Ouverture was arrested, imprisoned and taken back to France; the following year, he died in prison.[55] Wordsworth's 1803 sonnet 'To Toussaint L'Ouverture' praised his legacy: 'Thou has left behind / Powers that will work for thee . . . Thy friends are exultations, agonies, / And love, and man's unconquerable mind'. (Two hundred years later, the British-Guyanese poet John Agard would write a poem in reply to Wordsworth's, in which he imagined the exiled leader's response: 'I have never . . . had a close-up view of daffodils. / My childhood's roots are the Haitian hills.' The poem draws to an end with the line 'So, thanks brother, for your sonnet's tribute.')[56]

During this time, William produced an early draft of 'I Wandered Lonely as a Cloud', now one of the most well-known lyric poems in the English language. Although the poem depicts a solitary male wanderer, its inspiration and wording originated from a walk with Dorothy, whose journal describes daffodils which 'tossed and reeled and danced'.[57] While William was composing these poems, John again set sail for Canton on the *Earl of Abergavenny*, in 1803. His oldest brother Richard – the London lawyer – contributed £3,000 as an advance on the Lowther compensation money for investing in private trade on goods like tea and opium, but no money was made on this voyage either.[58] Being a commander was not sufficient in and of itself: John was desperate to secure the lucrative India–China sailing route and he kept his eye on the prize. He had witnessed the serious profits being made by shipping Indian opium to Canton, despite the various bans there. Opium addiction in Canton had by then reached epic proportions: around a tenth of the population were addicts.[59] The drug was wreaking havoc, but to East India Company officials this addiction represented an opportunity. Company ships smuggled it into China, then reinvested the profits in Chinese tea and silk, which it exported to Britain.[60]

Back home, the Wordsworths were watching their friend Coleridge's addiction with mounting alarm but, notwithstanding the known dangers of opium, John was determined to get in on the trade. Returning to Britain, he lobbied the East India Company long and hard to obtain the coveted Bengal–Canton sailing route. In doing this, he called on the family's company connections, and even persuaded William Wilberforce to intercede for him.[61] In the year of his fateful *Abergavenny* voyage, he finally got his wish. Officially, John's mission was to load Indian cotton in Bengal, and ship it to China; he was to reinvest the proceeds of its sale in luxury commodities for the British market. The *Abergavenny* was large and could carry a substantial and valuable cargo.[62] John, though, was more concerned with illegal opportunities. As he wrote to his uncle (phrasing it slightly oddly): 'I shall also have a chance of making by opium.'[63] On a previous voyage he had been disciplined and fined by his employer for trading illegally in silken fabric, an action which suggested his readiness to do whatever it took to make a profit.[64] John's purpose, as he himself wrote, was 'to get as much money as possible'.[65]

John's voyage was scheduled for February, to take advantage of favourable currents between Bengal and Canton. He would sail from Weymouth on the English south-west coast. Seeking investors, he once again called upon his family to invest. As well as putting up £400 of his own money, he obtained £277, 10 shillings from William and £80 from Dorothy, who were now flush with the first instalment of the repaid Lowther debt.[66] This was an act of trust on their part, as their investment represented a significant proportion of their savings. While they knew that their brother had previously been unsuccessful in his private trading ventures, the siblings likely felt assured of greater success on this voyage, given John's Bengal–China route, but they would have nonetheless been conscious of the risk. Altogether John raised an impressive £20,000 for the voyage. He planned to invest this money in his now considerable allowance in private trade and anticipated returning with a personal fortune of £6,000.[67]

Yet for John, profit was not an end in itself. In his mind, it meant affection, comfort and freedom. He thought of retiring in Grasmere, bringing home money to support his sister and to give his brother the freedom to write. It was a plan that he had discussed at length with his siblings. As William Wordsworth wrote in a letter to his friend James Losh:

> We had at that time little to live upon and he went to sea high in hope and heart that he should soon be able to make his Sister independent and contribute to any wants which I might have. He encouraged me to persist in the plan of life which I had adopted. I will work for you was his language and you shall attempt to do something for the world. Could I but see you with a green field of your own and a Cow and two or three other little comforts I should be happy.[68]

John's aims were, of course, nobler than his means. (William, it has to be said, rather glossed over his brother's trading activities, presenting him as a 'pilgrim of the sea', as though he were on a spiritual mission rather than an opium-trading expedition.)[69]

Ships gained trading advantages through speed – in this case, being the first to reach China.[70] Accordingly, John's preparations were hectic. He assembled a crew of 114 men. With the Indian Ocean rife with pirates, 'East Indiamen' like the *Earl of Abergavenny* doubled as armed passenger ships, including wealthy passengers who paid a premium for better accommodation and the right to dine at the commander's table – meaning, in turn, having to take livestock as cargo (the sailors and humbler passengers ate salt beef and pork).[71] John wrote to William that there would be almost forty people dining at this table, requiring considerable provisions which took up valuable cargo space. John asked company directors to reduce the number of passengers, as the ship was crowded.[72]

Also listed on the ship's manifest was a group of soldiers on their way to Bengal, among whom were several cadets:[73] these were the years of the East India Company's military campaigns and territorial expansion; to the south, Mughal rule was nearing its end and Delhi was soon to fall to the British.

From John's Grove, Ingrid and I descended to a road, where we found an ice-cream van. Despite the dreary weather, we bought ice-creams, and Ingrid held her double cone in front of her face for me to take a picture. (The photograph was, though I say it myself, perfectly composed, two round ice-cream scoops framing Ingrid's grey-ringed spectacles.) Cones in hand, we crossed a bridge over a stream made with giant slabs of local stone then puffed our way uphill, aiming for Rydal village.

We trod a stone path cutting through the hillside: the Coffin Route, once used to carry the dead to the churchyard in Grasmere for burial. The route follows the undulating shoulder of Nab Scar. Oak trees billowed overhead. Recent storms had left a trail of fallen trees, smashing through the dry-stone walls in places. Our conversation returned to Ingrid's landscape photography. She'd had some bad experiences in her early days, she said: once, she exhibited some originals which the gallery failed to return. Despite her persistent enquiries, nobody knew what had happened to them: perhaps someone threw them all away. She never saw any of that artwork again.

As we trod the stones of the Coffin Route, our thoughts went back, perhaps inevitably, to John Wordsworth's final days. In his letters John complained of interminable delays at port while awaiting favourable sailing conditions. He paid a rat-catcher to rid the ship of vermin.[74] Finally, he prepared to set sail in late January from the Isle of Portland, just off the Dorset coast. He wrote his last letter to William on 24 January 1805, telling his brother that his ship had collided while sailing in a fleet with the *Warren Hastings* – named after the governor of Bengal – but sustained little damage. He also praised *Lyrical Ballads* and listed his favourites among his brother's poems, as he was an attentive reader of William's work: 'the Leech gatherer, the Sparrows Nest and Butterfly and Cuckow'. He signed off, asking William to send his love to his sister-in-law Mary, to Dorothy and to give a kiss to his niece and nephew.[75] It felt almost like a valediction.

As we walked onwards, the woodlands to our right parted like curtains, and the sides of Nab Scar dropped down to Rydal Water. Beneath us the landscape rippled in verdant waves, nature's paint-sampler of paradise greens, jades and mints. Rydal Water absorbed the greenness of the hillsides and trees. It was no wonder William Wordsworth loved this spot so much.

While William's world was green, John's was blue. John Wordsworth knew the first part of his voyage was risky, with the *Abergavenny* needing to navigate past a notorious sandbank called the Shambles. A local pilot was due to guide the vessel through the danger zone. The pilot, however, arrived late, and by the time the ship weighed anchor, the tides were unfavourable. John was worried about this part of the route: he had, recalled the ship's fourth mate, quizzed the pilot over it; and had also written to a relative saying he hoped he met with no accident there.[76]

On 5 February at half past three in the afternoon the vessel was nearing Weymouth when the tide turned and the ship was drawn towards the Shambles. It hit some rocks but, though the impact was considerable, John thought the damage was superficial and ordered the pilot to aim for the nearest port. Distress signals were fired to alert people on the shore.[77]

By five o'clock it became clear that the ship's pumps had been damaged by the collision, and the ship was filling with seawater. An engineer tried to remedy the situation and officers and passengers lent a hand. Slowly but steadily, the ship was sinking, and all on board started bailing out water.[78] Night fell, and the winter seas turned rough. One florid account of the sinking claimed that when the ship's bell swung back and forth like a funeral knell, John ordered it to be resecured.[79]

By 8 p.m., one small boat set off with some crew, including a relative of the captain, Joseph Wordsworth, and a handful of passengers.[80] An allegation was then made which haunted the Wordsworth siblings long afterwards: lifeboats could have been launched, it was said, but they were not.[81] The fourth mate later testified that the ship's tilt did not allow it, as the main sail would have to have been lowered, an explanation supported by the archaeological evidence.[82] One maritime historian also believes that the crew reasonably expected assistance was near at hand and so the decision was understandable.[83] It was said that people headed for the liquor storage area as the ship went down, but officers calmly barred their way.[84] (The incident went down in literary history: Lord Byron dramatized it in his epic poem *Don Juan*, having the guard to the liquor shouting the same words as his real-life counterpart was reported to have used: 'Let us die like men.')[85]

When it became clear that the situation was hopeless, the chief officer went to inform the captain. One account of this moment said that John received the news calmly, replying: 'God's will be done.'[86] At around 11 p.m., the ship sank fast, pulling those who clung to her into the sea. Those who managed to stay afloat were pounded by waves. The passengers and crew were now entirely reliant on a single rescue boat which braved the rough seas and reached the site half an hour later, taking people out of the sea twenty at a time then returning to save more passengers. Accounts of this rescue tell stories of John Wordsworth clasping the ship's ropes as the vessel went down.[87]

In Weymouth, as dawn rose, people could see the *Abergavenny*'s top masts protruding from the Shambles. A ship was sent to guard the wreck and her valuable cargo, which included the investors' £20,000 in cash.[88] A messenger rode overnight to London's India House, arriving at half past six in the morning to convey the bad news.[89]

The corridors of India House soon filled with anxious friends and relatives of the passengers. Hours passed. Around mid-morning, a survivor of the wreck – a military commander – arrived and, though exhausted from his ordeal, nonetheless provided much-needed details. His assistance contributed to the first list of survivors. All in all, 263 people had drowned. Only 139 survived.[90] Among the dead were over fifty passengers and 159 East India Company and British Army troops.[91] Others who escaped with their lives were listed as '15 Chinese', initially identified by ethnicity rather than name.[92] Twelve of these surviving sailors – termed lascars, denoting South-east Asian sailors – subsequently sailed to China.[93] Other survivors included a 'black servant' Peter Thomas. Among the drowned was 'Mr. Routledge's black servant'. Mr Routledge survived.[94]

News of the sinking took a further day to reach the Lakes. On 7 February 1805, a letter arrived from Richard Wordsworth in London. 'My dear Brother,' it read:

> It is with the most painful concern that I inform you of the loss of the ship Abergavenny, off Weymouth, last night. I am acquainted with but few of the particulars of this melancholy Event. I am told that a great number of Persons have perished, and that our brother John is amongst that number.[95]

William's reply was less formal, more emotional. 'My dear Brother,' he wrote through his grief, 'The lamentable news which your Letter brought has now been known to us seven hours during which time I have done all in my power to alleviate the distress of poor Dorothy and my Wife.' As for himself, he added, 'John was very dear to me and my heart will never forget him.'[96] Dorothy too was grief-stricken. She wondered if any of John's items could be salvaged from the wreck, a book or anything else to remember him by. 'It does me good to weep for him,' she confided to her friend Jane Marshall, 'it does me good to find that others weep, and I bless them for it.' Her memories of John were vivid and painful: 'Many a time has he called me out in an evening to look at the moon or stars . . . then he was so happy by the fire-side, any little business of the house interested him, he loved our cottage.'[97] John had been at the heart of the Wordsworths' world. Inconsolable, Dorothy and

William now found memories of him everywhere in the life that surrounded them.

There were other aspects to the tragedy. William was especially concerned about the implication, in various reports of the shipwreck, that John committed suicide: one even claimed that John went down with a glass of claret in his hand – a lurid detail that, unsurprisingly, was picked up by newspapers. One was explicit: the fourth mate, it claimed, begged John to save himself, but he refused – though the author of this pamphlet later changed his story. Perhaps the eyewitness changed his mind, succumbed to company pressure to sanitize the tale, protect the company's reputation, spare the Wordsworth family's feelings, or a combination of all three.[98]

The family was especially concerned about the related charge of John's negligence in not putting out lifeboats quickly enough, as implied by eyewitness and second-hand accounts of the night of the sinking. Though the East India Company's Court of Directors cleared John's name in official documents which concluded he was not at fault, the Wordsworth siblings remained troubled by conflicting accounts of the shipwreck. They approached the writer Charles Lamb, a close family friend. Then a rising literary star, Lamb was making ends meet by working as an accountant for the East India Company. No enthusiastic employee – Lamb hated working for them[99] – he was happy to help the Wordsworths. Lamb pulled strings and interviewed surviving crew members. Initially, his conversations seemed to corroborate suggestions that John had, in Lamb's words, been 'careless of his own safety'. Lamb then obtained a copy of the fourth mate's report, and persuaded him to write a detailed account of events in response to some questions of William's relating to the apparent suicide and possible negligence. William's concerns, the fourth mate assured them both, were all unfounded.[100]

Then there were the financial worries. The ship had gone down with the family's life savings, and it was not then known whether John had insured the investments.[101] Fortunately for them, and other passengers, he had. On 17 March, Dorothy wrote that her

brother Richard believed they would get their *Abergavenny* investment back on the insurance. Richard was right because the siblings
recouped all their money.[102]

In the weeks following the shipwreck, bodies started to drift onto
the beaches near Weymouth. Three drowned Chinese sailors were
the first to be washed ashore; nine more bodies were beached soon
afterwards. A month after the ship had gone down, John's body was
found on the sands.[103] John was buried at All Saints Churchyard in
Wyke Regis, around the bay from Weymouth. Nearby, there are
headstones to two cadets who drowned in the wreck, aged fifteen
and sixteen respectively.[104] There is no burial record for the Chinese
sailors.

William could never bear to visit John's grave: his brother's
loss, he wrote to his friend James Losh, was irreplaceable.[105] William turned to his writing for comfort. That summer, he wrote
three poems in John's memory. In the first, called 'I only look'd
for pain and grief', a buzzard takes to the air, and the watching
poet thinks of John's fate: 'could he on that woeful night / Have
lent his wing, my Brother dear!' Retracing the steps of his final
walk with John, between Grasmere and Ullswater, the poet
describes finding a flower which became 'a ministrant / of comfort and of peace'.[106]

A second poem was 'Distressful Gift'. The 'gift' of the title was a
book of part-written pages intended to be filled with William's
poems for John to take on some future voyage; now, John's eternal
silence is lamentably expressed by the blank, inanimate 'book which
rests upon my knee'. Addressing his dead brother, the poet laments
that, 'Thou . . . / Upon the words which I had penned / Must never,
never look.'[107] Yet this poem is also evasive about his brother's destination. His brother's company trading activity is generalized to
'earthly hopes', and the poem is vague about the *Abergavenny*'s
route, simply saying 'whichever way his weary vessel went', when
William knew the ship's exact destination.[108] There were good reasons for William to be sensitive about his brother's work, with
public suspicion of the East India Company's commercial practices

increasing after the public corruption trial of the Bengal governor, Warren Hastings, a decade before John's death.[109]

William's third, revised, 'To the Daisy' poem is written 'in remembrance of a beautiful Letter of my Brother John'.[110] It quotes directly from John's letter written a few years previously from the Isle of Wight, which William treasured, altering the wording from 'daisies like little stars in a dark field' to 'a starry multitude'.[111] The poem implicitly recalls John's ambitions and hopes: to make enough money so that he could retire 'in manhood's prime / And free for life, these hills to climb'.[112] Though avoiding any of the specificities of John's voyage – the *Abergavenny* is described simply as a 'proud Ship' and a 'stout Ship'[113] – the poem hints at the two previous trading journeys John had already been on, and the trip to come, describing it as 'a way of life unmeet' or unfitting for a 'gentle soul' such as John. But for William, concerned to cherish his brother's memory, it didn't do to linger on the details of that 'way of life'.[114]

John's death impacted on Wordsworth's poetic activity in different ways. Poems about John were not simply ways of working out personal grief. William felt a moral compunction to continue on his poetic vocation. It was what his brother would have wanted. William rededicated himself to his poetic vocation because he was keen, he wrote, 'to shew him that he had not placed a false confidence in me'.[115] John's death also catalysed William Wordsworth's poetic development in other ways. In particular, the tragedy showed him how to turn life events into lyrical verse.[116]

The poems about John kept on coming. His 1806 'Character of the Happy Warrior', which was partly about his brother,[117] described the 'Happy Warrior' as 'the generous Spirit, who, when brought / Among the real tasks of life' follows these 'high endeavours' which 'are an inward light'.[118] In a letter, William observed of the poem that 'many of the elements of character here portrayed were found in my brother John'. In a similar way to his other poems about John, Wordsworth averts his eyes from the details of his brother's East India venture, which he converts into a 'high endeavour', a patriotic act of Nelsonian magnitude.[119] But the world has a

74

habit of intruding, and the sinking of the *Abergavenny* was not just a personal tragedy for the family: it ended all hope of financial ease. As Dorothy wrote to a friend, 'this loss of John is deeply connected to his business'.[120]

Wordsworth disliked tourists tramping around his beloved Lakes. He would doubtless have disapproved of the pleasure that Ingrid and I took in the various cafés along our route. Our second tea-drinking stop was at a village café beside the River Rothay, where a robin eyed up our scones. Rydal village was a regular picnic spot for William and Dorothy, who eventually moved – with the entire family, in 1813 – to Rydal Mount. Today, it remains a homely three-storey sixteenth-century house covered with climbing plants. We did not have time to go inside but peeped into its gardens, where William, like Dorothy, spent a lot of time, and which retains the rock pools and terraces that he created. We saw winding gravel pathways lined with stones and softened by rhododendron bushes. It was definitely a garden designed for reflective wandering, we decided. I told Ingrid about Wordsworth's daisy poems: my sister, I recalled, thought them ridiculous when she studied them at school, knowing nothing of the personal tragedy which inspired all three of them. I remarked that there were no daisies growing nearby but I was wrong: Ingrid's sharp eye spotted daisies in the verges around the house.

To reach Rydal Water we crossed the road at a seventeenth-century hotel and pub called Glen Rothay. We had now, I said to Ingrid, rejoined the route of my night-time walk. I pointed out all the spots I had scurried past and jumped at shadows. Now, in full daylight, it was a world transformed. In her journal, Dorothy described this very scene as 'extremely beautiful from the western side'. 'Nab Scar', she wrote, was just topped by a cloud which, cutting it off as high as it could be cut off, made the mountain look 'uncommonly lofty'. She described the lake that day as 'grave and soft', and this was just as it appeared to us now.[121]

It did not take long to walk to the end of the lake, and we topped the hill with the River Rothay to our right. By the time we arrived at Allan Bank, we would have traced a large oval from Dove Cottage to Rydal to the tea shop where we began. We stood at the crest of the hill, and the landscape layered into cloud, oak-leaf and bluebell. The small lake of Grasmere Water was below us.

In 1808 the burgeoning Wordsworth family left Dove Cottage for Allan Bank, which Wordsworth rented for a couple of years before the family moved to Rydal Mount. In 1809, Wordsworth's friend Thomas De Quincey became the new tenant of Dove Cottage. Then in his early twenties De Quincey, who had deliberately moved close by because he loved William's poems, had overstayed his welcome during a three-month visit to the family at Allan Bank. Dorothy maintained the personal connection over the years.[122]

Meanwhile, under the Lowther patronage, William Wordsworth became more and more the unwilling businessman, noting that he did the work out of duty to his family. He knew that the family's impending move to Rydal Mount (in 1813) would bring yet more money pressures and, by 1812, the financial repercussions of John's failed plan had begun to bite. He was unable to make money from his poetry, however, and *Poems, in Two Volumes* had proved a financial failure. As his father and grandfather had done before him, William turned to the Lowther family, writing to Sir James' heir, Sir William Lowther, for financial support. William knew that Lowther had previously discharged Sir James' debt to the Wordsworths and had at least shown some sense of responsibility towards the Wordsworth family. Blaming the national economic crisis – caused by expensive Napoleonic Wars – for his straitened circumstances, he wrote that he lacked the money to work on major poetry projects and needed to attend to the 'rational wants' of his family. Sir William, then a Tory MP, tried unsuccessfully to secure a government pension for William, then found him a civil service job as distributor of stamps in 1813, which he did for three decades. The job required him to receive postage stamps from the head office and supply these to post offices in his districts of Westmorland, Whitehaven and Penrith.

At a London auction house, in 2016, one of the items up for sale was an invoice headed 'Postage Stamps' bearing an 1840 blue stamp crossed with vermillion ink and addressed, by William Wordsworth, to the postmistress of Kendal.

Another means of addressing the family's financial requirements was to find a patron, but William knew that he was unlikely to strike gold: 'as to patronage,' he wrote in a letter, 'I hold it in little esteem for helping genius forward in the fine arts, especially those whose medium is words'.[123] In addition to finding Wordsworth work, Sir William nonetheless became his patron, offering support, which was insufficient to relieve him from his stamp-distributing duties, but enough to allow new poems to be published.[124] This patronage, though modest, certainly took the pressure off. A friend of William's wrote that Wordsworth could now write and print his poems without worrying so much about money.[125]

Having accepted Sir William's patronage, Wordsworth was compromised horribly. Whilst he had obtained greater financial security, he promoted his patron and presented a view of Sir William as a worthy, aristocratic paternalist.[126] A Tory politician, Sir William was regarded with suspicion by radicals, and the Lowther connection did Wordsworth reputational damage – just as it had done his father and grandfather before him. The association ultimately deepened the public image of Wordsworth as a political turncoat, ready to abandon his principles for personal gain. Lord Byron sniffed that, having accepted Sir William's patronage, Wordsworth brought his talents 'to the aid of a political party'. Percy Bysshe Shelley, a true radical, also thought that Wordsworth had sold out.[127]

When in 1818, a political rival, Henry Brougham, stood for parliamentary election against Sir William Lowther, feelings ran high. Locals in the town of Kendal believed, by supporting rises in the price of grain, Sir William made people worse off, and they turned against him. A crowd lobbed mud and stones at Sir William's contingent when it canvassed in Kendal. Wordsworth worked hard to defend his patron, lobbying a local newspaper called the *Chronicle*.[128] When his efforts failed, and the paper's editor declared himself neutral, the Lowthers set up a rival Tory newspaper, *The Westmorland Gazette*, and tasked Wordsworth with finding an editor.[129] He turned to the non-radical De Quincey, who – addled with opium and, terrible with money, deeply in debt – was both eager for work and keen to renew his friendship with Wordsworth. Predictably, however, the opium addiction interfered with his duties: his editorship didn't last long.[130]

Wordsworth, however, spared no effort in helping Sir William to restore his reputation and secure re-election. In an essay, Wordsworth presented the Lowthers' political dominance as the expression of a desirable social order.[131] He wrote to his patron every few days with regular intelligence updates on his conversations with newspaper editors, dined with Brougham supporters and reported the table-talk to his patron. He even provided Sir William with information about his friend, the anti-slavery campaigner Thomas Clarkson.[132] This detail was particularly telling. Despite William's association with figures like Clarkson – and of course Wilberforce, who had helped his brother John to become a commander – Wordsworth's own attitude to slavery grew ever more equivocal. As a younger man he had written his tribute to Toussaint L'Ouverture, and, in 1807, had paid poetic tribute to Clarkson when the British parliament finally legislated to abolish the slave trade. But slavery lingered on for decades, and during this time Wordsworth stayed quiet, preferring – by his own account – to leave the matter of slavery to politicians' consciences.[133]

When in 1824 Clarkson asked Wordsworth to distribute some anti-slavery papers for him around the local villages, Wordsworth refused, saying that local people had little interest in the matter and that encouraging anti-slavery sentiment would spread abroad and likely stir up violence among enslaved populations. This was a view the increasingly conservative Wordsworth continued to express[134] – and indeed, he now privately disapproved of Clarkson's single-minded commitment to the cause. Writing to Sir William, he described Clarkson as one of those men with 'much talent and little discernment' who did more harm than good when they 'meddle' with political matters and – presaging an argument that still lingers on today –[135] tried to marginalize the issue of Caribbean slavery by suggesting that reformers should focus on English workers' 'slavish toil' instead.[136] So while he had expressed anti-slavery sentiment in his poetry, his views on the topic were far from radical.

As we entered the final leg of our walk and descended to the lake at Grasmere, I realized I hadn't actually asked Ingrid what she thought of Wordsworth's poetry. 'Are you a Wordsworth fan?' I asked. Ingrid considered the question. It was complicated, she said finally. She wasn't really a poetry reader. And in many ways figures like Wordsworth marred her enjoyment of the Lakes. She included Beatrix Potter in this. In their different ways, both Wordsworth and Potter loomed so large that Lakeland visitors were confronted with them everywhere and Ingrid couldn't help wondering if they obscured – as much as revealed – things about the area's past. Their fame was merited, Ingrid acknowledged, but it was hard to see past Wordsworth's Romantic landscapes, and the naughty rabbits, impertinent squirrels and pastel shades of Potter's picture book world. Sometimes, Ingrid said, you just want to ignore all that and get on with your walking.

We sat down by Grasmere Water. If you discount the busy Ambleside–Grasmere road on one side, the lake looks much the same as it did in Wordsworth's time. There was, however, no accessing the lakeside. The shoreline had been claimed by landowners, and a forest of signage didn't let us forget it. 'Have you noticed', I said to Ingrid, 'how many PRIVATE and KEEP OUT signs there are?' I pointed out that the signs seemed to both mock and manifest *Pastoral Interlude*, with its wry commentary on the barriers to Black rural belonging which she had explored four decades earlier. There was only one quiet place to access the lake: the little stone beach we had descended to a few minutes earlier. As we lingered at the water's edge, the irony was clear to both of us. Wordsworth's Romantic poetry drew us to the wildness of a landscape enclosed by a series of forbidding gates and signs.

Being back at Grasmere took Ingrid back to the 1980s, when she'd stayed nearby at Little Langdale, a hamlet 3 miles to the south, which she used as a walking base with her friends. As we reminisced, the drizzle started again. Ingrid received a text message on her phone, and I smiled at the ringtone, an insistent 'cuckoo!'

We looked across the lake towards Dove Cottage on the opposite shore. Ingrid reminded me that Dorothy mentioned a 'merry African' who came begging at Dove Cottage, and of the presence of the 'silver-collared negro', a figure who condemns slavery in *The Prelude*.[137] But the later Wordsworth, she remarked, was hard to come to terms with. After all, as we had discussed, once Sir William Lowther became his patron, he mixed in wealthy social circles – some prominent Lowthers were slave-owners – and the worldviews of this new social set gradually entered his political bloodstream.[138]

Adding to Ingrid's misgivings, I told her that the Wordsworth family subsequently developed its own stake in the slavery business. Far away in Mississippi, slave-owners and investors were establishing ever more cotton plantations by the 1830s. As Mississippi's population of enslaved people swelled, demand for associated banking services rose exponentially, and the Bank of the State of Mississippi made loans to land-purchasers and slave-owners to buy enslaved people, clear land and expand the cotton plantation system. Such fevered financial activity promised enticing returns for English investors – including William Wordsworth's sister-in-law – who bought Mississippi bank bonds. As with much frenzied speculation and over-promising, it wasn't long before the bonds were in jeopardy. In 1837, the Planters Bank asked the State of Mississippi to bail it out, but the state refused, and financial chaos ensued.[139] The Wordsworths were affected: by then,[140] William's sister-in-law had died and bequeathed her Mississippi bonds to Wordsworth's daughter, aunt and uncle. In 1840, William Wordsworth wrote to the financial agent: 'You will be sorry to learn that several of my most valued friends are likely to suffer from monetary derangements in America,' and in a subsequent letter wrote that he had lost hope in his daughter's profiting from the Mississippi bonds or even getting her money back. Angered by this financial loss and having failed with his financial agent, William activated his church networks and had a letter published in *The Banner of the Cross*, an official church publication. In this letter he complained that 'My daughter, through the perfidy of the State of Mississippi, has forfeited a sum, though but small in itself, large for her means,' and later on in the letter he said he hoped that this 'injury' might be righted if 'even common humanity exists'. The letter was reprinted in the *Philadelphia Gazette* and the *National Intelligencer*. William later notified his agent that he needed to know if all was lost because 'I have a special reason for desiring to have knowledge on this point, as it would in some degree govern my distribution by will of my property among my children.'[141]

Ingrid, of course, agreed that the incident sat uncomfortably with the poet's ire, expressed in *The Prelude*, towards 'traffickers in Negro blood'.[142] By the time he was writing the letter about his daughter's Mississippi bonds, his outrage had shifted from inhuman treatment of the enslaved to inhumanity to investors in the slavery system. All of which further illustrates that the concerns of Wordsworth the young poet differed greatly from those of Wordsworth the ageing husband and father. Around this time, he dismissed the idea of investing his own money in Alabama bonds and invested in India bonds instead, that same year.[143]

Nearly all his life, William Wordsworth longed for greater financial stability, which only came twenty years before his death. For his last eight years he was awarded an annual government pension of £300 for his services to poetry. In 1843, he received a paid laureateship. He died at home on 23 April 1850 and was buried at the nearby churchyard of St Oswald.

We walked past Allan Bank, which had closed just a few minutes earlier. 'It is ugly,' Ingrid said. It was true: despite its lovely setting, the large white house was spoilt by awkward, functional extensions. We headed to St Oswald's graveyard, the burial place of William and Dorothy. The mossy churchyard was shrouded with large yews, which deepened the impression of gloom. We found the graves behind railings, the dedications clearly legible, one stone to William and Mary Wordsworth, one to Sarah Hutchinson, William, Dorothy and Mary.

Emerging from the churchyard, our thoughts turned to the pressing matter of Grasmere Gingerbread. Beside St Oswald's is a tiny shop which sells this spicy, chewy sweetmeat, made from a secret recipe by its founder, Sarah Nelson, who began serving her product to tourists in 1854, some four years after William Wordsworth's death. Grown in the West Indies, ginger was shipped from Barbados to Whitehaven on the Cumbrian coast, a few miles from Grasmere.[144] Gingerbread was already well established in the Lakes in William Wordsworth's time – and the poet loved it. His sister Dorothy, writing in her journal that 'Wm. had a fancy for some ginger bread', describes buying sixpence-worth at a local house.[145] Grasmere Gingerbread Shop claims that the origins of its other product – rum butter – are 'shrouded in mystery', though the mystery is easily cleared up. Rum was also shipped from the Caribbean to Whitehaven, a port which had been inducted into the transatlantic slave trade by Wordsworth's patrons, the Lowther family. Gingerbread is familiar to people the world over and is a culinary favourite in places like Virginia as well as Grasmere. Rum butter has a more distinctively Cumbrian twist.[146]

We munched our gingerbread. Sitting by the churchyard's overgrown yews, we surveyed one of England's loveliest landscapes. We had mixed feelings about the Lakes. As we'd passed the long section of Grasmere's shores from which almost everyone is barred, we'd remembered that Wordsworth himself disliked tourists. We had also, of course, spoken about all those iconic postcards in which Black hikers never appear.

Perched on the churchyard wall, we could just make out John's Grove above the other side of the lake, where Dorothy and William went to remember their brother after the sinking of the *Abergavenny*.

'You know what?' said Ingrid, looking across Grasmere Water to the grove, 'I can't see how Dorothy and William lay on the ground there: it was too steep!' I had to agree. Yet John's Grove had been strangely restful. As the rain fell, we remembered that William had compared lying on the woodland floor to being in a tranquil grave beside your friends.[147]

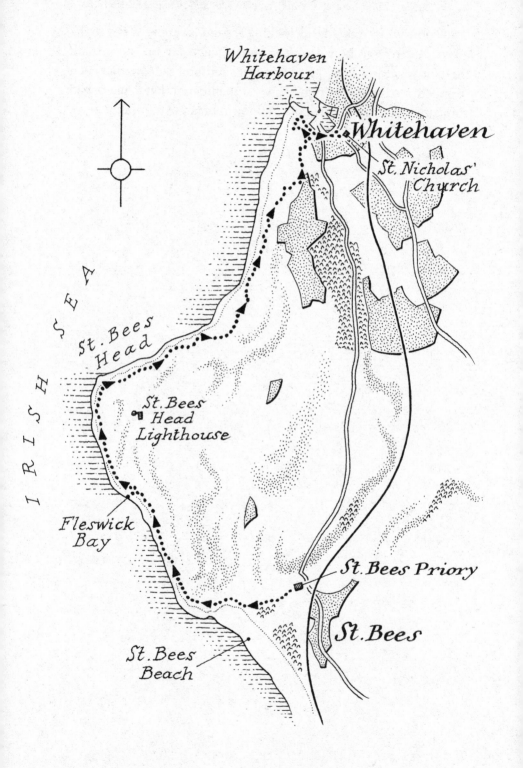

Whitehaven
Harbour

Whitehaven

St. Nicholas'
Church

IRISH SEA

St. Bees
Head

St. Bees
Head
Lighthouse

Fleswick
Bay

St. Bees Priory

St. Bees

St. Bees
Beach

3.

The Tobacco Walk: Whitehaven Coast

The Irish Sea churns against St Bees Head. This is northern England's most westerly tip, in a part of Cumbria once known as Cumberland. Here, giant cliffs face the Irish Sea; beyond it lies the Atlantic and North America. Today this is a designated Heritage Coast, its cliffs crowded with seabirds and rare species; the sea below is a marine conservation zone. The land tilts relentlessly seawards, and a cliffside footpath wavers so close to the edge that it would be folly to walk there in a gale.

The Heritage Coast is part of a gigantic coalfield, pock-marked with old mine works. Coal seams run for 14 miles north from St Bees to the coastal town of Maryport. Between them lies the Georgian town of Whitehaven. Once a huddle of fisherman's cabins and thatched cottages, Whitehaven became a major port with sweeping streets and generous mansions belonging to wealthy merchants. Nowadays, Whitehaven styles itself as the place where the Lake District meets the sea. From its harbour – now a marina – you can see the Isle of Man and Scotland's snowy peaks. The town's gentility has faded, and the peeling stuccoed houses rub shoulders with boarded-up shops.

Whitehaven's street names hint at the sources of former wealth. Irish Street is so-named because coal was shipped to Dublin from the 1600s. Roper Street refers to locally manufactured ship rope. The town was the territory of the Lowther family, a branch of the Lowthers whom the Wordsworths knew. Coal formed the bedrock of their wealth, as they monopolized its extraction and export to Ireland from the early seventeenth century.[1]

Over time, the Lowthers came to see Whitehaven as their

own – and with some justification. They owned most of the fields, woods and collieries round about, and provided much of the employment.[2] Little happened without their say-so, not just within the coal industry but in matters of politics and local governance. The family left its architectural stamp too. Today you can still see the Lowthers at every turn, from the turrets and battlements of their family seat at Lowther Castle to the road which runs from there to the bottom of the town: Lowther Street. From their castle, the family had a commanding view of Whitehaven's rectangular street-grids and extended harbour, all laid out according to Lowther instructions. It was the Lowthers, too, who secured parliamentary permission to levy taxes on locals and tolls for incoming ships, all of which funded town cleaning, sewerage, paving and the harbour extension.[3]

The Lowthers were coal magnates. But Whitehaven's story is not just about the coal trade to Ireland. Remote as the town was from other British urban centres, it nonetheless became Britain's second-largest tobacco importer and the nation's third-biggest slave-trading port. How did such an isolated coal town become such a major transatlantic port? In the seventeenth century, regular coal-voyages across the Irish Sea turned the heads of merchants and mariners towards the Atlantic, and they began to think of sailing to places like the West Indies, Maryland and Virginia to expand their trading options. To sail around Ireland's north coast, they knew, was to avoid enemy ships during Britain's interminable Anglo-French wars, which spanned the seventeenth and eighteenth centuries.[4] From the 1680s, then, Whitehaven's townspeople became tobacco traders, plantation-owners and slavers. In the fullness of time, these colonial figures became magistrates, customs officials, industrialists and politicians. They climbed the social ranks, married into wealthy families and gained local power and political influence.

Transatlantic profits were reinvested in local glassworks, coal mines, alcohol sales, tobacco processing, ship-building and philanthropy. The town's rich residents also paid for a turreted church tower at St Nicholas on Lowther Street. Located in the heart of Georgian

Whitehaven, the church stone glows pink at sunset, and you can walk – as the Lowthers once did – from this church to Tangier Street, past the bottle-green Tavern to the port.[5] Soon you reach Millennium Promenade, which runs along Old Quay, where coast winds sing through the boat masts. Beyond the cobbled inner harbour is Sugar Tongue Quay, and beyond that is the vast outer harbour, built for deep-water transatlantic ships.

This walk begins 7 miles south of Whitehaven, at the coastal village of St Bees. The route ascends northwards to clifftops at St Bees Head and follows the coastal path to a red sandstone gorge. Here, a stream rushes into the shingle of Fleswick Bay, and the air thickens with herring gulls and black guillemots. Steps lead from the beach, and a dust-red path skirts agricultural fields, fringed with yellow gorse in wintertime. The footpath passes near St Bees lighthouse and carries on past a quarry and some old mine works before descending into Whitehaven harbour.

My walking companion, the Mancunian writer Peter Kalu, knows Whitehaven well. His special relationship with the place began a decade before our walk. He'd visited the area to read some papers about Barbados in Whitehaven's local archive. Minutes after he arrived, he'd stumbled across a copy of a 1770s diary about plantation life in Barbados and, for the first time in his life, encountered the words and thoughts of a slave-owner. His response was to start writing historical fiction about British slavery. This was no easy challenge for, as he'd told me at the time, his own personal relationship to colonial history is complicated: his mother is Danish, his father Nigerian. 'The invader and the looted inhabitant,' he'd told me with a wry smile, though there's no doubt where his sympathies lie.

Peter and I have known each other for years. We first met while he was director of Cultureword, a nationally renowned centre for developing, discovering and promoting British African, Asian and Caribbean literary talent in Manchester. As a teacher and editor, Peter has had a galvanizing effect on the region's literary culture.[6]

Peter is always ready to talk about other people's writing, but I wanted to talk to him about his own work. History, race and class are prominent themes in his published writing, which spans poetry, fiction, folktales, plays, songs and film scripts. His crime novel *Yard Dogs*, for instance, references Manchester's cotton history and the origins of its wealth in the slave trade and exploited local labour.[7]

Now it was several years since Peter's original archival visit to Whitehaven but, by chance, I booked him into a place he'd stayed in before: Seacote Hotel in St Bees. When he arrived, they greeted him like an old friend. The hotel is near the beach, about fifteen minutes' walk from the church of St Mary and St Bega, an ancient priory built with giant sandstone blocks. The towering priory indicated St Bees' medieval importance as a religious and also economic centre: the monks themselves started coal-mining in the thirteenth century. Once a fishing hamlet, the village of St Bees now has around 2,000 inhabitants, three pubs and a train station.

The morning of our walk was bright, and Peter had already checked out of the hotel when I came to pick him up. I found him on the beach, enjoying the sea air and studying the red sandstone cliffs which had been 200 million years in the making. The priory's stone blocks, he said, must have been hewn from this very sandstone. Warmed by the winter sun, we stood and looked at the long beach, which swept from the glacial moraines at Seamill Beach some 150 miles north on the Scottish coast to the cliffs of St Bees Head. Peter was dressed for winter: padded coat and knitted grey hat pulled firmly down over his head, his white sideburns poking out below.[8]

We ambled along the beach towards the cliffs. He was a bit daunted by the hill, and I offered some vague reassurance that this was the worst climb. We puffed our way up a set of wide-spaced steps to the manicured edges of a golf course. Peter slung his red bag over his shoulder – he called it his *city bag*.

As we passed the golf course, Peter told me about a poem he'd recently written and performed for some schoolchildren. It was about a boomerang, reversing in mid-flight and coming back to

smack you in the face. The boomerang was a metaphor for colonialism, which returns with its consequences (looted museum objects,
controversial statues, repressed histories) – though, Peter laughingly added, the children were more interested in the boom, boom,
boomerang of his main refrain. But the metaphor well describes his
first encounter with the words of that eighteenth-century enslaver
in Whitehaven's archives. 'There I was,' he said, 'the son of a Nigerian father, hit between the eyes by an account of plantation
violence.' He explained that the diary belonged to a man called
Joseph Senhouse, who was well known to the Lowther family. He
was born in 1741 at the family home of Netherhall in Maryport,
14 miles north along the Whitehaven coast, where the Senhouses
dominated trade and held sway as landowners, in customs and as
developers and manufacturers.

Joseph's older brother William was active in the colonial trade.
Assisted into a lucrative customs post in Barbados by the White-
haven Lowthers (another branch of the Lowther family owned
Christ Church plantation in Barbados, and Robert Lowther, a dis-
tant relative, had earlier governed Barbados, between 1711 and 1720),
William became Surveyor General of Customs in Barbados in the
1770s and acquired a sugar plantation. Following in his footsteps,
Joseph became collector of customs on the West Indian island of
Dominica. There, Joseph owned a coffee plantation, which he
named Lowther Hall, in a nod to the dominant family.[9]

Sitting in the Whitehaven archives, Peter was stunned by Joseph
Senhouse's account of his visit to his brother's Barbadian estates,
written in his sloping eighteenth-century handwriting. 'What affected
me most', he told me, 'was the *thingification* of Black people.' What
Peter meant was that, even when detailing upsetting incidents,
Joseph Senhouse appeared to find it all a curious good yarn. He
describes the suicide of an enslaved man who, threatened with punishment for absenteeism, jumped into a vat of boiling cane sugar.
The diary made Peter wonder how a Black writer in the twentieth
century could even begin to work ethically with such unpleasant
material. His answer was a short story called 'The Keeper of Books', in

which a plantation-owner (loosely based on Joseph Senhouse) dictates his last will and testament in the presence of an enslaved woman called Morena. Wanting to avoid a painful plunge into slavery's trauma, Peter's approach to writing the story was to explore the absurd logic of colonial racism: in the story, the slave-owner disinherits his son for gambling but fails to perceive his own wrongs as an enslaver.[10] The blind hypocrisy of such logic was hard to understand. 'It's one of those strange moral compartmentalizations,' Peter said as we walked. Peter is fascinated by how, from the late seventeenth century onwards, Enlightenment philosophers emphasized tolerance, progress and personal freedom, yet this so-called Age of Reason saw the expansion of human enslavement on an industrial scale.

Our footpath was getting steeper. 'Bit of a workout,' I said, noting that the steep path was the same burgundy shade as the sandstone priory. We puffed our way uphill behind a line of walkers ahead of us, with a caravan park to our right and the sea at our backs. The path had been eroded, and we had to watch our step on the loose stones. As we climbed the shoulder of St Bees Head, brown waves tossed far below us. Ten minutes later, we had reached the top and swapped words with a couple of walkers, taking in the view. Below, St Bees glinted in the sunlight, its houses whitewashed and sandstone-red by turns.

St Bees had a particular significance for our walk because, following in the monks' footsteps, the Lowther family had started the local coal industry there. In the sixteenth century, St Bees was then a hamlet where people panned salt and fished salmon: an account from the 1550s said that the settlement consisted of six households and a ship called the *Bee of Whitehaven*.[11] But then, in the 1600s, Sir Christopher Lowther bought land at St Bees and in 1611 began exporting coal to Ireland. The area's coal journey had begun.

During those early coal years in St Bees, a trade was developing far away in colonial Virginia which would soon transform Whitehaven with an influx of wealth and motivate Whitehaven merchants to develop transatlantic trade routes. In the early seventeenth century, English colonists were developing a new strain of tobacco to suit European tastes, and tobacco soon drove the colony's economic development. (The most famous early adopter of tobacco was Sir Walter Raleigh, whose pipe-smoking so alarmed a servant entering with a tankard of ale that, seeing smoke coming from Sir Walter's mouth, threw the ale at him believing his face was on fire.)[12] By the 1620s, plantations were being cleared, and port towns and warehouses springing up. So valuable did tobacco become that its leaves were known as 'brown gold': in the Americas, they could even be used as currency.

From the early seventeenth century – while Lowther was developing his coal business in Whitehaven – the West Indian plantations were being worked by indentured labourers, who signed contracts of four to seven years, often in ignorance of the poor working conditions and risk of disease. As the century wore on and plantations became more established, the rising demand for labour saw the increased transportation of enslaved labourers to the colony of Virginia.[13]

Meanwhile, along the Whitehaven coast, the Lowther coal trade was expanding. Ireland proved a reliable market, and Sir Christopher was doing well. In the 1630s, he extended the harbour, building a new stone pier at the sizeable cost of £700 and purchasing the Manor of St Bees.[14] In keeping with the classic literary plot of the reprobate heir – which Peter had parodied in his story – Christopher Lowther disinherited his eldest son and namesake, leaving his property to his younger son, John. John inherited the estate, its surrounding coalfields and his father's sense of purpose.[15] He bought more coalfields and opened more mines. This burgeoning industry transformed Whitehaven from a fishing village to a planned town – designed by himself – and a major coaling port (three times bigger than Carlisle, which was 40 miles north-east).[16] Little is known of his character, but a portrait of 1680 shows him in purposeful middle age, holding town plans in his hand. His account books suggest that he was a man of great energy, living in London but travelling all over the country (and also buying many books).[17] Alongside his wealth, he obtained power. In 1664 he became Member of Parliament for Cumberland, a seat he held for three decades. He used his status as MP to push Cumberland's interests, especially in relation to coal – and Cumberland's interests were very much his own.[18] He financed an extension to his father's pier, a challenging construction which took twelve years.[19]

A parliamentarian and member of the Admiralty, Sir John (he had also picked up a knighthood) knew that colonial commerce was everywhere. During his annual stay in Whitehaven, he dined with ships' captains and the local gentry.[20] His head of collieries was a man named John Gale, who owned a Maryland tobacco plantation. Gale fed Lowther information about Whitehaven's tobacco trade and made him aware of his options as a future investor in transatlantic trading activity. Gale's sons became merchant mariners, one of whom also traded in tobacco.[21] The Gales were helped into colonial trade by the Whitehaven-born slaver Isaac Milner, who was a key networker and contact in London's slavery business.[22]

Alive to potential colonial profits, Sir John invested in the South Sea and East India Companies and in the 1660s explored the possibility of investing in the newly formed Royal African Company, set up by the newly re-established Stuart monarchy and London merchants. Refounded in 1672 after heavy initial losses, the 1672 company charter lists Sir John as a member.[23] The charter permitted the company to establish forts and factories on the West African coast, and – as with the East India Company – to maintain a standing army. In its quest for gold, silver and enslaved people, the company was also handed a monopoly on the increasingly lucrative trade in trafficking people from West Africa. Colonial investments, as well as coal, would form a significant portion of the Lowther family's wealth across the generations.

By this point, other regional families were involved in colonial affairs, including the aforementioned Senhouses of Netherhall in Maryport, with their links to Barbados and Dominica, and the

Curwens, connected to the East India Company, who presided over nearby Workington. Through the expanding port of Whitehaven, local people became well informed about colonial affairs in Virginia, Maryland, India and Africa – and the opportunities that presented themselves in these far-flung places.[24]

We were nearly a mile into our walk, heading north from St Bees along the clifftops towards Whitehaven. The path, which had levelled out, scored a wavy line across the fields ahead of us as we progressed along the coast. The sea was to our left; to our right, sparrows pecked at ploughed furrows in the bare fields. The sea was calm: transformed from the previous day, I told Peter, when the wind had whipped up the waves, sending ribbons of sea foam flying through the air and flecking the fields with bubbles. Peter remarked on the toughened, silvery grass that bordered the path, stretching to the cliff edge, whose sandstone edges constantly crumbled.

A mile further on, our coastal path descended to Fleswick Bay, forcing another climb by dipping towards this dramatic beach, dominated by red-raw rocks. Every beach, Peter said, has its own sound. Here, pebbles clattered like a thousand teeth and, despite the winter sun, the beach was deserted. Below the cliff the shingle receded into an expanse of swirled sand, sculpted by rough tides. We stood in the gully at the entrance to the beach. The silver-green grasses ended at cliffs which were layered unevenly with sandstone, like a clumsy red velvet cake.

We resumed our walk and climbed wide, steep steps back to the clifftop path. There, we saw black guillemots, angular as birds in an Escher painting. As we watched the guillemots from a bird hide, we returned to the topic of writing.

Being a Black writer in Britain, Peter reflected, is like being 'a stranger at the gates'. It's not just that Britain, like many other former empires, has tended to avoid, or even deny, the basic historical facts of colonialism. Rather, he continued, there is 'a racial empathy gap', in particular with slavery history. You find it in

Senhouse's diary, but it remains a phenomenon today. Writers like Toni Morrison have, he explained, said more or less the same. Peter described the problem he faced in his historical fiction: of somehow representing black-skinned people to groups of White readers who might well see themselves as 'universal', he said, quoting Morrison directly now, or 'race-free'.[25] This racial empathy gap has been observed more widely: in film and TV, for example, where researchers have found that White film audiences habitually and unconsciously disengage from Black characters.[26] How, I asked, did he tackle this empathy problem in his own work? Peter returned to his short story 'The Keeper of Books': here, he continued, he'd told it from the perspective of a White plantation-owner, enough to hold the readers' initial attention. In reality, though, the story's true protagonist is Morena, the enslaved woman, whose thoughts and words find their way into the slave-owner's dictated will: at one point, his slave-owning character accidentally details slavery conditions before asking for them to be crossed out. Formally, it's a brilliant idea: enslaved characters inevitably exist at the borders of a plantation-owner's narrative, because enslaved people were banned from writing. As a consequence, few first-hand accounts of slavery exist. The storyteller has to find ways around this: Peter's way was to frame the narrative in the dominant voice of a slave-owner, with other registers and voices bursting in, disrupting the legal language of the will, refusing to be suppressed. This effect is comic, the purpose serious.

Slavery, of course, was central to the tobacco trade – in Whitehaven, as well as elsewhere. And tobacco made Whitehaven rich. In the 1680s, a 94-ton ship called the *Resolution* entered Whitehaven port loaded with tobacco packed into large barrels, or hogsheads, marking the beginning of the town's colonial trade. Soon after, four more locally owned tobacco ships entered Whitehaven harbour: large vessels built nearby and fitted out for transatlantic voyages. The impact of these arrivals was significant, and Whitehaven was quick to adapt: that same year, customs officers requested a larger custom house to cater for 'the increase of our plantation trade'. Tobacco warehouses were soon built at Whitehaven port to weigh, inspect and store the hogsheads.[27] The ships kept coming. In 1693, customs officers logged ten vessels from Virginia; ten more arrived the following year, rising to twenty in 1697.[28]

In 1699, a clay pipe–house was opened (pipes had come into common use some fifty years earlier), and a tobacco processing plant began work in 1718.[29] Preparing a pipe was considered a comforting ritual. Clay pipes were disposable but, once pipes began being made from briar wood (in the nineteenth century), they became uniquely personal objects and poignant reminders of people after their death. Meanwhile, sailors quickly learned to chew tobacco: smoking was a fire risk on board ship, while chewing it freed up their hands while working. Although by the eighteenth century tobacco was widely consumed, good-quality tobacco remained a luxury for many, and those who could not afford it would roll home-made cigarettes using discarded cigars, pipe tobacco and snuff remnants. (Cigarettes were not otherwise smoked until the mid-nineteenth century.)[30]

By 1700, Virginia tobacco plantations were expanding rapidly. With the choicest locations beside the rivers long since occupied – riverside plantations were commercially convenient, traders sailing straight to the plantations to deal with growers direct – growers were moving inland. Creating a plantation was hard work. Land had to be cleared of trees, rocks and stones; roads had to be cut and waterways created through swamps. All this was done by gangs of enslaved people, working in terrible conditions. And there was an environmental as well as a human cost. The tobacco crop leached the soils, while the land clearance destroyed wildlife and deforested Virginia, to the tune of half a million acres by the end of the seventeenth century.[31]

Tobacco plantations typically consisted of a smokehouse, a slaughterhouse, a kitchen, stables, storage areas, huts for the enslaved and houses for the plantation-owners. The tobacco was planted in winter. Once established, the plants were transferred to fields in April or May, planted two feet apart. Enslaved field workers hoed and weeded them, ensuring quality by removing excess leaves. This was a labour-intensive process: one person tended three acres of tobacco. Once harvested, the tobacco was packed into hogsheads – barrels weighing about 450 kg when filled – and loaded onto carts.[32]

Whitehaven merchants dealt with tobacco from Maryland as well as from Virginia. In 1733, a Fulani Muslim named Ayuba Suleiman Diallo produced an account of his enslavement in Maryland, where John Gale of Whitehaven – among other townspeople – owned land. Diallo was from a noble family. He had himself owned enslaved people but had been captured by rival Mandingo people (he describes being pinned to the ground by captors who shaved his head and beard). Sold to the Royal African Company, he was put on board ship for transportation to Maryland. Although he convinced the ship's captain that he should not have been enslaved – in fact, Diallo told him, they had previously met whilst Diallo was himself a slaver – help didn't arrive, and the ship set sail with Diallo on board. Once in Maryland, he was put to work growing tobacco, but, being unused to such tasks, he soon became ill. He was assigned to cattle-tending instead, during which, he wrote, a young White boy would mock him whenever he entered the woods to pray. Eventually, he managed to get a letter to his father. Shortly after, as part of his exit plan, he boarded a ship to England, where he eventually won his freedom.[33] Accounts such as his were the hidden side of Whitehaven's global tobacco story.

By the 1740s, Whitehaven was second only to London for tobacco imports: 'tobacco', opined one local official, was 'the very life and soul of Whitehaven'. In that decade, the harbour was extended once again to accommodate the booming trade: in 1743 alone, fifty-seven tobacco vessels entered the port.[34] Coal and tobacco merchants began to jostle for supremacy: the coal merchants wanted to prioritize the inner harbour for coal ships; the tobacco merchants, led by a local family, the Lutwidges (of Irish origin), wanted the outer harbour rebuilt to accommodate more deep-sea tobacco vessels.[35] With funds for expansion limited, tensions mounted between the two groups. There were other discontents too. Like other goods, tobacco was commonly under-weighed to avoid import taxes and maximize profits; often, customs officials themselves were in on the act. Three years previously, in 1740, a new law had required tobacco to be stored in warehouses, making it harder to tamper with the hogsheads. Whitehaven merchants soon afterwards petitioned parliament to ask that tobacco import taxes be reduced, or for inspectors to be sent to Glasgow to stop Scottish tobacco merchants from cheating the system.[36]

Whitehaven merchants also had to consider the increasingly sophisticated preferences of their consumers. Virginia tobacco was more popular than that from Maryland; the same was true in France, a market to which Whitehaven merchants – Peter How, Captain Richard Kelsick and Thomas and William Gilpin – generally re-exported their product after it had made the journey across the North Atlantic.[37]

The heyday of Whitehaven's tobacco trade opened up opportunities, and not only for local merchants. Many worked on ships or found positions in booming businesses such as iron forges or fisheries to supply food to the growing population. Others found work as apprenticed clerks, an occupation which allowed young men to learn the tobacco business and to establish their own networks. In the 1740s, Peter Taylor, a Whitehaven man, was apprenticed to his uncle, a tobacco trader in the South Carolinan port of Charleston, then known as Charles Town (named after Charles II of England). His tasks included invoice-writing and letter-copying; operating retail outlets or transporting goods to the wharf; and accompanying his employers on port visits and voyages. Taylor, and men like him, trained on the job, studying manuals on trading, commerce and accounting as they worked. Peter Taylor returned to his native Whitehaven with substantial funds in around 1747.[38]

But there was, of course, another side to Charleston's history. In 2021, a mass grave was discovered in the city's downtown area by archaeologists, who analysed the bones and teeth of the formerly enslaved people who were buried there. Various details were revealed. They found people of various ages, including children, and they found both men and women. Analysis showed that the men had smoked tobacco. Coins and beads had been placed beside the deceased, who were later returned to the ground after being given African names.[39] In Charleston, then, those who were apprentices had their counterparts: those who were inventoried. All of which lay at the heart of my conversation with Peter as we walked.

The path beyond the bird hide narrowed, and we had to walk in single file. Peter stopped to take in the view behind him. Fleswick beach, lying beneath the cliffs, was all pinks and greys. The sea spray made rainbows in the gully we'd just left. Looking further back, we could see the clifftop path along which we'd walked and, inland, a neat patchwork of shorn winter fields partitioned with hedges. We continued our climb. Finally, the footpath levelled out, through fields which bristled with gorse.

We followed the path as it curved away from the cliff edge, and our conversation returned to the indifferent references to human suffering in Joseph Senhouse's diary. It was striking, Peter said, that Senhouse was a contemporary of Toussaint L'Ouverture, the leader of the Haitian Revolution. He spoke of his admiration for L'Ouverture, who enlisted words in his fight, leaving letters and books on colonists' desks. These contrasting characters used writing to different effects and ends. 'In their lifetimes,' said Peter, 'it was the mediocre Senhouse who won out.' Returning to England in 1779, the Lowthers helped him to obtain a knighthood.[40] L'Ouverture died in captivity. But, Peter continued, L'Ouverture ultimately won the day: after many twists, turns and complications, Haiti became the first nation to overthrow slavery. Peter's words took me back to the Lakes, and Wordsworth's own tribute to Toussaint L'Ouverture: 'Thou has left behind / Powers that will work for thee . . . Thy friends are exultations, agonies, / And love, and man's unconquerable mind'.

Peter may have admired L'Ouverture and detested Senhouse, but he dislikes telling readers what to think. Here, our conversation got to the heart of the matter: the tension between a writer's personal philosophy and their duty to historical fiction. For however repugnant an enslaver's acts, an historical figure is not just one thing, but many. For this reason, Peter wanted his depiction of Senhouse to be three-dimensional, to hold complex worldviews. His approach carries the risk – he was well aware – of privileging the voices of enslavers. The difficulty, though, Peter said, was acknowledging slavery's horrors without encouraging voyeurism. One particularly unpleasant passage in Senhouse's diary illustrates this dilemma well. On a neighbouring plantation in Barbados, Senhouse described seeing the 'head of a Negroe stuck upon a pole close to the roadside' as, he learned, punishment for making multiple bids for his freedom before this final recapture and execution. The principle behind this, Senhouse wrote, was that without a head the soul could not return to Africa: 'there are,' he continued, 'three other horrid spectacles of the like nature on the above plantation, having all been guilty of the same offence.'[41] Senhouse did not shy away from narrating these routine acts of murderous cruelty, but neither did he change his own ways as an enslaver. Not only was it upsetting to read such terrifying accounts, but the abiding image his diary left was that of a victim defeated. It was a challenge to draw on such sources and yet avoid presenting enslaved people as passive sufferers. This was why Peter found figures like Toussaint L'Ouverture inspiring, telling me that he embodied Enlightenment ideals as they *should* have operated.

Having rounded St Bees Head, we were midway to Whitehaven. By the early eighteenth century, as it became established as a hub of the tobacco and colonial trade more generally, the town made its almost inevitable entry into the slave trade. Local merchants found investors for slaving ships, which were fitted out for the purpose of transporting human beings as well as tobacco and other colonial goods. The Royal African Company maintained its monopoly on slave-trading, but there were many independent merchants and sea-captains who, setting themselves up in provincial ports like Whitehaven, wanted to get in on the lucrative slave trade. In order to operate as independent slavers, they were required to pay 10 per cent of their profits towards maintaining company forts in West Africa.[42] In Whitehaven, a temporary decline in tobacco trade coincided with this increase in slave-trading, with the Lutwidges the first among the family businesses to shift from tobacco to human trafficking. In 1707, the Lutwidge family commissioned the first of many slaving ships. One of these was the *Hannah-Maria*, which would sail to Jamaica and Antigua via the African west coast. By then, Sir John Lowther had been succeeded by his son Sir James (yet another Sir James: distinct from the Wordsworths' James Lowther), whose colliery overseer informed him that the *Hannah-Maria*'s maiden voyage would likely yield large profits, and he was almost certainly right.[43] Three years later, Thomas Lutwidge commissioned and owned the *Swift*, a heavily armed ship which reached Cape Coast Castle on the Gold Coast (now Ghana) but which – despite its armaments – was captured by the French as it neared Jamaica. The captors took ninety-five enslaved people from the vessel so as to transport and sell them themselves. Such incidents showed that, financially speaking, slaving was an unpredictable business: if the rewards could be huge, so could the losses.[44] The *Swift* made further voyages under the command of Captain Rumball, who ran Whitehaven's sugarhouse boiling works with a tobacco merchant called John Gilpin, a common Whitehaven surname. The vessel landed in West Africa and sailed across the Atlantic, disembarking enslaved Africans in Barbados and reloading with muscovado sugar.[45] Captain Rumball alone shipped 738 people and was responsible for eighty-nine deaths on Atlantic crossings by the *Swift* and *Fanteen Galley*.[46] The innocuous, even deliberately benign names of slaving ships often belied their horrific function. One was even named *Peace*.

The Whitehaven slave trade developed along its existing trade routes for coal and tobacco. In 1716, the *Whitehaven Galley* left the harbour loaded with coal, which was sold in Dublin. Here, the ship was filled with goods like Irish linen, salt beef, candles made from Irish tallow and other provisions. From Dublin the ship sailed to West Africa, where its goods were sold or traded. Crossing the Atlantic from West Africa with its cargo of enslaved people, *Whitehaven Galley* put in at Montserrat, Jamaica and Honduras, where it loaded up for the return journey with ivory, logwood and anatta dye[47] (which has orange hues and is still used as a colourant for products like Red Leicester cheese). Likewise in 1759, the locally built *Betty* cleared port, sailing to the Sierra Leone estuary; later, it disembarked 210 enslaved people in Charleston, where many Whitehaven tobacco merchants had connections.[48] Meanwhile, the Whitehaven slaver *Prince George* was built in tobacco-exporting Virginia.[49]

Whitehaven's slavery activities continued throughout the 1750s and 1760s. Slave-ships included the *Griffin*, *Providence*, *Betty*, *Unity*, *Wittington* and *Black Prince*, a fourteen-gun vessel built in Whitehaven, which transported enslaved people to the Caribbean from the Windward Isles, a collection of islands in the Lesser Antilles, and the Gold Coast, along the West African Gulf of Guinea.[50] [51]

Whitehaven's slave-trading business lasted some sixty years, petering out by the late 1760s, decades before the abolition of slavery in Britain. It's thought that there were insufficient quality goods made locally to trade in West Africa (hence the stopovers for Irish linen and tallow), while merchants were ultimately dissuaded from a trade that gave uncertain financial returns.[52] The decline in slaving also coincided with a surge in national demand for whale oil: some Whitehaven merchants, seeing the chance for greater and more reliable profits, subsequently diversified into whaling.[53] In other words, there was nothing particularly moral about Whitehaven's turn away from the slave trade: there were clear economic reasons for switching trades. Although it's conventionally claimed that Whitehaven had a minor slave-trading history, the town was once Britain's fifth-largest slave-trading port. The town's merchants trafficked over 5,739 people, and caused at least 906 deaths on transatlantic voyages.[54]

Incoming ships to Whitehaven port took careful note of the beam from the St Bees lighthouse, which now loomed above the fields ahead of us. Today, St Bees lighthouse's beam can be seen 18 nautical miles out to sea.[55] As we neared the whitewashed tower, Peter nodded at it: 'The ironies of Enlightenment.' It was an apt metaphor. The first lighthouse on this site had been built in 1718 by the local merchant Thomas Lutwidge, funded from the proceeds of his colonial trades, including slavery. Lutwidge had a clear interest in commissioning a lighthouse. The rocks thereabouts were treacherous, and a man like himself, who'd invested in the building of slaving and tobacco ships, feared losing everything by being wrecked along the Whitehaven coast.

Both coal ships and transatlantic ships relied on the lighthouse. Many of those coal ships belonged to Sir James Lowther, who in 1706, at the age of just thirteen, had inherited coal wealth and extensive lands from his father Sir John. Now a man, Sir James took up his father's parliamentary seat and pursued the same policies, opposing taxes on coal and applauding the removal of taxes on tobacco.[56] Sir James was cut from the same cloth as his father and grandfather before him, dedicating himself to business.[57] In 1711, he began investing in the South Sea Company, which had been set up as a joint-stock company (a business owned by its investors) that same year.[58] But, a shrewd and cautious investor, Sir James predicted disaster when the company won the right to transport and sell enslaved people to Spanish America, selling stocks at inflated prices and promising investors eye-watering financial returns. He was right; the company's collapse in 1720 precipitated the financial catastrophe known as the South Sea Bubble.[59] One man who lost out from this collapse was the Whitehaven slaver Captain Rumball. Having enriched himself by slaving, he was able to marry into a wealthy family and invest the substantial sum of £1,000 in South Sea stock. News of the 1720 Bubble reached him whilst he was loading timber from Stockholm on board his ship: he had lost the full amount.[60]

Sir James' own troubles lay closer to home. By 1720, Whitehaven port was clogged with shipping, a problem Sir James proposed to solve by reducing the number of transatlantic ships that came and went into the port, a proposal which showed quite how much power he had in Whitehaven. This solution would have worked for him, protecting his own interests by giving coal ships to Ireland priority over larger transatlantic vessels. Others were furious. A local war of words broke out, with anonymously authored pamphlets – nobody wished to incur Sir James' wrath – asserting that transatlantic tobacco ships subsidized the local coal trade and therefore deserved priority. (This was a reasonable assertion: tobacco funded local manufacture and development, while tobacco profits were also reinvested in coal.)[61] Sir James hit back with an anonymously authored pamphlet of his own, which he had printed in Ireland, to create the illusion that the pamphleteer was finan-cially disinterested. He instructed his steward to drop the pamphlets into people's gardens (including his own, to avert suspicion); and to distribute them widely in local pubs. It didn't work. The town's tobacco merchants won out, and the transatlantic traders con-tinued unabated.[62]

Transatlantic traders were pumping money into many local businesses, including ironworks and rope-making. They invested heavily in ship-building too: transatlantic vessels and slaving ships were built and repaired just north of Whitehaven. Sail-makers operated from the town, and Lowther leased premises to ship-wrights just behind Tangier Street. Local cloth traders expanded across Cumbria to supply the colonial trade, especially along the African west coast. A local business directory shows that linen, sailcloth, damasks, snuff and tobacco were all manufactured in Whitehaven.

Just as Whitehaven's harbour expanded, so too did the town. In the lifetimes of Sir John Lowther and his son James, the local popu-lation had increased from 250 to well over 3,000. This growing population needed infrastructure. The building of houses and fac-tories, and the constant upgrading of the harbour, provided jobs, as did the local brickworks, owned by Walter Lutwidge, the Irish-born slaver, tobacco merchant and lighthouse-builder. Whitehaven Glass-works Company was part-owned by the Lutwidge tobacco merchants (the bottles it made were considered of poor quality, as they kept breaking when corks were inserted). Of the nearby col-lieries, Walter Lutwidge also had a part share in Seaton Colliery, while Broughton Colliery was leased by East India Company fami-lies, the Christians (of Ewanrigg Hall in Maryport) and the Senhouses of Netherhall. Another tobacco merchant, William Hicks, who had 'lands in North America' (as his will put it),[63] ran a slave-ship, owned a local glassworks and invested in Low Mill iron-works along with the magistrate and tobacco merchant Peter How: each put in £2,000.[64] When this venture failed, a second ironworks was established by Humphrey Senhouse and Thomas Hartley, a rope-maker who invested in two tobacco vessels; other partners included the tobacco-trader Edward Tubman, and John Gale, whose sons were East India Company mariners.[65]

Additional local manufacturing was directly related to West Indies trade. A snuffery was built for Peter How and powered by a water mill.[66] Snuff was connected to the explorer Christopher Columbus, who'd come across it while on his second voyage to the West Indies in the sixteenth century. It puzzled him as much as smoking did. One of his shipmates, a Spanish monk, wrote that powdered tobacco leaf was sniffed into the nose through a tube. Snuffing became popular in Europe: during the seventeenth century it was the fashion in aristocratic circles and at royal courts. The snuff was fingered then inhaled, serving as a kind of purge. It was also kept in ornate snuffboxes. Snuffing was con-sidered daintier than chewing and spitting tobacco. There was no offensive smoke. Scented with flowers, herbs or port, it was an aromatic experience, warding off the stench of poverty, offensive odours from poor sanitation and the smell of other people's bodies.[67]

The East India Company also played a role in funding Whitehav-en's development, often in quite subtle ways, its profits extending well beyond the business domain. A dispensary was opened in 1783 to provide free medicine for families who could not afford it. At least four of its benefactors and subscribers who contributed to the dispensary's upkeep were from East India Company families.[68] Whitehaven's Ladies Charity, established in 1805, helped forty-three impoverished women to receive medical assistance during their pregnancies. Seven of the thirteen committee members had connections either to the East India Company or to the slavery business.[69]

Over a 200-year period, from 1600 to the early 1800s, then, Whitehaven prospered because of combined coal and colonial profits. But not everybody benefited. Wealth was concentrated in the hands of merchants and landowners, and poverty and hardship ran like a seam throughout these boom years. Many people, attracted to Whitehaven by the prospect of regular and reasonably paid work, went hungry. In 1728, amid grain shortages, a group of colliers attacked a ship which, loaded with oatmeal, was destined for Ireland. Troops were sent in from Carlisle to quell the riot.[70]

But Sir James Lowther flourished. In 1733, years after the South Sea Bubble, he was made a South Sea Company director. It was a short-lived caretaking role to steer the company clear of further disasters, but he continued to invest in the company as it re-established itself. Sir James had also invested in the Royal African Company, and in the East India Company, lending huge sums amounting to tens of thousands of pounds on the security of the stock he held in them.[71]

Much of Whitehaven's expansion was underwritten by Sir James' wealth. With credit hard to come by, he lent money to Whitehaven's tobacco traders, and more widely too: his debtors included Sir William Codrington of Dodington in Gloucestershire, whose vast fortune (and, later, the family's country pile, built in typical neoclassical style) came from Barbados sugar plantations.[72] Though Sir James Lowther was widely known outside Whitehaven, in the town itself he ruled the roost. In the election year of 1734, when Sir James made his biannual visit to Whitehaven, he was greeted like royalty. A party of gentry and local property owners headed by the High Sheriff of Cumberland met him at the town's limits, and made a grand entrance into Whitehaven, where crowds lined the streets that his family had constructed. Bells rang, cannons were fired, and ships put out their flags.[73]

Throughout this period, Whitehaven's poverty problems persisted. A workhouse for the unemployed and otherwise impoverished opened in 1741 and admitted sixty-four Whitehaven residents. Two years later, a smallpox epidemic in the town was caused by overcrowded housing: the town's doctor, William Brownrigg, wrote that in just one downstairs room he found one man dead, another dying and a third person seriously ill.[74] Such experiences were a world away from the likes of the Lowthers and the Senhouses.

Whitehaven's merchants served a population beyond their own town, transporting their valuable Atlantic imports inland from the sea, but the roads were poor, creating challenges for them. Sir James Lowther stepped in, leading a group of the town's merchants who agitated for improvements to roads for the cause of economic growth: in a petition to parliament they stated that the main road to Whitehaven was in terrible condition – in large part due to the increased traffic from the town's trading activity and so narrow in places that a horse and rider could not pass a horse and carriage. It was, they complained, almost impassable in winter. In 1744, the town's merchants, who were variously involved in tobacco, plantation ownership and slaving, used their influence and colonial wealth to persuade parliament to commission a turnpike road, charging tolls to travellers.[75] Two years later, a traveller to Whitehaven remarked that the road was now as good as London's best turnpikes.[76] Not only did these families contribute to local development, but their newfound wealth lifted them into the ruling gentry. Walter Lutwidge died in 1746, but his family's social elevation was part of his legacy. His son Charles became Supervisor of Preventative Officers in Cumberland, an important job in Customs and Excise, and his nephew and namesake Walter Lutwidge became High Sheriff.[77]

On his death in 1755, Sir James Lowther left a fortune. His canny investments in colonial stock had brought him around £19,000 in

East India annuities and bonds and £140,000 in South Sea stock (well over £16 million in today's money). By his death, coal profits accounted for only 23.8 per cent of his wealth, while East India Company and South Sea holdings, which made him the most money, made up a significant proportion, at 24.19 per cent.[78]

With the footpath now bringing us inches from the cliff edge, we continued to walk in single file, counting our blessings that there wasn't the faintest breath of wind. The path swerved inland again, past a quarry where giant machines conveyed sandstone blocks across the site. We crossed a bracken-covered hill, and the footpath broadened into a track past old mine works. Now, as the coastline descended to sea level, we approached the outskirts of Whitehaven. A housing estate lined the hill to our right, and we saw 'the candle-stick', a ventilation shaft poking out of a disused coal mine at Wellington Pit.

We'd arrived at Whitehaven harbour. In the distance, we could see the marina and the climb to Lowther Castle, a three-storey castellated building. The harbour itself was eerie. In front of us, the outer harbour jutted out like the disembodied claw of a cooked crab. The tide was out, which meant that we could enter the old transatlantic outer harbour and walk at sand level, craning our necks to look at the deep-water stone walls, also made of the local stone. Above our heads a couple walked along its cobbled walk-way beside some rusty capstans. The outer harbour was huge. A white lighthouse at the harbour entrance was dwarfed by the seaweed-covered harbour walls. Herring gulls soared above us, bringing to mind the moment in Peter's story 'The Keeper of Books' when enslaved people beat out a rhythm on their drums: 'See how the birds soar from the trees and fly wherever they wish? Why not us too?'

Beside the harbour was Whitehaven's Beacon Museum. We popped in to see a large goblet which commemorates a slave-ship called the *King George*. It has a twisted glass stem and a colourful engraving in red and gold. The goblet is engraved with the Royal

Coat of Arms and depicts a sailing ship with the words: 'Success to the African Trade of Whitehaven'. At the café beside the outer harbour we paused for a late lunch and, overwhelmed by our harbour and museum visit, discussed anything but slavery.

As we were soon to see, Sir John Lowther's seventeenth-century planned new town was impressive. He'd designed attractive terraces of three-storey townhouses, decorated with carved sandstone from the local quarry and roofed with Lakeland slate. Today, Whitehaven remains the most complete Georgian town in Europe, and 268 of its buildings appear on Historic England's list of the most important historic constructions. The streets are wide, the squares generous, the houses evenly designed. Through it runs Lowther Street, arrow-straight from Lowther Castle to the port, a statement of the family's dominance.

After lunch we wandered into the town, easily orientating ourselves amidst the parallel streets, walking past the inner harbour to the early nineteenth-century customs house, a broad, elegant building painted dove-grey and attached to a big warehouse. We headed for Lowther Street and our first destination, the mansion of Walter Lutwidge. Only part of it still stands but, even so, we got a sense of the grand house it once was. In Lutwidge's day, the house had two wings and twenty-six windows, topped with a cupola.[79] Living quarters were located in the centre with courtyards to the front and rear, where carriages could enter and carts unload.[80] It was of particular interest to Peter that Lutwidge's house was later sold to Joseph Senhouse following his return from Barbados, in 1801.

Across the street, we came across a mural commemorating the eighteenth-century satirical writer Jonathan Swift. Peter hadn't known that Swift had lived in the town as a very small boy, between 1668 and 1671: a Dubliner, he had been brought across the Irish Sea on those well-worn sea routes by his nurse, a native of Whitehaven. We talked about Swift's satirical essay of 1729, 'A Modest Proposal', in which monstrous ideas are presented in moderate, rational language: in this case, a proposal that starving Irish people, then in the midst of a terrible famine, should fatten up their babies for wealthy people to eat.[81] One of the greatest satires in the English language, its shock value remains. Peter is a fan – so much so that his own stories adopt a Swiftian approach to exposing callous and inhumane ideas, as with his parody of will-taking in Peter's short story 'The Keeper of Books'. As we contemplated the mural, I remarked that Jonathan Swift was one of the many investors in the South Sea Bubble. Did Swift know what his money funded? Peter shrugged his shoulders. 'There are no heroes in life,' he said.

We passed by the Rum Story Museum – a building fronted with bottle-green and arched white windows – but having previously looked in, I didn't have the heart to suggest we go inside. The museum does not yet close the 'racial empathy gap'. Perhaps inevitably so: the museum was established to celebrate the Jefferson family, which set up Whitehaven's rum cellars in the early nineteenth century. While acknowledging the connection between rum production and human enslavement, the museum focuses primarily on the succession of fathers and sons called Robert and Henry Jefferson, the first of whom – Robert Jefferson – worked as a wine merchant and sea captain on the customary sea routes to Virginia in the 1780s. His sons founded the family rum business in the early nineteenth century by trading with Virginia and the West Indies.[82] An Antiguan plantation ledger shows that the Jeffersons produced molasses on their Yeamon's, Yorke's and New Division estates, from which they made what they described as 'one of the best rums in England', sold from their base at 27 Lowther Street.[83] Today you can enter the old, barrel-filled cellars with their curved, backlit ceilings, to view rooms with displays of tropical forests, sailing ships, rum bottles and enchained Africans.

A great deal of know-how went into the production of rum, which was often produced using sugar cane damaged by hurricanes. In the eighteenth century it was distilled in the dry season, because damp conditions were not ideal.[84] Even so, it was difficult to make good-quality rum. In Barbados, plantations experimented with the froth from sugar-boiling vats, building distilleries – Still

Houses – on sugar estates. Through painstaking trial and error, Barbadian rum-makers became specialists, distilling the liquid twice to create a strong liquor. Rum-making then spread to other islands, including the Jeffersons' plantations in Antigua.

Enslaved people and indentured labourers in the British Caribbean sometimes received rum as part of their weekly rations and the drink offered temporary relief for those who produced sugar and rum. Rum was also given out as a reward for carrying out additional labour. Perhaps as a result, it took on a symbolic dimension, and was used for libation, poured out as an offering to African gods. For enslaved Africans producing rum in the West Indies, the drink expressed this connection to the homeland and helped to repair the spiritual bond with the societies from which they had been torn.[85] Rum was used as a commodity in trading negotiations in West Africa and with Caribs; mariners, too, consumed prodigious amounts aboard ship.[86] There were rum taverns for plantation-owners and military commanders, and the slave-owner Edward Long wrote in his 1774 *History of Jamaica* that freewomen sold rum-based drinks with sugar, water and fruit to soldiers.[87] Considered healthier than other spirits, it was believed to counter infections and illness. In 1775, the year of Sir James' death, rum merchants scored a coup when the spirit was made part of official British navy rations.[88]

Whitehaven's existing coal and tobacco routes explain why Ireland and Europe were major markets for the Jeffersons' rum – known locally as 'Whitehaven' rum – after it arrived in port, the spirit was re-exported to Dublin and then to mainland Europe. Whitehaven, indeed, was full of rum, with other merchants getting in on the trade. An 1816 advert in the local newspaper the *Cumberland Pacquet and Ware's Whitehaven Advertiser* proclaimed that rum could be bought at Mr Harley's counting house from the appropriately named Captain Barwise, whose relatives had set up a Whitehaven sugarhouse on Catherine Street.[89] Barwise, the advertisement states, was offering 130 puncheons of rum for sale.[90] This was no small quantity. A puncheon was a unit of between 70 and 120 gallons, so the counting house was selling thousands of gallons of rum. With so much rum sloshing around, people started to find other uses for it. Cumberland people developed a taste for rum butter – mixing rum and Caribbean sugar into butter – adding it to mince pies or sweet pastries.

Here again, Sir Joseph Senhouse cropped up. In 1794, seven years before Sir Joseph took over the Lutwidge house in Whitehaven's Lowther Street, he threw a birthday party at the family home of Netherhall for his twenty-one-year-old nephew. He wrote a song especially for the occasion, welcoming friends and neighbours to the party, and extolling the virtues of the drink on offer: rum punch. The young nephew was toasted with 'bowls of rich Punch, all fill'd up to the Brim'.[91] The anecdote only sharpened the contrast between Sir Joseph's gleeful enjoyment of a beverage distilled on a plantation and that same man's haunting diary account of a suicide in a copper vat of boiling sugar.

As we walked up Lowther Street to St Nicholas Church, I recalled that, when we'd set off, Peter had joked about his 'city bag'. At the time, I thought he just meant that he was no hiker but began to wonder if his joke about the bag expressed ambivalence about the countryside itself. I pressed him for more detail. 'The African continent was robbed,' he replied, 'and the fingerprints of the English countryside are all over the crime scene. No amount of warm beer, nuns on bicycles and thatched roofs can obscure that. So I always keep my hand on my wallet when I hit the green hills.' Characteristically wry, Peter evoked the nostalgic rural vision first expressed by George Orwell (and later by the former prime minister John Major), challenging such ideas by returning to the colonial era. Peter's own uneasiness, he explained, was nothing to do with his enjoyment of nature – he loved black guillemots as much as the next person – but he was well aware of how many country squires were also East India Company figures and plantation-owners, knowing well that Whitehaven's tobacco traders and enslavers had brought enslaved people back with them to Whitehaven. The town's history shows how the triangular trade, as it is sometimes called (British goods to

West Africa, enslaved people to the Caribbean, then plantation produce back to Britain) was far more complicated than the simple
three-pointed 'triangular trade' idea. Enslaved people were often
trafficked from island to island and from continent to continent.
The town's transatlantic ships did not just bring tobacco and sugar;
they brought people too.

We had reached the tower of St Nicholas, the church which
glows pink at sundown. Another fine sandstone building, it show-
cases the locally quarried rock, cut into immaculate blocks by local
stonemasons. The original tower still stands, though it was a little
overgrown with shrubs and tangled weeds. Standing beneath the
tower, we surveyed the elegant old square, seeing how impressive it
would have looked when its three-storey townhouses were smart
and new.

The main, rebuilt, church building was closed, but we wanted to
visit the site because many Black citizens were baptised, married
and buried at St Nicholas and at churches in Maryport, Workington
and St Bees. Between 1700 and 1815, I told Peter, at least sixty-six
people of African, and sometimes Indian, descent were baptised or
buried here and in the surrounding area.[92] In the eighteenth
century, then, Whitehaven was a truly multiracial town.

I had a copy of the archivist's list of parish record entries, and
together, Peter and I perused the names, previously identified by
local archivists. In 1753, the parish register of St Nicholas recorded
that 'Samuel, Son of a Female Negro Slave call'd Powers, a native
of Carolina in North America' was baptised there.[93] This brief
record notes that he was connected to a family in the Cumbrian
town of Kirkby Lonsdale. In 1758, St Nicholas Church also saw the
baptism of a man whose name and identity followed the now-
established tradition of renaming enslaved people after places in
the British Isles: 'Thomas Whitehaven,' reads the entry, 'a Negro
of ripe years.'[94] Eight years later, also at St Nicholas, the burial
took place of 'Othello, a Black of Mr. John Hartley', the slaver:
'Othello' reflected the equally common practice of giving enslaved
people literary names.[95] Just as Peter had examined in his story,

tiny information fragments like these testify to enslaved people's exclusion from the historical narrative. So many unanswerable questions sprang to mind: why were they here? What were their lives like? What did they think of Whitehaven and how did they change it? These glimpses of them are mediated by official figures. 'You could write sixty-six more stories about this place,' I said to Peter.

There are many other records of these unknown lives, men like Lewis Joseph Bichau, who, at the age of twenty-five, was: 'publikly Baptized the 3. of August. 1768. A Negroe.' This baptism happened on the occasion of his marriage at St Bees Church, though whether to a local woman it is impossible to tell.[96] In 1772, a twenty-one-year-old woman called Rosetta died of smallpox. Described as 'an Indian Black', her presence is explained by the town's extensive East India Company links, connected particularly to the Christian and Senhouse families of Maryport and the Curwen family of Workington.[97] In 1773, Cato Robinson,[98] another manservant of John Hartley, was baptised at Whitehaven. Five years later, Robinson married a woman called Mary Sharp in the newly built Georgian church of St James, on the town's high street. Their children, Mary and Joseph, were baptised in Whitehaven, and Cato Robinson became a brewer. His business seems to have been unsuccessful: burial records up the coast at Workington call him a 'Negro pauper' on his death in 1794.[99]

There were so many names. 'Samuel, a black man', born about 1774, was baptised as an adult at St Nicholas. Samuel, states the parish record, was 'Son of Quashy and Nimbo, Slaves on Locust Hall, Barbadoes'.[100] If his estimated birthdate was correct, he was buried at the age of thirty-three, in 1807. The Locust estate belonged at the time to the slave-owning merchant Osgood Hanbury II. From an Essex family, Hanbury clearly had a Cumberland association: his marriage was in the local paper, and the Locust Hall estate later came into the hands of John Wood, from a Whitehaven family.[101]

By the time the Act to abolish the Slave Trade was passed in 1807, the legacy of slavery had long since been felt along the

Whitehaven coast, which was proportionately more multicultural in the eighteenth century than it is in the twenty-first. When, in 1833, the Slavery Abolition Act was passed, a further Act of Parliament empowered commissioners to pay compensation money to enslavers for their loss of property – but not to the enslaved. In Whitehaven, the Hartley family claimed for 794 enslaved people in five Jamaican estates: Crawle, Trelawney, Dry Valley and Water Valley and Tillstone, estates that mostly produced sugar, molasses, rum and pimento. Major slave-owners, the Hartleys – whose 'servant' Othello was buried at St Nicholas – were respected townsmen, both manufacturers and bankers, and the compensation money was duly paid into the Hartleys and Co. Bank, for which Milham Hartley had inherited a fifth share from his father John Hartley.[102] To anyone versed in British slavery compensation records, these Whitehaven stories feel familiar, if more sinisterly intimate. 'But what really counts,' said Peter, 'is how places tell their stories.' This is why his stories explore and expose storytelling processes themselves. 'You can tell a lot,' he said, 'by looking at which stories get bigged-up and which are minimized or ignored.' These choices revealed a nation's philosophy.

I thought of the National Trust's description of the Whitehaven Coast, which illustrates how celebrations of the landscape can sometimes obscure historical truths. Whitehaven's mining heritage is mentioned, but the description focuses overwhelmingly on flora and fauna, including work by the Royal Society for the Protection of Birds to care for puffins and other seabirds. The sandstone cliffs, the Trust description reads, are among Britain's tallest. There is no mention of tobacco or slave-trading.

Our walk was over; it was time for us to part. I saw Peter to his car and wished him a safe journey back to Manchester. Then I set off to St Bees, back along the coastal path, retracing our steps to the lighthouse. I reached it at sunset and, leaning against its whitewashed walls, looked back towards Whitehaven, the provincial town transformed into a colonial trading hub by its deep-water harbour. I thought of all the ships which sailed from Whitehaven to West Africa, Maryland and the West Indies. And of all the missing stories.

The wind had picked up and darkness was falling. Peter liked the darkness, he'd explained, 'it erases the modern and surfaces the past.' I had to agree. I looked out to sea where navigational maps once joined the dots between continents. Then I looked back at the lighthouse. Here, each and every night, it flashes every twenty seconds, like an historical conscience.

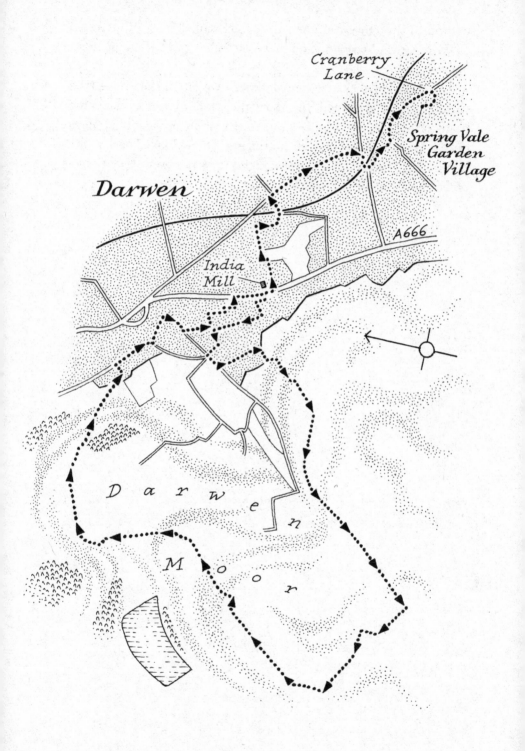

4

The Cotton Walk: East Lancashire

Bordering Cumbria with the Irish Sea to the west, Lancashire's old cotton mills lie within the urban triangle formed by Oldham, Bolton and Manchester. Cotton was vital to Britain's formation as an industrial nation, and Lancashire, the nation's textile manufacturing heart, was central to the story. Lancashire's workforce of spinners and weavers used raw cotton, which had been imported to the Atlantic port of Liverpool and transported eastwards to rural valleys, where tumbling rivers – the Irwell, Medlock, Croal and Roch – powered millwheels. These waterwheels allowed the textile industry to develop amid the West Pennine Moors and Rossendale Fells. Cotton cloth defined the region. Even today, almost everywhere you go, the Lancashire skyline is dominated by soaring mill-chimneys, boiler houses, spinning mills, weaving sheds, bleaching sheds and dye works. Mill-town streets are lined with workers' terraced houses. This iconic architecture testifies to the industry's colossal importance: by the 1830s, cotton textiles accounted for over half of Britain's home-produced exports.

Cotton mills epitomize Britain's industrial heritage. Textile manufacture was the mainstay of the nation's Industrial Revolution, driving the invention of engineering technology, mass production and the factory system. The region's textile history has wrought some expressive phrases: cotton was white gold, cotton was king. Manchester was Cottonopolis. Lancashire clothed the world.

Lancashire's cotton story is not just a matter of local history. The manufacture of cotton cloth had a vast intercontinental geography reaching from India to America's Southern states. At the nineteenth-century height of Britain's cotton export industry, cheap raw cotton came from plantations worked by enslaved people in places like Tennessee, North Carolina and Mississippi. But Britain's relationship with cotton actually began back in the early seventeenth century, when the East India Company established a textile factory in the Indian region of Gujarat, the birthplace of cotton cloth. By the late seventeenth century, the company began importing brightly coloured Indian cloth. It dazzled English consumers, who quickly acquired a taste for light, washable cotton fabrics.

Many of us have been taught the domestic history of Britain's cotton manufacture. Before the mid-eighteenth century, it was a cottage industry. Textile merchants sent raw cotton from ports like Liverpool and Manchester to local producers, who were paid to make cloth. Cotton was spun and woven in people's homes or in rented rooms, then dispatched to fullers, who thickened it to improve its quality; the fabric was then dyed. In the 1760s, mechanization transformed what had essentially been a domestic industry. This process was hastened by innovations which replaced processes that had previously been done by hand. Despite fierce resistance by radical groups such as the Luddites – who smashed Lancashire's looms[1] – cotton production was by the 1830s almost entirely mechanized within the factory system.

Mills were hot, dangerous and unhealthy places to work. William Blake's exhortation to eradicate the country of its 'dark Satanic mills' sums up the region's vertiginous descent into the health-wrecking indignity of factory labour.[2] Elizabeth Gaskell's famous 1855 novel *North and South*, about a family which moves from an English village to an industrial mill town, conveys the idea that hell was pure cotton white.[3] There are many disturbing eyewitness accounts of ailing workers inhaling cotton dust and children being mangled by industrial machinery. We might recall these details from the classroom – less so, perhaps, the huge impact that global events had on Lancashire's labour history.

These global stories have been explored by my walking companion, the artist Bharti Parmar. East Lancashire holds special significance for her: its moors and river valleys bring her own family story to life. Bharti's father was a textile worker who came from India to work in a northern English mill in the 1960s. She remembers him putting in long factory shifts.

Bharti's upbringing made her an experienced traveller between parallel cultural worlds. She spent her preschool years at home speaking Gujarati. When she first went to school, she had no English and could neither understand the teacher nor read. Confronted by the meat-and-two-veg of school dinners, Bharti had to learn to eat with a knife and fork rather than her hands. (Being from a Hindu background, Bharti did not eat with her left hand and was puzzled when a teacher swapped her knife and fork around.) Each day she peered at her lunch, always fearful that it might contain forbidden beef and longing for her mother's flavoursome cooking. Placed in a remedial class at school, Bharti only learned to read when she was ten. It was like opening the door onto a different, wider world – and it set Bharti on her path of academic study.

Bharti is from Leeds, across the Pennines in Yorkshire, but her father came from Surat in India's Gujarat region. Gujarat was the birthplace of Mahatma Gandhi, whose place in global cotton history fascinates Bharti. Cotton became a pivotal issue in the Indian independence movement, for which Gandhi was the figurehead. In 1920s pre-independence India, cotton became a symbol of the country's enforced dependence on British rule – and British-made cloth. In these years Gandhi advocated that Indians free themselves from their dependency on British-made fabric by spinning their own cotton for half an hour per day. The anti-colonial Swadeshi movement was born, founded on a philosophy of self-reliance and peaceful resistance.

The interwoven histories of Lancashire cotton manufacture and Indian resistance are bound up with Bharti's personal family history, but cotton textiles also hold a special meaning for her professionally. An acclaimed visual artist and academic, she works with embroidery and is an expert in fine art. Our walk was inspired by Bharti's 2021 exhibition *Khadi*, the Hindi name for the homespun cotton

cloth that came to represent self-sufficiency, self-assertion and freedom from the glut of expensive foreign goods then deluging India.[4]

The day before our walk, I met up with Bharti in Blackburn, a
cotton town a few miles north. *Khadi* was showing in the Blackburn
Museum and Art Gallery, an impressive cotton-era civic building
with handsome wrought-iron gates. Bharti's exhibition was in an
airy gallery on the upper floor. Illuminated cabinets displayed local
archival documents, and her own artwork hung on the surrounding
gallery walls: delicate paper sculptures on hand-made Indian cotton
paper. This paper was itself made from recycled cotton T-shirts,
Bharti told me, discarded products of the fast-fashion industry.
'Made on cotton, about cotton,' she said as we looked around the
exhibition. *Khadi* does not focus solely on Blackburn's Indian connection but explores the full intercontinental sweep of Lancashire's
cotton story, from the sourcing of raw cotton from nineteenth-
century plantations in America's Southern states to the eventual Indian
rejection of British-made textiles in the early twentieth century.

As part of the installation, a film ran on loop, showing interviews with local people who worked in the factories. The film-maker,
Sima Gonsai, also has a father who is a textile worker called Ranjitgiri
Gonsai, the son of a tailor who came to Darwen as a student in textile technology. Gonsai's own family story is woven into the film.
Born in Surat, Ranjitgiri remembered cotton being picked by hand
and, in Blackburn, the making of Manchester cloth stamped MADE
IN ENGLAND. This cloth, he said, was worth forty times as much as
the original cotton bale. Ranjitgiri made clothes with Lancashire-
spun fabric. For six months he worked in a mill, finishing, bleaching
and printing the cotton cloth. After working as a factory supervisor,
he became Blackburn's first full-time Asian lecturer. 'Blackburn has
given me everything,' he says in the film.[5]

There is also footage of Bharti making her own artwork, a process
which draws her closer to her father's experience of factory labour.
Hammer in hand, she punches holes in rough cotton paper so that
delicate, tactile patterns are produced across the page. The sounds of
the punch and hammer are amplified in the film, so as to evoke

cotton's long association with all kinds of conflict, from opposition to enslaved labour in the Southern states of America to British rule in India and, of course, to the factory system in Britain itself.

As we left the gallery, Bharti pointed out one of her artworks, which references Jacquard loom cards from 1801, a chain of punched cards which allowed complex patterns to be woven. 'Like an early form of computing,' she said. This development, of course, hastened the growth of the factory system. But Bharti was keen to celebrate the skill involved in cotton work, which is why her exhibition concentrates closely on individual manufacturing processes to emphasize the dignity of handwork, not just as a general principle but in tribute to her family history of labour.

Inspired by Bharti's *Khadi* exhibition, the following day we planned to walk from the mill town of Darwen, in a fold of the West Pennine Moors some 20 miles north-west of Manchester. Darwen was one of Lancashire's cloth-producing 'cotton towns', including Blackburn to its north and Bolton to the south. The town has much in common with other mill towns in Lancashire's cotton story. Uniquely, however, in the twilight of British Indian rule, Darwen received a visit from Mahatma Gandhi himself. He was in Britain to negotiate Indian independence with the British government and, while in London, received an invitation to the town from Darwen's mill-owners, keen to show him that Lancashire millworkers were suffering because of his Swadeshi movement. To their astonishment, he agreed. At this moment, in 1931, Darwen became intimately bound up with the conversation about Indian independence.

Before leaving for Darwen, I asked Bharti how she'd characterize herself as a hiker: wildly keen or mildly so. 'I'm definitely in the mild category,' she said firmly, 'especially when it comes to hillwalking' – and this was wise, because she knew full well that I was an enthusiastic walker with a habit of underplaying walks' distance and difficulty. We planned a short circuit of about 4 miles: one that would take in Darwen's old mill and workers' terraces, joining a moorland path before descending to Garden Village at the edge of the town.

Darwen was mostly built during the nineteenth-century cotton manufacturing boom; today, its grand buildings, canals and railways reflect its former textile wealth. The town hall has a roofed clock tower, and there is an elegant domed library. Today, the town remains bustling, with a fierce sense of community as well as its share of busy roads, betting shops, greasy spoon cafés and pubs (including one called the Spinners' Arms). Our starting point was the River Darwen, which flows through the town. As we set off, Bharti remarked on the views of the surrounding countryside, which could be seen from almost everywhere in town. To the east, parks and playing fields lead to the old Roman Road; to the west, paths climbed onto the moors.

It was late May, but the sky was overcast, and we hoped it wouldn't rain. As we passed a string of charity shops and clothing stores along the high street, my eyes were caught by the great brick chimney of India Mill, which stands a dizzying 303 feet tall. This, Bharti reminded me, was where Ranjitgiri Gonsai worked, the father of the film-maker for the *Khadi* exhibition. The mill's commanding chimney is square, like an Italian bell tower, and it just forces your feet to walk towards it. It was completed in the 1860s, during the steam age. Attached to the boiler house, the tower's practical function was to carry away smoke, smuts and ash. But it was built to impress, for India Mill was among Lancashire's most important textile manufac-tories, a spinning mill which did not cease working until 1991. Before our walk Bharti had described how the mill dominates the town and towers above the rooftops. Seen up close, the massive structure transfixes, resting on its enormous block of quarried stone.[6] It can be glimpsed on every street corner, down every alleyway: the whole town gravitates towards it.

The lower storey of the mill was a boiler room, the first and second floors were used as carding rooms, while the top three floors were used for spinning. Today, the building serves as a business centre. Bharti was keen to show me inside. Entering, we remarked how the building had retained its original character. The smart interior pillars were painted blue, while illuminated brick ceilings showcased its architectural drama. We were greeted by a security guard, who showed us to a desk and brought a box containing photographs of the mill and a book of millworkers' reminiscences. I turned to Bharti. 'You told them we were coming?' She smiled. I might have guessed, because she's the most organized person I know. As I looked through the box, she leaned towards the window. 'Look at the view from here!' she exclaimed and we gazed up at the chimney through the glass. But where smoke once billowed, peregrine falcons now nest. The security guard told us that one day a juvenile falcon plunged from the chimney's top ledge during its first flight. The staff rescued the bird. He scrolled through his phone, showing us photos of the chick with its huge yellow talons.

In an unillustrated book of reminiscences, the millworkers' punishing regime was vividly described. There were accounts of early-morning knocks on each and every millworker's window, and the clatter of millworkers' clogs on the cobbles. In later years the rapping at people's windows was replaced by a five o'clock morning factory siren, which made labourers stream along the streets to the factories. For these townspeople there was little hope of any other career: mothers, fathers and their children tended to work in the same mills.[7]

We repacked the box, returned it to the security guard then peered outside again. Clouds had deepened the day's gloom. Anticipating rain, we dawdled through the town, walking Darwen's hilly Victorian streets. We climbed sloping terraces of weavers' cottages, built during the period when cotton cloth was still made in people's houses: these were narrow back-to-backs – terraced houses with walled backyards – characterized by rectangular windows on the upper storeys. Bharti stopped for breath and gestured at one of the houses. 'Those long windows allowed light to shine on a weaver's loom,' she said, telling me how weavers sat beside them to optimize the daylight.

We followed a path that snaked up through the rows of houses, passed a playground and grinned at the ecstatic screams of playing children. Soon, the houses thinned; the town fell away. Rows of sycamores marked the path, guiding us along a series of paddock fences, which I charted with the help of an Ordnance Survey map. We cleared a buttercup meadow and, suddenly, found ourselves in open moorland with sooty clouds sweeping across the sky. This was Darwen Moor. 'The wind's picked up!' I said. But Bharti's attention had already switched to the lush moorland growth. A proficient and knowledgeable gardener, she identified sere grass, lurid clusters of loosestrife and wiry pink persicaria, native to the Himalayas. Alongside these unruly grasses, the hill was dressed in elderflower, ferns and moss. As we continued to climb, the moor expanded into galaxies of shining cotton grass. Bharti told me that the plant was native to Britain and that we were lucky: May was the best time to see it. We watched its fluffy fronds waving in the wind. 'Do you know its other name?' she asked. I didn't. 'Bog grass,' she said. 'It likes waterlogged ground, so wherever it grows, we shouldn't walk!' We steered well clear and continued up the hill.

The story of India's relationship with Darwen – and all Lancashire mill towns – reaches back to the late seventeenth century. Indian cotton cloth has been woven and exported since antiquity, with different regions producing a range of textiles: calico came from Calicut, muslin from Bengal, and the Gujarati city of Ahmedabad was full of weavers, artisans and merchants selling brightly coloured cotton fabrics.[8] These fabrics were desirable: muslin in particular was said to be so fine as to be made by fairies or butterflies.[9] Having established factories in Gujarat in the seventeenth century, the East India Company fixed local market prices by binding the weavers into contracts which forced them to sell exclusively to the company, at a price dictated by them. Using these methods, the company gradually expanded their Indian cotton territories until, later in the century, it was able to supply English consumers en masse with Indian cotton fabrics.

The influx of these cheap fabrics into English markets angered the country's textile manufacturers. They went to the East India

Company headquarters to complain, wanting people to buy their own home-made wool and silk materials, not this imported cloth. English manufacturers lobbied parliament to safeguard their businesses by charging protectionist import taxes. Weavers protested outside calico shops, and demonstrations turned violent: there were cases of acid being poured over fashionable calico-wearing women, who had the fabric ripped from their bodies.[10] The writer Daniel Defoe characterized calico as a 'Foreigner by birth: made the Lord knows where, by a Parcel of Heathens and Pagans, that worship the Devil and work for a Half-Penny a Day'.[11] The Calico Acts of 1700 and 1721, parliament's response to these petitioners, were laws designed to protect domestic manufacturers against Indian cloth. This did not open the doors to British cotton manufacture, however, because the ban extended to British-made cotton cloth in order to favour domestic wool and silk goods.[12] Further legislation banned the importation of Indian cottons entirely: from 1721 anyone who smuggled in foreign cotton was punished by law.[13]

It was Bharti's *Khadi* exhibition which had first drawn my attention to Darwen's Indian history. As we walked up the hill, she told me that Darwen's India Mill was so named because the factory used Indian cotton during the American Civil War. I thought of this while we ascended, the horizon expanding as if the moor itself wanted to impress the region's vast cotton geography upon us. I stopped and gazed at the surrounding hills. Bharti was only too glad to catch her breath, because the resting bench I'd promised her had failed to materialize. 'What colour would you call the hills around us?' I asked her. 'Pea green,' she said, and we resumed our climb a few moments later.

When the Calico Acts were repealed in 1774, the stage was set for the growth of England's domestic cotton textile industry. Mechanical innovations like carding machines, Arkwright's water frame and, in the 1780s, the spinning mule made British cotton manufacturing competitive and gave consumers the fine Indian-style chintzes and muslins for which they had developed a taste.[14] Mechanization and the factory system allowed Britain a further competitive advantage. Soon, British cotton manufacturers had far outstripped Indian supply, and India began to import British-made cotton cloth.[15] By the 1830s, the manufacturing fortunes of India and Britain had completely reversed: cotton fabric from Lancashire mills had become India's main import. By the following decade India was Lancashire's largest global customer, so much so that twenty-three of the county's mills were dedicated to the exclusive production of turbans and loincloths.[16]

American cotton bales were first imported into Liverpool in 1784. The Southern states were now the main source of Lancashire's raw cotton, and, as the industry grew, railways and canals were built to connect the cotton towns between Liverpool and Manchester; 1.5 million American cotton bales were being shipped to Liverpool by 1850, before being transported out to local mill towns.[17] By 1860, 88 per cent of Britain's raw cotton imports came from the United States.[18] As this high percentage suggests, the region depended heavily on the American South for its cotton bales.

With the cotton trade of paramount economic importance and possible civil war brewing in the United States, it was clear that reliance on a single source of raw cotton – which, since the 1780s, was the American South, produced cheaply in the Southern plantations by enslaved labour – carried obvious risks to the economy should anything happen to cut off the supply. Identifying alternative sources of cotton was a British priority and a particular concern of cotton merchants from Liverpool and Manchester. Others had less pecuniary reasons for supporting such a measure: abolitionists favoured 'free-grown cotton' from India, because they hoped it would hasten the end of slavery. Yet 'free-grown' cotton proved no triumph of personal liberty for Indian cultivators. The British state became centrally involved in cotton policy-making during this period, and the crop was overwhelmingly produced by impoverished and indebted smallholders or tenants working under coercive control.[19] But in the meantime Britain continued to source its raw cotton from the southern United States.

*

Out on the moor, we cast about for Witton Weavers Way, a long-distance trail extending in a 32-mile loop which begins and ends at Witton Country Park with its 480 acres of nature trails. For centuries, these old paths were used by weavers, pedlars, farmers and labourers, until – in 1870 – their way was blocked because the Reverend William Arthur Duckworth, then lord of the manor, wanted to remove their right to roam, and to use the moors for game hunting. After a long struggle, the local townspeople took him to court and defeated him. The ancient rights of way were opened up again in 1896.[20]

As though the Reverend Duckworth had risen from his grave to block our route, we promptly got lost. 'This might explain why I couldn't find the moorland bench I'm looking for,' I said. After stumbling around, we cut across country, forcing our way through heather and sliding into peaty troughs. From behind me came Bharti's faint voice: 'This kind of walking is out of my comfort zone.' And, so it transpired, mine too: I tumbled over, landing with my feet in the air. I righted myself and, poring over the map, we discussed our options and decided to keep going rather than returning to the place where we'd gone wrong. Angry clouds scudded across the sky.

After fifteen long minutes of battling the undergrowth we jumped a ditch, found the Witton Weavers Way and followed it to the top of Darwen Hill. The historian David Olusoga recently rekindled Bharti's interest in Darwen when he shone a spotlight on Lancashire's connection with American cotton. A man of British and Nigerian heritage, Olusoga was taught that cotton history spoke to his White, working-class roots, about the factory system and appalling labour conditions; and about workers' acts of resistance to a system in which machines were replacing their jobs. But, Olusoga realized, Lancashire's cotton story was every bit as much about the experience of enslaved people labouring in the cotton fields of the Southern states of America. As the anti-slavery campaigner Thomas Clarkson had warned, back in the early nineteenth century, a new cotton factory opening in Lancashire created a corresponding demand for enslaved people on plantations. As he anticipated, this was long after Britain's 1833 Slavery Abolition Act had outlawed enslaved labour in most British colonies.[21] By contrast, slavery remained legal in the United States until 1865. This is why Clarkson – whose anti-slavery efforts were praised by a Wordsworth sonnet – fulminated against Britain's reliance on Mississippi's 'blood-stained cotton' and angered Southern growers by suggesting Indian cotton instead.[22]

Though these 1.8 million enslaved workers lived far from British shores, their story is integral to Britain's cotton story. As Olusoga puts it, the Confederate states were Lancashire's economic siblings because plantation-owners and cotton manufacturers were joined at the hip.[23] For the financial beneficiaries of the cotton business – from merchants to producers – the key to success was maintaining a reliable supply of raw cotton bales.

Lancashire's cotton industry boomed during these years. All told, there were some 2,300 mills in operation in the county, employing some 450,000 textile workers. Moreover, for every cotton worker there were three times the number of associated hosiery-makers, dockworkers, mechanics, dealers and speculators.[24] Lancashire's entire economy was underpinned by the supply of cheap American cotton. But then, in 1861, when the American Civil War began, the supply of American cotton was cut off.[25] It was as though someone had flicked a giant switch.

As in Lancashire, mechanization was transforming the American South. Whitney's cotton gin, splitting the cotton pods with dry air, was a game-changer, separating seed from fibre eight times faster than a single pair of human hands.[26] Meanwhile, as they worked the thorny cotton plantations, enslaved people dealt with their oppressive conditions as best they could. They grew fruit and vegetables, ran markets, created informal economies and banks and offered their services in healing, herbal medicine, crafts or music. Some made bids for freedom on the Underground Railroad, a network of clandestine escape routes and safe houses between the Southern states, 'free states' and Canada.[27]

For plantation-owners, there was much to be gained from an economy dependent on slavery: in 1860, two-thirds of the nation's wealthiest people were Southerners. When Abraham Lincoln was inaugurated as president in 1861, eleven Southern states seceded from the Union and the fast-industrializing North to establish the Confederate States of America (1861–65). Civil war broke out soon after. It would last four years and 'emancipate' four million enslaved people. Allocating $2 million to pay troops, Lincoln was determined to hit the Southerners where it hurt, ordering a naval blockade of Southern ports. Now, the Confederate states could no longer export their plantation-produced cotton to Lancashire.[28]

At first, Confederate leaders believed that Lancashire's cotton dependence would encourage Britain to intervene in favour of the South. However, deputations of Southerners sent to England were dismayed to find that mill-owners, anticipating war, had stockpiled enough cotton to last at least a year.[29] The British themselves were also divided on the Civil War's central issue: slavery. Despite the 1833 Slavery Abolition Act, many Britons still felt that slavery was justified in the American South. To some, it was divinely sanctioned. An 1863 tract produced in Britain, 'The True Interpretation of the American Civil War and of England's Cotton Difficulty, or Slavery from a Different Point of View', argued that the violent Civil War was a holy judgement on those who broke God's natural laws by considering Africans as equals. (The same tract also called the Northern states hypocritical for siphoning off cotton wealth through their agents, brokers and bankers.)[30] All of which echoed widespread opinion in the Confederate states: the notorious Southern plantation-owner, slave-owner, rapist and US senator James Henry Hammond repudiated the idea that all people were born equal, opining that slavery was God's commandment.[31]

The Civil War was not initially all about emancipation: it was only towards the end of the war's second year that President Lincoln issued the Emancipation Proclamation, declaring 'that all persons held as slaves . . . are, and henceforward shall be, free.'[32] The historian Kris Manjapra observes that Lincoln thought slavery could be stopped by compensating enslavers as Britain and France had done.[33] Meanwhile, it was not until the 1862 Militia Act that

Black people could even fight in the Civil War. By the end of the war there were 180,000 Black soldiers, commanded by Whites and fighting with inferior equipment. Yet, on the battlefields the stakes were high for Black soldiers: if captured by the Confederates they faced enslavement or, in many cases, re-enslavement.[34]

The Civil War and its accompanying debates were closely followed by Lancashire people. With entire towns dedicated to cotton manufacture, the Union blockade of cotton ports had dire consequences. Following the outbreak of war, the mill-owners' first response was to cut mill operatives' pay: the owner of Low Moor mill near Rochdale was fairly typical in his ultimatum to his textile workers: if they didn't like it, he said, they could leave. Factory owners rationed their cotton supplies, introducing shorter hours and job-shares to avoid people losing their employment. But most measures failed. By October 1862, the stockpiles of cotton were exhausted. By mid-winter, 70 per cent of textile workers had been laid off, and poverty began to bite. A fifth of Lancastrians were on poor relief. The Lancashire Cotton Famine had begun.[35]

Contemporary accounts of the famine's impact are vivid. Visiting Blackburn in 1862, one visitor noted that the chimneys were not smoking and the air was unusually fresh. But the place, he wrote, had lost its life; people walked aimlessly through the streets.[36] In Wigan, another mill town some 15 miles south of Darwen, a local man wrote to newspapers under the pseudonym 'A Lancashire Lad'. He described dwindling shop supplies and bare houses, described families hiding their meagre meals of porridge at the arrival of visitors. It was desperately cold. In one house, a woman sat on a box by the fire, having already burned her wooden furniture. She gradually broke off bits of her box to feed the flames. Starving families used up their meagre savings, sold their furniture, pawned their belongings, wore out their clothes and ran out of shop credit. The Lancashire Lad wrote of 'glum', unemployed fathers watching their children 'whimper for bread which they cannot have'. Formerly, he added, the better-paid millworkers had a reputation for eating well.[37]

Responsibility for alleviating poverty lay with Poor Law Unions throughout Lancashire. Each union was connected to a workhouse governed by a board of guardians. These boards were responsible for administering 'poor relief' in their districts. Poor relief was then a legal obligation discharged not by central government but by local parish authorities. Two high-profile figures – Chancellor of the Exchequer William Gladstone and the novelist Charles Kingsley – were unimpressed by the way this system operated in practice during the Cotton Famine. They said that the Lancashire board of guardians should have made the wealthy dig deeper into their pockets to relieve the poverty on their doorstep.[38]

The sufferings continued with a lack of nutrition wrecking people's health. Deaths from poverty-related diseases like typhoid increased, driven by insanitary, overcrowded conditions that developed when rent-defaulters were forced to move in with family or friends. Darwen's relief committee sometimes paid rent if a landlord did not want to give rent relief or proved intractable.[39] A doctor's survey of Lancashire mill towns found that scurvy became widespread among millworkers, with vegetables, fish and eggs disappearing from people's diets.[40]

In Darwen, as elsewhere in Lancashire, poor relief decisions got personal. The connection between wealth and power was exacerbated by extreme poverty, and those who were stricken by it were commonly condescended to. Recipients of poor relief naturally wanted to better control their own situations and repeatedly requested actual money rather than goods. Meanwhile, donations by wealthy locals indicated the donors' ignorance of local life, with the relief committee secretary recording wildly inappropriate contributions, from venison and deer's heads to dancing shoes, opera cloaks and parasols.

This ignorance extended to the relief committee itself. Rather than handing over funds that had been donated, it made moral decisions: assuming that people would spend it on gambling or drink, they refused to distribute cash, instead handing out blankets, clothes, clogs, coal and tickets to redeem in shops.[41] The secretary of Darwen's relief committee, Mr Nichols, recorded that every piece of clothing or blanket was stamped with: 'Lent By the Darwen Relief Committee' to ensure such items were not pawned for money. The worst week, he recalls in his account, was in December 1862, when provision tickets were given to 494 local families, or around 1,974 people from a total population of 16,492, about 12 per cent of the town's population, but then – as critics noted at the time – this was likely to have been woefully inadequate. Darwen poor relief expenditure for March 1863 was just over £493, roughly £29,150 in today's money.[42] After considerable protest by suffering families, the committee eventually relented. They gave 2 shillings 6 pence per week to each single person, whilst families of five got 1s 9d per person. Unemployed townspeople were sent to school. Women and girls attended sewing, reading and writing classes, which very much reflected middle-class domestic ideals.[43] A men's school soon followed, where a fire was kept burning and board games were provided on condition there was no disorderly behaviour. Outside these permitted leisure hours, men underwent five hours' daily instruction in reading and writing.[44] For Darwen's factory workers, it seemed, the richest thing they had was the view of the moorland above their town.

As it happened, upper- and middle-class attitudes were (as so often) wide of the mark. Working people had a very clear sense of the complexities of the global economy – and of how relative even their own suffering was. Some months after Abraham Lincoln's Emancipation Proclamation was signed, George Burnett, a draper in the mill town of Chorley – about 10 miles west of Darwen – remarked on the proclamation in a diary he kept. It was, he wrote, a 'wondrous' example of the way God brings good out of evil: 'The slave obtains his freedom at the expense of a fratricidal and bloody war.'[45] At the same time, he was troubled by the hardship caused by the Cotton Famine. 'The state of business,' he wrote, 'is depressing in the extreme. As much attention is required now as ever, without the least stimulus in the way of profit.'[46] Quoting from official trade reports in Blackburn, he recorded that, of the town's 72 cotton mills, only 16 were operating as normal; 28 had stopped altogether and the rest were operating at far reduced capacity. In Blackburn, 10,990 of the town's 23,624 factory operatives were now unemployed, and in Darwen a third of looms had stopped altogether.[47] The situation was bleak.

Darwen's Cotton Famine lasted five years, just beyond the length of the American Civil War. As long as the blockades held, there was little hope of things improving in Lancashire – 'trade is as bad as ever,' wrote a miserable George Burnett.[48] Around this time, the Public Works Act of 1863 allowed the authorities to pay for 'outdoor relief'. This was harsh, outdoor labour, stone-breaking in quarries, building and repairing roads: in March 1863, 113 men were asked to work on local footpaths. They repaired these with spades, picks, hammers and a roller[49] for a shilling per day, a drastic reduction in income for households accustomed to 30 shillings a week. This was a truly vicious circle. Unable to access sufficient protein and calories, and with lungs damaged by cotton-dust, millworkers struggled to adapt to hard labour in the cold air.[50] One visitor to the quarry wrote how men rested frequently, leaning on their tools until they heard warning shouts at the approach of the foreman, at which work recommenced with feigned enthusiasm.[51]

Even in the midst of famine, Darwen's people managed to find some joy. In 1863, New Year's Day celebrations were attended by about 200 people, and the secretary of the committee was impressed by 'a negro conjurer', a 'man of colour' who was an unemployed factory worker who attended the adult male school. His tricks were 'most expert', and he 'gained deservedly much applause'.[52]

On Darwen Moor I thought of the millworkers who repaired the local footpaths. And I remembered George Burnett too, as we braved the blustery weather conditions: during the Cotton Famine, the Chorley-based diary-writer took a great deal of solace from his country walks. On a far warmer day than ours, in early March 1863, Burnett described the countryside round about. 'The primrose and daisy . . . bespangle the verdant fields,' he wrote, and 'birds sang merrily as I came along, the voice of the Throstle conspicuous in the harmony.'[53] By 'throstle' he meant a song thrush, but today there were no songbirds up here on Darwen Moor.

The hill wasn't overly steep, and there was enough breath for conversation. Bharti told me about her visit to a cobbled road on Rooley Moor near Rochdale, 20 miles from Darwen. She'd visited with her film-maker and described how it bears the scars of labour: grassed-over tramways, drainage channels, mineral deposits and slots chiselled into the rock. A sum of £500 was secured in mid-crisis for twenty-five Rochdale men to lay square stones in the ground. In that chilly place poorly shod, ill-clothed workers from Rochdale's factories were hired to make the 'Cotton Famine Road', a name which reflects the role of cotton shortages and factory stoppages in impoverishing local people. This road was built along an old packhorse route almost 1,500 feet above sea level. Another group built a workhouse.[54] Bharti told me about Rochdale's reputation for radical thinking; looking across Rooley Moor, she'd seen nearby Lobden Moor, where labourers once gathered for clandestine night-time meetings about wages and workers' rights. Meanwhile Rochdale's weavers, she told me, were early pioneers in establishing cooperatives as businesses to benefit all members.[55]

Everything that Bharti and I had read and seen in the archives suggests that there were radical sympathies all across Lancashire. Here, Abraham Lincoln's anti-slavery message – communicated in newspapers and speeches – fell on fertile ground among communities that had proud traditions of calling for democratic rights and workers' dignity. It was not just workers who were anti-slavery. Some leading mill-owners and manufacturers did give speeches against slave-produced cotton, comparing slavery in the United States with poor working conditions.[56] Despite the growing poverty, many millworkers refused to work with what little Confederate cotton was available. Moved by such support, New Yorkers reciprocated in kind, raising money to send ships loaded with barrels of flour and other food aid to Lancashire. Twelve prominent New York merchants raised the money;[57] city stevedores worked for free to load the goods onto a ship, the *George Griswold*, which was the first of nine such relief ships.[58] The ship's arrival in Liverpool – with 11,236 barrels of flour, 50 of pork, 125 of bread and 300 bushels of corn[59] – was commemorated with shanties and songs.[60] In Rochdale Museum, Bharti had seen one of the *George Griswold*'s food relief barrel remains on display, stamped with the words: 'I am one of the thousands that were filled with flour and sent by the free states of America in the ship George Griswold to the starving people of Lancashire whose miseries were caused by the aggressive and civil war of the slave owners in 1862–3–4.'[61]

When Mancunians wrote to Abraham Lincoln to express their support for the Unionist cause, he responded with a letter in January 1863. In it, he explained, 'I know and deeply deplore the sufferings which the working men of Manchester, and in all Europe, are called to endure in this crisis.' He added, 'Under the circumstances, I cannot but regard your decisive utterances upon the question [of slavery] as an instance of sublime Christian heroism which has not been surpassed in any age or any country.'[62] The letter was widely published and read out in public meetings throughout Lancashire. It had a galvanizing effect across the land, and pro-Union resolutions – no matter what the local deprivations – were passed in many urban centres.[63]

During the Cotton Famine, the British government adopted a neutral stance on the American Civil War, neither formally supporting the Unionists nor recognizing the Confederacy. Rochdale millworkers were firm in their anti-slavery beliefs, but some other Lancastrians actively supported the plantation-owners of the American South: the hundreds of Cotton Famine poems printed in local newspapers reveal a range of stances on the American Civil War.[64] Some pro-Confederate poets just wanted an end to the war, and to Lancashire's suffering.[65] Meanwhile Liverpool, having transitioned from sugar to cotton wealth, overwhelmingly supported the Confederacy. Liverpool Southern Club energetically promoted the Confederate cause across Lancashire mill towns. Three out of four Liverpool newspapers sided with the Southern states.[66]

Despite the support of some for slavery, the Emancipation Proclamation also reawakened Britain's older anti-slavery traditions.[67]
The Chorley draper, George Burnett, was inspired to read *Uncle
Tom's Cabin* and declared afterwards that the novel made him detest
slavery. He wrote in his diary that, connected as it was to the horrors of enslavement, Lancashire's suffering was a form of divine
retribution for profiting from slave-produced cotton.[68]

Now 1,220 feet above sea level, we could see across the wide
plains, as far as Manchester, the old Cottonopolis. Here, the path
divided and dropped away to a cluster of firs, but we continued
along the main path to follow the exposed curve of the hilltop. Now
we felt the full force of the wind, which roared in our ears and made
conversation impossible. All around us the violet hills quivered in
the gale. By instinct, we turned our faces away from the wind
towards the Jubilee Monument, a crown-like hexagonal tower
topped with a circular glass observatory. The monument overlooks
Darwen and was built in 1898 to celebrate Queen Victoria's Diamond Jubilee, another great orientating landmark for inept
map-readers like me. We left the hillside and approached the tower.
Clouds billowed under its buttressed entrance, and I shouted, over
gusts of wind, that it looked like a stone space rocket about to lift
off in the gale.

Reaching the 86-foot tower, we saw its weathervane swing wildly
from the top of the observatory. Bharti had heard the monument
had a spiral staircase inside. We were eager to climb it, but as luck
would have it the tower was fenced off due to renovation works.
Blocks of sandstone lay about its base. Bharti spotted a plaque nearby
and went over to read it, then called me over to look. 'This has a radical history too!' she said. Though dedicated to royalty, the plaque
explained, the monument also commemorates the townspeople's
rights-of-way victory over the nimbyish Reverend Duckworth two
years previously. Having just trekked along one of them, we were
pleased to learn that Darwen Moor remains public property to this
day. Walking around the tower, Bharti spotted scores more paths
looping around the hill. 'I wonder why there are so many?' she asked.

Their excessive number seemed to defy the meddling Reverend. Keening bird-cries made us look up, and we saw two lapwings surfing the wind, their wings fully extended. Far below them, and us, Darwen huddled in its valley.

It felt like time to seek shelter and, as we left the tower behind, we reflected on the bleak day. 'I know it sounds strange,' I said, watching the wind tug at the tiny beards of cotton grass, 'but this unseasonable weather seems right for the walk.' Bharti felt the same. Everything about the history of this place seemed to insinuate itself into our walk, from Darwen's slavery connection to its local stories of Cotton Famine and blocked footpaths. 'That's called the pathetic fallacy,' Bharti said, 'life imitates art.'

We climbed a stile and picked our way down the glassy hill. 'Look!' said Bharti, pointing in the direction of India Mill, 'we don't need a map any more.' It was true; the giant brick finger beckons you back to Darwen. Bharti said the chimney reminded her of a panopticon, regulating the lives of its inhabitants.

We reached a lane and saw a neat stone farm set among the hedgerows. A Union Jack flew from its dry-stone wall in preparation for the Queen's Platinum Jubilee. We followed the lane to the cobbled terraces, stained black by the smoke from that gigantic chimney.

Bharti and I had completed a big loop leading from Darwen, across the moor and back again. Now we descended into the town, past the weavers' terraces and along the main road back to India Mill. Despite its dominance, the mill had an uncertain start: built in 1867 by the Lancashire industrialist Eccles Shorrock, it was opened as Darwen Cotton Spinning Company Ltd, and soon closed. 'He chose an inopportune moment to build it,' said Bharti, 'right at the start of the Cotton Famine.' The mill fell silent until it was opened again in 1933 with the new name of India Mill, its name – as Bharti had told me earlier on during our moorland climb – reflecting Darwen's history of using Indian cotton during the American Civil War. Desperate for other sources of cotton, mill-owners had turned to India to help close the gap. By 1862, 75 per cent of the cotton used in British mills was Indian. Back in the United States, this troubled the Confederacy because British manufacturers now had less motive to support their cause, no longer being reliant on supplies from the American South.[69]

Yet Indian cotton didn't bring instant relief. Lancashire's machines were unsuited to Indian cotton, which had short fibres and was more liable to snap than American cotton. Weavers constantly had to stop to change the thread, which given that they were paid by results, was more than a mere inconvenience.[70] With much Indian cotton coming from the city of Surat, that name quickly became a Lancastrian byword for anything of inferior quality: a 'surat beer' was a poor brew. In a poem called 'Th' Surat Weyyer', the Lancastrian poet and millworker William Billington compares the torment of working with Surat cotton to being put in debtors' prison or being transported to the penal colonies. Poverty, the poem went, was a certain outcome of weaving with Indian cotton, which the last line curses: 'To hell wi' o t'Surat!'[71]

The British prime minister at the time, Lord Palmerston, felt that Indian cotton was rescuing Britain's textile industry from ruin. He saw political advantages too: a secure supply of Indian cotton meant that Britain could better afford to take sides in conflicts like the American Civil War rather than sitting on the fence to protect its own economic interests.[72] But men like Palmerston were far removed from the realities of snapping thread, and – far worse – cotton-growing in India.[73] In Berar Province, in central India, cotton yields doubled between 1861 and 1865. This was a success story for British supply – by 1869, a Liverpool merchant could order Indian cotton and have it delivered via the newly completed Suez Canal within six weeks[74] – but it was India's loss. British price-fixing so undercut local cloth prices that large swathes of skilled and semi-skilled workers were pushed from cloth manufacture into agriculture, cultivating cotton for the global market. Spinners and weavers became agricultural labourers. Needing capital to buy seed and equipment, and forced to pay crippling taxes, cultivators were plunged deep into debt: even before it ripened in the fields, their cotton crop was generally pledged to local moneylenders. Indian cotton growers were now subject to the mood swings of the global economy, something over which they had no control. Once the Civil War was over and the American cotton crop slowly started flowing again, cotton prices fell and in 1876 food prices soared due to a drought which led to a terrible famine, affecting nearly 60 million Indians. This catastrophe made Lancashire's cotton famine pale by comparison. India's cotton districts were devastated by famine in the 1870s and again in the 1890s, when, amid more drought and further crop failures, 8.5 per cent of Berar's population died of starvation because people could not afford grain.[75]

This deterioration of living standards in cotton-producing districts came as no surprise to the British. When railways were built to carry Berar's cotton to the ports, in 1865, the British cotton commissioner bluntly hoped that the railway would enable European goods to 'be imported so as to undersell the native cloth'. The impact of this, he continued, would not only result in 'a larger supply of the raw material' – for, he explained, 'what is now worked up into yarn would be exported' – but would make available for agricultural labour 'the larger population now employed in weaving and spinning'. And so, he concluded, 'the jungle land might be broken up and the cultivation extended'.[76] This was deliberate underdevelopment. The commissioner's prophecy came to pass – and where India suffered, the Lancashire mills reaped the benefit. It was a zero-sum game, and India's once-renowned global cotton industry never recovered. By 1914, some half-century after the Lancashire Cotton Famine, India was the world's biggest importer of Lancashire cotton goods, with 3 billion yards bought annually.[77]

Cotton cloth, once the pride of India, had become a symbol of British dominance and oppression. By the early 1920s, those leading the movement for Indian independence from British rule were determined to reclaim it. Central to Gandhi's Swadeshi movement, which emphasized self-reliance as a way of resisting colonial rule, was the boycotting of British-made cotton cloth. On 30 July 1921, the

Bombay Chronicle carried a notice that a 'bonfire of foreign clothes' would be 'performed by Mahatma Gandhi' and that all who attended should wear 'Swadeshi Clothes of Khadi'.[78] Bonfires of British-made cotton clothing raged all over India.

Reaching across class, caste and region, from urban centres to remote rural regions, and across languages and cultures, the cotton movement, coordinated by the All India Spinners Association, emphasized collective action on a national, epic scale and homespun *khadi* was a major milestone on the road to independence: Gandhi's own image, wearing only a *khadi* dhoti, or cotton loincloth, embodied the Swadeshi philosophy.[79]

With Bharti having arranged for us to meet the owner of one Darwen house, linked to this history, we took the backstreets from India Mill and walked about a mile to Spring Vale Garden Village. Along the way Bharti told me about a record of a public meeting held in Blackburn on 28 April 1931, concerning the India cotton boycott, that she'd come across while preparing her exhibition. By this time, the boycott had really begun to bite, and the meeting was an attempt to fuel opposition to Indian nationalists boycotting Lancashire cotton goods. The local industry, it was said, was suffering from a lack of 'open competition', and millworkers were suffering too much because their 'purchasing power is already too low'.[80]

What happened next explained Bharti's fascination with Darwen, because she'd spent some time with Blackburn library's archivist exploring exactly why Gandhi came and what happened when he visited. Just a few months after the Blackburn meeting, in September 1931, he arrived in England for roundtable talks with the British government about Indian Independence. Old newsreel footage shows him walking down a gangplank in Europe – he stopped first in Marseille – with a voiceover by a British commentator who remarks that he is 'dressed as he says he would be, in just his loincloth, even in the chilly climes of Europe'. The newsreel also shows him walking off a ship at Folkestone port in England, with the following commentary: 'And here comes the little man, still scantily clad with an extremely wet blanket around his tiny frame.' It cuts to Gandhi in a car, sitting beside the driver rather than being chauffeured in the back.[81]

And now, we were walking through Darwen's backstreets towards Garden Village, which lies at the heart of the town's Indian story. Bharti was excited to show me where Gandhi stayed, and where he walked too. Gandhi was invited to Darwen in the first place by the mill-owning Davies family. The Davies, who were Quakers, wanted to show Gandhi that the Swadeshi movement was harming local livelihoods – even hoping that a visit to Darwen might persuade the Indian National Congress to relax its cotton boycott.[82] Late in the evening of Friday 25 September, thousands of people gathered at Darwen station but were disappointed to find that he was not on the train. He'd got off at Spring Vale station, where he was welcomed with cheers by a second crowd and driven to Spring Vale Garden Village, where he was to stay. Built by another Quaker, the local mill-owner Charles Haworth, the 'model' village had been completed just a few years earlier, designed according to the Quaker principle of providing attractive environments for workers.

The limestone millworkers' cottages were simple but generous, arranged around a grassy square with blossoming apple trees in the centre. Number 3, Garden Village, where Gandhi spent the night, looked like all the other houses. Bharti knocked on the door, and we chatted with the owner. 'Do many people knock on the door like this?' I asked. Locals were really interested in the house, she told us, and back in 1931 people were pleased that Gandhi had put their model village 'on the map'.[83] She showed us a commemorative blue plaque which she'd recently managed to have put up. We were burning to look inside the house but we weren't cheeky enough to ask. The owner pointed to the attic room where the independence leader had slept. Later, we read that Gandhi's host had commented on his simple wants: his only special request was goat's milk, rather than cow's, and a goat was kept in the back garden to supply him with milk.[84]

During Gandhi's visit, people remarked on the attention he paid to those who were normally beneath the notice of dignitaries: the workers, rather than the textile owners. He talked with his chauffeur, with the policeman who guarded him, and the postman who brought him mail. A local journalist from the *Northern Telegraph* who followed Gandhi around Darwen wrote how impressed he was that Gandhi asked for a chair to be brought for this reporter as well as for Gandhi. The journalist called him a 'clever, powerful, discerning leader', despite his humble appearance.[85]

During his brief visit, Gandhi appeared outside Darwen's Municipal Offices to rapturous crowds. A small number of locals – who opposed the Indian cotton boycott – challenged the crowd, saying that he was Lancashire's worst enemy. The overwhelming mood, though, was one of excitement. In the meeting that followed with mill-owners and local dignitaries, Gandhi emphasized the need for Indian self-sufficiency. He stressed that poverty was comparative: Lancashire's unemployed millworkers, he pointed out, at least got unemployment payments. In India, millions of people had no income at all and were reduced to beggary. Gandhi was careful throughout his visit to emphasize the starvation conditions in India. He contrasted Britain's grim unemployment figures – three million – with India's far grimmer 300 million total.[86] The mill-owner Charles Haworth said that Gandhi wanted to communicate this contrast to as many English people as he could.[87] What was more, Haworth said, the effect of the Swadeshi movement had already done much to alleviate poverty: there were already 100,000 more Indian women employed in spinning, and 10,000 men in weaving, bringing prosperity not just to themselves, but to their communities.[88]

When Gandhi walked to the Haworth family house, his way was lined with onlookers, many of whom reached out to touch his hands. Inside the house he participated in a silent Quaker prayer meeting and afterwards reported himself impressed by the power of silent communal prayer. He also expressed his wish for reconciliation between Lancashire people and impoverished Indians.[89]

All in all, Gandhi's visit to Darwen did a great deal to communicate the nationalist cause and India's plight, both to Lancashire people and to the English public more broadly. Quiet but resolute,

Gandhi acknowledged that the Swadeshi movement inevitably reduced the demand for Lancashire cotton – but he promised, too, that a more prosperous India would in time produce trading benefits for the people of Darwen.[90] All present praised him for his respectful directness in letting Lancashire people know where they stood.[91]

Bharti and I had just one more stop on our walk, Cranberry Lane, which was a couple of minutes away on foot. 'We can't do a walk featuring Gandhi,' she said, 'without retracing his footsteps,' because Darwen's surrounding hills had tempted him out for a country walk. I readily agreed, and we set off up Cranberry Lane, a steep road lined with hawthorn blossom. By 1931, Gandhi was a well-known pioneer of epic marches, having led a 24-day Salt March against the British monopoly on salt the previous year. As I said to Bharti, his 'stroll' along Cranberry Lane was more of a speed walk, his host Charles Haworth commenting on the rapidity of his pace up this lane: his companions, especially his police escort, had difficulty keeping up. Doubtless the pair of us, puffing and panting up the lane, would have been left far behind in his wake, though he didn't go right out into the countryside.[92] Apparently, so Haworth and his coterie were told, this was Gandhi's normal pace: he was then in his sixties.

Gandhi's visit ended with a trip to Charles Haworth's Greenfield Mill. Smilingly, he was asked if he wanted to wear a piece of Greenfield's mill-cloth. Knowing that a picture of him wearing Lancashire cloth would go down like a lead balloon in India, he jokingly gestured as if he were deaf. Talking to the press nearby, he spoke of the warm reception, the 'affection', that he had received from his hosts at Garden Village and Greenfield Mill, as well as from Darwen's people. He also declared himself saddened by the poverty he'd seen in the town and heard about from locals: 'It distresses me further to know that in this unemployment I also had some kind of share,' he said. 'That distress is relieved, however, by the knowledge that my part was wholly unintended.'[93]

Not everyone was impressed by Gandhi's visit to Lancashire, nor persuaded by his arguments. In the years after his visit the fascist MP Sir Oswald Mosley gave speeches in Blackburn, a few steps from the gallery which showed Bharti's *Khadi* exhibition. There, he declared that Lancashire was suffering because Britain's journey into internationalism was dragging the country down to the 'coolie' level. Mosley also visited Darwen, on 9 January 1935, giving a speech at Darwen Baths to an audience of around 800 people. A leaflet given out at these events said that a fascist government would remove Indian tariffs on Lancashire's finished cotton cloth and give work back to local millworkers.[94]

After the Second World War, Lancashire's cotton industry went into terminal decline. The world wars left global markets in disarray, economic disorder that coincided with a worldwide increase in demand for cotton fabric. With buoyant markets of consumers who now preferred good-quality cloth from South Asia and the Middle East, Lancashire mills – which produced cheaper varieties – were disproportionately hit.[95] Insufficient investment in British mill machinery and new technology added to the problem. As the newly independent nations of India and Pakistan quickly invested in new automatic looms and spinning machines, making their mills more efficient and productive, the tables had turned one last time: cotton fabric from India and Pakistan – alongside Egypt and China – now reigned. One further advantage these four nations had was their labour costs, which were vastly lower than those of Lancashire, where the old mills no longer justified the investment. Many closed down and the cotton textile workforce fell by a third. By the late 1950s, Britain was importing cotton goods once again.[96]

Yet this decline was due in large part to rising living standards in Britain. In the post-war years, textile work was no longer an attractive prospect for many Lancastrians: other industries offered better wages and better working conditions. While factory owners knew that the 24-hour working cycle optimized productivity, working through the night didn't appeal to people in Darwen and the Blackburn district. So, in the 1950s and mid-1960s, factory owners found a new workforce: skilled South Asian textile workers took up employment in Lancashire's mills.[97]

Bharti's own father arrived in Bradford in the snowy winter of 1962. He'd already been on his travels, sailing from Gujarat to the Yemen – a popular route for people from his region who often started up businesses there. Finding nothing in the Yemen to keep him, he embarked on a ship to England. There he joined his two brothers, who had already responded to an open call for immigrant textile workers. The three brothers shared working men's lodgings. Bharti's father found work as a machine setter, helping to make industrial parts for the textile industries. Soon, he moved to nearby Leeds, where in 1964 he married his wife, Bharti's mother. There were no Hindu priests in Leeds, so they married in a registry office and bought a house: with immigrant textile workers not paid enough to save a deposit, he'd borrowed the full asking price – £900 – from a Hindu elder. Two years later, Bharti was born. As a child, Bharti remembers her father returning late from the 2 p.m. to 10 p.m. shift, which was better paid than the morning shift.

Immigration to textile factories took on a new pattern after the 1968 Commonwealth Immigrants Act, which severely restricted opportunities for coming to live and work in Britain. Now, South Asians could only enter Britain as dependents of relatives who were already there. It had an unintended consequence, with young men under the age of sixteen joining their fathers in Britain: as with previous generations of millworkers, fathers and sons worked together in the factories.[98]

Poor treatment was common in Lancashire mills. What was more, although South Asian workers joined unions en masse, those same unions showed a lack of sympathy and support, in particular over their need to calibrate holidays differently to take account of religious requirements (especially Eid) and to return to family back in the Kashmiri or Mirpuri regions. The result was a high turnover of staff, who moved from mill to mill as their circumstances demanded.[99] All this, amid a period of social change: between the late 1960s and 2000, the population of Oldham – another textile town some 20 miles south-east of Darwen – rose from about 700 to 11,000.[100]

Working conditions were hard. One Oldham textile worker, Razak Ahmed, whose job was to bring cotton from the carding room to the spinning room, recalled emerging from the night shift for the 1 a.m. tea break to meet his father who had come to visit: his father failed to recognize him because his skin, hair and clothes were covered with cotton dust. Britain, he told Razak, had turned him into a ghost. In this regard, things hadn't changed much since the mid-nineteenth century.[101]

The late 1970s and early 1980s brought recession, and with it the closure of most remaining Lancashire mills. Racism and non-transferable skills caused particularly high unemployment rates among textile workers of South Asian heritage. Language was another obstacle to work: night shifts provided limited opportunity to improve their English, and, with written language tests now common prerequisites for other kinds of available work, this group was three times more likely than any other to be unemployed.[102] In Lancashire, their options were limited. With the wider economic trend moving away from industrial work to services, the most viable jobs for former millworkers were in retail, markets, restaurants or takeaways. A flexible option was taxi-driving, which could be combined with other types of work.[103] The experience of one Oldham millworker, Attique Rehman, was common enough. Made redundant in 1982, he was sent by the job centre to a warehouse to pack boxes. The sole Pakistani worker, he was badly treated and left to work in a small textile business. The pay was terrible, and he eventually found alternative work as a taxi driver. Another man, Cheema, was made redundant the same year. He borrowed his friend's taxi to save enough money to buy a car, which he drove for two years. He then took over a relative's business, but had to leave because he and his family were targeted by racists. From that point on, he divided his time between taxi-driving and working at the Rose of Kashmir takeaways, also in Oldham.[104]

Today, in Lancashire, the mills are silent but the air is cleaner.

The major legacy of South Asian textile workers is demographic change: 2021 Census figures show that 35.7 per cent of Darwen-with-Blackburn residents identified with the category 'Asian, Asian British or Asian Welsh'. Of this number, 80 per cent were born in England; they are the children and grandchildren of people like Bharti's father.

The chill on Darwen Hill had brought home the reality of outdoor labour during the Cotton Famine; rock-breaking and path-building in the bitter cold. Walking through central Darwen, Bharti and I sought out the nearest café and cradled our mugs of tea. I asked her about a local woman who'd appeared in Bharti's exhibition film. Eileen Entwistle had been a cotton winder at India Mill, whose job was to load empty bobbins onto the machines and remove them once full of thread. Back in 1931, Eileen's grandmother was photographed beside Gandhi among the cheering crowd.

Leaving the café, I followed Bharti along the high street, away from the steep streets surrounding India Mill and past the Spinners Arms. Darwen is no small town to Bharti. Despite her unpromising school beginnings, her expansive consciousness has illuminated cotton's transnational cycle, with its global chains of cultivation, harvesting, processing, manufacture and export.

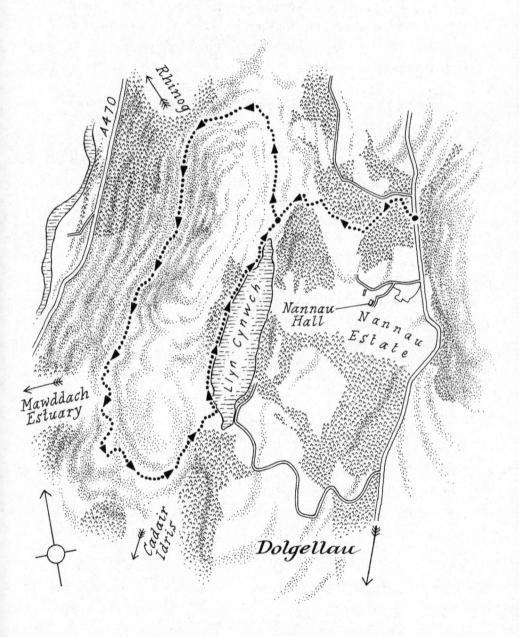

Rhinog

A470

Mawddach
Estuary

Llyn Cynwch

Nannau
Hall

Nannau
Estate

Cadair
Idris

Dolgellau

5.

The Wool Walk: Dolgellau and the Americas

Dolgellau is a thoroughly Welsh town. Situated 10 miles inland, on a tributary of the River Mawddach, whose estuary works its way east from the seaside town of Barmouth, Dolgellau lies in the historic county of Meirionnydd, which takes its name from Meirion, a fifth-century king who ruled over part of north Wales. Nestled in the Mawddach valley, Dolgellau's cottages fan out from the tiny centre and climb into the foothills of Snowdonia, a land of mountains, plunging rivers and remote lakes. To the south, the peaks of Cadair Idris and Rhinog loom above its cobbled streets. The town itself is bisected by the Wnion, a small river that burbles through crooked lanes and weaves between the cottages. The houses themselves are a uniform grey with neat, white sash windows. Pressed close together along narrow, winding lanes, they seem to provide refuge from exposed pastures and chilly shearing sheds.

In the Middle Ages Dolgellau was a serf village. Today, the oldest surviving houses are seventeenth-century gabled cottages, built with dark, irregular blocks of dolerite, the local stone. Standing one-and-a-half storeys high, these cottages curve around old field boundaries, marked by stone walls with projecting stones to protect them from being knocked over by laden carts. As the town's prosperity grew throughout the eighteenth century and into the early 1800s, handsome new three-storey stone and slate houses were built, dwarfing the earlier dwellings, while pubs like the Golden Lion and the Unicorn were erected using smart, dressed stones. A turreted, square-towered church, St Mary's, was also built. If you look closely at Dolgellau's buildings from this period, you can see how elaborate they are. There's an exaggerated chimney here, a miniature tower there. During this period, the grand and wide Eldon Square was built to replace the old marketplace, together with a fashionable line of elegant houses called Eldon Row. This wealth came from wool, and it continued into the early nineteenth century, with the building of imposing new infrastructure: a new jail, courthouse, town hall and other civic buildings.

During this time, wool was almost entirely responsible for the town's rising fortunes, architectural flourishes and swelling population. By the early eighteenth century, Dolgellau had become the wool-making capital of Wales. Everybody, including those who had previously earned their crust from agricultural labour (which was in any case seasonal), got in on the act. Back then almost every household had a spinning wheel. Today, you can still see weaving lofts high at the top of Star House on Meyrick Street, and there's an old loom shop along the same road.[1] Walking the streets, it's easy to picture the weavers arranging threads at their looms, then throwing the shuttle between them. You can almost hear their feet moving the pedals and the rhythmic clatter of the wooden frames.

With the building of a new turnpike road in the 1770s, a trickle of English travellers began to access Dolgellau. By the 1820s, the prosperous town was an established tourist destination.[2] Drawn to Snowdonia, Victorian tourists stayed at places like the Royal Ship, a double-fronted hotel with dormer windows on its slate roof. Snowdonia was, and remains, the ultimate Welsh tourist destination, popularized by landscape painters, poets, botanists and geologists, whose works fuelled the post-Romantic mass enthusiasm for awe-inspiring natural landscapes that had been memorably and influentially fêted by poets like William Wordsworth.[3] Attracted to the dramatic landscapes around Dolgellau, artists also painted local mills and cottages. Among them was Thomas Gainsborough, who painted the town in the eighteenth century.[4]

Today, sheep still roam the hillsides around Dolgellau. The landscape is still crisscrossed with walled fields, old shepherds' footpaths and remote drovers' roads, along which wooden carts once bore woollen cloth to Shrewsbury, Dolgellau's dominant market just across the English–Welsh border (until the mid-eighteenth century).

Dolgellau's homespun cloth was distinctive to the region. Sometimes called 'Welsh plains' (for plain it was), this woollen cloth was produced by local people and, as production grew, by incoming wool workers too. Also known as 'webs', which had many wool-scraps woven into it, Dolgellau's woollen cloth was cheap, coarse and durable with a raised nap – drawn out fibre-ends – and it was a strong fabric.[5] At the height of production, 718,000 yards of webs were produced almost entirely for export with around eighteen mills operating in and around Dolgellau.[6]

The town's wool history is first and foremost a global story, as the town grew to accommodate global demand for its locally made woollen fabric and it prospered because of it. The markets for Dolgellau woollen textiles were not simply drapers in the English border town of Shrewsbury, some 50 miles to the east, or the capital city of London. A major market for Dolgellau's woollen cloth lay across the Atlantic Ocean.

In the late seventeenth century, wealthy West African traders wanted dyed Welsh plains, in bright colours. Blues and greens fetched different prices. In 1683, an agent at Cape Coast Castle on the Gold Coast requested green-coloured Welsh plains; further along the coast, African slave-traders wanted blue plains as gifts before starting business negotiations.[7] By the early eighteenth century, the Royal African Company was a major buyer of the cloth, which it used to barter for enslaved people. In 1718, one merchant ordered over 5 miles of Welsh plains for this purpose in a single month. Such vast orders were not uncommon: another merchant, the Londoner Samuel Monck, obtained nearly 6 miles of white Welsh plains for the Royal African Company two years earlier.[8] But the main global purchasers of woollen plains were slave-owners in the Americas, who bought Dolgellau's coarse, plain cloth to clothe enslaved people on American and West Indian plantations.

Demand grew as the slavery system expanded, and the amounts of material ordered by slave-owners were staggering. The historian Chris

Evans estimates that, around 1690, Welsh plains clothed 97,000 enslaved people in the Caribbean and North America, amounting to 388,000 yards of cloth. By the mid-eighteenth century – the period when Dolgellau's smart houses started going up – this number grew to just under 2 million yards for some 279,000 enslaved people, and by 1812 the region was producing nearly 8 million yards.[9] If Dolgellau is a quintessentially Welsh town, its distant Atlantic connections were crucial in making it what it became. Transatlantic slavery permeated the lives of rural working people: sheep-shearers, wool-carders, spinners and weavers. Not that these people were made rich by slavery: on the contrary, their lives were often harsh. The money was being made by people far higher up the economic ladder: landowners with sheep-grazing pasture, wool-merchants, slave-traders and their backers.

I invited Charlotte Williams to walk with me around Dolgellau. Charlotte is an academic who has explored the colonial connections of Wales for decades, eventually beating a path to the door of the Welsh government, advising them on educational and equalities policies as well as on the educational curriculum, where it is now mandatory to study Welsh colonial history. We felt that the Precipice Walk would be a good way to explore Dolgellau's Atlantic-based prosperity. Created on pastureland belonging to a vast country estate, it became a particular draw for Victorian tourists in search of sublime panoramas. Making a 3-mile circuit around a hill above Dolgellau called Foel Cynwch, the walk starts in deciduous woods 2 miles beyond Dolgellau, before passing Nannau Hall, a grey-stone mansion in the midst of meadows which plunge into the deep Mawddach river valley. The Nannau estate belonged to the region's major landowners, the Vaughans, who, masters of all they surveyed, created the walk for family and friends to enjoy the spectacular views. Climbing 800 feet above sea-level, the route passes through walled pasture then circles the hill, which offers long-range views of the Mawddach estuary and the mountain range of Snowdonia. If you look down from the narrow path around Foel Cynwch – and nervous walkers might well prefer not to – there is a treacherous drop to the Mawddach river, which wriggles like a silver snake through the valley far below. On the way back, you descend to Llyn Cynwch, a lake by a woodland path which leads you back to where you began.

For Charlotte, north Wales is home. Her maternal family came from the slate-town of Bethesda, and she grew up in the windswept Victorian seaside resort of Llandudno, about 50 miles due north from Dolgellau. But, with a Welsh mother and a father from the sugar-producing country of Guyana, Charlotte struggled with a feeling that Wales did not accept her. Growing up, Charlotte was referred to as 'Black', so imprecise a term that it implied she was without history and vaguely other, a curiosity.[10] (Charlotte used to wonder if she should just tell local Welsh people that she came from Africa 'the long way round', because she did once sail to Africa as a child on a cargo ship called the *Prome* before returning to Wales, her birthplace. Her father had taken her to live in Sudan for a few years. There, as a six-year-old, she remembers the smell of neem, mimosa and camel dung.)[11] Racism tainted her childhood. Neighbours and acquaintances would say that they couldn't tell when she was dirty – and in any case perhaps she didn't need to wash too often, because no one could tell the difference. They complimented her 'suntan' and asked to feel her hair. Because she had a White mother, locals would assume she was adopted and think she was from a Barnardo's children's home. Her first date turned out to be a dare by one of the teenager's friends to drive a Black girl around in his car. He told Charlotte that he didn't fancy her.[12] Charlotte's attempts to fit in had only harmed her more: it was, as she describes it, 'death by assimilation'.[13]

In the end, though Charlotte felt disowned by Wales, she had no intention of disowning it. Her sense of feeling only 'half home' in Wales – 'feeling that,' as she puts it, 'somehow to be half Welsh and half Afro Caribbean was always to be half of something but never anything quite whole at all' – was given expression in her powerful memoir *Sugar and Slate*, a title that combines both her Guyanese and Welsh heritages (as she was growing up, the local slate quarry was the world's roofer). Sugar and slate are interconnected commodities in north Wales, where the profits of Jamaican sugar plantations funded slate-quarry excavation. In its heyday, Penrhyn Quarry, owned by Richard Pennant, employed over 3,000 people, and its main shaft was over a mile wide. Charlotte's book title also takes literal form in a photo of her great-grandparents, who owned Quarry View Stores near Penrhyn. The photograph shows them in their shop, surrounded by foodstuffs for sale, including demerara sugar from Guyana.[14]

Charlotte is not the first in her family to explore Welsh slavery links. Her painter-archaeologist father imparted to her his knowledge of the connection between Welsh iron and the slavery business. Welsh ironworks made chains, manacles, neck collars, thumbscrews and branding irons for plantation owners,[15] and also produced iron bars for export. Her father became interested in iron because he was long haunted by an historical question about the slave trade in Africa. He knew that the continent had a long history of enslaving the captives of West African battles but wanted to know why anyone would sell their fellow Africans to European slavers. Through his archaeological explorations he found some answers in the old smelting centres of West Africa. Throughout Europe's slave-trading years, West Africans used iron to make farm tools, weapons, fashion items and money. Iron was also used to fashion figurines for ritual worship and to connect to people's ancestors. The need for iron was so great that supply outstripped demand and traders began exchanging items and people for iron bars. The bars were brought on slave-ships and made in Merthyr Tydfil in south-west Wales.[16] This didn't answer his moral question, but it better explained why the Welsh commodity of iron was in so much demand.

At the beginning of *Sugar and Slate*, Charlotte writes that her local community was bounded by a sea which few ever crossed, meaning that many locals never left Wales.[17] Yet their forebears clearly did travel: Welsh colonial figures were the economic migrants of the eighteenth century. There are place-based reminders of Welsh involvement in wider colonial activity everywhere, from New South Wales in Australia to Llandudno in Cape Town and Fort St David on India's Coromandel Coast. There were East India Company ships called the *Earl of Abergavenny*, *Cardigan*, *Carmarthen* and *Monmouth*.

It was a Welshman who first coined the phrase 'British Empire'.[18] Yet even today, few Welsh history books contain the words 'empire', 'colonial' or 'imperial' in their indexes.[19] Charlotte's book presents an autobiographical challenge to insular versions of Welsh history, which concentrate on local people's experiences of industrial and post-industrial Wales without mentioning the country's vital connection with the British Atlantic world.

When Charlotte arrived in Dolgellau, she greeted me not with a handshake but with a hug. We made a quick plan, deciding to take her car up to a carpark at the start of the walk, and I jumped straight in. As we drove up the hill, she immediately reeled off a list of historians who, she said, would know far more than her about this wool-making region of Wales. I smiled. You'd never know from talking to her that Charlotte is the author of the most popular book on Welsh colonial history of all time, but – in my experience – the truly knowledgeable are self-effacing and ever-curious. As we got out of the car, she added, 'I made a list of questions about wool-making here,' holding up some copious notes she'd made about Meirionnydd.

Outside, autumn leaves trembled in the wind. There was a cold sunlight, 'the best sort of October weather,' Charlotte remarked. She zipped up her turquoise anorak, put an orange rucksack on her back then pulled on a knitted woollen hat and pushed it back to reveal a band of curly hair. We easily found the damp, leaf-filled woodland track through the woods which, we had read, soon tapers into a narrow path with drops so steep that anyone with vertigo should avoid it.

The woodland was dense, and the tree trunks were covered with lichen-speckled moss. 'Clean air,' Charlotte said. The dry-stone walls which lined our route were similarly painted by nature: the mossy stones were splashed with lichen and had manes of ferns. We stopped to photograph the velvety walls that rose unsteadily from the bracken. When the path emerged from the woodland, we saw that bracken had grown rampant in the fields and remarked on the way its rust-colour matched the path's layer of autumn leaves. As we walked, we chatted about the Nannau estate, whose impressive gatehouse straddles the lane in a wide arch, just off the road we'd driven in on, the dry-stone walls curving towards it on either side. 'I could live in that,' I'd said, pointing to its window, ostentatious chimney and clock which ornamented the stone structure. 'And that's just the gate-house,' Charlotte had laughed. We were curious to see the main house. After a few hundred yards, we turned a corner, and there, across meadows, was Nannau Hall: an elegant grey Georgian building on rising ground which obtains one of those perfect views which money buys. Built with the same dolerite stone as the houses in Dolgellau, the hall is on three floors with a pillared entrance, topped by an elegant stone balustrade. The symmetrical façade, made with expensive square-cut blocks, is punctuated by perfectly proportioned windows. You would never guess that the house, now abandoned, is dilapidated inside. 'It hasn't lost any of its grandeur,' said Charlotte. It was true: the wooded hills around set off the slate roof and smoky stone. The house, we agreed, encapsulated Dolgellau's golden age.

Our woodland path continued through the estate grounds, owned by the Nannau family from the Middle Ages. Its position was consolidated in the late thirteenth century after it wisely sided with the powerful medieval king Edward I when he conquered Wales. ('Treacherous!' Charlotte remarked with a smile.) From then on, the family's prominence in the region continued, successive generations expanding their lands and holding local government posts. In the late seventeenth century, a descendant of the first Lord of Nannau, Colonel Hugh Nanney, became a Member of Parliament. His daughter married into the influential Vaughan family, from which a succession of owners came. The house that still stands was rebuilt by the Vaughans in the late eighteenth century, by which time the family were the biggest resident landowners in the region, also owning Dolgellau's Hengwrt estate and mansion (no longer standing) and Rûg, a town in the same parish.[20]

The mansion, I told Charlotte, comes with its own supernatural story. According to local legend, a ghost haunted the estate for some four centuries. Back in the early fifteenth century, a Welsh nobleman, Hywel Sele, was invited to Nannau by his cousin, the Prince of Wales

Owain Glyndwr, then fighting a war of independence against English overlordship. Sele, however, was close to the English king, Henry IV – and opposed Glyndwr's uprising. The Nannau invitation was Glyndwr's attempt to broker a reconciliation with his cousin but, as the pair went out hunting, Sele was shot (accounts differ as to whether he was trying to kill Glyndwr at the time) and killed. His body was hidden in a nearby oak tree, from where it subsequently disappeared. The oak, and the site, remained haunted for almost 400 years, with Dolgellau locals giving it a wide birth. On 27 July 1813, the vast oak – its circumference measured a whopping 27 feet 6 inches – was hit by lightning and felled. At that point, Nannau belonged to Sir Robert Vaughan, who had inherited his father's baronetcy and considerable lands some twenty years previously. By now, the Nannau estate alone was 12,000 acres, complete with two farms, ten cottages, a deer park and a fishing pond as well as being surrounded by a 55-mile estate wall. As Dolgellau's largest owners of sheep-grazing pasture, the Vaughans benefitted from the upsurge in demand for woollen plains destined for enslaved people across the Atlantic.[21]

It was the energetic Sir Robert who commissioned Nannau Hall to be rebuilt, from 1788, as well as Eldon Row, the elegant houses around Dolgellau's wide square. Indeed, Sir Robert took charge of rebuilding and developing the town, being pivotal in commissioning the jail, courthouse and a new school. Estate maps of 1760 and 1794 also show bursts of development around Mill Street. The prison, also guided by Sir Robert's hand, was built in 1811. The town hall and courthouse followed in 1825. Weaving rooms were set up in Meyrick Street, named after a family which had dominated the town's wool production since the late eighteenth century.[22] All this building activity happened whilst Atlantic demand for Welsh plains was at its peak, between 1760 and 1840.[23]

Sir Robert also ordered many miles of footpaths, drives, walls and follies to be constructed around the Nannau estate (declaring that he wanted to relieve unemployment during the economic depression which followed the Napoleonic Wars).[24] As a Member of Parliament, by contrast, he was an inactive speechmaker (addressing the House of Commons only once over a period of forty-four years), preferring to spend his time in and around Dolgellau on his farms and in his deer park, which he had expanded into a designed estate. Sir Robert lived lavishly. In 1824, he held a banquet for his son's twenty-first birthday celebration for 193 guests, who ate 165 pounds of beef, four haunches of venison, four mutton legs and ten plum puddings.[25] He was a physically imposing man, standing at six foot and with a stout figure; when petitioners and constituents surrounded him, they resembled railings around a monument. Locals called Sir Robert the Golden Calf of Dolgellau and joked that he could see Mount Snowdon's massive bulk from his house but considered it smaller than himself.[26]

Sir Robert was not a slave-owner and did not make his money directly through Atlantic trade. Nonetheless, he seems to have been ambivalent about slavery and was in fact disliked by the anti-slavery campaigner Thomas Clarkson, who complained in his diary that it was hard to mobilize the Anti-Slavery Society because the members were all under Sir Robert's thumb. Clarkson may have thought this, but Sir Robert did present parliament with anti-slavery petitions from Barmouth and Dolgellau, which suggests some local strength of feeling from townspeople who were likely aware that the region's woollen plains were linked to Atlantic slavery.[27] He did this in 1824, ten years before the Slavery Abolition Act, while the anti-slavery movement was growing. On the other hand, many local people had a vested interest in slavery's continuance, including himself as the owner of extensive grazing lands. The prospect of abolition worried local wool manufacturers and clothiers because, as one contemporary observer put it, Dolgellau people were 'excessively anxious about Affairs in America', an anxiety which reflected the Atlantic market for their woollen cloth.[28]

Four years after presenting the anti-slavery petitions, Sir Robert made one of his rare interventions in parliament. His wool-making constituents wanted protective tariffs on foreign wool imports.[29] Wool manufacturers and local clothiers were keen to see off any threat to their wool-making dominance and, should plantation owners stop buying woollen plains in the wake of possible anti-slavery legislation, it was now doubly important that woollen manufacturers would be able to adapt to and compete in domestic woollen markets instead.

'Sir Robert stipulated that everyone who attended his funeral,' I said to Charlotte, 'wore woollen cloth around their mourning hats.' We considered this for a moment. Going to the trouble of ordering wool to be worn at your own burial seemed to underscore wool's significance in Dolgellau, a place where wool mattered in death as it mattered in life.[30]

From the Nannau estate, Charlotte and I made the short climb to the circular path around Foel Cynwch. Stone walls wandered off in all directions, and the path was lined with thick bracken and bilberry bushes. 'This is an old sheep track here,' Charlotte said, picking her way around a dry-stone wall. The path narrowed and curved, so I dropped behind her as we rounded the hill. The field to our right sloped down to a purple cloud of trees, and beyond that was a hill of evergreens. In the clear autumn light, we could see Barmouth Bridge 9 miles away. We continued across some grazing land, the going easy, offering walkers panoramic views for very little effort. 'Perfect for female walkers in Victorian dress,' as Charlotte put it. Nonetheless, our eyes focused frequently downwards, as the path was scattered with little rocks and stones: potential tripping hazards. And, while we weren't yet at the edge of the precipice, the hillsides were starting to drop away from us.

Passing some rowan trees, we paused to admire their glowing orange berries. Charlotte made out the gleaming estuary with its mustardy sand, remarked on the red-brown hills and identified the purple peak of Cadair Idris.

As we rounded the hill, Dolgellau stretched out below us, snug in its valley. From high above on the mountainside, we could see how the demand for Welsh plains in plantations across the Americas had transformed the old medieval village of Dolgellau. You can pick out the contours of the original ancient settlement, the boundaries delineated by curving rows of the oldest houses; then, with the arrival of woollen wealth, the town's expansion, overspilling these old boundaries.

As we walked, I told Charlotte that, in February 1767, seemingly a world away from Dolgellau, a slave-owner in Northumberland, Virginia, placed a newspaper advertisement in the *Maryland Gazette*. He wanted to recapture a man called Solomon who, nineteen years old, had made a bid for freedom, running away from the plantation on which he worked. Among Solomon's distinguishing features, as listed in the advertisement, was his 'WELSH cotton jacket'. The jacket, though, was not cotton: it was made from Welsh plains.[31] 'The itchy fabric with the raised nap,' said Charlotte, and shuddered. 'Rough, drab clothes, like prison wear.'

Plenty of runaway slave advertisements of the age mention Welsh woollen clothing. There is Ben, or Toomer, described as a heavy-set man who made his bid for freedom from Lake Washington, whose enslaver believed that he was wearing 'Welsh plains pantaloons'.[32] (A later notice in the *Vicksburg Register* indicates that he was recaptured and imprisoned.) Another escapee, Violet, was unwell when she fled carrying 'about ten yards of Welsh Plains, to make up into a dress'.[33] Charles, who had a stutter, was also sought through the pages of the *Maryland Gazette*, where he was described as likely wearing 'a Welch cotton jacket'.[34]

Charlotte told me that people are generally shocked when presented with the fact that so many enslaved people wore woollen textiles made in north Wales. She told me they immediately ask: 'How?' and 'Why?' We agreed that the answer was unpleasant to give. Inadequate clothing was a contributing factor to high death and sickness rates among enslaved populations in West Indian and North American plantations – something hinted at in the advertisement for the fleeing Violet, above. A sick workforce was an unproductive workforce, and – to the enslaver's mind – the death of any enslaved person represented a lost investment. For plantation-owners, clothing enslaved populations was a pragmatic act. As one plantation-owner on Nevis observed bluntly, working hours lost by sickness 'amounts to a greater loss than the price of Cloaths'.[35] Meanwhile, legislation such as the Barbados Slave Code of 1661 legally obliged plantation-owners to supply enslaved people with new clothes annually, even as this same code allowed enslavers to maim and murder them as punishment for misdemeanours or for running away. The Jamaican Slave Code of 1696 imposed a penalty of five shillings if enslaved men were not provided with 'jackets and drawers' and women with jackets, petticoats or frocks by Christmas day each year, although this law was lightly policed.[36] Nonetheless, such legislation, combined with voluntary precautions against illness and death – through clothing enslaved people to reduce this risk – meant that Welsh plains became the second-most-favoured material for plantation-owners: the material was, as one Virginia plantation-owner commented approvingly, 'Good Welch cotton'.[37] Demand was high: by 1815 the enslaved population in the Americas was well over a million. That is a lot of cloth.

The historian Marian Gwyn found that in 1806 just three plantations in Clarendon, Jamaica, ordered over 8 miles of fabric; 15 per cent of this was woollen and from north Wales. Alongside this order came a request for 181 pounds of thread to stitch garments together. Jamaica had 800 plantations altogether, and Antigua, Barbados, Grenada, St Kitts, Nevis, Carolina, Georgia and the Deep South all used woollen plains.[38] In 1812, around 4,395 miles of Welsh plains were sold.[39] Sewn together, this cloth would reach from Wales to Jamaica.

A long-tailed sheep grazed at the shorn grass. These hillsides were once crowded with hardy mountain flocks herded by shepherds who lived frugal lives. Remarking on the impact of woollen plains and the associated slavery business, as still seen in Dolgellau's buildings, landscape and heritage, Charlotte said, 'What I really wonder is what enslaved people thought of Welsh woollen plains.' There was, she added, something disturbingly intimate about the woollen cloth produced in the Dolgellau region. Welsh plains were worn against the skin: this was the only layer of clothing enslaved people would wear. The plainness of the clothes bothered her too, their regulation dullness contributing to the denial and erasure of each person's unique cultural identity. While people were transported to the plantations from diverse societies across West Africa, she said, on the plantations, dressed in Welsh plains, they were reduced to enslaved uniformity. Regulation clothing is generally disliked, even in the best of circumstances. What we do know is that all over the Americas, enslaved people made colourful clothes and established Sunday markets where bright garments could be bought and worn outside labouring hours. But slave-owners sometimes saw the wearing of colourful clothes as worryingly self-expressive and rebellious, and laws, such as the South Carolina Negro Act of 1735, were passed, requiring that the enslaved must wear dreary clothing, even going so far as to recommend Welsh plains as an ideal material to purchase. An historian in the late nineteenth century called Philip Sidney even went so far as to say that the quality of these woollen plains was appreciated by plantation-owners across the Americas who were not satisfied with anything else but cloth woven on Dolgellau looms, although these plains were produced in at least two other towns, and the figures suggest that around a third of the webs used by slave-owners came from Dolgellau.[40] Either way, it is no surprise that, when emancipation finally came, this Welsh fabric was immediately cast off in favour of bright garments and light cotton clothing.[41]

Far above Dolgellau, our path now encircled the hill like a thin leather belt. Everything plummeted – the hill-flank, the pink heather and the dry-stone walls. The peaks of Rhinog and Cadair Idris rose on either side of us. We had to imagine that once this land would have been carpeted with multitudes of sheep awaiting the shearing shed. These pasturelands paid landowners like Sir Robert Vaughan rich dividends. Charlotte asked me if Sir Robert made any colonial investments with his wealth, but I told her that, though it didn't seem unlikely, I hadn't found any record of it. What was clear, from his building work, was that Sir Robert was awash with money. 'Just goes to show: even this walk came about because of the town's wool prosperity,' Charlotte said. This was true: the walk was created by a major estate owner at a time when pastureland was at a premium and at a moment when the turnpike road brought tourists and still more money into Dolgellau. We remembered a phrase we'd each heard used by the Welsh historian Marian Gwyn: these lands are slavery landscapes.

Yet in eighteenth-century Dolgellau, the manufacture of Welsh plains was a lifeline. With wages low, rents high and agricultural work exceptionally poorly paid,[42] poverty plagued the entire Meirionnydd region. Woollen manufacture by and large insulated Dolgellau people from hunger and vagrancy. The Dolgellau parish books – packed with references to wool-making occupations – show that, in 1797, 116 people were receiving weekly money or help with rent despite being in work, benefits that were almost certainly a redistribution of wool-wealth.[43] Wool's pervasiveness bears restating, since nearly every impoverished townsperson and every tenant farmer took part in woollen production.

Despite its plainness, Dolgellau's woollen cloth was the product of skilled artisans and underwent many processes. Fleeces were initially removed using hand shears, and the level of expertise involved meant that shearers sat at the top of the wool-working hierarchy and could negotiate their terms and wages.[44] Woollen collection was done by women and children, ready for carding and spinning.[45] Sorters selected the best-quality wool, a skilled task. There are many grades of wool in a fleece. Handling the wool was hazardous in the days before wool-washing, because dirty fleeces exposed people to disease.[46] Carding prepared the wool for spinning. Woollen fibres were straightened into *rolags* ready for the spindle. Carding was done by children on the cottage hearth. They used leather-backed implements filled with wire teeth. It was a boring task, and children found ways to relieve the tedium, such as naming the metal spikes of their carding implements after their neighbours. For these child workers, nonetheless, conditions were better than for their counterparts in Lancashire's cotton factories.[47] Spinning was then done in the home.[48]

Weaving generally took place in winter when farm work dropped off.[49] People brought their spun thread to weavers in farmhouses or rented rooms (handlooms – unlike spinning wheels – were expensive).[50] The novelist George Eliot recreates the experience of sitting at the loom, describing its rhythmic sound and the weaver watching the slow growth of his web and moving his limbs in time with the machine-parts. The sensation conveyed is one of monotony and concentration combined, like a hypnotic 'treadmill'.[51] This was repetitive but, at least from George Eliot's description, not unpleasant work. Moreover, before mechanization, weavers had a degree of independence and at mealtimes might easily go out into the surrounding woods and fields.[52] There was considerable literacy among weavers, who were at the forefront of the struggle between economic self-reliance and the loss of autonomy associated with industrialization.[53] Small traders like weavers and woollen workers were also prominent in the call for fairer labour conditions, pay and better political rights.[54] (There was certainly plenty of subversive reading going on in Dolgellau at the time: local printers supplied William Cobbett's pamphlets against wage suppression and poverty and in favour of democratic electoral reform. These pamphlets had been translated into Welsh.)[55]

Wool was dressed, thickened and felted at fulling mills around Dolgellau, where wet cloth was beaten with hammers to clean and thicken it. Lots of water was required, and townspeople would have heard loud thuds.[56] The name 'pandy' indicates the presence – or former presence – of a fulling mill, and there are eighty-two places called 'Pandy' in and around the Dolgellau area. Between 1725 and 1851, there were some sixty-two fulling mills in the wider Meirionnydd area too.[57] After this process was complete, the wool was hung on tenterhooks for drying and dyeing.[58]

Transporting the wool to market along drovers' roads and paths across the steep, exposed hills was arduous: men and women sometimes hired themselves out as human packhorses to carry the finished wool across the mountains.[59] With the Shrewsbury Drapers Company initially dominating the woollen business,[60] most profits went to them and to London's Welch Hall. Wool-makers themselves just scraped a living.[61] Towards the end of the century, with Liverpool becoming Britain's largest slave-trading port, the city's merchants came direct to weavers in Dolgellau so as to secure their supplies in advance. Life improved somewhat: there was no longer an arduous trek to market, while weavers were paid by agents in Dolgellau – where they then spent the money, which was good for the town's prosperity.[62] Looms became more obtainable because Liverpool merchants lent weavers the money to buy them.[63] The eagerness of Liverpool merchants for plains also meant that cloth was increasingly finished in the local region. Dyers and other specialist wool-workers moved into the area. Unsurprisingly, then, the town's rising population figures coincide with Liverpool's dominance in buying Welsh plains for export to Africa and the Americas.[64]

Dolgellau's fortunes remained closely connected to events across the Atlantic. The 1833 Slavery Abolition Act had an immediate and dramatic impact on the local woollen industry. The corresponding drop in demand for Welsh plains from the West Indies and British colonies meant that, almost overnight, Dolgellau's spinners and weavers were out of work.[65] From around 1840, the town's population slowly declined, with wool-workers drifting away to seek work elsewhere. Poverty crept up, reaching some of the highest levels in the country.[66]

The Dolgellau Poor Law Union was formed in 1837 and was overseen by an elected board of trustees known as guardians: their minute books show Dolgellau consistently distributing more poor relief funds than other local parishes. Examples include the money given to two destitute people in Dolgellau and a weaver called John Jones; the one-off payment of 4 shillings' worth of fuel allocated to the wife and children of one Dolgellau weaver, John Thomas, said to be 'out of his mind'; and the payment of 10 shillings given to another unemployed weaver, Humphrey William, who had lost his daughter to smallpox. Other financial relief was ongoing, such as that paid to an unemployed Dolgellau weaver called Robert Owen, who had a wife and three children to support. Other relief money was spent on medical prescriptions, rent, clothing and funeral expenses, often, tellingly, for the children of destitute families. The minute books also show that, typically of the age, guardians equated poor relief with morality: were individuals, they discussed among themselves, 'deserving' of relief?[67] Given the growing issue of unemployed wool-workers, it was perhaps inevitable that, in 1854, a workhouse was built in the town. The Dolgellau gaol records suggest that, in the 1860s, many crimes of theft were related to rising poverty in the town: people stole spoons, cash, watches and everything from a rabbit trap, a piece of timber, a pocket knife, to cats and jackets, fodder and hay.[68] The domestic market was entirely unable to make up for the shortfall caused by the disappearance of the trans-atlantic market. The fall in global demand for woollen plains coincided with the boom in fine, washable cotton fabric produced in Lancashire's factories for which rough webs presented no competition. Hated though woollen plains were on the plantations themselves, Dolgellau people had, until the 1840s, kept hunger away from their own doors by producing them.

These connected histories are only now being explored by new generations of researchers like Charlotte. Through their work, we are beginning to understand the full significance of slavery to wool-workers, wool-merchants and ultimately to the development and decline of places like Dolgellau – as well, of course, as to enslaved people themselves.[69] And now we were approaching the most perilous stage of our walk at the edge of the Nannau estate.

You take the precipice walk at your own risk. If you lost your footing, you'd bounce down the mountainside. From here we could see the Wnion River which powered the woollen fulling mills, criss-crossed with stone and iron bridges.

The path encircled the crown of Foel Cynwch. We were dazzled by autumn's jewel-box colours; the bracken-covered hillside had turned amber, and the rain-dampened mountains glowed ruby and gold. Charlotte has deep knowledge of the Welsh hills and she picked out two autumn shades – mauve and fox-red – and explained how these are incorporated into Welsh knitting and patchwork blankets. 'The patterned woollen quilts of Wales are inspired by these changing seasonal colours,' she said. She and her sisters collect Welsh quilts: one made by their mother has pride of place in their collection.

From the high path we could see the estuary flowing seaward

towards the continents in which Charlotte has spent her life: Europe, Africa and the Americas. Completing her journey through all three points of her global family history, she visited her father's homeland in Guyana: there, she'd made a trip to Wales village, on Demerara's west coast.[70]

In *Sugar and Slate*, Charlotte makes a point raised by my other walking companions: White British people don't readily associate Black people with the countryside. I asked her if, two decades after she wrote the book, she thought things had changed. 'No,' she replied. 'I wish I could say differently, but I don't think it has.' Since we were walking so close to Dolgellau, we compared notes on Black people from the eighteenth century who'd lived in the local area. Charlotte knew of a kidnapped African who was trafficked to Wales in the 1760s and ended up in the town. His name was John Ystumllyn, transported as a child from the West African coast and brought to the local area to become a servant. He was baptised, received an education and, literate and fluent in Welsh and English, became an accomplished gardener and a favourite of young women, who sought his affection. Charlotte laughed at this detail, and we commented on how evocative these personal details are, especially when the records of such figures are so sparse. 'You just get glimpses,' she said. But we do know that John chose Margaret, whom he married at Dolgellau church in 1768, at the peak of the region's trade in Welsh plains. They had seven children, one of whom married a Liverpool musician. Charlotte wondered if, in the case of this couple and their children, the Liverpool trade in woollen plains created a point of connection: this, after all, was the period when Liverpool merchants were frequent visitors to Dolgellau. But Charlotte – who has researched Christianized African figures in Wales – was interested to learn of another detail about John: he became a strict Christian and regretted, on his deathbed, having played the fiddle on the Sabbath. 'And there's another Black figure associated with Dolgellau too,' I told her, as we stepped over a tumbled-down dry-stone wall. 'Samuel Coleridge-Taylor.' Charlotte already knew about the composer, born in England to an English mother and a father from Sierra Leone. In

1907, the English composer Samuel Coleridge-Taylor made regular visits to Dolgellau as a conductor and musical adjudicator, as he earned some of his money touring and judging musical competitions. We laughed because his impressions of the place were unfavourable: apparently, he considered the locals to be 'a very rough class of people'.[71] 'Oh dear,' said Charlotte, 'I suppose Dolgellau was a far cry from the Royal College of Music,' since this was where he studied as a young teenager.

Well might she sympathize, given her own family's experiences. When Charlotte's sister succumbed to the strain of responding to racism – assimilating and asserting herself by turns – she ended up in Denbigh psychiatric hospital (formerly known as the North Wales Counties Lunatic Asylum): a grand Victorian pile, now disused. The irony of the hospital's location is hard to ignore: Denbigh was also the name of the Jamaican sugar plantation belonging to Richard Pennant, the owner of Penrhyn Castle near Bangor. Charlotte says that her sister was incarcerated behind a door with an eighteenth-century lock, closed with an eighteenth-century key.[72]

In her book, Charlotte had expressed her pain that Wales rejected her.[73] I reflected on all this as we reached the narrowest part of the path, with the most vertiginous drops.

'Do you mind heights?' I asked, belatedly. Charlotte laughed. She didn't mind the alarming drop to her right, she said, because the hillside was reassuringly close to her left. Watching her sure-footed progress, the metaphor surfaced in my mind. Wales failed to claim her. Left without a path, she cut her own precarious line across its landscape. In doing so, she gained a panoramic view of herself, and of Wales, soaring above her life-story to reveal its vast, intercontinental patterns.

Charlotte understands Wales as being both intimately local and sweepingly global. She connects Welsh ports with African sailors, Welsh iron and copper with West African slave-trading. As we picked our way along the narrow mountain path, we talked about Penrhyn slate quarry, in her neck of the woods, which was then the world's largest, and the main local employer. The quarry was founded back in the late eighteenth century by Richard Pennant, who inherited his

Jamaican wealth in 1781. He immediately turned local slate producers off his land and opened the quarry the following year. Within a decade, 500 men were employed there. In a sinister echo of conditions in Jamaica, the men's barracks resembled huts for enslaved people on the Pennant family plantations.[74] Many years later, the quarry saw the great strike of 1900–1903, caused by Pennant's opposition to the North Wales Quarrymen's Union. Charlotte was very close to this history, since her grandfather John William Hughes lost his slate-based employment because of the intransigence of the slave-owning Pennants.[75] The strikers lost, and 2,000 hungry, impoverished quarrymen left for south Wales.[76]

Our path broadened; we descended the hill and could no longer see that amazing view. But there was one more treat in store. We passed through a wooden gate to reach the remote Llyn Cynwch, an oval lake enclosed by woods. I remembered then that Charlotte says in her book that, in her best moments, she feels indistinguishable from the trees.[77] 'Let's stop here,' I said. We sat among oaks and watched their reflections ripple across the water's surface. The trees seemed topsy-turvy, the trunks moss-green, their foliage brown as bark. Everything was still, at peace. In that place and at that moment, culture wars seemed stranger than ever. Charlotte broke our silence: 'Talking about slavery is nothing to do with finger-wagging,' she said. 'Our task is to understand history more than judge it.' She was right, of course, and that is the job of historians. But those historical wounds can run deep. Those who are descended from former colonies are justifiably alienated by those who do not accept that colonialism caused much damage. 'Accept,' said Charlotte, 'or even know.' I nodded. 'And those who don't know that history,' I continued, 'struggle to see why it is so important to understand and acknowledge it.' Some mutual suspicion is inevitable, but there is no need to push each other into the abyss.

But that afternoon it all seemed so easy, really. There we were – Charlotte descended from colonized people, me from colonizers – sitting beside this peaceful lake, feeling like we'd just flown over Snowdonia. The path was precarious, but the horizon was wide.

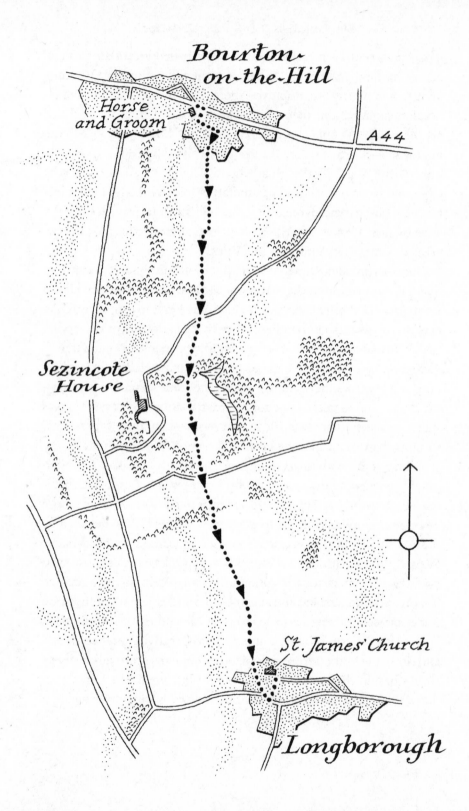

Bourton-
on-the-Hill

Horse
and Groom

A44

Sezincote
House

St. James' Church

Longborough

6.

An Indian Walk in the Cotswolds

How did an Indian palace come to be built amidst Gloucestershire's rolling hills? The construction of Sezincote House, a dazzling Mughal-style palace built in Cotswold limestone in the early nineteenth century, was a question that had long absorbed me and my walking companion, the curator and historian Raj Pal. In quest of an answer, we set out for Sezincote – pronounced 'seas-in-coat' – along the Heart of England Way, which runs 100 miles roughly north–south through some of the country's most prized landscapes: from the woodland and heath of Cannock Chase (once a royal forest) to the Cotswold hills. There, it passes through the villages of Bourton-on-the-Hill and Longborough, which lie north-east of Cheltenham and Gloucester – the nearest large towns – and north-west of Oxford, the closest city.

Towards the path's southern end, amid the region's scenic villages of honeyed stone, and set on a sweeping 3,500-acre landscaped estate, Sezincote House features peacock arches and a copper dome, mixing Islamic and Hindu references in a jumble of minarets, pillars and lotus flowers. Its octagonal pavilion was designed as an aviary for exotic birds. Water gardens trickle under a stone bridge decorated with Brahmin bulls; above it sits a pool, fed by a spring gushing from a limestone grotto, framed by a temple dedicated to the Hindu sun god Surya. Ornamental pools abound, and the sound of trickling water is everywhere; the effect is hypnotic. It feels like a nineteenth-century tourist's visual impressions of South Asia, mixed up and given architectural form. Which, in a way, it is.

Raj and I weren't about to embark on the whole hundred miles of the Heart of England Way. Our more modest route began at the pretty village of Bourton-on-the-Hill, then headed south to Sezincote, past woods and across ploughed fields to the twelfth-century church of St James at Longborough, where the owners of the Sezincote estate had – as was common among rich local families – their own private chapel. It was early autumn and, mindful of the shortening days, we tailored our walk accordingly, allowing time to meet Sezincote's current incumbent, who had invited us to tea, to talk about the house's unusual history.

In the late eighteenth century, John Cockerell – descended from the adopted heir of the diarist Samuel Pepys – returned to England from Bengal, where, a generation or so after Francis Sykes of Basildon Park, he had made a fortune working and fighting for the East India Company.[1] Back in England, Cockerell, a West Country man, converted his Indian money into land. Sezincote fitted the bill. For John, location was key: the neighbouring estate of Daylesford was owned by his mentor and close family friend, the former governor general of Bengal, Warren Hastings. But ill-health meant that John had little time to enjoy his new estate. When he died in 1798, his fortune passed to his younger brother Charles. Also an employee of the East India Company, and a banker, Charles returned to England. Influenced by his close social circle – relatives and friends who were company artists, architects and administrators – he had the old Jacobean house at Sezincote restyled as a Mughal fantasy palace.

If Britain's architecture rarely reveals its colonial heritage, then Sezincote House is the exception which proves the rule. Palladian houses like Basildon Park, as we've seen, say little about the Asian origins of the wealth that funded their construction. Indianized buildings like Brighton Pavilion – for which Sezincote served as an inspiration – were uncommon.[2] Gothic and neoclassical architecture was exported to former colonies, but for the most part, at home, empire was kept out of sight if not out of mind. (It was prudent: at the time, there was widespread public distrust of the East India Company, whose figureheads were on trial for corruption.) Yet Sezincote House flaunts its original proprietors' Indian connections. Why did Charles Cockerell wear his Indian wealth as a badge of pride, even as he refashioned himself into an English country gentleman?

Raj, my walking companion, was born near the old British hill-station of Shimla in the Himalayan foothills; his family links with Britain go back three centuries. Raj and I are near neighbours in Birmingham, and we have a shared interest in colonial history. Raj was on the team of historical advisors on the Colonial Countryside project, my child-led history and writing project with the National Trust; like the rest of the team, his work was the subject of hostile newspaper coverage. In one piece, whose headline spluttered 'Are they impartial historians – or is there a political agenda behind their interpretations of the past?', a commentator drew attention to Raj's Twitter handle at the time, *Raj Pal damn black*. Yet the commentator omitted to mention its source: a comment by the television historian David Starkey, who contended that slavery couldn't be construed as genocide, because 'otherwise there wouldn't be so many *damn* blacks in Africa or Britain, would there?'[3] In the commentator's view, however, Raj's mockery of this racism became evidence of his own historical bias.

Raj's Birmingham home overflows with history books. In his front room, tomes on ayahs, lascars and princes jostle for space with his collection of global teapots. Raj loves his books so much that he hates parting with them, even temporarily. Once, on lending me his copy of E. P. Thompson's *The Making of the English Working Class*, he actually wept.[4] Quoting from Thompson's Preface, about the need to rescue Britain's labouring past from unsympathetic and socially privileged historians, Raj explained that these books were his intimate companions: parting from them was like parting from a close relative. For him, history is not just academic: he feels it personally. Something about Sezincote intrigued him: he had been once before, and was keen to return.

It was a shimmering autumn afternoon. We joined the Heart of England Way at Bourton-on-the-Hill, a village with traditional stone cottages and an old tithe barn. Picking up the footpath near the Horse and Groom pub, which crowns the steep main street, we crunched along a gravel lane lined with cottages painted in heritage blues and greens. The well-pruned front gardens bristled with restrained autumn growth. I warned Raj that the path to Sezincote was muddy, but he waved his hand good-naturedly. His mind was fixed on blackberries in the fields beyond, and the instant we reached a hedgerow, Raj-the-Forager sprang into action. Raking through it for wild berries, he found low-hanging apples instead. He picked one for me, one for himself and threw ten more into his rucksack to make an apple crumble for his son Kabir.

The surrounding fields were striped with ridges and furrows: remnants of a medieval open-field system, Raj remarked, in which each strip of common land was farmed by a family. The strips were created by many generations of ploughing, and when the open fields were enclosed by landowners, the old ridges and troughs remained. Presently, the fields gave way to an avenue of stately oaks with saffron leaf-sprays. Through the trees, the Mughal dome of Sezincote came into view. The dome's copper had greened and, as we continued along our path, it was echoed by a verdigris-coloured lake at the estate's lower reaches; the autumn woods beyond the house gave it a fiery crown. Beyond the sloping lawns we glimpsed paradise bridges and climbing plants amidst flowing waters framed by ferns and softened by moss. Neglected during the world wars, this water garden was lovingly restored by the Kleinwort family in the 1960s. It was beautiful: no wonder Sezincote has been called an Indian idyll.[5]

Back in the eighteenth century, a ship took between four and six months to make the sea journey to India and the ports of Mumbai, Kolkata and Chennai (or Bombay, Calcutta and Madras, as they were known), depending on the weather and speed of the vessel. It was a long journey, but worth the effort for people like the Cockerells. For Britons of all classes – not just the elites – late eighteenth-century India was a land of opportunity. British people working for the East India Company as seamen, soldiers, surgeons, civil servants, even artists could return to England with their social and financial status transformed. Sezincote's history illustrates how well this system worked in practice for John and Charles Cockerell, who took different routes through the East India Company, John earning money as a soldier and Charles as a financier. Theirs is a story of fortunes made, rising status and mixed-heritage relationships.

Born in 1752 to a family of modest wealth, John Cockerell joined the Bengal Army European Infantry Regiment, part of the East India Company, as a cadet aged just fourteen. His voyage to Calcutta took around twenty weeks,[6] and he arrived there at a pivotal moment in the company's history. Two years earlier, in 1764, company forces had defeated the Mughal ruler Shah Alam II at the Battle of Buxar in the eastern state of Bihar. With this victory, the company effectively ruled all of Bengal. This rule was sealed by the 1765 Treaty of Allahabad, which allowed the company to act like a government by minting coins, administering justice and declaring war.[7] The victorious commander-in-chief and first British administrator of the region, Robert Clive, set about extracting as much tax revenue as he could from the newly conquered territories, a process enforced by 250 tax collectors and a 20,000-strong army. (In the process, Clive 'of India' helped himself to gold and jewels from the Bengal treasury.)[8] Accompanied by widespread company corruption, this massive wealth extraction inflicted considerable harm on the Bengal economy. The people of Bengal – including peasants, farmers and textile-producers – suffered as a result of swingeing tax 'reforms'; many were brought to subsistence-level poverty.[9] Tax defaulters were punished, some by execution, their dead bodies placed on public display as a warning to others. Local merchants had to work for the company on sufferance. Those who refused likewise ran the risk of punishment.[10]

John Cockerell, then, arrived at a time when the vast, rich state of Bengal – encompassing modern-day Bihar, Jharkhand, Odisha, Assam, Tripura, Mizoram, Meghalaya, Nagaland and Manipur – was ripe for the plucking by its new British rulers. Cockerell was assigned to General Robert Barker, whose role was to protect the Nawab – or governor – of Oudh, a compliant princely state in northern India which was used by the East India Company as a buffer state against its enemies. According to military records, Cockerell embraced the culture and immersed himself in local politics.[11] The year after his arrival, aged just fifteen, he was promoted to lieutenant.

All this seemed so historically and geographically remote from the Cotswold countryside in which we walked. As we strolled through the woods which fringed the Sezincote estate, Raj, whose wife Roxana is Romanian, quizzed me about the relationship between John Cockerell and an Indo-Portuguese woman named Estuarta, with whom John would go on to have four children called Sophia, John, Charles and Samuel.[12] We don't know exactly how or where the couple met, but – as far as can be seen from John's fond allusions to Estuarta in his letters to his brother Charles – theirs was a love match of sorts.[13]

In 1769 and 1770, famine devastated Bengal. Monsoon rains had been light, the ground was hard, and the rice fields looked like straw. There was widespread crop failure. Anyone without a store of grain was immensely vulnerable to starvation. The company failed to offer tax relief, while much of the available rice went to feed its private armies. The famine was exacerbated by a smallpox epidemic. In just twelve weeks, 76,000 people died in Calcutta alone.[14] One Englishman stationed near the town of Rajmahal described foul-smelling air and desperate cries for help from the dying population.[15] Amid the chaos, John thrived. In 1770 he was promoted to captain.

As we tramped through the long grass, Raj had plenty to say about the great Bengal famine. The local Mughal rulers were doubtless far from perfect, he said, but at least they had had some sense of duty towards the people they ruled. In previous times of famine, Raj believes, even the most indolent Indian princes made efforts to stave off mass starvation, easing tax collection and creating public building projects to provide jobs and alleviate poverty. What angers Raj most was the contrasting laissez-faire attitude of many East India Company officials who, as people died in their millions, simply threw up their hands as if there was nothing they could do. During these famines, Raj added, the company's indifference to humanity was laid bare. With a few honourable exceptions, he said, profit was the bottom line: both for the company and for its employees. By now, indeed, this hunger for profit was out of control, even threatening economic instability back in Britain. In 1773, a Regulating Act established greater parliamentary control over a company whose spiralling debts and rampant mismanagement was causing widespread concern, especially to those who had heavily invested in it.

The man appointed to turn Bengal's fortunes around was a longserving company employee, the experienced and erudite Warren Hastings, who became the first governor general of Bengal, its colonial administrator in effect if not by right. Now one of Hastings' close allies and servants, John Cockerell knew that Hastings wanted, in the words of the governor general himself, to 'reconcile' English and locals through cultural exchange and governance of 'ease and moderation'.[16] John Cockerell, then, had been mentored by two men – Barker and Hastings – who spoke Indian languages and were fascinated by Indian art, history and religions. Both men had clearly seen something in John, who likely absorbed some of their views.

In 1776, a decade after John had first disembarked in Calcutta, his 21-year-old brother Charles arrived in Bengal. Warren Hastings befriended Charles as he had John, and the connection served Charles well. Starting out as a writer in the surveyor's office, he had a meteoric rise through the company ranks, becoming a towering figure in the world of colonial finance and commerce. Forged in India, this association between Hastings and the Cockerells would continue in Gloucestershire when the three men returned to England.

Bypassing our eventual destination of Sezincote, we trudged through the wide stubbly fields towards Longborough village. We spotted an owl's head, severed from its body, placed upright on a bank of ploughed soil. The eyes resembled round, empty lamps. Raj and I wondered what had befallen it: was this the work of a larger owl? A fox? Or something more sinister? Walking on, we turned to the less macabre task of guessing what crop had recently been gathered in from the fields: Raj was sure it was cabbages – and he felt he ought to know, given that he comes from a family of Punjabi farmers. Indeed, around the time of our walk, Raj was campaigning passionately on

behalf of hundreds of thousands of farmers in India whose livelihoods were threatened by proposed new farm laws that would likely
place them at the mercy of private firms, driving down prices and
threatening their livelihood.[17] The farmers' protests sparked intergenerational, pan-continental concern about their plight: Raj had taken
his son Kabir to public meetings and demonstrations in Birmingham;
father and son both shouted themselves hoarse. Raj's own mother,
also living in England, emerged from a deep Covid-induced depression to rally on the farmers' behalf. After a year of protest and
confrontation – in which several farmers lost their lives – the farmers
succeeded in blocking the farming reforms. When he learned this,
Kabir shouted in triumph: 'We won!' The boy's identification with his
farming heritage meant everything to Raj.

There was deep resonance, Raj said, between this modern-day
opposition to Hindu nationalist government reforms and historical
legislation passed by the colonial authorities, such as the 1793 Permanent Settlement. As Raj saw it, this piece of colonial agricultural
reform created a class of Indian landowners who were loyal to the
British authorities: they were allowed to keep their existing status in
exchange for relinquishing their previous powers as magistrates or
law enforcers.[18] Other historians, too, have argued that the Permanent Settlement meant that, whereas land had previously been held
by local leaders and their families, the new absentee landlords were
civil servants, bankers and merchants for whom land was a commercial venture.[19] These new landowners also pressured their tenants to
grow cash crops like indigo rather than food, a policy linked to subsequent famines.

As we passed a row of bare fruit trees, Raj scolded me for not
scheduling our walk a few weeks earlier, to coincide with the wild
plum season. I laughed. We trod the soft soil towards Longborough,
a picturesque village gathered around a green. On our left was its
twelfth-century church, ancient amid a grassy graveyard. In 1822, Sir
Charles Cockerell had a family chapel incorporated into the building, complete with family pews, a private entrance and a burial
vault.[20] The Sezincote chapel is set within a specially built north

transept, whose perpendicular design matches the rest of the church: decorously in keeping, unlike the flamboyance of Sezincote House. We climbed the chapel stairs and saw where the Cockerell family would have sat, on the upper floor, looking down on the congregation below.

The autumn sun provided little warmth, and we were glad to dive into the nearby Coach and Horses pub, where we ordered lunch and continued chatting about the British in India. When our food arrived, Raj was in full flow on the contrasting styles and attitudes of two successive eighteenth-century company figures: Robert Clive and Warren Hastings. Clive, whom Raj despised, took little interest in Indian history but plentiful interest in Indian wealth; the more responsible Hastings was certainly interested in wealth, but also fascinated by Indian cultures and religions. Raj reluctantly admired Hastings. The two men were like chalk and cheese, he said between mouthfuls. 'The trouble with conversations about history these days,' he said, stabbing the air with a chip, 'is that there's no f*****g nuance!' We burst out laughing, then hushed as our laughter echoed round the virtually empty pub.

Our giggles had drawn the attention of a solitary diner. Amused by our animated discussion, he struck up a conversation with us. Now retired, he'd once worked as a gardener at Sezincote. He vividly recalled shooting a rabbit in the grounds, mistakenly believing his employer to be away. To his alarm, he heard a shout behind him, 'Good shot! I nearly bagged that rabbit myself!' Luckily for him, Sezincote's proprietor at the time – the current occupant's grandfather – found it amusing. The new owner, as we were to discover, was equally affable.

Our talk returned to Bengal, and the Cockerell brothers' continued rise. In the early 1780s, John Cockerell, now a major and trusted personal assistant to Governor Hastings, was embroiled in the Second Mysore War in southern India. The war was fought against Hyder Ali, father of the powerful, independent ruler of Mysore, Tipu Sultan. Both father and son considered the British a serious threat to India's stability and prosperity.[21] During this period of conflict, John kept in touch with his brother Charles, based more than 1,000 miles north in Calcutta. He wrote almost daily: letters full of brotherly affection, vivid descriptions of the war's progress and – underscoring Raj's point that these Indian ventures were primarily about profit – about money-making and the trade in Indian diamonds.[22] But while the Second Mysore War was finally brought to a close with the Treaty of Mangalore, signed by Tipu Sultan and the East India Company in 1784, neither side was satisfied. The treaty forced the East India Company to return to Tipu Sultan the lands they had conquered, a humiliation for the company; for his part, Tipu wanted the British out for good. It wasn't long before, in 1790, war broke out for the third time. Now a lieutenant colonel, John Cockerell fought under the command of his third governor general, Charles Cornwallis. (Hastings, by this time, had retired to England and his estate of Daylesford, not far from Sezincote.) John complained about his small tent, more suited for sheltering from rain than heat: the company canvases, he wrote, 'boil my brain almost', while the marching distances were hard, supplies ran low, and the surrounding lands were 'infested with Wild Beasts' (though, regrettably, he did not elaborate).[23]

Two years later, the war ground to a halt outside Seringapatam, Tipu Sultan's fortified capital known for its thick walls, impressive architecture and beautiful gardens. When the East India Company besieged the fortress, Tipu Sultan requested peace negotiations. In the resulting Treaty of Seringapatam, Tipu signed over significant sums of money and half his kingdom to the East India Company, along with two of his sons, aged eight and ten, as hostages to guarantee that the Treaty terms were met.[24] (Later, Charles Cockerell would buy a painting depicting this very scene, which hung in his London residence at Hyde Park Corner, a neoclassical house with Robert Adam interiors.)[25]

Away in Calcutta, Charles was himself rising through the ranks.[26] In 1789, he was appointed to the influential role of postmaster general of the Bengal Postal Service. Initially established to assist the East India Company's commercial and military undertakings, the service had, during the governorship of the brothers' mentor Warren Hastings, been transformed into a service for the general public. But Charles Cockerell, it turned out, had an eye for the main chance. Responding to Governor Cornwallis' crackdown on private trading by company personnel, in the 1780s he went into business with an associate named John Palmer. The pair set up an 'agency house', a business for handling people's financial affairs (what today might be called a fund manager) to cater for company employees looking to invest their profits, and to transport their wealth back to England. John Palmer and the Company of Calcutta provided various services including banking, ship-building, shipping and investment in commodities like indigo and sugar; the handling of wills, trusts and estates; and the cashing of funds for company personnel as they returned to Britain.[27] Like other similar agency houses, they also organized receipts to be paid into the East India Company's Canton treasury to fund the opium export trade to China. This in turn oiled the wheels of commerce, securing funds to buy Chinese tea, porcelain and silk for British customers. Agency houses such as Cockerell and Palmer's drove commercial activity across the entire region. They had sister companies in the City of London to enable intercontinental financial collaboration, creating commercial networks which helped move goods and capital around the world. Attracting immense capital, including loans and investments from Indian merchants, John Palmer and Company became the richest and most prestigious of Calcutta's twenty-five agency houses.[28]

John Cockerell, though, had finally had enough. After the Siege of Seringapatam, he returned to England in 1793. He was forty-one and had spent a quarter-century in India, much of it fighting. Living between various lodgings and at his brother's London residence at Hyde Park, he retired on a company pension of £1 a day (worth about six days' wages for a skilled labourer). This relatively modest income was augmented by considerable savings from his earnings as a colonel serving during the Third Mysore War, his East India Company stock and an allowance from a family trust.[29] With these combined resources he cast around, as retired company employees tended to do, for a country estate: a 'promising purchase in land' where he might establish his main residence, as he put it in a letter to Charles.[30] John had particular reasons for doing so, however.[31] Desperate to shake off a listlessness that had overcome him since his return to England, he wrote that he wanted to 'run from town [London] to recover my mind from this excessive idle habit that has come upon me since my arrival in England'. He wanted 'quiet and ease': the change of scene and country air, he hoped, might do him good.[32]

The estate that he would buy was Sezincote, with its original Jacobean residence – though he worried it was too damp to suit him or to please Estuarta, who he hoped would follow him to England, along with their children.[33] He did, however, hope that the purchase of Sezincote would tempt his brother back home – and was anxious for Charles to return, reminding him in a letter that 'you may not hazard your health, a day more than necessity calls for, in a climate which never agreed well with you'.[34] He also mentioned that he would 'stock my cellars' in anticipation of his return from India.[35] Nonetheless, having bought Sezincote, John seemed unsure what to do with the house. It would be Charles who fully embraced the place.

Lunch over, Raj and I retraced our steps to Sezincote, past the allotments, the owl's head and the bare plum trees. We were full of anticipation for our meeting with the house's owner, Edward Peake. Crunching our way up the gravel drive, we rang the doorbell. Moments later, the door was flung open, and we were greeted like old friends. Dressed in a wool waistcoat and soft blue jacket, the owner – tall, kind – showed us into a wide, light-filled entrance hall, with elegant chairs, a polished side-table and, over it, a painting of the estate done for Sir Charles Cockerell. 'I've laid everything out for you,' Edward Peake said, smiling, and ushered us into a bright, homely sitting room in turmeric hues, lined with antique books. 'I've really been looking forward to this!' he added.

Edward is not descended from the Cockerells, but Sezincote has been in his family for three generations, all of whom have embraced the house's Indian history, and he has a longstanding fascination with his predecessors at Sezincote.

Edward gestured towards a generous, comfortable sofa and poured us tea. Then he showed us four colonial-era history books, but, afraid to disturb their flaking pages, we left them unopened. Then he carefully unfolded his prize possession: the original architectural plans for Brighton Pavilion, drawn up by Humphry Repton, the celebrated eighteenth-century landscape designer who also proposed plans for Sezincote. His (unrealized) Brighton Pavilion plans were on thick, oversized paper, the ink drawings – faded, now – neat and precise, a sense of artistry conveyed by water-coloured flourishes. Repton's plans for Sezincote itself, however, were rejected in favour of a design by Samuel Pepys Cockerell (who was perhaps inevitably awarded the commission, given that he was Charles Cockerell's brother as well as a reputed architect).[36]

Interested in the concept of Indianized buildings on British soil, Repton thought that Britain might soon embrace a new architectural style to mark its colonial dominance over India.[37] While it didn't come to fruition, Repton's prediction wasn't wholly wide of the mark. In the preceding decades, a handful of English buildings had been given elements of Indian styles because of their East India Company links: they included a 1767 Margate home, modelled on a house in Calcutta; a Hindu-style temple at Novar estate, which resembled Government House in Bombay; and a 1793 Indian temple on a Middlesex estate. A similar structure was built in 1800 at Wiltshire's Melchet Park by another East India Company official, John Osborne (incorporating a bust of his friend, Warren Hastings). Repton's ideas were echoed elsewhere. In an address to the Asiatic Society of Bengal back in 1785, the Indologist William Jones expressed a wish that the 'correct delineations' of Indian buildings by artists like William Hodges might inspire British architects to experiment; Joshua Reynolds, the celebrated artist, likewise hoped that such drawings would allow the 'Barbarick splendour' of Indian buildings to provide 'models' and ideas for Indianized buildings and a 'new field' of British-Indian architecture.[38]

Putting aside Repton's drawings, we dived into the Cockerells' story, comparing notes and references. Of the two brothers, Edward said, he felt more drawn to John, who seemed less interested in money and more interested in Indian culture – which, he added, 'might seem strange given that it was Charles who had commissioned the building of Sezincote'. Edward was sure that, not long after his arrival in Bengal, the young John Cockerell had been introduced to the royal court of Oudh, where he would have picked up his Persian, and would have experienced artistic and musical performances of the highest order. As talk turned to John Cockerell's return to England, Peake spoke of John's listlessness. I agreed: John's letters to Charles during this time, in which he described himself understatedly as 'a little felled in disposition', were revealing.[39] Did John Cockerell, we wondered, worry about being thought of as a 'nabob', the pejorative term for company retirees? If so, he wasn't alone: many did.[40] Clearly unsettled, he wrote to Charles about returning to India, given sufficient financial 'enducement' – before adding emphatically that nothing besides money would make him return, a sentiment he repeated in a later letter.[41] John Cockerell's relationship with India, we all felt, was complicated. He had spent most of his life there and found it hard to adjust back to life in England: we agreed that he must have suffered from some kind of reverse culture shock. I told Peake about the relentless focus on money in the Cockerell brothers' letters which, though personal, make fleeting mention of India itself. Profit, as Raj had asserted, was the brothers' major concern.[42]

As we covered everything from East India Company sailing times and the court of Oudh, to Mysore and the design of Sezincote, I couldn't help wondering at our warm reception. I glanced at Raj: like me, he was probably imagining how different things could be if, like the open-hearted Edward, other landowners were so sincerely interested in their property's colonial connections, so ready to inform and be informed.

Our host was especially interested in Raj's account of his own first visit to Sezincote. Raj had, he said, brought with him his goddaughter, Shaana Toor, and the place had a powerful effect on her. Before she saw Sezincote she didn't feel that England's heritage, or its countryside, had much to do with her: it was other people's heritage, White people's heritage. She'd been to Snowdonia and other rural places but never felt she had a right to be there. The Cockerell estate had finally changed her perspective, Raj said. It was Shaana's first glimpse of a country house which represented England's relationship with the rest of the world. She was astounded that Sezincote existed. She told Raj that seeing two aspects of her heritage – India and England – in a single place felt like a homecoming. It was a response that Edward understood. Couples from mixed religions and heritages often held weddings in the house, he said. It seemed in keeping with India's interwoven histories, traditions and architectures.

Edward shared our regret at the house's un-Indian interior, but the strange thing was that Sezincote reversed the usual pattern of neoclassical exterior with the private interior serving to showcase owners' global collections. Sezincote wore its Indian-ness on the outside; inside, it was all eighteenth-century neoclassicism.

But there was an exception, Edward said. Guiding us across to the octagonal pavilion at the end of the north wing, he showed us Charles Cockerell's bedchamber. Here, Charles slept with a tent hung over his bed in the style of a Mughal ruler. Solidly 'English' in his public persona, in private Charles Cockerell seemed to cultivate something of an identification with South Asia's powerful rulers – ironic, given his financing of the wars that overthrew them.[43]

Edward also invited us up an elegant wrought-iron staircase and onto a narrow balcony to enjoy a view of the Alhambra-style fountain with its long channels. 'Now let me show you the gardens,' he insisted. Edward seemed most at home outside. He was eager to explain the rationale behind the garden design by Samuel Pepys Cockerell, restored to its former glory by Edward's own grandmother. 'The garden was very carefully thought-out,' he said. It was all designed to uplift and inspire, to simulate Mughal ideas of paradise. More than this, he explained, the original design made informed and knowing reference to Indian religions. As we followed the garden downhill towards the lake, Edward showed us the Temple Pool, dedicated to the Hindu sun god Surya. 'It was even designed to face the rising sun,' he said and invited us to peer into a hidden underground spring – one of his favourite features – within which we saw a backlit temple concealed inside the grotto.

Down we continued, across some stepping stones through the water gardens and along winding paths to a weeping hornbeam, one of Edward's favourite trees. We stood admiring its curving branches, which bent to the ground. In India, Raj said, the hornbeam symbolized the art of ageing with grace: the lowering branches shade others.

Alongside his wife Camilla, Edward continues to enhance these paradise gardens. They had recently planted cedar trees to evoke the Himalayas, a detail inspired by one of their own Indian visits; and added new stones carved with Sufi sayings, which they felt would add to the spirit of the place and reflect India's multi-religious history and character. As we walked back towards the house, Edward pointed to some towering trees, cedars of Lebanon; then, inside again, stopped in front of the oil painting of Sezincote that we had seen earlier. Charles Cockerell had commissioned it, he said, from the landscape painter Thomas Daniell: there, in the picture, were the very same cedars of Lebanon, newly planted and far smaller than they are today.

It was growing late. As we said warm farewells in Sezincote's porch, I took a selfie of the three of us: Raj, me and the tall Edward Peake, leaning into the photograph and smiling.

Raj and I retraced our steps to the Horse and Groom at Bourton-on-the-Hill, back across the ridges and furrows. I told Raj that, before we left Sezincote, Edward had mentioned to me that the Cockerell family had instructed their land agent to buy up the land around Bourton-on-the-Hill shortly after Sezincote came into their possession, so as to benefit from anticipated enclosures of the surrounding lands.[44] The consequent entitlement of Charles Cockerell to a portion of lands that were formerly in common use is indicated on legal documentation when the land was finally enclosed by an Act of Parliament in 1821.[45] Before this enclosure, there were 2,526 acres of common meadow and hillsides in the parish of Bourton-on-the-Hill and, usually, the old medieval strip farming system was still in use. After the 1821 enclosure, major changes in land access and use meant that the number of locals employed in agriculture declined, and 1831 census figures show that twenty-five village women went to work as servants in local mansions, including Sezincote.[46] Raj shook his head, not at all surprised. I told him that my very next walk, through East Anglia, explores the use of imperial profits – like Cockerell's – on land enclosures, the privatization of land that was formerly in common use.

Crossing the ridges and furrows, we reflected on our conversation at Sezincote. Before we'd parted, Edward had expressed embarrassment about the culture wars waged by politicians and – occasionally – by other country-house owners. He'd heard, he told us, about the hostility we had experienced as a result of our work with the National Trust: he did not feel, he said, that investigating heritage sites' colonial histories was something to be resisted or opposed. Raj and I wondered if, somehow, Edward had wanted to give us a different impression of country-house ownership: to show us another way of doing things. We remarked on his openness, his ideas about how to attract and welcome Britons of all heritages to the house and gardens. He wanted to tell visitors the fullest possible history.

All of which returned us to the topic of John Cockerell and his relationship with Estuarta, the Indo-Portuguese mother of his children. It's clear from John Cockerell's letters that he had to persuade Estuarta to join him in England.[47] When she got to London, he informed his brother of the safe arrival of 'her and all her flock', by which he meant the children and possibly some servants.[48] At the time, around a third of all British men in India established relationships with Indian women. But when they returned to England, such relationships generally ended or remained hidden, both the women and any children of such unions being left behind (though, some-times, children were brought back in the guise of 'servants'). John was unusual. He, Estuarta and the children all lived openly under the same roof for a time in his brother's palatial Hyde Park resi-dence, John converting the parlour into a study for himself, while Estuarta and the children occupied the upper floor.[49] These were unconventional living arrangements, and John ruefully confessed in a letter that Estuarta had advised him to replace his brother's furni-ture after all the children's 'dancing, jumping and rioting!'[50]

In John Cockerell's day, British rule in India was focused primarily on trade, battles and tax; the 'civilizing mission' of the British Raj came later in the nineteenth century. But things were already chang-ing. In 1792, just before John's departure from India, rules were created to exclude the mixed-heritage children of these couples from high company office, thereby directly discriminating against people with British and Indian parents. Now, children of such inter-cultural unions could only work in menial or low-ranking positions. This policy had a long legacy: when India came under direct British rule after 1858, this remained the only kind of work Anglo-Indians could obtain.[51]

As John and Estuarta entered London society, they re-established contact with Cockerell's friend and mentor, the former East India Company governor Warren Hastings. For the previous seven years, Hastings had been the defendant in what would prove the political trial of the age. Impeached for misgovernment and corruption during his time as governor general, he was tried in the cavernous West-minster Hall, a process which attracted widespread public attention and subjected company activity to detailed scrutiny.[52] While, legally speaking, the trial did not hold water, its exposure of company excesses and corruption shocked many Britons at the time.[53] Hast-ings, some believe, was the wrong target: he had a reputation for avoiding corruption, and at least thought – in contrast to many other company officials – that those who governed should be know-ledgeable about the places they ruled. He particularly questioned traders' fitness to rule.[54] His letters condemn company abuses of

Indians, although it is unclear how actively he opposed them in practice.[55] Hastings also contributed to a new translation of the Bhagavad Gita and wrote in the preface that the holy book would endure long after the British Empire had come to an end.[56] When in 1795 Hastings was finally acquitted, John Cockerell was duly delighted, opining that his mentor had been much wronged.[57] 'I encourage myself with the hope of taking Estuarta to a Grand Ball' (in Hastings' honour), he wrote, which 'is to be a very grand and superb business.'[58]

Hastings' public image had nonetheless been tarnished by the trial. Widely understood as a fabulously wealthy figurehead of East India Company corruption and excess, he was portrayed by the cartoonist James Gillray in a turban with loose Indian pyjamas and shoes with upwardly curled toes like a despotic prince.[59] With their South Asian wealth, customs, and (in Cockerell's case) mixed-heritage children, the likes of Hastings and Cockerell were perceived as a societal threat.[60] Indian eating preferences were mocked, even while they gained popularity: Britain's first curry powder advert appeared towards the end of John Cockerell's military career. (The late eighteenth-century play *A Wife in the Right* depicted one governor – Anderson – as refusing to dress for dinner, rejecting his bland English meal and wanting to make curry the 'common food' of Britain.)[61]

Three years after Hastings' acquittal, John Cockerell's health deteriorated. Having struggled with illness ever since returning from India, he died in the summer of 1798, aged forty-six, at an affluent London residence in Mayfair.[62] His will stated that 'Seasoncote' be divided between his two brothers and his sister Elizabeth. To Estuarta, he left nothing – despite John's desperation to bring her to Britain, the length of their relationship and the affectionate references to her throughout his correspondence with Charles. He left 80,000 rupees to be shared among their four children.[63] After this mention in John's will, the children disappear from the historical record. They remind us, however, that empire left a demographic legacy in Britain itself, as well as in the colonies.[64] Given the number of Anglo-Indian relationships at the time, this legacy would have been significant.

Charles Cockerell was still in India when his brother died. By this time, his agency house had played a key role in the ongoing conflict between the East India Company and the ruler of Mysore, Tipu Sultan.[65] Determined to crush Tipu Sultan's alliance with France, the new governor general, Richard Wellesley, turned to Charles Cockerell, among others, to supply the funds for an army of 60,000 troops, artillery and supplies. Charles Cockerell obliged with a loan of £1 million: an astronomical sum at the time.[66]

With Charles Cockerell's finance, the company was able to pay its soldiers four times what Tipu paid his men.[67] On 4 May 1799, Wellesley's army captured Seringapatam. Tipu Sultan had declared that he would 'rather live a day as a lion than a lifetime as a sheep' and had no wish to become 'a miserable dependant on the infidels, in their list of pensioned rajas and nabobs.' He abandoned his midday meal, climbed onto the battlements, fought and was killed.[68] In August that year, Governor Wellesley was presented with a letter of congratulations from the English in Madras, Bombay and Calcutta. Charles Cockerell was among the signatories.[69]

Charles returned to England in 1801, around the same time as an Indian scholar-soldier of Persian heritage called Mirza Abu Taleb Khan. Abu Taleb had reluctantly agreed to serve the East India Company as a tax collector in the northern Indian city of Lucknow. Collaborating with the company would, he knew, make him many enemies – but he had been reassured by promises of protection from company employees, chief among them Governors Hastings and Cornwallis. The promises were never honoured, and Abu Taleb was left a pariah. He fell into debt, abandoned by friends and family alike. With all those company men whom he knew now back in England, Abu Taleb realized he had no choice but to follow them.[70] There, he re-established contact with the two company men who had, as he put it, 'marred my fortune, by forcing me to accept of an employment in that [company] government'.[71]

Meanwhile, the newly repatriated Charles Cockerell had lost no time mobilizing his East India Company networks. He rapidly converted his Indian wealth into political power, his former East India

Company contact Richard Barwell helping him to secure the parliamentary seat of Tregony in Cornwall. Tregony, and Cockerell's next seat in Lostwithiel, were both rotten boroughs, with so few voters that the seat in parliament could easily be bought or attained through bribery – which Cockerell duly did. Entering parliament, he joined a substantial body of MPs with East India interests.[72] (John Cockerell, by contrast, had attributed his own lack of political ambition to 'the hurrying scene of my past life' as a military man who'd 'never had the power over my own time, & not entirely of my actions'.)[73]

During the early 1800s, Charles Cockerell shuttled between the original Jacobean manor house at Sezincote and his palatial Hyde Park residence. At Hyde Park, Cockerell was surrounded by a tight-knit community of former company officials, foremost among them the former governor general Richard Wellesley, whose magnificent Apsley House faced Cockerell's home. This was convenient, given that Charles Cockerell acted as banker to the Wellesley family; he also remained an East India stockholder and served as commissioner on the board of control for India, which oversaw East India Company business and Indian affairs.[74]

Now in London, Abu Taleb wrote an account of his experiences there. His warmest words were reserved for Charles Cockerell. 'Had I been his brother,' he wrote, Cockerell 'could not have behaved with more kindness', inviting Abu Taleb to dinner weekly and lending him money. Cockerell's lifestyle was lavish: Abu Taleb described attending a banquet with hundreds of guests of high social rank, at which exotic fruits were served (these, Abu Taleb speculated, must have been grown in artificial heat under glass).[75] Cockerell also took Taleb on a tour up the Thames valley, through Berkshire's 'English Hindoostan', to Windsor, Oxford, Blenheim Palace and Sandford Park, as far as Sezincote. The two men went hunting, sometimes on horseback, sometimes on foot: on one day alone, Abu Taleb recalled, they shot twenty partridges and five hares, noting that two servants led their horses and carried their game.[76] During these outings, Charles Cockerell impressed on Abu Taleb English landownership laws. In England, he told Abu Taleb, 'game is considered as private property; and if any person kill it on the land of another, he is liable to a severe penalty.' Unlike his more relaxed successor at Sezincote, Charles Cockerell applied the law strictly and made a point of prosecuting poachers.[77]

While at Sezincote, the pair went to see Warren Hastings at nearby Daylesford, where Abu Taleb stayed a week. Daylesford had been recently remodelled by the company architect Samuel Pepys Cockerell. Abu Taleb remarked that Hastings, who disliked London life, was happily occupied in rural pleasures and had spared little expense in beautifying the estate. Such liberal spending did not escape the eye of more hostile observers. In the last year of the Hastings trial, one journalist sarcastically quipped that Hastings might easily have paid his massive legal bills had he not spent £50,000 on shrubberies and gravel walks.[78] Again, Abu Taleb showed no sign of ill-feeling over Hastings' former treatment of him in India (or if he did, he didn't commit it to writing). For his part, Hastings – perhaps remorseful over the episode – offered to fund the rest of Abu Taleb's England trip, an offer which he declined.[79]

Plans for the redesign of Sezincote's Jacobean house took shape in 1806. The obvious path was neoclassical, the style in which so many country piles were then being rebuilt – and which, given that Charles Cockerell was (like many nabobs), busy building a British façade for his Asian wealth, might have seemed appropriate. Having made his Indian fortune, he had secured 'rotten' parliamentary seats back in England. (Later, he swapped far-flung Lostwithiel for the more convenient Surrey constituency of Bletchingley, which he held until 1812.)[80] That year, too, he married into the aristocracy, wedding the Honourable Harriet Rushout, daughter of the first Baron of Northwick, whose seat of Northwick Park was just 5 miles from Sezincote. Cockerell then made a successful bid for a baronetcy, supported by his Hyde Park neighbour, the former governor general Robert Wellesley.[81] With Sezincote's plans in progress, he was well on the way to refashioning himself as a gentleman on an English country estate. Except, of course, that those plans were for a very different style of house.

It was perhaps at Daylesford that Charles Cockerell found inspiration for his own Mughal palace. His close friend and neighbour Warren Hastings had already made significant efforts to introduce Indian culture into Britain. While still in India, Hastings had commissioned the artist William Hodges to produce a large number of landscapes.[82] Hodges was an established painter of colonial scenes and cultural encounters: he had previously accompanied Captain Cook on his second Pacific voyage as the expedition's artist.[83] Accompanying Hastings on his official travels through India, Hodges sketched. On his return to England he had turned these sketches into a collection of aquatints: *Select Views in India, Drawn on the Spot, in the Years 1780, 1781, 1782 and 1783*.[84] Significantly, Hodges was heavily influenced by current ideas of the picturesque. His aquatints and drawings represent Indian architecture in the soft style of the English pastoral – which gave impetus to Hastings' vision for Daylesford.[85] For not long after, Hastings dined with Charles Cockerell's brother Samuel Pepys Cockerell to discuss designs for a new exterior of his own house at Daylesford. Inspired by Hodges, Hastings settled on an Islamic-style dome and a conservatory with Eastern-style windows. For the interior he had selected fireplaces depicting Indian scenes.[86] At Daylesford, then, everything came together. Here, in more muted fashion, was an architectural style that would find its fullest expression in Sezincote.

Charles Cockerell drew on the same close-knit company circle: on its expertise in Indian architecture (Pepys Cockerell), an interest in Indian history and languages (particularly Hastings) and landscape painting (Thomas Daniell, who like his contemporary Hodges had spent years in India and who became a consultant on Sezincote's design).[87] It was Daniell – whose *Oriental Scenery* featured Indian architecture with mixed Hindu and Muslim elements, Sezincote's hallmark – who ensured the house's fidelity to Indian architecture.[88] Sezincote's transformation took a full fifteen years – and, Cockerell confessed, phenomenal expense.

Sezincote and Daylesford may have been isolated examples of Indianized architecture in Gloucestershire, but they did have some local architectural influence. You can see Sezincote motifs locally, in the old Spa Cottage of nearby Lower Swell, and Mughal influences in Cheltenham's old marketplace.

In 1819, at age sixty-four, Charles Cockerell – who had continued his peripatetic parliamentary career, inheriting his father-in-law's former seat in nearby Evesham – had his portrait painted by George Taylor. Dressed in black, Cockerell stands beside an elaborately carved table, gilded with gold. In the background are wintry clouds, pastoral hills and an old stone church. Charles holds papers in his hand; architectural drawings lie around his feet. His cheeks rosily English, his hair wavy and grey, he is the picture of a respectable Englishman, a figure of reassuring civic authority. It was an image he continued to cultivate, donating money to nearby charities and supporting the local Heythrop Hunt. During these years, too, he designed the additions to Longborough church, creating the family's private entrance and lofty pews. His business interests also took a domestic turn. He reinvested his Asian wealth into British energy, became director of the Arkendale and Derwent Mining Company and acquired a gas and coke business whose ambitious aim – unsuccessful, as it turned out – was to supply London with gas lighting.[89]

There were many Charles Cockerells: the British parliamentarian, the squire, the East India returnee with his social set and the global businessman. Partnering with the London banking house of William Paxton, another East India figure, Cockerell was a banker to Britons and Indian businessmen alike; he was also in shipping, transporting commodities and passengers to and from India. (Confusingly, this enterprise changed names from Cockerell, Trail and Company to Trail, Palmer and Company, eventually bearing only Palmer's name by 1810.)[90] Cockerell's relationship with John Palmer, co-founder of their agency house, meanwhile, came under increasing strain, the house running up debts to Cockerell after a series of setbacks. Theirs had always been a risky venture: failed indigo crops, fluctuating opium markets, shipwrecks, stolen cargo and fraud perennially threatened profits. As attitudes towards Indians became ever more hierarchical, the East India Company's increasing reliance on

Indian commercial and financial networks also eroded British confidence and affected Palmer's business standing. With his investments now firmly repatriated, and his own offices moved to Austin Friars, near the Bank of England, Charles Cockerell demanded that the bad debt be repaid: Palmer and company duly collapsed.[91]

Not all Cockerell's business activities were transferred to England, however. After the 1833 Slavery Abolition Act, Cockerell diversified into the indentured labour business, shipping Indian labourers to work Mauritian plantations.[92] The first labourers arrived from Calcutta in 1834. Escaping famine and starvation in India, they worked under harsh conditions for a period of five years or more, supposedly in return for wages and their return passage. Wages were low, and return journeys relatively rare. Their experience would have been grim from the start. The outward voyage to Mauritius lasted months. Death and disease were common.[93] Critics of the Mauritian indentured labourer system accused Indian-based recruitment agencies of corruption, kidnapping, ill-treatment and a lack of legal redress.[94] Charles Cockerell's involvement in the mass transportation of people was among his last business activities. He died at Sezincote in 1837.[95]

The cases of John and Charles Cockerell laid bare the tensions and contradictions experienced by East India Company employees. Many immersed themselves in Indian culture, formed relationships and even had children; when they returned home, their lives were immeasurably altered, and they found themselves impelled to recreate in England what they had found in India. Yet, in the end, their fortunes were founded on ransacked wealth, as employees of a company that stripped Indian assets bare in the quest for profit and power, an instinct that was ingrained in both John and especially Charles. As John put it to his brother, when back in England, nothing would induce him to return to India – except perhaps money. Yet in Sezincote and in Edward Peake that afternoon, Raj and I had seen something different: an openness and a willingness to acknowledge and accept a full version of the house's past – and, perhaps, a way forward.

★

It was late by the time we got back to Bourton-on-the-Hill, but we had to make the short drive over to Daylesford to see Warren Hastings' house. After all, it was where Sezincote all began. Raj wanted to imagine the old journey by carriage, to picture the Cockerells visiting their old mentor and to glimpse the house.

On the edge of the Daylesford estate, we parked the car by a stile and continued on foot. The footpath to Daylesford came tantalizingly close to the house, but the building was hidden behind a high perimeter wall. Skirting some pasture where thoroughbred horses grazed beside woodlands carpeted with autumn mulch, we walked around the wall to an orchard. To Raj's annoyance, there was no scrumping the fruit trees under the watchful eyes of nearby gardeners.[96] Surrounded by 'Private Property' signs, we gave up, returned to the car and headed for the nearby Daylesford Farm Shop.

Inside the farm shop complex we marvelled at the cheese room, with its immaculate rows of organic Double Gloucester, Waxed Adlestrop and Penyston Brie. Wandering into a nearby clothes shop beside the courtyard, Raj inspected the price tag on a sweater and let it drop as if he had been stung. It was £500. 'What kind of money would you need to have to buy a jumper that expensive?' he burst out. We recalled our earlier chat with a regular at the Coach and Horses in Longborough. Cotswold house prices were now beyond unaffordable, the man had said. A two-up, two-down house in Longborough had recently sold for half a million pounds. Villages were emptied of their long-time inhabitants; many homes were now rented to holidaymakers. Most of the shops were gone, too, and community centres were closing along with local transport links. Cars ruled, the villager had told us. And a local mansion had gone for £6 million – the new owner, it was rumoured, planned to live there for just three months a year. Now, as then, new money changed everything.

The sun began to set. Driving along narrow lanes, we talked about place, about who belongs and who has the power to define the past. Our conversation turned to a more recent period of history: the participation of Commonwealth soldiers in the two world wars.

Raj's grandfather, Bulaka Singh, fought on the Western Front. Raj and his son Kabir had recently visited the battlegrounds of Ypres in Belgium – Raj described these battlegrounds to me – and said that the experience was still raw. As he walked with his son through those small, 'Punjabi-looking fields', they talked of the experience of trench warfare, of the violence and shell-shock; they also spoke of his uncles, who fought in the Mediterranean during the Second World War. A third relative had fought in Burma. 'They put their lives on the line,' said Raj, 'to secure freedoms they themselves had been denied.' 'By colonial rule?' I asked, and he nodded. What affected Raj and Kabir most, though, was their visit to the Belgian war museum. There was no commemoration of Indian soldiers; indeed, no mention of them at all. Raj could not find anything to say that they had fought, any mention of their sacrifice. 'That silence just prolongs the insult and deepens the wound,' said Raj. He sighed.

As we continued on past the hedgerows on either side of the road, Raj's thoughts drifted back to the Indianized palace with its paradise gardens. Places like Sezincote, he said, can potentially promote broader representations of British history. He'd been heartened by Edward Peake's account of the mixed-faith weddings which take place there: weddings that, Raj felt, resisted narrow nationalisms, whether the imperial nationalisms of Western Europe, which had redefined entire peoples as 'civilized' or 'barbaric', or the nationalisms of today. We drove on in silence. Then, just beyond another of those honey-coloured Cotswold villages, Blockley, we braked sharply. There, an avenue of stately beech trees stood like a copper portal in the fading light.

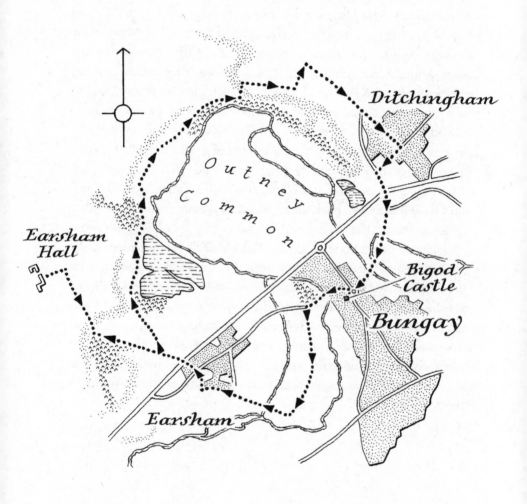

7.

The Enclosure Walk: Norfolk and Jamaica[1]

If you head about 150 miles north-east from the Cotswolds, through Cambridgeshire, you come to East Anglia, which bulges out into the North Sea. Unlike the Atlantic coastline on England's western edge, its counties of Norfolk and Suffolk are notably flat: a mixture of sandy heathland, fens and marshes (many drained over the centuries for farmland). Norfolk's rich pastures are dotted with ancient villages and farmsteads. Willowy lanes meander through salt marsh, reclaimed from the sea over a thousand years ago using dykes and ditches.[2] People have grazed livestock for centuries amid the water meadows and lowland lakes of the East Anglian Fens. These wetlands teem with fish and eels; otters and bitterns continue to thrive.

The names on old maps reflect the management of these landscapes: First Fen, Second Fen, the Thirteen Acres. Others, like Bullock Shed Close and Duck Lands Lane, suggest how land was used. Names convey observations of the natural world too: Toads Lane, Birds Hill and Thistly Close, whilst Devils Lane, Fairy Hill and Hedenham Mermaid give a flavour of folklore and superstition. These old local names tell a messier story than today's managed landscapes suggest. They tell a more intimate story of land that was well known and well loved long before it was regimented and regularized by enclosure – the fencing-off and privatization of land that was formerly under common ownership, and the consequent loss of people's former right to graze livestock and grow crops there.

In the later Middle Ages, Norfolk and Suffolk landowners became immensely rich through wool production. This explains the grand medieval churches, known as wool churches, which can be found throughout the region, and many fine buildings in Norwich,

Norfolk's capital. I wanted to walk in Norfolk, both because it remains one of England's most rural regions and because of its unique place in the history of enclosure which, in the early nineteenth century, was linked to British slave-ownership in the West Indies.

We generally think about enclosure as the wholesale privatization of land that went on – with parliamentary approval – from the early seventeenth century onwards. But wool production, and its attendant wealth, was a major driver of enclosure because it provided a motive for converting land into pasture. Enclosure actually started long before the seventeenth century. So, too, did the fight against it. In 1549, in the manor of Wymondham south-west of Norwich, a local turf war escalated into something bigger. The landowner Robert Kett, infuriated at the enclosure of common land by a rival, tore down the fences and then, impelled by a new-found sense of social justice, helped local commoners tear down his own. The protests escalated, and soon Kett found himself at the head of a popular army of 16,000 marching on the city of Norwich. The rebels' demands focused on curbing the power of the landed elites to exploit common resources. Though, in taking Norwich, the rebels were moderate and restrained, the rebellion's end was predictably violent. The teenage king Edward VI – son of Henry VIII – sent a strong army to Norfolk. There was a stand-off for two months, ending in the deaths of thousands of rebels, defeat and Robert Kett's hanging.

Norwich's radicalism continued. In the late eighteenth century it was reputedly dubbed by Prime Minister William Pitt the Younger a 'Jacobin city', a place of revolutionaries – with distinct echoes of the French Revolution – owing to its protests at legislation restricting the freedom of speech.[3] From the time of Kett's rebellion, too, the city had a long tradition of religious dissent, with Quakers and Baptists to the fore.[4] But the region's radical history is not confined to Norwich. Thirty miles to the south-west, the town of Thetford was the birthplace of Thomas Paine, advocate of democratic reform, republican, supporter of the French Revolution and author of the influential *Rights of Man*, published in 1791. A bestseller then, it continues to influence ideas about democracy and rights today. But in the late eighteenth century, Paine's freethinking alarmed politicians, the aristocracy and the monarchy. One of his fiercest opponents was John Reeves, an ultra-conservative civil servant, legal historian and magistrate (and Newfoundland's first colonial chief justice). A year after the publication of *Rights of Man*, Reeves founded the Association for Preserving Liberty and Property against Republicans and Levellers, which aimed to suppress popular dissent, quell unrest and prevent radical publications like Paine's, often through intimidation and violent means.[5] But in Norwich – as in London, the industrializing north of England, revolutionary France, the Thirteen Colonies and elsewhere – Paine's ideas fell on fertile ground. Especially so among the county's weavers, who were both more radical and more educated.[6]

By Paine's time, Norfolk's radicalism went far beyond England's shores. A strong anti-slavery movement in the county persisted into the nineteenth century, with figureheads like anti-slavery campaigners Thomas Clarkson and Harriet Martineau. Black abolitionists visited the region, including Benjamin Benson – born into slavery in Bermuda in 1818 – who was freed after the 1833 Slavery Abolition Act and came to lecture in Norfolk, a place where his anti-slavery speeches likely fell on fertile ground.[7] He spoke about slavery to the pupils of Crimplesham School, south of King's Lynn. Norfolk people were among the subscribers to Olaudah Equiano's narrative detailing his experiences of slavery. The purchase of slave-produced sugar was also widely discouraged in Norwich, one newspaper noting that city dwellers commonly banned such products from their tea tables.[8] Anti-slavery petitions garnered thousands of signatures. The longest such petition, measuring over 200 feet, was signed in 1824 by 17,000 people at Norwich's St Andrew's Hall.[9] In the early nineteenth century, the radical Norwich MP William Smith campaigned against slavery with William Wilberforce; he also negotiated the slavery compensation scheme, which – notoriously – involved state-funded pay-outs to slave-owners rather than to enslaved people. (It was this compensation scheme that finally got MPs to support the 1833 Slavery Abolition Act.)[10]

Yet it was the slavery business itself that shaped Norfolk's radical politics, its land use and agricultural practice. For Norfolk, as many other places in England, was home to returnee slave-owners with plantations in the West Indies, who were zealous in the protection of their interests and properties abroad and at home. And in Norfolk – again, as elsewhere – slave-owners were landowners who enclosed the commons, took away people's commoning rights, blocked rights of way and aggressively legislated to control access to land and to protect their newly expanded estates. In Norfolk, the links between slave-ownership and domestic enclosure were particularly striking.

In tracing this history, I planned a walk along the Norfolk–Suffolk border, which bisects East Anglia from east to west. Here, a footpath weaves its way across the boundary. The walk would begin in the historic Suffolk town of Bungay, follow waterways back into Norfolk and then take quiet lanes to Earsham Hall, a red-brick residence that was once home to Sir William Windham Dalling, an encloser and slave-owner. Doubling back to All Saints church – which contains the usual stock of colonial memorials – the route would lead through the ancient village of Earsham, then across Sir William's formerly enclosed lands of Outney Common and along a footpath which overlooks Waveney Valley's water meadows. Finally, the walk loops back to Bungay through the nearby Norfolk village of Ditchingham.

This part of East Anglia was as new to my fellow walker as it was to me. Keeping me company was the broadcaster, writer and DJ Zakia Sewell. Zakia shares my interest in enclosure and was likewise curious about Norfolk's history of resistance to it as well as the county's links with slavery. Her own rural journey of discovery developed through a love of English folk songs, which in turn led to a deep interest in folklore and lost rural knowledge. Her Radio 4 series *My Albion* began in a Herefordshire churchyard, where she explored remnants of a pagan past where people practised pre-Christian rites.

Zakia is captivated by folk cultures which emerged before people were literate, or belonged to nations, or to an empire. My youngest walking companion, her generation has inherited an environmental crisis, which has only intensified her keen interest in old rural ways, when people honoured the seasons and connected deeply with the land. As she pointed out to me during the walk, it is necessary to understand ancient relationships with nature in times of polluted air, overworked soil and dwindling biodiversity.

A Londoner, Zakia's father's family are Welsh; her mother's parents came from Carriacou, a Grenadine island in the south-eastern Caribbean Sea. I knew that Zakia would find Norfolk's neat, partitioned countryside a marked contrast with the land of her father. For Zakia, west Wales is a mystical landscape filled with ancient forests and castle ruins, the land of myth and Merlin, of bards, dragons, druids and harp music. Her Grenadian mother similarly loves Wales – everything slows down there, she says – and, echoing Dylan Thomas (she's a fan), feels that the lanes at nightfall really are 'slow black, Bible black'.[11] But Zakia knew well that other areas of rural Britain had their own colonial histories. Given her own Caribbean connections, she told me she felt ready to look the countryside's slavery history in the eye.

I stood in the blossom-filled, buttercup-studded churchyard of St Mary's in Bungay, awaiting the bus from Norwich. Tall and slim, Zakia stepped off the bus, her hair in a full, centre-part Afro, dressed in shorts and a lime-coloured shirt to match the unseasonably warm weather. We exchanged a hug and, bathed in birdsong, exclaimed over the warm day.

I got out my map as we stood beside the church tower, a local landmark which stands over 90 feet high and is decorated with grey flint. 'Are we on the Suffolk side of the border here?' she asked. I confirmed that we were. Showing her the route, I explained that it was loosely based on an existing walk but I'd added an extension to allow us a glimpse of Sir William Windham Dalling's Earsham Hall along the way. 'The local walk I found makes no mention of the hall's connection with slavery, though,' I remarked.[12] 'I wonder if the locals know about it?' Zakia replied.

But before we left the churchyard, Zakia mentioned the Black Shuck legend associated with St Mary's. I smiled, not in the least surprised that she knew about it. In 1577, the story goes, a black hound lurched into St Mary's church in Bungay during a lightning storm. There was a loud clap of thunder. The creature had flaming eyes and, some said, was as tall as a calf or a horse. It attacked the congregation and killed a man and a boy. The church tower collapsed. The animal, known as Black Shuck, reappeared 12 miles away in Blythburgh church and repeated its savage actions, killing and maiming more people. The creature is said to stalk the region's lonely footpaths and coastlines. If you hear its gruesome howl, your fate is sealed.

We went inside, the church interior cool after the spring heat; light streamed through plain glass windows. We passed a wooden cupboard near the entrance, used to collect bread to feed hungry locals in the late seventeenth century, and wandered among the pews. Zakia pointed out a griffin, and carved angels, eagles and a lion on the roof, and we came across a seventeenth-century Flemish wood carving of the resurrection, gifted by Sir Rider Haggard, the author of late nineteenth-century colonial adventure tales who lived in nearby Ditchingham.

Leaving St Mary's behind, we set off through the old marketplace and Butter Cross (where local traders used to sell dairy), then took a back lane to the thirteenth-century remains of Bigod Castle, its hulking gatehouse a towering reminder of Norman landownership. It took just five minutes to walk out of town, but we soon stopped on an old stone bridge to take in the Monet-like waterlilies and weeping willow above the Waveney river, which flows through the town. A walker passed us, calling out cheerfully that Zakia won the prize for the best hairstyle. 'I considered a more conformist hairstyle for our country walk,' Zakia said with a smile, 'but decided against it.' It was, she said, a decision she always has to make: whether or not to fight the instinct, as a Black woman, to modify her appearance when she visits the countryside: people invariably look twice.

We continued along a busy road for some minutes, leaving it with some relief at the Roaring Arch Bridge (which, nondescript, didn't live up to its magnificent name) and passed through lowland pasture beside a watery drainage ditch, white clouds of cow parsley waving us on our way. Long pastures extended over half a mile, then we turned onto the Angles Way towards Earsham village. Pausing in the sun, we looked back at the fields we'd walked through, Zakia pointing out the 'assorted colours of cow'. Some were roan, others white and some were splashed with grey, as though someone had thrown a tin of paint across their backs.

I asked Zakia how much she'd looked into Norfolk's colonial history. 'I do know there were plantation-owners in Jamaica and Grenada who ended up in Norfolk,' she said, 'but I've tended to bypass the colonial period, really.' I asked her whether this meant she was avoiding it. 'Well, yes,' she replied, laughing, 'it might spoil things. Ancient Britain is less disturbing to me than the days of empire.' And because she felt ready, we focused on the names and details of Norfolk's slave-owners as we followed the Angles Way. Prominent among them was Thomas Walpole, nephew of Britain's first prime minister. An MP for the Norfolk borough of King's Lynn between 1754 and 1784, Thomas Walpole was a thoroughly colonial figure: a major property speculator in the American colonies, he was also a slave-owner with estates on Tobago and Grenada.[13] When an Edinburgh firm with whom Walpole was financially involved defaulted on a sum worth around £93,000 today,[14] there was a downturn in his personal fortunes. Walpole's exact financial relationship with the firm remains unclear, but he took legal action to recover its Grenadian assets, the Bacolet and Chemin plantations. However, these estates instead went to the Bank of England, in payment of the debt owed to it. Researchers recently discovered documents in the bank's archives which relate to the plantations' eventual sale. They show that the bank owned 599 enslaved children, men and women from these estates, which it sold on in 1788.[15]

'It's incredible, really,' I said to Zakia, 'because in 2021, the bank mistakenly said it was "never itself directly involved in slavery", but actually it was!'[16] Archivists later discovered that the bank not only owned enslaved people but also provided underpinning credit for the slavery system.[17]

A second example I mentioned to Zakia was a soldier called William Tooke Harwood, who owned a Grenadian plantation. He was from Thompson village, 32 miles west of Bungay. He owned Diamond estate in Grenada with his uncle. When his uncle died, he inherited the remainder of the plantation, which he left to his wife when he died in 1824.[18] This example of slave-ownership is a reminder that it was not just prominent politicians who were slave-owners; East Anglian slavery connections were linked to more obscure figures too, including – as we would find out – local clergymen.

We crossed a ford and followed a hedged track to the Anglo-Saxon settlement of Earsham village, where the River Waveney once powered a flour mill. The village lies in the Waveney valley, where the river marks the border between Norfolk and Suffolk. All Saints was the site of the original village, near the old mill. Our tree-lined track was dappled with sunlight, with chocolate-box cottages and trees either side. We passed the fourteenth-century parish church of All Saints. With plenty of distance to cover, and unsure of the timings, we decided to visit the church on our return loop from Earsham Hall. Leaving the village behind us, we continued along Five Acre Lane towards the Earsham country estate, a good 3 miles distant along the hedgerows.

The trees thickened into woodland beside Pheasants' Walk – named after hunting pursuits of old, we speculated – and we spotted a deer's white tail flitting between the trees before vanishing, startled at our approach. Wood pigeons crooned, hiding among the newly unfurled spring leaves. The land around us was less lush and green than we'd expect for this time of year; we remarked at the parched verges and bleached fields. 'Where's the Green Man when you want him?' I joked. We passed a clearing where felled trees had been dismembered into logs and chippings. We turned into the old Norwich Road. Thin hedges marked the edges of the enclosed Earsham estate, and we passed flowerless meadows planted with gigantic oaks. A tunnel of spindly hawthorn arched above our heads, then, a few steps further on, we reached a smart metal sign announcing Earsham Hall, now a family home and business centre. I apologized to Zakia for all the lane-walking. 'In the eighteenth century,' I said, 'we could have got here on direct footpaths across fields, but they were blocked during the land enclosures,' and I spotted a private road just beyond the mansion, which had just come into view. Conscious that it was a family home, we nonetheless lingered by the hedge at the end of the drive. The house was built on rising ground with mellow red brick and well-proportioned sash windows (Georgian, as the original seventeenth-century house was rebuilt in 1784). 'It doesn't have one of those long, pretentious drives,' I said, and we looked at the house's parapet, hipped roof and moulded stone cornice. 'It's very elegant, though,' I added, as we looked on at the smart white stone entrance. Right on cue, a peacock crowed, and we laughed. To the British, nothing evoked the aristocracy more than the nasal cry of this regal bird, regardless of the peacock's Asian origins.

There, at the edge of Earsham estate, Zakia told me more about her family history. 'My mum was born in England,' she said, 'but her two older brothers were born in Carriacou and stayed behind on the island until my mother was older.' Zakia explained that her mother's prolonged separation from her brothers, the pressures of surviving in England, the racism she and her family experienced unsettled her for life. By the time Zakia was born, her mother was seriously unwell. Though she didn't have the photograph to show me there and then, Zakia described a picture of her mother holding her as a newborn baby. 'She looked disturbingly spaced out in that picture,' Zakia said. As it turned out, her mother was experiencing her first symptoms of schizophrenia and was hearing voices in her head: some near, some far. Some seemed to come from her neighbours, saying bad things about her. All this took its toll on Zakia, since she felt she spent her first quarter-century without really feeling that her mother was there at all. This experience of disconnection also placed Zakia at some remove from her Caribbean heritage. Still more disturbingly, she said, her mother believed that some of the voices she heard – screams and cries – expressed the violence inflicted on her enslaved relatives long ago, as though they were communicating with her from beyond the grave. Her mother's schizophrenia, Zakia feels, expresses slavery's disturbing intergenerational and psychological legacy, 'unresolved ancestral trauma'. Her mother's experience, and by extension her own, has made Zakia think deeply about the long-term impact of slavery: violence, migration and separation, but, by the same token, she has found herself reluctant to make explicit connections between slavery's disturbing history with rural England, somewhere she's found peace throughout her life. 'I've found the countryside soothing,' she says, 'even if I've been unsure of my place in it.' 'No wonder,' I replied, 'that you've preferred to focus on ancient rural Britain.' It was true, she acknowledged, 'but I feel I'm ready to look into these slave histories now.'[19] I already had a sense of this shift in her focus because – I told her – I'd heard her say that we need to think about British history from beyond the shores of England, Wales and Scotland to understand 'the way', as she'd put it, 'that culture has flown out of this place and the echoes come back.'[20] That was why, she responded, our East Anglia walk was timely for her.

We sat on a dry verge overlooking the mansion and talked about its long association with slavery in Jamaica. Earsham was bought in 1720 by Colonel William Windham, a local landowner who was a rare winner in the South Sea Bubble of the same year. Just over a decade later, his daughter Catherine eloped with, then married, the son of a Bungay apothecary. Their son, John Dalling, had a taste for adventure that took him to various British colonies: North America, where he fought in the British army; Jamaica, where he became governor; and Madras (now Chennai), where he commanded British troops. It was in Jamaica, however, where he made his fortune. Marrying into the slave-owning Pinnock family, which was prominent in Jamaican politics, he rose rapidly thanks to his in-laws' influence.[21]

In Jamaica, Sir John Dalling was governor during the infamous hurricane of 1770, which destroyed coastal communities and killed hundreds of people. He confirmed in a letter, dated twelve days later, that he had sent to Kingston for provisions, asking merchants to help. The merchants had agreed to assist but also appealed to the Crown to do something, so he was clearly responsive to the colonists' humanitarian situation, at least.[22]

During his time in office, Dalling was faced with an intermittent insurgency by 'maroons' – people who had escaped slavery and lived in the great and inaccessible mountain range of eastern Jamaica, the Blue Mountains. One famous maroon who coincided with Sir John's time in office was the leader Jack Mansong, who acquired a terrifying reputation among European slave-owners.[23] He raided plantations by night and organized an insurgency, hiding guns and ammunition in the Blue Mountains. In 1781, Governor Dalling went after Mansong. Publishing a proclamation listing his misdeeds (which included assisting the escape of enslaved people), Dalling placed a £200 bounty on his head and offered a list of other rewards relating to Mansong's group of insurgents, together with rewards for anyone who could deliver a person from Mansong's band of maroons to an island gaoler.[24] Shortly after, Mansong was located and killed.[25]

Obstructed and troubled by maroons, Sir John also found himself out of his depth with administrative affairs, and he began to make himself unpopular towards the end of his governorship. He took executive decisions on affairs which affected the British population. Before making major decisions, governors were supposed to consult the Island Council, elected assembly and local naval commander.[26] When Dalling embargoed shipping routes and imposed martial law during his second term, the island's governing bodies initially complied but later felt that the measures were no longer necessary. Plantation production had ground to a halt, and trade routes were obstructed. Even Dalling himself began to say that he was 'unequal to the task' of governor. He was recalled to England in 1781, the year he seemed most angry about Mansong in particular and maroon activity in general.[27]

Back in undignified retirement in England, Sir John joined the pro-slavery lobby and was a witness quoted by a 1792 publication inveighing against the abolition movement, entitled *A Country Gentleman's Reasons for Voting Against Mr. Wilberforce's Motion for a Bill to Prohibit the Importation of African Negroes into the Colonies*. Enslavers on Jamaica, Dalling claimed, treated their charges with care. (The cruellest slave-owners, he suggested, were formerly enslaved men.) According to him, enslavers were 'humane', going out of their way to ensure that food supplies never ran out, actions he attributed to fellow feeling for the enslaved workers on their plantations. No expense was spared to provide adequate housing and suitable clothes, he said, a claim that has been consistently contradicted by statistical evidence of deaths and disease on Jamaican plantations. According to Sir John, plantation labour was not unpleasant work, enslaved people were treated with compassion and as they grew old were only allocated minor tasks. Accounts of ill-treatment were exaggerated, he added, and it was these false reports that had provoked enslaved people to violence.[28] These were the standard claims of men who stood to gain personally from slavery's continuance and who defended the slavery system to the last.

In fact, the Dallings stood to gain a great deal. In 1810, the Dallings' son and heir, Sir William Windham Dalling,[29] inherited the Norfolk estate of Earsham Hall. On his father's death back in 1798, he had also inherited his father's Jamaican plantation of Donnington Castle: between 1799 and 1840, it brought him the huge income of £150,000. Flush with these funds, Sir William, an absentee plantation-owner, acquired many new paintings and, in 1818, he added a new library to the house.[30] Inventories show that he filled it with books about the West Indies. Without any apparent sense of irony, the family book collection also contained volumes of poetry by William Cowper, a well-known abolitionist (and the favourite poet of Jane

Austen).[31] Like his father, Sir William lobbied politicians to maintain the slavery system. In 1831 he had a meeting – alongside others with slavery interests – with the prime minister, the first Earl Grey, and the secretary of state for the colonies. Members of this delegation of slave-owners all had interests in West Indian plantations.[32] (Even after the 1833 Slavery Abolition Act, as the Donnington Castle profits began to dry up. Sir William was awarded £3,500 compensation for 176 enslaved people. He also claimed for 11 enslaved people from St Mary's Parish in Jamaica, for whom he was paid £239, 18s, 11d.)[33]

Such histories make it easy to see why those who love Britain's countryside might want to avoid such information. Yet even as we spoke about the house's Jamaican associations, Zakia told me that the cooing of pigeons in the surrounding trees was consoling, and that her mother similarly appreciates nature's calming effects and communes with nature just like her distant ancestors once did in Africa. Beaches, in particular, appeal to her mother's desire to be free. This shared love of rural places has helped to reconnect mother and daughter. 'I think the countryside is a potential source of healing,' Zakia said. To her, natural settings like these were good places to address Britain's slavery history. 'Ancestral trauma can be handed down through the generations and it can inflict all kinds of damage if it's left to fester,' she told me. Then she laughed and said, 'Britain needs therapy!'

We were soon back in Earsham village. All Saints churchyard – Sir William's local church – was wild around the edges. Bees droned in the early-afternoon sun, and a red admiral fanned its wings. The church's fourteenth-century tower has a shingle spire, added at the turn of the eighteenth century. Inside the building was cool and airy. We were the only people there. Zakia noticed black dogs carved in stone on the floor and wondered if it was a reference to the Black Shuck legend.

Examining the church walls, we found an array of colonial memorials, and photographed a marble wall plaque dedicated to Sir John Dalling of Earsham Hall, detailing his titles of governor of

Jamaica and commander-in-chief at Madras. A second large plaque commemorates the death of Sir John's eldest son, killed during a battle in Madras aged seventeen, with an inscription to the effect that he was a dutiful son with fine manners and an upright character. The second son also died and is memorialized there, though we were unsure how he met his death. 'That explains why Sir William inherited Earsham Hall,' I said, 'even though he was the third son.' We took a seat in the wooden pews. 'The Church of England is talking about its associations with slavery at the moment,' I said. 'They could include the local story here,' Zakia replied. We were thinking of a recent announcement by the Church of England, in 2020, pledging to explore and reflect on its relationship to the slavery business. The General Synod, the church's governing body, had just begun to advocate honest explorations of complicity with historic slavery, going beyond the obvious pride in anti-slavery churchmen like William Wilberforce.[34] At the time of the walk, the Church was at the beginning of this journey. Early initiatives have included an exhibition at Lambeth Palace, in 2023, about the Church's slavery links together with a focus on the many memorials to slavery advocates and beneficiaries which can be found inside churches in the cities and in the countryside. For the theologian Robert Beckford, however, the Church has a long way to go because it needs to recognize 'how the church's theological ideas made slavery possible'.[35]

As All Saints church illustrated so well, churches and parish records are invaluable resources for anyone interested in finding local slavery connections. The church in which we stood was a case in point: a former rector, Reverend George Sandby,[36] who lived in nearby Denton Lodge, was a slave-owner who shared substantial compensation, with nine others, for 314 enslaved people on the Tryall estate in Jamaica, where Sir William Windham Dalling's father had been governor. Sandby had taken up his position at All Saints in 1810, the year Sir William inherited the hall. Another neighbour of Sir William, the Reverend George Day, was also a slave-owner and investor on the Tryall estate (his name appears alongside Sandby's in the slavery compensation records).[37] These three were near neighbours and acquaintances – Day was a correspondent of Sir William[38] – and their collective slavery interests meant they held sway over the lives of 811 enslaved people in Jamaica. 'You'd never know all that, looking at this peaceful place,' I said. Zakia sighed and said that the church was getting cold, so we stepped outside into the sun.

The relationship between colonial activity and authority in rural England itself is little understood, but Sir William and his associates are good examples of how things worked in and around Bungay. One of Dalling's contemporaries and neighbours was Thomas Hoseason, a slave-owning magistrate who was put on trial for prosecuting one of his own agricultural labourers who insisted on taking a lunch break during the harvest. For a magistrate to prosecute and punish one of his own labourers was a clear conflict of interest, hence Hoseason's trial, but he got out of trouble by activating his old colonial networks; two naval officers testified to his good character and this led to his acquittal.[39] A few years later, Hoseason attended a meeting at Shirehall, 15 miles north of Bungay, to debate whether or not parliament should bring about an immediate end to slavery in British colonies. Also in attendance were two slave-owners who'd sold land to Sir William so that he could consolidate his Earsham estate: the Reverends George Sandby and George Day.[40]

We continued along the quiet lane. In the sixteenth century, we would have seen marshland fowl and many more deer, because these were the old hunting grounds of wealthy landowners. 'Now all this land is owned by the Earsham estate,' I said, gesturing at the rolling pastureland, 'and farmed by tenants.'

Today, Earsham village is tranquil. We left the sleepy old cottages behind and reached a rose-coloured pub called the Queen's Head, which stands on the Old Railway Road. We did not stop there and so left the village behind us. In years gone by there was a station in Earsham, serving the local Waveney Valley Line. The station was part of the Great Eastern Railway, a company which built the branch line running from Tivetshall through Bungay to Beccles, which opened in stages during the 1860s. The line connected local people with routes to Norwich and London as well as to commercial centres and ports. 'The village must have felt far busier once,' Zakia commented. 'Earsham must have been transformed by the coming of the railway.' As the celebrated landscape historian W. G. Hoskins pointed out, railway earthworks themselves came as a shock, being the largest in Britain since pre-Roman times, while railways were of course accompanied by infrastructure: stations, shops and hotels.[41] Inevitably, the profits of slavery found their way into the construction of Norfolk's railway network, which was part-financed by slavery compensation money belonging to people who lived outside the county.[42]

By contrast, the Bath Hills represented a peaceful retreat, and this was where we were now heading. These hills once invigorated the locals with spa water at Cold Bath House, though it no longer stands. In the eighteenth century, drinking – and bathing in – pure mineral water was used as a medical remedy. Having crossed a busy main road, we were glad to turn into a back lane which led us through the hills. We walked beside a beech hedge and, by some red-brick cottages and a crooked fir, our view opened out onto ploughed fields, bordered by woods, the bare earth folding into chestnut-brown layers dotted with trees. The lane dipped into a copse and then rose up as though to entice us with the promise of views over Outney Common. Today, Outney Common, also known as Bungay Common, extends over 400 acres within the northern loop of the Waveney river, its low grazing lands ascending to higher ground along which runs the Angles Way footpath. Parts of the common have been bought back from the old estates, and some rights of way have been restored.

As I told Zakia, the common comes close to the heart of Sir William's Jamaican wealth, which brought tracts of this land into private ownership. 'It's not obvious from just looking,' she said, 'that slavery changed the landscape around here.' Zakia was spot on. It was not just the Acts of Enclosure which allowed land to be privatized in Britain, but slavery wealth helped provide the capital to pay for it. Sir William was upwardly mobile (two generations previously, his paternal grandfather had been an apothecary), and Jamaican profits secured his social standing, a status tied up with his expanded estate. As the case of the Dallings shows, land enclosures in Norfolk were deeply intertwined with the slavery system and the benefits it delivered to enslavers like themselves.

Over the centuries, enclosure effected a slow transformation from peasant farming to capitalist farming, and from smallholding to large-scale landownership.[43] Although enclosure describes the planting of hedges or building of walls and fences to section off pieces of land, its legal significance was to remove land from common ownership, instead allocating it to a proprietor who controlled the way the land was accessed and used. This process accelerated rapidly in the eighteenth century, when, between 1750 and 1820, over 21 per cent of England was enclosed by parliamentary decree. Enclosure coincided with colonial expansion – but in fact this was no coincidence at all. A great deal of land in England was bought and enclosed using wealth from the West Indies, and through investment in the slavery business by entities like the Virginia and Royal African Companies.[44]

Piecemeal enclosure relied on local agreements and sales – and, often, a liberal dose of coercion. General enclosure happened when proprietors collaborated to enclose large estates in a single stroke. Parliamentary enclosure was a form of general enclosure, in which land and rights over its use were awarded by commissioners, who adjudicated over a process of land allocation in which ordinary villagers were invariably the losers. In Norfolk, as elsewhere in Britain, this process had a devastating impact on the countryside and on the rights of rural people.[45] In a 1797 map of the county produced by the cartographer William Faden, based on surveys done between 1790 and 1794, commons, heaths and warrens were a pronounced feature of the landscape. Within fifteen years of the map's publication, all the commons were gone.[46] Compensation to those deprived of their rights was often minimal: a so-called poor allotment, or small plot of land to grow food. Sometimes, there was no compensation at all.[47] Most women, along with others, could not legally prove their ties to the commons and were excluded from the compensation process altogether.[48]

Landowners themselves presented enclosure as a 'civilizing mission', a concept with distinct colonial overtones. Though colonial occupation and enclosure differed markedly in nature and degree, it is important to note that Britain's accumulation of overseas colonies coincided with seventeenth-century parliamentary acts of enclosure back home and, by 1788, more than half of mainland Australia had been claimed by British colonists on the grounds that it was uninhabited and uncultivated land, though it had been occupied by Aboriginal Australians for some 50,000 years. It is hard to ignore the fact that powerful British figures involved in these land grabs – colonization abroad and enclosure at home – evoked similar pretexts for occupying domestic land, laying legal claim to it by declaring it empty, unowned or unproductive wasteland.

Norfolk looms large in Britain's story of land privatization. In 1646, one Norfolk pamphleteer complained that land was being misrepresented to parliamentarians as 'useless quagmire' when it was actually being used for producing dairy products, collecting thatching reed and making baskets from sedge-grass.[49] Parliamentary petitions which proposed enclosure of various lands drew heavily on these mischaracterizations of the commons. In this way, wealthy landowners reconfigured, commanded and ruled the countryside. Prominent in their rhetoric was a claim to be 'tidying up' common land because it attracted people who existed at some remove from the system of wage labour, such as Romani Gypsies, travellers and squatters. Proprietors argued that enclosing these lands deterred gatherings of undesirables, a narrative that still resonates today.[50]

Often, those who enclosed land did so with funds derived from their colonial plantations. Enclosure maps of 1812 and 1816 show that Sir William Windham Dalling used his Jamaican wealth to consolidate and expand his estate. Two years after inheriting Earsham Hall, he was a petitioner on the 1812 'Act for Inclosing Lands in the Parishes of Earsham, Ditchingham, and Hedenham, in the County of Norfolk'. Involved in this enclosure petition was his neighbour, the Duke of Norfolk, whose agent told Sir William that the duke approved of the proposal: it would, he wrote, very likely pass through parliament without many problems.[51]

The lands due to be enclosed by this Act included Outney Common and Dole Meadow, the term 'dole' suggesting lands which had been habitually given over to people without a stable income as an act of charity. These commons, Sir William and the other petitioners argued, were 'uncultivated . . . wasteland' that would be 'improved' through enclosure. Like British colonists, they suggested that the commons were situated too far from anyone to practicably use them.[52] This claim is undermined by the petitioners' promise to award appropriate costs to displaced users of the land. Compensation was, the petition said, to be awarded to the owners of cottages or buildings. Any objectors were instructed to employ an attorney, which of course was beyond the means of most. The commissioners' judgement was always final in the enclosure process, and any who disputed the outcome of their appeal were to be evicted. As a result of the successful 1812 enclosures, the commissioners allocated just five acres as 'poor allotments'. These small plots were to be leased to tenants who would now pay rent twice a year, having paid nothing previously.[53]

Newly enclosed lands were strictly off-limits to locals. One of Sir William's neighbours, J. Bedingfeld, complained that people were fishing with nets in the broads – as they'd done from time immemorial – and vowed to prosecute anybody he caught doing so.[54] Sir William was equally draconian. Anybody caught on his new enclosures cutting turf or carrying off gorse, rocks or flagstones without permission would be fined. Non-payment would result in bailiffs recovering the full amount. Sir William also claimed exclusive rights to all the timber, standing or fallen, on the enclosed commons.[55] This was, of course, bad for anyone who had previously collected firewood or used logs for furniture-making or building. (Landless people were not the only ones to resent Sir William asserting this right. The Duke of Norfolk's agent wrote to Sir William to inform him that the duke alone had that right, historically.[56] The duke was from an old propertied family. Sir William's money came from Jamaica. Such antipathies arose as new slavery wealth usurped the settled aristocratic order.)

Lip-service was paid to due process. The 1812 enclosures were indeed contested by locals after notices were placed on church doors and printed in the *Norfolk Chronicle*.[57] A public meeting was held to hear objections put by an attorney – but, predictably, only a handful of complainants could afford one. Among these was a local man called Alexander Adair, who claimed 2 acres in the Dole Meadows as his by right, but his claim was overruled when the Act was passed regardless.

Hand-drawn local enclosure maps showing Sir William's new land resemble dense webs. Spindly demarcation lines show the proposed new land plots – numbered in red – and existing buildings are shaded in dark pink. Within these plots, the names of the new and former landowners are written in tiny, immaculate letters. The 1812 map shows that Sir William vastly expanded his land portfolio. He bought 280 acres around the perimeter of his estate, gobbling up lands around Earsham Hall which were deemed by the commissioners to have 'unfixed and uncertain' boundaries.[58] The map shows private roads created from High Green, close to the Hall, for the use of Sir William and his heirs. A second private road was laid out from Earsham churchyard to Priest Meadow (like the private road that Zakia and I had noticed leading across the Earsham estate), for the use of Sir William and two other landowners, running to and from All Saints church. Public lanes and footpaths which previously passed through Sir William's estate were blocked off. The footpaths ran from Earsham Hall to the Bath Hills, from Earsham Street to Earsham Hall, and from Summer House Hill to Burnt House Wood: now, all these were off-limits to locals, who were forced into time-consuming detours as they walked the long way round. Other paths were blocked between Earsham Hall, via Dirty Lane, to the Norwich Road Piece and from the Duke pub to Sir William's land.

Water courses and dykes were created along the land belonging to the Duke of Norfolk and near the Waveney River, as part of a bid to drain and consolidate farmland. Wooden bridges were built over the ditches wherever they were crossed by private roads. Gates and fences were erected, and a directive given to keep them in good order.[59] Access to these enclosed lands was then severely restricted. Today there are no public byways from Denton (2 miles to the west, but now just over 3 miles by road) or from Earsham village across the estate, though the 1816 enclosure map indicates that a new footpath had been planned, although Zakia and I were unable to find the footpath on our modern map.[60]

One local worthy who was permitted access to the newly privatized roads was the Reverend George Day of Earsham, Sir William Windham Dalling's slave-owning neighbour. In Norfolk, the Reverend sold Sir William plenty of land (which had previously been adjacent to, or within, the present-day Earsham estate) but he also bought large amounts himself, including fen and common land. Though locals were allowed to continue grazing livestock on Outney Common, and to grow beans or sow hempseed, they were now ordered to pay a tithe, a tax due to the Church, for the privilege.[61]

The links between slavery and enclosure resonate strongly in estate management far away in the West Indies, where provision grounds were created for enslaved people, and where mapping and surveillance practices echoed agricultural and land management practices back in Britain.[62] Both at home and in the colonies, British landowners embraced pastoral aesthetics. In the late eighteenth century, Sir George Cornewall used cattle for practical purposes on his Grenadian plantations – to turn the sugar mills – but surrounded his house with pasture to evoke the feeling of an English estate.[63] Like Sir William, other slave-owning enclosers of land identified as polite improvers of their British estates. They saw their land management as stewardship, especially with respect to managing tenants and labourers. Estate improvement involved buying and intensively farming land, creating large farms, leasing land to new tenants and landscaping. The enclosure of this period, bound up in the agricultural revolution of the time, was characterized by new mechanized practices, and new approaches to crop rotation, husbandry and fertilizing.[64] A prominent figure in this activity at the time was Sir Thomas William Coke, known as Coke the Improver. Also the trustee of a Barbados plantation who claimed compensation for 325 enslaved people on behalf of family relatives,[65] he had water meadows constructed on the land around Holkham Hall in north Norfolk, creating a water management system for which he became a renowned agriculturalist.[66]

By the time Sir William took up residency at Earsham Hall, pastureland had become fashionable in landed society. Evoking tranquil scenes, the placid wellbeing of grazing livestock emitted a sense of rest, calm and plenty.[67] Pasture culture had been around for centuries, but now it gained new impetus, championed by, among others, the celebrated landscape designer Humphry Repton (who, among many other projects, had drawn up plans for Sezincote's redesign). Reflecting this craze for the pastoral, many images from the period depict livestock around local country houses.[68] An engraving of Sir William's Earsham estate, created while he lived at the Hall, reproduces this pastoral aesthetic, showing cattle grazing beside the house. But while cattle grazed beside Earsham Hall, in 1816 there were food riots across Norfolk, conflicts which reflected rising food prices and diminishing opportunities for people to grow their own food. For all the pastoral celebration of pastureland on Earsham estate, the enclosure of Outney Common by Sir William and his neighbours drastically reduced common pasture from 402 acres, in 1707, to 150 acres by 1842.[69] Enclosure was compounded by long working hours for low wages. By 1821, midway through Outney Common's enclosure, the population of the local workhouse – 'Shipmeadow', on the Beccles to Bungay Road – rose almost 150 per cent in just a decade.[70] In the 1820s, with jobs and wages threatened by mechanization, people rose up, destroying machines across Norfolk (and across the country). In 1822, a year of considerable unrest, there was machine-breaking in Bungay, Ditchingham and Woodton. Military assistance was requested from Norwich, and in Bungay, troops were attacked outside the Three Tuns pub. Protesters refused to leave until the riot act was read out.[71] In Attleborough, people brought an agricultural machine into the town centre, where they publicly destroyed it to music provided by an accompanying band; in nearby Shelfanger, a machine was thrown into a pond.[72] All in all, 123 local people were tried in East Anglian courts for their apparent roles in the 1822 disturbances. Sentences for such crimes varied wildly from modest fines to hard labour in the Australian penal colonies.[73] The penal colonies, I told Zakia, were the focus of my walk in Dorset.

We stopped to drink water. As we sat on a raised verge and talked, a hare careered down the furrows. We watched it race into the distance, exclaiming at its speed, its powerful hind legs and black-tipped ears. 'A sign of spring if ever there was one,' Zakia said. She explained that the hare was once seen as an otherworldly and mystical creature which embodies legends and old ancestral ways. Associated with the peasantry, these beliefs and outlooks were remote from the worldviews and lives of the landed gentry. Yet, Zakia suggested, looking down on folklore was also integral to the colonial mindset. 'Colonizers,' she said, 'saw the folklore of colonized people as backward and inferior.' As for enslaved people's religions, like *obeah* and *voodoo*, these were considered by imperialists as an active threat to the colonial project.

As we set off, we heard a cuckoo, a song that was once commonplace but is now relatively rare. This iconic bird, as we both knew, heralds the start of spring. As it happens, one of Zakia's favourite tunes is an English folk song called 'The Cuckoo'. When Zakia first heard the song, its otherworldly quality appealed to her instantly. In its dreamy way, it evoked and accessed the natural world. 'I was still at school,' she said, 'so I listened to the song secretly.' In the song, the cuckoo sucks sweet flowers to keep her voice clear, though it is also about infidelity and lost love. When I asked Zakia why she listened in secret, she said she was hyper-aware that it would seem incongruous with her cultural heritage, and even asked herself whether such music could belong to a woman of mixed heritage.

We talked about the way songs travel, are performed, shared, adapted and transformed: after all, Zakia remarked, 'sea shanties were carried across the Atlantic by sailors and translated into steel pan,' testifying to the call and response of cultures across time and space. And, of course, such exchanges travel in different directions. 'The Cuckoo' itself is a good example: there's an American version of the song when the cuckoo only calls on 4 July, Independence Day.

Long before our walk, Zakia has thought long and hard about how a woman of mixed heritage, like herself, can claim a sense of English rural belonging. She is therefore intrigued by the fact that, as in other largely rural counties, Norfolk has seen a continuous rural Black presence for centuries. In Norfolk's case this goes back to at least 1589, with the appearance of an African in Yarmouth whose name was simply given as 'John'.[74] In the early eighteenth century, Holkham Hall (later the home of Coke the Improver, who played a key role in developing farming techniques) had kept African servants, probably through the family's colonial associations with the Anson and Vernon families, well-known families with interests in the West Indies. One record of 1727, from papers belonging to Holkham Hall, refers to a servant known as 'Captain Uring's Black', which maps onto the voyages of the Norfolk sea captain Nathaniel Uring, sent by King George I to help colonize the Caribbean islands of St Lucia and St Vincent in 1722.[75] Uring, the son of Walsingham shopkeepers, wrote an account of his voyages, which shows him sailing the classic triangular trade route to West Africa, the Leeward Islands and Jamaica. Uring transported hogsheads of sugar on Atlantic vessels throughout that period, so was trading in goods produced by enslaved people.[76] He also wrote how, back in England, he shuttled between London and his native Norfolk – making it reasonably straightforward to work out how this Black servant, of whom no other information is known, reached Holkham Hall.

From the mid-eighteenth century onwards, there is a steady stream of evidence for the presence of Black people in East Anglia. In 1754, the owner of Garboldisham Hall, Crispin Molineux – himself born in St Kitts – came to England and settled in Norfolk, presumably bringing with him Black servants.[77] The Garboldisham records reveal several generations of Black people settling and marrying, their children growing up in the area. While the 'Three Blacks' mentioned in 1766 is not especially informative, it's possible that Charles Molineaux, a Black servant who was sixteen years old in 1777 (almost a quarter century after Crispin Molineux settled in Garboldisham) was himself born in Norfolk. So too, perhaps, was Mary Molineux who, described as 'a mulattoe', married a local man in 1791. Another married couple were Robert Taylor, 'a mulatto', and Mary Driver, a White woman, a couple who had six children, born between 1793 and 1810.[78] A few years earlier, in 1787, the parson of Weston Longville met a Black French-horn player, who told him about his previous occupations and dwelling places in the locale.[79] His itinerant wandering and music-making hints at the possibility that other Black locals had their own stories of adaptation and creativity.

By the mid-eighteenth century, too, Africans even lived on Bungay's Earsham estate. Among them was Barlow Fielding, 'a negro servant at Earsham Hall', his wife, the local butler's daughter, known as Ann, and their sons. A decade later, another Black servant, called John Fielding, worked at Earsham Hall: the historian Richard Maguire convincingly argues that many such servants may already have been local to Norfolk.[80] Indeed, there were Black presences in the region well before the Atlantic slave trade and even after it, and they often had no connections to slavery. Pablo Fanque, who lived between 1810 and 1871 (during Sir William's lifetime), is remembered on a blue plaque in Norwich. He was born in Norfolk to an African father and local White mother and owned a travelling circus which is referenced in the Beatles' song 'Being for the Benefit of Mr Kite!'. The lyrics include the lines: 'Late of Pablo Fanque's Fair, what a scene / Over men and horses hoops and garters / Lastly through a hogshead of real fire!'

We were both particularly heartened by the story of the Black horn-player. Zakia loved this glimpse of a man travelling around with his fellow musicians, a local person just getting on with his work. I agreed.

Norfolk had an old history of mixed-heritage people too, showing everyday relationships, people doing ordinary jobs and bringing up their children in these quiet places. Stopping for another drink of water, Zakia stood on a ridge and gazed at Outney Common.

This footpath had survived, yet many of the old footpaths are still blocked off and remain inaccessible to all but landowners. This is enclosure's legacy around Bungay and Earsham, and indeed in rural places throughout Britain. Many wonderful writers lament the land privatization which restricts our access to nature – from Roger Deakin's *Waterlog: A Swimmer's Journey Through Britain* to Nick Hayes' *The Book of Trespass: Crossing the Lines That Divide Us.*[81] Yet, Zakia and I agreed, the enclosure history of places like Bungay provides an additional layer to the analysis of Deakin and Hayes: transatlantic slavery forms the hidden backdrop to the more familiar theme of enclosure's ills. Few ever blame slave-ownership for our legally sanctioned exclusion from Britain's old footpaths, woodlands and waterways today. 'The link is far from obvious,' Zakia said.

We stood on high ground beside a (private) golf course looking down onto the lowlands of Waveney Valley, where cattle grazed: a classic pastoral scene. We could see why the villagers of Bungay and Earsham must have resented losing their commoners' rights, not just because it deprived them of necessities such as free pasture and firewood, but also because of Outney Common's serene, dreamlike quality. The spindly aspens and waterways below looked like a scene out of a John Constable painting. Outney Common was way north of 'Constable Country', but it felt tailor-made for the painter – even more so, Zakia remarked, because Constable was the son of a miller and nearby Earsham village grew up around its mill. He painted everyday people engaged in agricultural tasks. We looked out across the pastureland: the woad-blue sky, the puffy clouds, the river's gleam.

Yet, as I told Zakia, Constable wasn't isolated from the wider world. He had family connections to the East India Company, sailed on a company ship and painted scenes on board. After he died, his iconic paintings later became integral to Britain's colonial education system too; Constable's works were reproduced in Caribbean school textbooks. The Trinidadian author V. S. Naipaul recalled studying the painter at school, making England's beech-lined water-meadows seem uncannily familiar to him when he visited them as an adult.[82]

These reflections on Constable made me remember another local artist I'd read about from Banham, 20 miles west of Outney Common. His name was Edward Thomas Daniell, a clergyman. Daniell's father was the attorney general of Dominica, who died in 1806 and left his wife a Dominican estate, together with £2,000 and 100 enslaved people, to be passed on to his son, Edward Thomas, then still a toddler.[83] Edward Thomas' painting of Back River in Norwich resembles Constable's limited palette of blues and greens. The sky is milky calm, and a river runs through lush meadows where shining beeches create languid reflections.[84] The painting is of Norwich, but it could just as easily have been of Outney Common because it conveys the same feeling. Paintings like these are part and parcel of the aesthetic branding of Englishness, so it can be disconcerting to learn that even these artists had a colonial dimension.

And so our view over Outney Common was disturbed, as though the paint had cracked and the canvas gaped through.

It was late afternoon. Leaving Outney Common behind, we walked along Angles Way towards Ditchingham village. Here the old path sinks into the earth, worn down by centuries of use: shoes, hooves, cartwheels. Soon, we found ourselves in meadows. The wind had picked up and the swishing trees, meadow scents and waterways were, Zakia said, like a balm to the soul. All around us were rivers and water-filled ditches. As we passed through the landscape, I felt I had a sense of Zakia's approach to loving such places. She's managed to carry them close to her heart, she explained, by concentrating on the unique histories and ecologies of rivers and hills. The land, she said, is older than people, older than the empire, older than books. It does not discriminate or judge, but simply lives, breathes and nurtures. Nature's character, as Zakia sees it, is the opposite to the colonial figures who altered the course of British rural history.

We passed Ditchingham House, the former home of Henry Rider Haggard, born in 1856. His story, as I mentioned to Zakia, is yet another local illustration of the forgotten link between colonial rule and British agricultural history.[85] The first part of Haggard's adult life was spent as registrar of the High Court of Transvaal and he is primarily remembered for authoring *King Solomon's Mines*, a colonial adventure tale published in 1885. This Victorian tale journeys into 'darkest barbarism', as the protagonist Allan Quatermain calls it, where the South African landscape is overtly represented as a female body awaiting conquest and possession.[86]

Returning to England, he and his wife eventually settled in Ditchingham, where he entered the world of agricultural reform. He farmed his own Norfolk estate and produced *Rural England*, a thousand-page survey for policy-makers and reformers, which detailed agricultural challenges in twenty-seven counties at the turn of the twentieth century. In this, and in his other agricultural writing, he focused on the benefits of working the land, which he saw as a solution to poverty and urban ills. He felt, though, that British land reform should be considered in tandem with settlement policies in the British Empire.[87] Haggard set out some of these ideas in a report, which led the colonial secretary to establish a committee to consider the author's proposals.[88] Workhouses and poor-relief schemes were not advisable, Haggard felt, perhaps thinking of Shipmeadow workhouse between Bungay and Beccles. He proposed emigration by impoverished Britons to Canada and Australia to cultivate land in the colonies as an additional solution and as part of people's patriotic duty to create a Greater Britain, meaning that its territories expanded across the world.[89]

Haggard's pastoralism resonated with eugenicist ideals of racial purity. He drew on established ideas about the countryside which juxtaposed the unvirtuous city with the 'virtuous' countryside, addressing contemporary fears about urban racial intermixing by emphasizing the countryside's invigorating and purifying quality. Haggard even referred to rural Britain as 'the nursery of our race'. Haggard's ideas moved away from the old dominance of aristocratic estates, instead advocating a social order composed of farming land-owners, yeomen and smallholders.[90]

We admired Ditchingham's cottages, painted in cheerful pinks and blues. The bells of the village church were pealing. Called St Mary's, the church has a lofty fifteenth-century tower, one of the tallest in Norfolk.

We glanced at our watches. The walk felt about the right length, certainly in this pleasant weather. Bungay and Ditchingham were a tiny distance apart, so we soon found ourselves back at our starting point. Meanwhile, as we'd seen in this small corner of East Anglia, the connection between colonizing countries and enclosing land was now plain enough, though they were by no means equivalent processes. Zakia pointed out that words like *settle* and *enclose* might sound benign, but they have disturbing resonances.

As we climbed up the sloping main street into Bungay we chatted about the cuckoo we'd heard and the hare we'd seen. At the top of the street we peeped into windows, a sweet shop, a hardware store, a wholefood supermarket. 'We're in plenty of time for the bus after all,' Zakia said. We slowed our pace. I'd enjoyed the day's conversation and valued Zakia's unique perspective on things. Since our walk had taken place in the midst of Britain's history wars, she'd simply commented that we should avoid narrow nationalisms by deepening our knowledge of local history whilst fostering global perspectives, not just on history but on climate change.

The bus was dead on time. The fields around us were hedged, clipped and ordered, but the hedgerows were alive: history bursts forth like a vigorous hare that refuses to be contained.

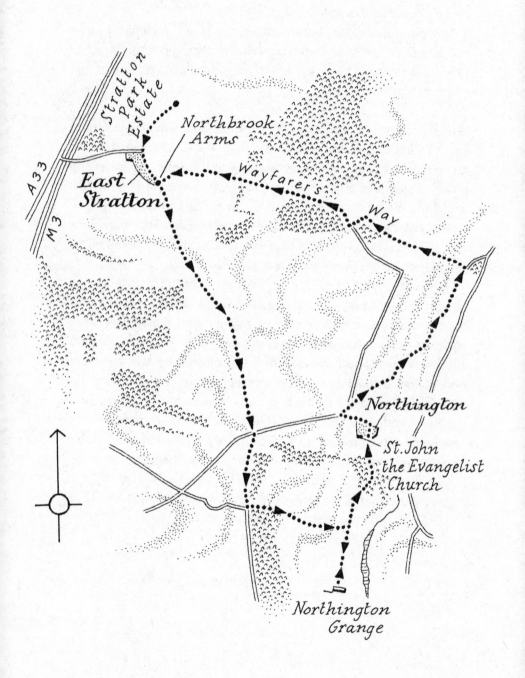

Stratton Park Estate

A33

M3

East Stratton

Northbrook Arms

Wayfarers Way

Northington

St. John the Evangelist Church

Northington Grange

8.

The Bankers' Walk: Hampshire and Louisiana

The English county of Hampshire links south-east England with the West Country. Lying between West Sussex and Dorset on the Channel coast, Hampshire is bordered by the home counties of Berkshire and Surrey to the north and east and Wiltshire further west. The rolling chalk hills that stretch through England's south-east continue here, with 3,000 miles of footpaths crossing its downs, scarps and vales. These paths run through the national parks of the South Downs and New Forest. With its woods and pasture, the latter endures as one of the largest areas of common land (whose name, famously, refers to its 'new' creation by William the Conqueror as a royal hunting forest, in the decades after he seized the English throne). In Hampshire, England's far older histories of human habitation are evinced by Bronze Age farmsteads, Iron Age hillforts and Roman settlements.

This walk would begin a few miles north of Winchester, in a bucolic village called East Stratton, and continue through a succession of villages and hamlets encircling Stratton Park, an estate once home to the powerful Baring family. At the turn of the nineteenth century, the wealthy banker Sir Francis Baring – founder of the eponymous bank – acquired a baronetcy, the Stratton Park estate, and (following a pattern that you might now find familiar) set about converting himself into an English country gentleman. With ambitions to create what he called 'the kingdom of Stratton', he had the original house rebuilt in the neoclassical style favoured by the age, and its 1,000-acre grounds were designed by the celebrated landscape gardener Humphry Repton.[1] An 1809 etching of Stratton Park conveys a similar pastoral feel to artistic images of Sir

William Dalling's Earsham Park near Bungay; the etching of Sir Francis' property shows cattle chewing the cud with sheep grazing in the foreground. The pastoral theme continues in an 1820 aquatint of Stratton Park by the German artist Rudolph Ackermann, in which cattle graze at the front of the house, with a flock of sheep behind.[2]

Barings Bank was founded in 1762 by three sons of John Baring, a Bremen wool merchant who'd settled in the West Country city of Exeter. The bank was led by Sir Francis and, from the early nineteenth century, his son Sir Alexander.[3] By this time, Baring Brothers and Co., as it was then named, was the most powerful merchant bank in Europe. Specializing in international trade and loaning money to states, corporations and wealthy individuals, it was known as 'the sixth great European power', the other five being the nations of Britain, France, Austria-Hungary, Russia and Prussia.[4] If, today, Barings Bank jogs your memory, it may be because of its collapse in 1995, when fraudulent investments by a rogue trader called Nick Leeson lost £827 million of the bank's money.

In the luxuriant tapestry of Barings Bank are knotted threads which lead to Senegambia, an ancient region between the Senegal and Gambia rivers, from where enslaved people were trafficked across the Atlantic to Louisiana. Barings helped finance the slavery system in Louisiana: Sir Alexander Baring negotiated, financed and profited from the Louisiana Purchase of 1803, the world's largest ever land purchase, which allowed the slavery system to develop in the American South. The merchant bank also lent money to Louisiana plantation-owners and, by 1833, a quarter of its income came from cotton produced by enslaved people.[5]

These historical connections – between Senegal, Louisiana and Hampshire – led me to invite Ibrahima Seck to walk with me through the lush green Hampshire haunts of the Baring banking dynasty. Originally from Dakar in Senegal, he works as a curator and senior researcher at Whitney Plantation on the west bank of the Mississippi River. For years, Ibrahima scrutinized Louisiana archives to find the stories of the enslaved people whose labour made the Barings and their peers so rich. He examined wills, baptism, burial and court records, sales documents, leases, inventories, debt records, death reports, travel accounts, newspapers, diaries and interviews done back in the 1930s with the direct descendants of formerly enslaved people in Louisiana. What Ibrahima discovered reawakened awareness of the Afro-Louisiana connection in his home country. It also set in motion the development of an old Louisiana estate called Whitney Plantation as a museum which focuses on the lives of enslaved people rather than on the enslavers who lived there. Whereas other former plantations in the American South host weddings and celebrate plantation house architecture and opulent lifestyles, Whitney Plantation centres the experience of enslavement.[6]

Walking with Ibrahima through Barings country in Hampshire would enable us to join three points of an historical triangle. The first two points are Senegal's enslavement story and Louisiana's plantation story. The third concerns the Hampshire-based bankers whose lending enabled Louisiana's plantation system.

Ibrahima made the long journey from Louisiana to join me in Hampshire. At the end of an unseasonably warm September, we found ourselves standing on the green at East Stratton in the mid-morning sun, surrounded by a village of mellow brick and photogenic thatch: a quintessential English scene. Ibrahima was used to very hot weather, so he wore a winter jacket and had no intention of taking it off. Apart from two women heaving huge laundry bags out of the bed-and-breakfast next to the Northbrook Arms pub, there was no one around. Ibrahima gestured sweepingly at the village. 'So no one is coming out to ask us who we are and why we are here? It must be the English way,' he smiled.

Unfolding an Ordnance Survey map, I traced the walking route for Ibrahima. Here we were, I showed him: East Stratton village lies at the edge of Stratton Park, Sir Francis Baring's expansive estate. We'd head there first, then backtrack along lanes to footpaths leading to the meadows of Northington Grange, where Sir Francis' son

Alexander Baring, following his father's example, converted an existing seventeenth-century house into a similarly splendid home.

Ibrahima bent over the map, all 6 foot 2 of him, dressed in blue with a checked shirt, navy cap and tie-dyed indigo scarf. 'How far are were walking?' he asked. 'Just under 8 miles,' I replied, to which he let out a mock gasp: 'You're going to kill me! I normally drive everywhere!' I laughed and said that, though the road surface can be hard on the feet, we'd be treading soft footpaths for the second half of the walk. He nodded. 'I am ready.'

In front of us was a row of identical thatched cottages, designed by the architect Charles Dance for Sir Francis Baring after he bought Stratton Park in 1801. Banking wealth – including slavery profits – was commonly used for philanthropic purposes in villages like these, producing model cottages for village workers. An information board on the green explained that East Stratton remains an 'estate village' to the present day. Over a century before Sir Francis Baring bought the estate, a previous owner, William Lord Russell, had part of the village pulled down and its inhabitants relocated; the land was enclosed and incorporated into his deer park. (Russell was keen that his house be surrounded by 'wildernesses': villagers were not part of this scene.)

We set off through the village beside the cottages. Fascinated by the thatched roofs, Ibrahima stopped to inspect the packed, trimmed straw, held in place by netting. One cottage, covered in scaffolding, was having its roof redone. A van was parked beside it with the words 'Jack the Thatcher' painted on its side. Fresh straw was heaped on the scaffolding boards, and a man was hard at work on the roof. Ibrahima strolled over and shouted up: 'Are you Jack the Thatcher?' 'Yes,' the man smiled. 'It's a messy business, thatching.' Ibrahima praised his work: 'You should come and do some of our African village huts!' Laughing, Ibrahima and Jack exchanged goodbyes, and we walked on towards the ruins of Stratton Park.

Soon, we were out of the villages, ambling along Embley Wood Lane. 'And is there still a wood?' Ibrahima asked. As if in reply, trees soon spread out to our left, arable fields climbing the slopes to our right. As we walked, a shotgun popped and echoed close to the lane. A deer leaped through the hedge directly in front of us, followed by another, and another: we counted fourteen in total. Round hooves drummed the asphalt and then, springing into a field, the herd was gone, as though we had imagined it. Ibrahima was struck by their size – 'There is plenty to feed them around here,' he observed – and was equally impressed by their powers of concealment.

A lane swung off to the right, and the trees thinned out to reveal the old pleasure grounds of Stratton Park (now privately owned). We couldn't go near it, but, thanks to a footpath which skirts the old estate, we could view the house from afar. Today, the only visible remains of Sir Francis Baring's neoclassical pile is the pillared portico, which stands, Ozymandias-style, in the grounds. Knocked down in the early 1960s by his descendant John Baring – whose predilection for demolishing historic buildings earned him the nickname 'Basher' – his impressive mansion was replaced by a modernist house that now shows distinct signs of dilapidation. You'd imagine that Sir Francis, with his stately pretensions, wouldn't have been impressed. We considered the old portico from afar. 'So Francis Baring liked the Greek style,' Ibrahima pondered, 'just like the original plantation-owners in Louisiana.' He stood there for some minutes, lost in thought. A faint breeze stirred the surrounding trees.

The portico was built in 1803, I told Ibrahima – to which he replied instantly, 'The year of the Louisiana Purchase.' I nodded, wondering if the house and grounds were commissioned in anticipation of the profits made by Barings Bank on that eye-wateringly vast land sale. 'The money would have come in handy for the furnishings and fittings at the very least,' I said. We eyed the distant ruin across a shorn wheatfield. As we both knew, it was not Sir Francis but his second son, Alexander, who took Barings to international prominence by managing the Louisiana Purchase, though his father and his banking partners shared in the profits. Alexander had been educated in Europe and the United States, and his experience of life in America, in Massachusetts and Maine, between 1795 and 1801, was key to his banking vision.[7] In 1796, he married Anna Louisa, daughter of William Bingham, an exceptionally wealthy senator who traded in tobacco, molasses and enslaved people. The marriage made Baring even richer: following the marriage settlement of £20,000, a further third of his father-in-law's gigantic estate came to Alexander through his wife's inheritance when Bingham died in 1804.[8]

By then, Alexander Baring had already bought – on behalf of his bank – over a million acres of Maine from Bingham. He was aware of some land struggles associated with this sale. He acknowledged that there were objections to the sale by 'Indian tribes' with a prior claim: for Baring, however, this was not a matter of conscience but a potential risk to be factored into the sale. (He considered the risk to be low.) What particularly excited him was the potential profit from financing – rather than actually buying – land of this nature, noting that a single purchase of 20 million acres elsewhere in the United States had recently brought a $25,000 commission to the lender.[9] For bankers, he knew, land speculation reaped great financial rewards.

The Maine transaction was a dry run for Alexander Baring's financing of the Louisiana Purchase, a sale which doubled the land mass of America. In it, the nascent United States bought from France a vast swathe of land. Extending from the Gulf of Mexico to Rupert's Land (around the Hudson Bay drainage basin which extends across Montana, the Dakotas and Minnesota) and from the Mississippi River to the Rocky Mountains, it encompassed an area covering a million square miles, two Canadian provinces and no fewer than fifteen present-day US states.[10] Emperor Napoleon Bonaparte wanted to sell, and President Thomas Jefferson wanted to buy. Key to Jefferson's plan was the port of New Orleans, which the French had occupied two years previously, and which steamboats had made into America's second-biggest port (after New York).[11]

Alexander Baring's connections positioned him perfectly to arrange the Louisiana Purchase. Through him, the bank worked its way up to becoming the American government's official London banker. Alexander managed the negotiation in Paris, bargaining down the sale price, overseeing the shipping of gold to France, and the sale of US government bonds (on the handling of which the Barings and their partner, Hopes, made a vast profit). The US general Horatio Gates later congratulated Jefferson for ridding America of European dominance and buying Louisiana 'for a song': $15 million.[12] The Louisiana Purchase massively boosted US cotton and sugar cultivation, and, in consequence, slavery was vastly extended across the lands which had been newly acquired from France.

The Louisiana Purchase turned these former lands from a French colony with relatively minor slave-trading ports to a major sugar and cotton-growing region. Between 1810 and 1860, some 280,000 enslaved people were transported from other states such as Virginia to work on its plantations, since buying enslaved workers from outside America had been illegal since the 1807 Act Prohibiting Importing Slaves.[13]

For Barings Bank, the Louisiana Purchase brought a financial bonanza. The bank subsequently facilitated the transportation and sale of cotton which was planted, tended and picked by enslaved people in Louisiana, and extended loans to plantation owners.[14] One such was the £6,000 loan to the New Orleans cotton planter Vincent Nolte so he could buy land, start a cotton export house and build a warehouse. Some years later, in 1820, Sir Francis' grandson and namesake visited Nolte in New Orleans – 45 miles from Whitney Plantation – and noted with pride the 'cotton bales on which were stamped the marks of my firm'.[15] In 1828, Sir Francis' other grandson, Thomas Baring, sailed to New Orleans to arrange a loan with the Planters' Association of Louisiana, receiving $285,000 of bonds in return. Thomas Baring, too, was closely involved with discussions about Louisiana plantation management.[16] Though Whitney Plantation itself was not financed by Barings Bank, the

Louisiana plantation economy of which it was an integral part relied on loans like these to thrive. Barings Bank would go on to finance cotton's transportation to Lancashire mills, establishing a commercial Liverpool hub which bolstered the merchant bank's success.[17]

Before the walk, I'd shown Ibrahima the 1820 etching, by Rudolph Ackermann, of Stratton Park, with its pastureland and grazing sheep. Now we were at the edge of the parkland, I asked whether he thought the estate resembled that old etching. The sun was now directly overhead, and Ibrahima shielded his eyes with his arm to look out over the scene. 'That portico is still white,' he observed, 'but dirty,' and I noticed that a pillar was missing from the right-hand side of the structure. 'And,' Ibrahima added, 'the trees were small in the etching, and now look at them!' He gestured towards the giant trees dominating the portico.

Barings Bank earned around $1 million in commission from the Louisiana Purchase, at least $26 million in today's money.[18] The banking partners each got a share of the profits. That year's account books of Sir Francis suggest that the land sale profits helped furnish a lavish lifestyle at Stratton Park, which had an exceptionally grand interior, including an enormous library. In 1803, Sir Francis spent £2,000 on jewels, £6,000 on furniture and £15,000 on works of art.[19]

Stepping back onto Embley Wood Lane, we doubled back to East Stratton, then took the path towards Northington Grange, which was acquired in 1817 by Sir Francis Baring's exceptionally wealthy son Alexander. (During the War of 1812, Alexander Baring supplemented his wealth with $200,000 of US government bonds as security on a $16 million loan to the US government. In Britain, there was uproar: *The Times* newspaper accused Baring of supplying dollars to men who were cutting English throats. But the Barings, it seemed, were by now too big to fail.) Northington Grange was only a 3-mile carriage ride from his father's Stratton estate: appropriately so, given how closely the banking family worked together.

Walking up Stratton Lane, and passing a narrow way to our right called Baring Close, we found ourselves in a landscape of newly ploughed and hedged fields. Ibrahima nodded appreciatively: 'Fertile brown earth. It's too easy to grow food here.' Back in Senegal, he added, the soils were relatively dry and barren. We passed some sheep on our left, and he joked that I should send him some British lambs to graze in a Senegalese village where he plans to retire, a place north of Dakar called Djilor. 'Those lambs will start out nice and fat,' he went on, 'but after a week in my country they'll be thin!'

The fields around us were indeed luxuriant. 'They grow watercress near here,' I said, because chalk streams trickle through fields of the peppery, nutrient-rich plants. Watercress was an ancient crop: grown in the county since Roman times, it was cultivated commercially in Sir Alexander Baring's day, and, picked from the surrounding streams, formed part of the local diet.[20]

Ahead of us, a mouse weaved back and forth along the lane. As we watched it disappear into the verge, we caught sight of a hare grooming itself just yards ahead, unconscious of our presence until an approaching car disturbed it.

Further on, we came across a woman with her eyes fixed on the road. Ibrahima asked her what she was doing. It was mating season for frogs, the woman told us, and she was trying to rescue these vulnerable creatures from the path of passing vehicles as they headed to their mating grounds (with, so the evidence showed, only partial success). 'What kind of frogs are these?' Ibrahima asked, pointing to one of the flattened victims. 'Common frogs,' she replied, 'now increasingly *uncommon*.' Leaving the woman behind, we reached a T-junction and located our turnoff, a footpath almost obscured by undergrowth. With the sun hot, we followed our footpath and entered the shade of some ferny woods with some relief. Our track passed between beech trees beside high walls and forbidding 'Private, Do Not Enter' signs, then, it opened out into a wide field which gave a fine view of an impressive church tower. 'That's St John the Evangelist, a Baring church,' I said. 'We'll reach that later on.' Ibrahima pointed at the furrows and asked what they grew there. 'Rapeseed,' I told him, that lurid yellow summer crop which has become so familiar all over Britain.

As we walked over the ploughed earth, I asked Ibrahima how he came to research Whitney Plantation. 'I was a teacher in Dakar,' he recalled, 'then I went on an exchange visit to New Orleans.' There, he'd heard an old Delta Blues singer and felt an immediate resonance with the music of his homeland. Wanting to know more, he attended a talk about the West African origins of enslaved people in Louisiana. The topic gripped him and, back home, he enrolled for a PhD. 'My mother wanted me to be a doctor,' he joked, 'just not that kind of doctor.' He told me that his PhD had explored African cultures and slavery in the lower Mississippi valley. 'I've divided my time between Whitney Plantation in the United States and Senegal ever since,' he said. For part of the year, he teaches history at the University of Dakar.

What particularly intrigued me was how Ibrahima became involved with Whitney Plantation after having researched it. He explained how, back in 1999, a trial attorney from New Orleans named John Cummings bought Whitney with the aim of turning it into a piece of lucrative real estate. With Ibrahima's help, local protesters persuaded the landowner to think again and, learning about the site's historical significance, Cummings realized what his own education had never taught him. The museum was born.

Ibrahima's research was instrumental to the painstaking restoration of the plantation, which is designed to show that slavery's legacy is – he said as we turned out of the field, following the footpath onward to Northington Grange – 'not only one of racism, suffering and poverty but also of names, relationships and a burgeoning culture.' A key element of Ibrahima's work is telling the stories of ordinary enslaved people. Heroic figures like the abolitionists Frederick Douglass or Harriet Tubman, who rescued so many people from slavery, are both inspiring and familiar but, Ibrahima believes, it's equally important to research the unexceptional experiences of those who neither made bids for freedom nor learned to read and write. This philosophy lies at the heart of the plantation's educational policy.[21] 'And,' he continued, 'enslaved people transformed Louisiana. You can see their influence everywhere, from cooking to music,' especially, he said, the Africanized musical forms of jazz, blues and rock and roll. 'New Orleans in particular was changed for ever by enslaved people and their descendants.'

As we approached the Grange, Ibrahima explained that Whitney Plantation was originally bought by Ambroise Heidel, a German immigrant in the 1720s, when many German labourers and artisans were settling in the territories of the Taensa people, an area on the east bank of the Mississippi River that became known as the German Coast.[22] When Heidel first arrived with his mother and siblings, there were insufficient crops to feed the colonists and a real risk of starvation. Searching for a reliable crop, the colonists in Louisiana introduced West African rice to the region. Seedlings from Senegambia were transported to Louisiana, along with 570 Senegalese who knew how to cultivate them: in this way, rice crops were successfully established to feed people like Ambroise Heidel and his family. 'This was a transfer of knowledge from Senegambia to Louisiana,' Ibrahima told me, 'those Africans established a reliable food supply, enabled the mass cultivation of cash crops.' Plantations like Whitney, he explained, could only be established in this food-secure environment.[23] Ibrahima pointed to the tie-dyed scarf around his neck. 'Heydel's chief crop was indigo at first,' he said. 'Processing the plant into dye relied on West African expertise.' (Most slave-ships came from the two main indigo-growing regions of Senegambia and the Bight of Benin, whose peoples held ancient knowledge of how to process indigo.)[24] But, in the last decades of the century, the indigo trade was undercut by competition from India and collapsed. As a result, the Heidel plantation switched to sugar production.[25] By the early nineteenth century, the plantation was a leading sugar producer, with sugar mills, a granary, a handsome mansion – and huts for the enslaved.

Reaching an avenue of giant limes and fir trees that marked the entrance to the Grange estate, and now around halfway through our walk, we decided it was high time for lunch. 'How are your feet?' I asked Ibrahima. 'They are dead!' he exclaimed.

When Sir Alexander Baring bought Northington Grange in 1817, the house had recently been done up in the most fashionable of styles by its previous owner, the banker Henry Drummond (who wanted to outdo his neighbour over at Stratton Park). The architect William Wilkins, then fresh from designing East India College in Hertfordshire – a school for future East India Company employees – rebuilt Northington as a Greek Temple. Today, having narrowly survived the attentions of their descendant, 'Basher' Baring, the house is managed by English Heritage.[26]

We could not enter the house, as it is kept locked up, but, finding ourselves alone in the grounds, we went in search of a picnic spot. A grassy slope met a long and narrow ornamental lake which shimmered in the sunlight; a swan swam serenely across it. This whole scene – meadow in the foreground, ribbon lake and pasture beyond – had been carefully designed for Alexander Baring, who lavished money on the estate:[27] in 1823, he contracted the architect Charles Robert Cockerell, the son of Samuel Pepys Cockerell, to landscape the grounds. (This was the same Cockerell family which had transformed the Cotswold manor of Sezincote into a Mughal palace.) The grounds were planted with cedars of Lebanon and mixed deciduous trees. They were landscaped with terraces which dropped towards the river below the house. Water features were introduced, with a fountain and two narrow lakes (Ibrahima and I could only see one) which extend along the entire valley, flowing southwards from the main driveway for over a mile. The lakes are separated by a dam and a waterfall, and are spanned by bridges with parapets of brick and flint. Between the lakes, Sir Alexander had a two-storey folly built, a crenelated tower finished in flint and, today, covered in moss.[28] Cockerell considered Northington Grange to be as close to Arcadia as any earthly place – and this was more than just flattering his wealthy client (and, by association, himself).[29]

But the place was eerie. The meadow was studded with

oversized daisies, their white petals quivering in the light wind, their yellow carpels seeming to stare at us. Absent presences, it seemed, spoke in whispers: leaves rustled from the surrounding copses for the duration of our visit. On rising ground, the house dominates its grounds. Its triangular portico has eight giant, round pillars and the neoclassical theme continues along the sides of the building with plain, square pillars. Ibrahima went very quiet. Finally, he said, 'So this fine estate is connected to Louisianan people.' He wanted to walk around the house, he said. I took out our sandwiches while he did a circuit of the Grange. The house's massive structure resembled a stone forest which dwarfed Ibrahima as he passed beneath it.

Alexander Baring also commissioned Cockerell to add a massive conservatory to the house, which was subsequently filled with Asian plant species. (Much of it built offsite in Birmingham, the conservatory is one of the earliest examples of prefabrication.) Cockerell also designed Alexander Baring's Greek revival drawing room. Based on a real Grecian temple, it was designed to convey Baring's scholarly credentials.

The Grange was just one of Alexander Baring's many countryside purchases.[30] Boosted by his wife's inheritance and his commission from the Louisiana Purchase, he bought no fewer than three estates in southern England – in Hampshire and Ashburton in Devon and Buckenham Tofts in Norfolk – and also had a London property in Piccadilly. But that portion of the Barings' wealth which came from slavery didn't just come from Louisiana. The Barings Archive, near Moorgate in central London, holds a colonial ledger, a narrow accounting book from 1803, where the pages need to be turned slowly as they are ruffled with age. An inch thick, the ledger details the slavery system's importance to banking profits. The financial transactions recorded in the colonial ledger in turn show that there were many clients in Jamaica who were shipping products like coffee and sugar and rum from their plantations, which included (among many others) the Bogue estate, the Windsor estate, Success estate and Dunkley estate alongside many others.[31]

Having circled the house, Ibrahima returned to the meadow. We ate then cleared up our picnic things and lingered in the sun for a while, drinking in the landscaped Arcadia. Finally, we got to our feet: the afternoon was now getting on, and we had footpaths to find. As we left the grounds along the elegant gravel drive, Ibrahima told me that, though he appreciated the beauty of the place, he was glad to leave: the estate's associations with the slavery business, he said, made him feel uneasy.

Ibrahima's comments echoed those of a much earlier visitor to the area. During the 1820s, the radical campaigner William Cobbett rode through England observing rural life at first hand: he wrote up these observations in *Rural Rides*, the book that brought him lasting fame.[32] In Hampshire, he wrote, newly enriched families now dominated rural affairs. The Barings in particular had 'swallowed up' small farmers and the local gentry.[33] East Stratton village and the hamlets round about now lay within the bounds of the Stratton Park estate, while Northington Grange covered a quarter of Itchen Stoke and Ovington parish. Cobbett saw this Baring dominance in the planting and landscaping of Sir Alexander's grounds, writing how the imported trees – those towering cedars of Lebanon – were as oversized as Baring's funds. He felt that they ruined the estate's natural beauty, representing the worst excesses of colonial wealth. (Today, you feel, Cobbett would hate it even more, given the mature cedars and limes that dominate the drive and the lake.) Suspicious of foreign wealth, Cobbett lamented the way in which colonial profits were reshaping the social order: they had displaced 'old' families at both the Grange and Stratton Park, even if those families were no great loss to many locals (it was, after all, Lord Russell – not Francis Baring – who had demolished part of East Stratton village to extend his deer park).[34] The profits of empire had 'flooded the countryside', he concluded, appalled: this new wealth 'brought in on the back of African and Indian labour, was the same money that partitioned English commoners from their livelihoods and land'.[35]

Cobbett's position was not straightforwardly subversive: he was suspicious of anti-slavery campaigners because he felt that they worried more about slavery overseas than poverty on their door-steps.[36] Nonetheless, his acute mind joined the dots between the activities of rich merchant bankers abroad and at home, and their use of colonial wealth to buy up the countryside and preside over rural affairs. In this, too, *Rural Rides* is notably critical of the Barings, among them Alexander's older brother Thomas, who had inherited Stratton Park from their father Sir Francis. Noting that Thomas Baring had put his name to a magistrate's judgement for a reduc-tion in local poor relief, Cobbett commented on Sir Thomas' hypocrisy: he had a local subscription to an association (the Consti-tutional Association), focused on opposing civil liberties, which aimed to prevent – in the words of its founders – 'the daily weaken-ing of the bonds of union between the humbler ranks of society and their natural guardians and protectors',[37] these 'natural' leaders supposedly being people like the Barings. According to him, Thomas Baring's subscription to the Constitutional Association amounted to a labourer's annual wage.[38]

During the first decades of the nineteenth century, as Louisi-ana's sugar trade boomed, Alexander Baring's career went from strength to strength. As a politician, he was suspicious of demands for wider political enfranchisement. After the infamous Peterloo massacre of 1819, in which fifteen peaceful campaigners for parlia-mentary reform were killed when cavalry charged at a crowd of thousands, Baring sided with the politicians and landowners by saying that their use of force was justified. Linking property own-ership to voting rights, he pronounced, maintained social order – although, he added, politicians ought to consider the needs of impoverished people since they did not have a vote. William Cobbett, who had criticized Baring's overly tall trees in *Rural Rides*, was unconvinced by this patrician expression of concern for those in poverty: Baring, he wrote, was a 'loan-monger' who lent money to oppressive figures and who opposed anyone who stood up for working people.[39]

Indeed, standing up in parliament, his brother Sir Alexander had stated that reports of widespread poverty among agricultural labourers were exaggerated, even claiming that Hampshire was free of protesting labourers. By this time Hampshire was a centre of both rural poverty and rural protest. In the summer of 1830, workers throughout southern and eastern England, worried about poor working conditions, declining wages and the mechanization of agricultural work, rose up. Landowners and farmers received threatening letters, ordering them to destroy their threshing machines – and, if they refused, the workers would do the job themselves. Many of these letters were signed 'Captain Swing', the name of the protest movement's fictional figurehead. The first attacks took place in Kent and spread swiftly – though Baring at first professed himself unconcerned by the 'Swing Riots', as they became known. As winter drew in, cold and hunger fuelled the anger of agricultural labourers who destroyed three barns at Barton Stacey, about 10 miles from Alexander Baring's Northington estate. The trouble came closer. Seven hundred labourers damaged threshing machines in nearby Micheldever.[40] Then, on 19 November that year, Northington Grange itself was attacked by 250 protesters. While events remain shadowy and little architectural damage was sustained, Baring was apparently present, and his safety was reportedly threatened. The culprits were dealt with severely by the Duke of Wellington, then Hampshire's lord lieutenant.[41] Baring himself doubled down, backing the 1834 Poor Law Amendment Act, which decreed – after the theory of Thomas Malthus – that poverty was best solved through emigration to the colonies, and that poor relief should be reserved for older people. In effect, the Act stipulated, if you were poor you should emigrate, accept lower wages or go to the workhouse.[42]

Alexander Baring's wealth was indeed, in Cobbett's words, obtained on the back of African labour. During these years of relative repose at Northington Grange, Sir Alexander continued his Louisiana association, financing Louisiana banks: as a banker for banks, he helped operationalize the slavery system. In just one year,

1832, he sold over £1 million of stock for the Union Bank of Louisiana and in 1834 lent £6,500 to the Consolidated Association of the Planters of Louisiana. These were years in which enslaved people were transported to Louisiana from other states, many of whom were involved in the backbreaking practice of planting sugar cane and cotton.[43] Harriet Beecher Stowe immortalized the phrase 'sold down the river' in *Uncle Tom's Cabin,* referring to this internal transportation of enslaved people to work on plantations in the American South.[44] Sugar was a major Louisiana cash crop, and planting began in January and February; harvesting took place between October and December. Enslaved people spent the intervening months collecting wood and maintaining drainage canals and dams: essential maintenance to prevent flooding by the great Mississippi. After harvesting came the sugar processing. First, canes were crushed by cogs with brass rods, a hazardous process in which enslaved people risked losing a limb as they fed cane into the rollers. Sugar was boiled in open cauldrons of different sizes and the scalding liquid transferred to copper coolers using long copper ladles.

Sugar, not cotton, became the main crop at Whitney Plantation. What struck me most about my conversation with Ibrahima about Whitney Plantation was his sense of his own past and his own calling. 'When I'm at the Louisianan plantation,' he told me as we walked towards the church where the family of Alexander Baring once worshipped, 'I feel my ancestors close by.' When I pressed him on this, he said, 'None of this happened by chance, you know. Sometimes I think about it beyond science: I feel like I was elected, I was put on a mission by the ancestors.' This feeling drove him on, giving him the persistence to accomplish everything that he did at Whitney. It took fourteen years before the museum eventually opened. The displays and memorials there aim to recover Louisiana's human stories amid the economic details. When I thought about how this had all begun – with Ibrahima recognizing the strains of Senegalese music in a piece of blues music, I couldn't help marvelling that he could hear all this in a single song.

Ibrahima told me how, inspired by oral histories collected by an

African American named Robert McKinney in the 1930s, he studied the experiences of enslaved people who escaped Louisiana plantations, called – as in the West Indies – maroons (from the French *marron*, originally meaning 'feral' or 'fugitive'). In Louisiana, people had been resisting enslavement long before the Barings became involved with the slavery economy. Maroons had built communities in the 'bayous', the wetlands, where, at the time of the American Revolution, they controlled a large area between Bas du Fleuve and New Orleans. Here, they'd eked out a living, gathering fruit and cutting wood, fishing and hunting, growing corn, rice and squash – and pilfering supplies where necessary. Maroons hid in the woods and swamps, returning to plantations after dark to find food, steal from the meat house or kill a cow. To throw off the plantation bloodhounds, they tied bay leaves to their feet and walked in manure. Sometimes maroons sold stolen goods to impoverished Whites, even venturing into towns and cities to do so. Freedom was a risky business: recapture brought severe punishment, execution sometimes followed a third attempt to escape.[45]

We were thankful for the woodland shading our way between the Grange and nearby Northington village. The day remained unusually warm, although – having just arrived from the heat of Louisiana – Ibrahima kept his coat on throughout the walk. Our thoughts turned back to the lands around Whitney Plantation. During Sir Alexander's retirement years[46] at Northington Grange, away in the American South the cruelty of slavery continued. In 1841, the abolitionist who wrote *Twelve Years a Slave*, Solomon Northup, was captured and shipped to New Orleans. From there he was transported to the Red River region in central eastern Louisiana, 170 miles north-west of Whitney Plantation. On the steamboat he calmed himself by devising 'a hundred plans to escape'.[47] The whole region, Northup related in his book, was characterized by marshy lowlands, and he identified white oaks and yellow pines as he passed through the landscape. The 2013 film of Northup's book was partly shot in Whitney Plantation, and it imparts a sense of the landscapes Ibrahima has come to know so well; menacing swamps of crooked cypresses draped with hanging Spanish mosses, a feature which is also described in North-up's book: 'From every tree,' he wrote, 'hang long, large masses of moss, presenting to the eye unaccustomed to them, a striking and singular appearance.'[48] Northup also described alligators lurking on the river banks thereabouts.[49] He described the process of harvesting cotton, in which the Barings invested so heavily. Women and men preparing the ground for cotton planting, working around soil beds six feet wide, whilst a mule-drawn plough broke the soil and girls dropped in the cotton seed. The seed was covered with soil and hoeing began when the cotton plants sprouted. All this time, Northup observed, the enslaved workers would be followed on horseback by an overseer who carried a whip, whose 'lash is flying from morning until night, the whole day long'.[50] Reading this description of labour in the cotton fields reminded me of a trip I'd made to see Ibrahima in Dakar: he'd shown me round the city's Museum of Black Civilizations, and we'd stopped in front of a sculpture of cotton plants, the stems represented by tall metal rods containing iron pods filled with fluffed-up wool to serve as cotton lint. 'That's a clever sculpture,' I'd said. Ibrahima stared at the sculpture for a moment. 'Yes,' he'd replied, 'but actual cotton plants are much lower. They make the pickers stoop.'

The cotton and sugar plantations of Louisiana were so geographically removed from the vicinity of Hampshire, but of course the two landscapes, and their creation, were once profoundly interlinked. Along the woodland footpath we saw the square tower of St John the Evangelist, which, every August, peeps above a tangle of yellow rapeseed. We threaded our way between trees until a clearing opened up at the edge of a graveyard and the church tower loomed above us. Sited at the edge of Northington village, this ostentatious church is known as the Cathedral of the Valley, and – as I now told Ibrahima – it was built with Baring wealth. Finance, the building seemed to say, was next to Godliness. In 1890, this Baring-funded building, with its handsome tower and beautifully ornamented stonework, replaced the previous church dismissed by the architect Sir Thomas Graham Jackson as 'a little mean damp building of brick and stucco'.[51] The funding was put up by Francis Baring Junior, the grandson of Alexander Baring, whose financial contribution is chiselled into the porch for posterity. As we walked into the church, I pointed out two stone bears carved into the church entrance: the Baring family emblem. Stepping inside, we found the Baring theme continues: another plaque commemorating the Baring donation; family pews with their accompanying bears; a neoclassical memorial to various Barings buried in the nearby crypt; busts of Thomas Baring's father and mother.[52] In the bell tower hangs the original tenor bell of 1602: a bell that would have regulated the days of the Barings and villagers for miles around,[53] and which pealed triumphantly when King George III passed near the old church in the year of the Louisiana Purchase.[54] When I mentioned this detail, Ibrahima reminded me that, thousands of miles west across the Atlantic, Whitney Plantation retains its bell from slavery times. Like the bell of St John's, its toll signalled the stages of the working day – though its purposes were more sinister, also assembling enslaved people when bodily punishments were inflicted, usually by the whip. Nowadays, visitors to Whitney Plantation are asked to ring the bell to commemorate the enslaved: the bell, wrote one visitor, has a reluctant metal tongue and heavy-hearted chime.[55] Punishments were an everyday event, meted out for everything from work deemed inadequate to attempts to escape – or, simply to set an example, or to assert the dominance of the punisher. But they didn't stop enslaved people from rising up – and in 1811, they did so, all along the 'German Coast' in and around Whitney Plantation, inspired by Toussaint L'Ouverture's Haitian revolution nine years previously.

Following the events on Haiti, plantation-owners and public figures in Louisiana decreed that no enslaved people should be transported from Saint-Domingue – modern-day Haiti – in case they provoked similar rebellions locally. But the soaring population of enslaved people and some of the most brutal working conditions in North America made revolt inevitable. In January 1811 insurgents led by an enslaved overseer named Charles Deslondes marched across the Louisiana plantations with stolen rifles, sharpened sticks and work tools, drumming and carrying banners towards New Orleans. Joined by hundreds more enslaved people as they went, they attacked plantation-owners and burned houses and crops. The rebellion didn't last long. Within forty-eight hours it had been put down by local militias.[56] The resulting executions of rebels were horrific in their ferocity. A naval officer called Samuel Hambleton described a long row of stakes with decapitated heads along a Mississippi levee all the way to the coast. He described the heads as crows on fence-posts.[57] Today, Whitney Plantation commemorates these violent executions unflinchingly, with a line of sculpted ceramic heads on poles. Ibrahima wanted no hidden knowledge. After all, he told me, 'No one who was there at the time was shielded from it.'

Ibrahima said that an inventory of Whitney Plantation, drawn up in the following year, 1812, reveals nothing of the horror of the rebellion's aftermath. It does show that sixty-one enslaved people lived there, nineteen of whom – mostly men in their twenties and thirties – were African-born; the rest were born into slavery on Louisiana soil.[58] Many retained African names and used African words to name the world around them. Nicknames were particularly important because they were believed to afford protection from harm: in West African folk culture, names had a mystical power, the Senegambian influence also clear in the naming of people after days of the week, particularly Friday (Aljuma) or Monday (Altine); others were called Joly Coeur, sweetheart, or Sans Soucy, carefree.[59]

At Whitney, as elsewhere, women's experience of slavery was marked by sexual violence. Today, at the museum, a granite wall displays the names of enslaved women, together with accounts of their treatment, ranging from rape by sailors during the Middle Passage to sexual violence on the plantation itself (state law was on the side of White sexual predators, not enslaved women).[60] Ibrahima explained how he was able to trace individual stories across multiple archives, including parish burial records. He discovered that, of twenty-one women listed in the plantation inventory, fourteen children were sold alongside their mothers. Local Catholic Church records reveal high infant mortality rates, equivalent to one child dying every year per household. Of thirty-nine babies born on the plantation between 1823 and 1863, only six reached the age of five over a forty-year period. 'Now,' he said, as we walked away from St John the Evangelist, 'we have a place dedicated to the many children who died at Whitney. We call it the Field of Angels.'

We walked through the hamlet of Northington, where the site of the old, simpler church – now replaced by the Cathedral of the Valley – is marked by a Baring memorial. Following a little lane lined with cottages and pretty gardens, we passed an elegant house. Ibrahima stopped, partly to eye up the steep hill ahead – 'the only hill, I promise!' was my assurance – and partly to admire the artistry of its red roof and wall-patterning of flint and Victorian brick. 'Fit for the chief of my village!' he exclaimed. We reminisced about my own recent visit to Senegal, when Ibrahima had taken me to the House of Slaves Museum on Gorée island, the place where captured Africans were kept before being taken across the Atlantic. 'The so-called Slave House,' Ibrahima said, because he didn't like the name. Language matters. To call someone enslaved emphasizes what has been done to them by others, rather than to imply – however unintentionally – that it is someone's natural condition. Inside, we saw cells where people from the Senegambia region were kept before being transported by ship: bare, cramped rooms with slits in the walls for ventilation. The most sinister of these is a low-ceilinged cell underneath a flight of stairs, where people would have sat hunched on the hard ground, awaiting their passage through a door which led to the sea and, from there, across the Atlantic. It is called the door of no return.

Walking out of Northington, we climbed a steep lane and, at the hill's crown, stared out across the rolling hills. Puffing, Ibrahima laughed: 'This *is* the only hill, right?' When he'd regained his breath, we followed the road along a flat ridge lined with trees, crunching beechnuts underfoot. We were now a mile from the Northington estate, and the high ridge provided panoramic views of the Hampshire hills, dotted with small villages in the direction of an attractive town called New Alresford. Ibrahima remarked on the neatness of the beeches, planted at regular intervals along the ridge, and pointed out a planted row of coppiced trees half a mile or so away, his finger tracing the lines of enclosed fields and their even furrows.

We soon turned off the road to take another tangled path towards the village of Brown Candover and its old manor which – perhaps inevitably – once belonged to another Baring, Francis, the fifth Lord Ashburton, who died in 1938. 'This is the Wayfarer's Way,' I said, 'hard to find,' relieved that I hadn't got us both lost and thus added to our mileage. 'Who used these old footpaths?' Ibrahima asked. They were, I told him, old farmers' tracks for driving sheep to market in the nearby towns of New Alresford and Farnham. There are far fewer footpaths today than in the unenclosed landscapes of earlier centuries, I added. 'Now,' I told Ibrahima, 'we can only access a fraction of our countryside.'

As we entered a field, a cloud of red admirals rose from an ivy bush they'd been feeding on. 'I see forty butterflies there, maybe fifty,' Ibrahima exclaimed. The air was thick with them, and we disturbed plenty more wildlife all along that old path, where it seemed nobody had passed for some time. We pushed aside the long grass: a pair of partridges squawked in alarm, and pigeons clattered out of the undergrowth. Beside the path, a chalk stream gurgled undisturbed, accompanying us along the way. We stopped to pick some wild plums and ate some. Another twenty minutes' walk brought us to the edge of Brown Candover, which lies on the old road between Winchester and Basingstoke. The Wayfarer's Way turned off before the village; beyond, the houses stood silent in the warm, still afternoon. We glimpsed a willow arching over a chalk stream as we turned onto the Wayfarer's Way – which, I saw with dismay, headed up quite a steep hill. 'You said there was only one hill!' said Ibrahima in mock accusation – and I mumbled something about being terrible at reading contour lines.

As we climbed, we saw a dead partridge trapped on a barbed wire gate, its beak red, its eyes glassed over. The path narrowed. I walked ahead for a few minutes, then stopped by a disused quarry to drink water as I waited for Ibrahima to catch up. 'How are your feet now?' I asked as he approached. 'They are still attached to my legs,' he said, then added, 'I'm enjoying it!' Only a mile and a half to go, I assured him, and we pressed on.

As the path levelled out, hedgerows opened out onto arable fields and we spotted feeding stations for pheasants and partridges, which flocked around the food. A quarter of a mile further along the track we came across a field of dead thistles where beaters scare the birds from their hiding places. 'So they feed them to shoot them,' Ibrahima wondered. A longstanding preserve of the landed classes, I acknowledged ruefully.

As we approached the outskirts of East Stratton, our conversation returned to the topic of Sir Alexander Baring. As a parliamentarian, Sir Alexander positioned himself as impartial and informed on the topic of enslavement.[61] Impartiality, presumably, lay in the eye of the beholder. In parliament, Baring defended the trade in slave-produced cotton, in which he and his family had heavy and longstanding investments.[62] With their major financial stake in cotton imports from America, the Barings' Liverpool office bought cotton from commission houses in New York, Philadelphia, Charleston and New Orleans and gathered vital information about raw cotton supplies, manufacture and demand.[63] By 1833, the Barings, in addition to their activities in finance, were the fifth-largest British importer of cotton, produced by the labour of approximately 70,000 enslaved people.[64]

'I am not myself a West India proprietor,' Baring told the House of Commons. While technically true, his assertion belied Barings Bank's intimate association with the plantation system. One letter in the Baring archive, dated 1824, relates to the death of a plantation-owner in Trinidad and discusses the measures being taken to pay his Baring creditors by selling the estate, its enslaved people and associated properties.[65] Three years later, the Barings entered into a legal dispute with plantation mortgagees on the Caribbean island of Saint Croix (belonging to Denmark); a Danish court in Copenhagen awarded the plantation to Barings Bank.

Baring had, he told parliament, personally observed enslaved people at work in Georgia and the Carolinas. He said he could vouch for the plantation-owners' humane treatment of enslaved people, claiming that they were 'treated with justice and kindness'. He even argued that the 'name of slave is a harsh one; but their real condition is undoubtedly, in many respects, superior to that of most of the peasantry of Europe'. Again, he professed his neutrality: he was, he suggested, simply an eyewitness, stating that 'the accounts which have reached us in various publications of the condition of Negro slaves are essentially false'.[66] He was still finding arguments to oppose slavery in 1831, telling parliament on 15 April that year that the consequent rising price of sugar brought about by abolition would encourage the enslavement of Africans by other European nations in an attempt to maintain profits.[67] Yet in the same breath, Baring declared himself to have 'always been a sincere abolitionist'.[68] By the mid-1830s, Barings had a whopping £250,000 invested in mortgages on West Indian estates.[69] Following the 1833 Slavery Abolition Act, when slave-owners were compensated for the loss of their enslaved workforces, Alexander Baring made his own compensation claims for plantations in St Kitts, to redeem the plantation owner's unpaid loan as his creditor and three further estates on the same island.[70] The Barings also counter-claimed for enslaved people on Spring Garden estate in British Guinea and in Belair, additionally making seven further joint claims as mortgage lenders to plantation-owners in British Guinea, mortgagees who had fallen into debt.[71] All in all, seven members of the Barings family, including Sir Alexander, claimed £75,377 for 1,717 enslaved people. For enslavers, compensation was a profitable business.[72]

Yet the Barings family had plantation business of various kinds in locations not subject to British anti-slavery legislation. Eighteen years after declaring himself an abolitionist, Alexander Baring still owned enslaved people. There exists in the Baring archive an 1841 register of 500 'unfree' people living on the Barings' Upper Bethlehem estate in Saint Croix, the Dutch West Indies, where slavery was not abolished until 1848. The record makes sober reading. One column, headed 'Moral Character', describes enslaved individuals variously as 'indifferent' or 'insolent' and 'not good'. One man, aged forty, is described as 'good' under the 'Moral Character' column. His name is written neatly in swirls of brown ink: 'Baring'.[73]

Meanwhile in 1834, Alexander Baring's son-in-law wrote to the bank about his South Carolina plantation. He regretted the idea that enslaved people were considered as his personal property, he wrote, but he nonetheless wanted to mortgage the plantation and its unfree population. In line with Alexander Baring's own self-presentation as humane, he proclaimed that the enslaved children on his estate were more informed about Christianity than many of their White counterparts (and by implication, so was he, their owner).[74]

Walking back up the main street of East Stratton, our walk had come full circle. 'A saying comes to mind,' said Ibrahima, 'that He-Goat makes the gumbo, but Rabbit eats it.' This was, he said, a proverb from the days of plantation slavery in Louisiana: the goats were the enslaved, the rabbits the enslavers and their financiers. (Louisiana's rabbit stories originate in the Wolof region of Senegal, where the rabbit is associated with cunning. It's no coincidence, Ibrahima found: between 1751 and 1775, over half of enslaved Africans came from the Wolof region. Both in Wolof and in Louisiana, these tales begin and end with a call and response.)[75] 'You know,' he continued, 'the story of slavery is not just a story of bad treatment.' He told me that the guiding philosophy behind the interpretation of Whitney Plantation, all its displays, has been to highlight the pivotal role of African people and their descendants in the region's formation, and – ultimately – in the cultural and economic development of the United States as a whole. This, he added, is not 'Black history' – something separate from the histories of White Americans – but the history of people throughout the United States, a perspective which many people share. The purpose of Whitney was to help people to understand that Africans and their descendants did not just build the US economy, as they did throughout the Western hemisphere, but, Ibrahima said, 'They defined the culture, and what makes American culture so attractive across the world was born on those plantations.' Though the pain behind this is essential to acknowledge and understand, Ibrahima continued, 'I call it a story of resilience, of the civilization of America itself.'

As we headed to the eastern end of the village, where stands the Baring-built church of All Saints, Ibrahima expanded on his theme. 'Africans came to America with many skills,' he said, 'including agriculture.' In Louisiana, enslaved people grew crops and nutritious African vegetables like okra – a staple of gumbo – on provision grounds, patches of land allocated for subsistence crops. Gumbo is made using a roux, whereas its African counterpart has a different thickening base: both, though, are served on a bed of rice. Black-eyed peas, also grown in Senegambia, were grown by enslaved people in Louisiana: the peas are bonding, Ibrahima laughed, because they cause flatulence. Cooking creatively, enslaved people adapted this food to make new dishes. Jambalaya – which uses rice, meat (usually shrimp, chicken, and andouille sausage), and Cajun spices – is a Louisiana variation of a dish cooked in coastal Senegal, known as Jollof rice, which typically also contains black-eyed peas or peanut butter sauce.[76] Then there's pounded millet, another Senegalese influence, known in the American South as grits. In Africa, women pounded the millet with grindstones, also moistening and steaming it: a laborious task. The rub-a-dub beat of Jamaican reggae, Ibrahima added, recalls the rhythm of pestles and mortars in villages throughout the Bight of Benin. The early-morning thud awoke the residents, he said, like the village bells of the local churches would have woken the residents of Northington.[77]

Slavery wealth, I told Ibrahima, continued to provide luxury to the Barings. When Alexander Baring died in 1848, Northington Grange was inherited by his son, William Bingham Baring, who lived there with his wife Harriet.[78] There, they held literary salons, among whose frequent attendees were their close friends Thomas Carlyle and his wife Jane. During this period, Carlyle published his influential post-abolition essay called 'Occasional Discourse on the Negro Question',[79] a pamphlet that infamously censured economists and the British government for leaving Black people without sufficient paternalistic care. Another guest, the writer James Froude, blamed Caribbean underdevelopment on the Black population itself.[80] Meanwhile, the guests praised their serene surroundings and their hosts' hospitality. Jane Carlyle observed that the park extended for 5 miles and wrote that she had not just one bedroom to herself but an opulent suite. The exotic wood and Turkish carpets, she added, reminded her of the Arabian nights.[81]

It was one of those early-autumn afternoons, when shadows stretch across the road, and the light bestows silver halos on the trees. All Saints church was designed in 1888 by the same architect who worked on the church at Northington. It was paid for by Francis Baring, 1st Baron Northbrook – the grandson and namesake of the original Sir Francis Baring – with a similar end in view: to reaffirm the Barings' pre-eminence and to direct the spiritual lives of the villagers. Both churches include the architect's signature chequered pattern on their exterior walls. We had the churchyard to ourselves. In the calm afternoon light, I fancied I could see the ghost of William Cobbett, who rode through East Stratton village in the 1820s and met a little girl dressed in her Sunday best, consisting of a 'camlet gown, white apron and plaid cloak'. The girl carried a book, Cobbett wrote, and 'told me that Lady Baring gave her the clothes, and had taught her to read and sing hymns and spiritual songs. As I came through the Strattons I saw not less than a dozen girls clad in this same way.'[82]

The church was open. Inside, the low evening light illuminated the dark pews and white arches. We found a stone memorial to the church's funder, the first Earl, which listed his various titles: between 1872 and 1876, he was governor general of India, following in the footsteps of Warren Hastings of Daylesford almost a century before.[83] It felt incongruous to find the title here, in the quiet of this country church, but then, as I said to Ibrahima, 'village churches so often contain these sorts of memorials'.

We recalled the details of the day's walk, the thatched cottages, the pillared ruins of Stratton Park, the herd of deer, the hare washing its ears in the lane. 'Hampshire is definitely the missing piece of the jigsaw,' Ibrahima said. It is true. This southern county adds an English dimension to Ibrahima's journey to reconnect the pathways between Senegal and Louisiana, a journey on which he has been so long engaged. In the thick colonial account books of the Barings, their loans and investments, you can see where the quest for wealth and power all ended up: in ostentatious porticos and landscapes, certainly, but also in the churches, enclosed fields and the model village.

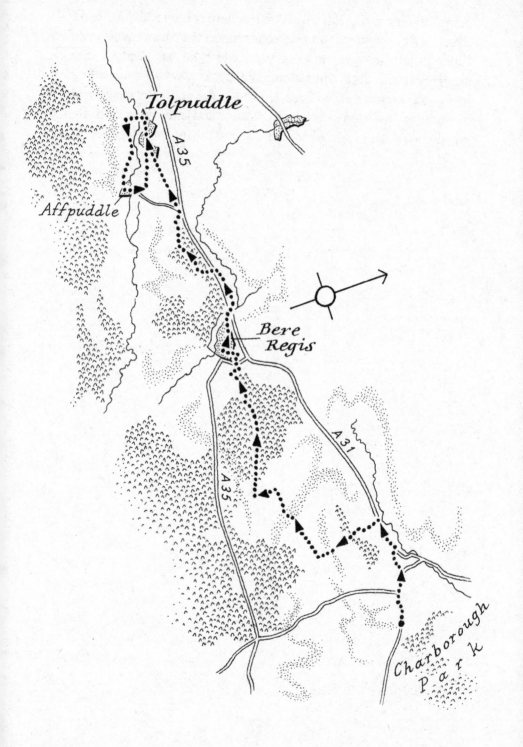

9

The Labourers' Walk:
Tolpuddle and British Penal Colonies

West of Hampshire, Dorset pushes inland from the southern English coast towards the borders of Wiltshire and Somerset. Here, you are deep in the West Country, the epicentre of Thomas Hardy's Wessex. Tourists flock to its dramatic Jurassic coastline, which, two centuries after Mary Anning's pioneering discoveries of dinosaur skeletons, remains a magnet for fossil hunters. Inland, its wide vales, floodplains and clay valleys are punctuated by Neolithic, Roman and Saxon settlements.

The Dorset ports of Poole, Weymouth, Bridport and Lyme Regis are all sited at the western end of the channel as it opens out towards the Atlantic. Unsurprisingly, from the late seventeenth century onwards, they participated in the slavery business: exporting wool and importing sugar, tobacco, cotton and indigo, ships also made slaving voyages from Dorset ports.[1] Central Dorset, meanwhile, has its own unique colonial geography, with six prominent slave-owning families living within a 13-mile radius. Of these families, two residences at nearby Fonthill Abbey and Iwerne Stepleton belonged to the Jamaican plantation-owning Beckford dynasty. The family at Kingston Lacy was connected to Leeward Islands plantations – Frances Woodley was an heiress to these plantations, where her father was governor – and Merley House was built by the St Kitts plantation-owner Ralph Willett. All these country estates were a carriage drive away from the biggest estate of them all: Charborough Park, with a formidable seventeenth-century manor at its centre. Today, it remains home to its historic owners: the Drax family, also still owners, since the mid-seventeenth century, of the Drax

Hall estate on Barbados, which cultivated the first sugar cane in the West Indies.[2]

I planned to start here, at the gates of Charborough Park, and walk 7 miles through the Dorset countryside: a walk that would take me into the heartlands of Dorsetshire labour history. I would end at Tolpuddle village, from where, in 1834, six agricultural labourers were transported to Australia as punishment for organizing an agricultural workers' union.

In Tolpuddle, as elsewhere in Britain, colonial history and labour history are two sides of the same coin. From the early seventeenth century Dorset people were shipped to Barbados plantations to work as indentured labourers, selling their employers a set number of labour years and receiving a lump sum, or its equivalent in sugar or land, at the end of their contract.[3] By mid-century, these indentured servants were being replaced by enslaved African labourers. Plantation profits flowed back into Dorset, enriching landowning families, which became locally and nationally influential, occupying political and legal positions. By the early nineteenth century, a time of recession and depressed wages, the Swing Riots reached Dorset, moving westward from Hampshire, and agricultural labourers rose up in protest. Among them were the villagers of Tolpuddle who, refusing to accept lower wages, formed a 'friendly society' or union in protest. Convicted under obscure laws, their story would become one of the most celebrated in British labour history; each summer, trade unionists flock to the village and celebrate these men at a festival, where people hear lectures, watch radical films and listen to music.

Tolpuddle's interlinked histories of race and class resonate with the personal experience of my fellow walker, the writer Louisa Adjoa Parker, who lives and works in Dorset. The child of a Ghanaian father and an English mother, Louisa started life far from the West Country, in a council flat in the Yorkshire city of Doncaster. Her love of England's rural south-west began when her grandparents moved to Devon when she was six and she used to visit them on family holidays by the sea.

I stood outside Charborough estate. The April morning was full of promise, casting a warm light over the ploughed earth fields, turning them golden brown. Teasels bristled from the hedgerows, and dandelions puffed like seed factories. Hawthorn shook its blossom over the verges, which were full of starflowers. Louisa stepped out of her car wearing sunglasses and gold hoop earrings. She looked well, but her voice was hoarse. 'Oh no!' I exclaimed, dismayed. 'You're ill!' She acknowledged she had a terrible cold, but hadn't wanted to let me down. 'In any case,' she said, 'the fresh air might help, and it's warm too.' We paused to plan our route, holding the map up to the light, then made our way along Charborough Park's wall to a minor gatehouse on the south approach to the estate. This was a small building with elaborate stone features, but – as I said to Louisa – nothing like as ostentatious as the main gateways to the estate, with their grand arches and stone beasts.

As we wandered along the wall, I asked Louisa about her holidays at her grandparents' Devon home. She had many happy memories of playing in their apple-tree-filled garden by the sea, she said. 'Home didn't feel a safe place at the time because of domestic violence,' she continued, 'but that garden was a refuge.'

When Louisa was twelve, her parents split up, and she and her siblings moved close to their grandparents' home, to the south Devon town of Paignton in a house near arable fields and a river. They had very little money and her mother didn't own a car, so Louisa walked everywhere and got to know the surrounding paths, woods and fields. Though Louisa loved the countryside, she felt it didn't love *her*. In 1970s Devon, very few locals had seen children who looked like her. To them, she was unusual – and she came to view herself as unusual too, a feeling which marred the landscapes of her childhood.

These were the days of the National Front, a political party which advocated a Whites-only Britain. Its rhetoric dominated Louisa's formative years. When she was a teenager, a former classmate, attracted by the National Front's ideology, put a stink bomb through her letterbox. What really wore her down, though, was the drip feed of banal everyday comments, typified by one schoolmate's remark that she was 'quite pretty for a coloured girl'. Her peers' subtle but relentless commentary on Louisa's physical difference gradually eroded her sense of self, a feeling made worse by a complete lack of acknowledgement of her mixed heritage. 'It was as if I didn't exist,' she told me.

Louisa didn't mention specific instances of racism to her parents – though she does remember her Ghanaian father having once told her that she'd have to work harder than White people to attain similar goals because she was Black. Finally, as a student at Exeter University, she found the words to articulate her lifelong experience of racism. There, too, she learned new things about Dorset's history. 'Before I attended university,' she said, 'I had no idea that Black people lived in the region before my family did.' Dorset's long association with people of African and Caribbean descent made Louisa feel she wasn't alone, and she wrote a book called *Dorset's Hidden Histories*, which details 400 years of rural Black experience. 'We have been coming here for centuries,' she wrote, 'as enslaved African "servants", soldiers, entertainers, refugees, visiting royalty, writers and, more recently, students, migrant workers, care and catering workers.' I hoped, I said, that our walk would add to her work by exploring yet more of Dorset's colonial stories. With her interest in colonial history, working-class stories and rural settings, Louisa was the perfect walking companion.[4]

We walked on and on, the estate wall at our side. This mid-nineteenth-century structure is quite something. At 3 miles long, and comprising some 2 million bricks, it's among the longest in England. Covered in mosses and white lichens, it curved away from us. The wall seemed surprisingly low, easily scalable. But its original function was as a boundary marker to delineate the course of the main Wimborne–Dorchester road when it was diverted to extend the Drax family parkland – and turnpiked, so that the Draxes could make money by charging tolls to all who used it.[5] We peered over the wall and between the trees but couldn't catch a glimpse of

Charborough House itself. Relatively few people get to see it, outside or in. A dove-grey seventeenth-century manor with large windows and elegant Ionic columns, the house has – according to reports – a mural-adorned staircase and a picture gallery, while its library takes up a whole wing. The Draxes invested the profits of slavery in both house and grounds. Following the 1833 Slavery Abolition Act, John Samuel Wanley Sawbridge Erle-Drax received the large sum of £4,293 12s 6d in compensation from the British government for 189 enslaved people.[6] His wealth paid for the estate's two really imposing entrance gates further along the wall – one topped by a stag and another by a lion – as well as for the estate wall itself. (It was he who diverted the road and installed the turnpike.) He also added a Georgian façade to the house, employing the noted architect John Nash, and rebuilt Charborough Tower, an octagonal Gothic tower that stands on rising ground to the house's south-east, after it was damaged by a lightning strike.[7]

Charborough's current owner, a Conservative Member of Parliament, is Richard Grosvenor Plunkett-Ernle-Erle-Drax, or Richard Drax for short. His massive portfolio of property still includes the Drax Hall estate on Barbados, which, founded by the Draxes in the 1650s, still cultivates sugar cane today. His plantations, historically, were worked by enslaved people. Following the 2019 United Nations declaration that the slave trade was a crime against humanity,[8] in 2022, the Barbadian government invited Drax to a private meeting with the country's prime minister to discuss reparation payments. In that meeting, the PM proposed that part of the Drax Hall estate be set aside to house impoverished Barbadian families. Her other suggestion was to turn the Barbadian estate into a museum focused on African history. As I said to Louisa, this suggestion mirrored the National Trust's recent emphasis on the slavery connections of families which owned country houses that are now under its management. Opening up Drax Hall in this way would mean that, no longer screened from public view, the house would tell the history of the enslaved people who worked on its plantations. It would also show how the Draxes helped formalize and systematize enslaved labour in

Barbados by taking a leading role in sugar growing, pioneering enslaved labour and involving themselves with law-making on the island. The Barbadian authorities made it clear that, in the event of failing to reach an agreement with Richard Drax over Drax Hall, legal action would be used to secure reparations from the family. Meanwhile, that same year, the Jamaican government – through its National Council on Reparations – was considering similar proposals regarding the Draxes, who had also owned a plantation (another Drax Hall) on the island.

Throughout this process, which has yet to be resolved, Richard Drax has said that the family's slaving history was 'deeply, deeply regrettable'.[9] He also once complained that people 'pick at bits of my family history' – meaning the slavery part. Meanwhile the chair of the Caribbean Community's Reparation Commission (CARICOM for short), the historian Hilary Beckles, stated that the Drax Hall estate is 'a massive killing field with unmarked cemeteries'. He has argued that 'Sugar and Black Death went hand in glove. Black life mattered only to make millionaires of English enslavers and the Drax family did it longer than any other elite family.' The response from Charborough was that the family couldn't 'be held responsible for something which happened 300 or 400 years ago'; Beckles's rejoinder was that, as the owner and inheritor of this land, the issue had everything to do with Richard Drax.[10] Archaeologists have also intervened in the conversation with the deputy director of Barbados Museum and Historical Society, the historian Kevin Farmer, saying that experts need access to Drax Hall, so as to learn more about the burial grounds of enslaved people and discover further details about how they lived.[11]

As we walked, Louisa and I discussed the Drax involvement in slavery, which spans continents and generations. It began in Barbados, the easternmost island in the West Indies, where powerful trade winds once drove the island's windmills. Drax Hall lies in St George's Parish in the island's central district. Towering above it is Gun Hill, from where islanders could spot the approach of both enemy ships and hurricanes.

In 1627 a London-based merchant group, William Courteen and Associates, began to colonize Barbados, whose indigenous population had already been captured and turned off the land by the Spanish in the previous century. These new English settlers spent considerable funds preparing the island for tobacco production.[12] Among them was James Drax, ancestor of Charborough Park's current owner, who, arriving in Barbados in 1645 with £300, bought a large tract of land and purchased the labour of twenty-eight indentured servants from the British, mostly impoverished labourers and convicts.[13]

Tobacco was no easy venture: prices were unstable and profits uncertain. Plantation-owners also tried growing indigo and cotton, but a glut in the global supply led to falling prices. However, the climate and soil conditions on Barbados were ideal for growing sugar cane, and growers turned instead to producing sugar: the first English colony to do so.

Within a decade, Barbados' dense forests and luxuriant growth were mostly gone, eradicated to make way for sugar cane crops. Aside from the environmental damage, this treeless landscape left plantation-owners with a logistical headache. Cane juice, extracted then milled from harvested cane, required boiling in order to form sugar crystals. Boilers needed timber as fuel. James's son and heir, Henry, relied on a combination of his remaining trees and milled cane stalks, which burned more quickly than wood. Moreover, as Drax observed, importing timber or coal was expensive. Deforestation was causing soil erosion, and so walls and weirs were being built to prevent it.[14] The soil, too, was quickly depleted. Whereas the first sugar cane plots had once harvested three successive crops, planting sites had to be rotated to rest the exhausted soils.[15]

Nonetheless, sugar profits were vast, and Barbados' plantation-owners were soon rich – none more so than James Drax. With wealth came political power: Drax had a seat on the Council of Barbados, responsible for passing laws on the island.[16] A decade after arriving in Barbados, he was the island's richest plantation-owner, with a sugar product known for its quality.[17] He lived a regal lifestyle in a house which remains today the oldest colonial house in the Caribbean. In his 1657 account called *A True and Exact History of the Island of Barbados*, an English plantation-owner named Richard Ligon said that Drax lived 'like a Prince'. Attending a feast hosted by Drax, Ligon rhapsodized about fourteen beef dishes (beef was, Ligon noted, rare on the island) and the profusion of meat courses, including suckling pig.[18]

Many others who sailed from Britain to the Americas were at the opposite end of the social scale.[19] In the early years of growing tobacco, cotton and indigo, Barbados plantation-owners relied almost entirely on indentured servants: the indigenous Caribs resisted labouring for colonial planters, and it was then hard to obtain enslaved Africans, since the Spanish and Portuguese held a slave-trading monopoly, and Britain's own slaving activities would not develop into the industrial-scale transportation of enslaved people across the Atlantic until the 1660s.

James Drax and his fellow plantation-owners led the island's shift to sugar production, which soon dominated the island's exports and reshaped the regional economy.[20] Growing sugar was labour inten-sive, but, by the 1640s, the number of indentured servants was dwindling, people avoiding the island because of its terrible work-ing conditions.[21] This raised the price of indentured service to as much as £14 per head by the mid-1650s. Drax Hall estate had ini-tially relied on indentured labour, but James Drax made an early switch to slave labour, a decade earlier than most plantation-owners. His swelling profits meant that he could afford enslaved people – who were more expensive – but, unlike indentured servants, their labour was lifelong. Enslaved women also had children, which – in the minds of enslavers – reproduced the labour force and increased its value.[22]

The road forked, and, turning our backs on Charborough's long estate wall, we struck out along the forbiddingly named Vermin Lane, towards the village of Bere Regis. The hedgerows fizzed with white blackthorn, wild cherry and pink-tinged crab apple. Sparrows brought the hedges to life, and a brown wren held its tail aloft within the thicket. Elderflower scented the air.

With Louisa suffering from her cold, we stopped frequently for restorative breaks. 'I really miss walking through the countryside,' Louisa said. 'I've been cooped up indoors too long, having online meetings on my computer.' She'd love to buy a country cottage one day, she admitted wistfully, and we wondered how much one round here would cost. 'Too much,' she said decisively, as we set off again.

Looking out onto the ploughed fields, Louisa said: 'I've never seen anyone who looks like me driving a tractor!' We agreed that the absence of Black Britons in such settings was an issue of representation as much as a reality: who typically appears in such landscapes and who does not. 'Even now,' Louisa told me, 'people commonly assume I'm from somewhere else, a city. Whenever I go out to places like this, people ask me if I'm from Bristol or London.'

It's taken many years for Louisa to embrace a sense of rural belonging. She recalls how, at university, she came across a photograph of the Lake District that brought her up short, by Ingrid Pollard, with whom I'd walked through that same landscape just days earlier. 'I'd never seen a photograph of a Black person in the countryside before,' she said. 'It was such a striking image too. She was a Black person in the Lakes, and that was just fine by her.' The instant she set eyes on Ingrid's photograph, Louisa realized that she'd spent years explaining her presence in rural places, 'almost apologizing, letting people know why I was there, reassuring them that I wasn't a threat, that I was a nice person.' Nowadays, she told me, she feels more at ease in the countryside. 'When I take a train to Devon I relax and feel like I'm going home.' Still, Louisa feels anxious visiting an unfamiliar village and instinctively scopes it out to be sure that she is safe. If she walks into a village pub, heads often turn to look. On those occasions, she explained to me, she feels uncomfortably visible, 'seen but not heard'. Then, earlier, as she drove to meet me, she'd spotted a Black dustbin worker chatting to someone in the street and felt reassured that she wasn't alone.

Louisa has written poems about her experiences and believes – as I do – that the arts produce personal and social transformation of all kinds. She's a poet of skill, courage and clarity, sharing her knowledge and craft with school pupils, library visitors and prison inmates. 'One of the biggest challenges is convincing people that rural racism actually exists,' she said; having the experience of prejudice denied or doubted is a wearying experience. She told me the story of a Black actor who, on the day he was due to perform in a play about racism, was stopped by local police and told that he looked like a drug dealer.

About a mile into our walk, our conversation returned to the history of Barbados and indentured labour. From 1630 onwards, I told Louisa, over half of the White people who travelled to the West Indies were indentured servants. Between 1624 and 1750, over 30,000 such servants travelled to the English Americas. 'Many of these were from Dorset,' I added.[23] In 1643 alone, 836 indentured workers were shipped from the county to Barbados.[24] Some went voluntarily, hoping for a route out of poverty: when their time was served, they received either a plot of land, or increasingly – with the choice plots already taken – a lump sum in payment. Others went out of dire necessity, being homeless or unable to pay their debts.[25] Others still were refugees of the English Civil War, or political prisoners. The Civil War played out in colonies like Barbados. As a parliamentarian, James Drax was close to Oliver Cromwell, who sent captured enemies to work on colonial plantations. When, in 1651, a Royalist faction had temporarily retaken the island, Drax recaptured it.

In his 1657 account *A True and Exact History of the Island of Barbados*, the (Royalist) plantation-owner, Ligon, described how indentured labour worked. Newly arrived labourers were transported to the plantations, where they were told to construct their shelters and given a small meal of potatoes and water. Typically, the working day was from sunrise to sundown, all under the watchful gaze of an overseer, with a break at 11 a.m. for a meal of maize porridge with beans or more potatoes. Labour conditions were harsh, although

Ligon claimed that conditions improved over time, with warmer accommodation and better hammocks and clothing.[26]

There was an inevitable conflict of interest: plantation-owners wanted cheap labour, while indentured labourers sought social and economic advancement.[27] This advancement was hard to come by: indentured servants were listed on plantation inventories, taxed as property or used as currency, and their remaining years of service were passed on in people's wills. Some servants were mortgaged or gambled away. One woman was bartered for a pig: both were weighed on the scales. Servants could be part-exchanged for land or used as part-payment for debts. While in theory they had legal rights, in practice rulings invariably went against them. Their movements, too, were restricted: servants needed a pass to leave the plantation.[28]

In 1661, the governor of Barbados informed the colonial office that the shortage, and cost, of labour would ruin plantation-owners.[29] Now, the transition from indentured labour to enslaved labour began in earnest. It is important to distinguish between indenture and chattel slavery because British labour and union leaders habitually compared the two during this period, sometimes referring to 'white slaves'. But this comparison does not bear scrutiny now and neither did it then. It was true that, until the 1660s, indentured labourers and enslaved people commonly worked alongside one another on Barbados plantations. But the two groups received very different treatment. Servants who had worked their period of indenture were free to go. This was not the case for enslaved people. In 1661, the island's government drew up 'An act for the better ordering and governing of Negroes', which provided the island's legal basis for chattel slavery, conferring the right to own human beings. The 1661 Slave Code, as it became known, gave enslavers the legal right to torture and murder their human property. According to this law, an enslaved person's murder was not punishable by prison sentence but by a fine, paid to the treasury or to the legal owner (should the culprit not be the owner).[30]

Although indentured servants and people in chattel slavery

sometimes worked in the same fields, enslaved people made the servants' food.[31] Indentured labourers received payment at the end of their contract. Enslaved people who received their freedom – and most did not – got nothing but the occasional reward or concession.[32] Indentured labourers' whereabouts were controlled during their period of indenture; enslaved people's movements were restricted until death. Although the legal system didn't always work in their favour, indentured labourers had contractual entitlements and the right to appeal to a court of law. The 1661 Servant Law, drawn up alongside the Slave Code, required a letter from parents or guardians for children under fourteen to be landed on Barbados. Servants under eighteen could not serve for more than seven years, and married servants could not be separated. None of this was the case for enslaved people.

According to the island's legislation on indentured labour, servants could be whipped, and often were. Nonetheless, punishments differed markedly for servants and enslaved people. On Barbados, the penalty for assaulting an employer was a year's additional indenture. For the same crime, enslaved people were whipped for a first offence and had their noses slit and faces burned for a second. Theft by a servant was punished by two additional years' indenture. Enslaved people could be put to death for the same crime. Seventeenth-century slave-owners on Barbados could legally decapitate, castrate or burn enslaved people alive. They could fetter escapees and place spiked iron collars around their necks.[33]

Neither I nor Louisa have ever visited the Barbadian Drax Hall mansion built in the 1650s by James Drax: like Charborough Hall, it remains screened off to visitors. From photos, we could see that the seventeenth-century house remains imposing, with red gable roofs, though its masonry is stained with age. Inside, the house has grand staircases, carvings and fine balustrades.

We reached the end of Vermin Lane, which gave way to a busy main road, the A31. At this junction, we were relieved to find a pub, the Botany Bay Inn (its name a nod to the place where the first Australian penal colony was founded), with its nautical livery of navy blue. We took a pitstop in the adjoining beer garden, where red and blue parasols flapped merrily.

Our thoughts turned back to the Draxes. In 1663, I mentioned to Louisa, the Company of Royal Adventurers of England Trading to Africa (later the Royal African Company) shipped more than 5,000 enslaved people to Barbados; this large-scale operation enabled it to sell transported human beings for £18, undercutting the Spanish and Portuguese competition.[34] State papers of 1677 reveal that James Drax's son Henry sat on a Council of Barbados session which voted to keep the 1661 Barbados Slave Code, a law which was subsequently used to legally codify slavery in Jamaica, Carolina, Georgia and Antigua, and also influenced the slavery laws of Virginia and Maryland.[35] Very little information remains about enslaved individuals who lived on the Drax estate. One detail caught my eye: a request by Henry Drax to give one 'Moncky Nocco' extra fish or meat, a new hat and set of clothes annually. He intended to promote the man to the position of overseer.[36] The name 'Moncky Nocco' made me shiver, I told Louisa. My own distant French ancestor was Jean-Baptiste de Caradeuc, a notoriously cruel enslaver who owned Croix-des-Bouquets plantation on Haiti (then Saint-Domingue). After fighting the first Haitian Revolution as governor general in the 1790s, Caradeuc had fled to South Carolina with some enslaved people who were part of his household, including a wet nurse he called 'Mama Monkey'.

Henry Drax hadn't been on Barbados long before instructing his plantation manager to use enslaved people rather than indentured labourers. This broke Barbadian regulations, which mandated that plantation-owners on the island use a larger proportion of indentured labourers than enslaved people.[37] Henry Drax, it turned out, would often be accused of rule-breaking. Factors – men who sold enslaved people to plantation-owners – accused him of allowing enslaved people to be disembarked illegally,[38] while he was also alleged to have under-reported the weight of ships' cargoes for export (the balance therefore being smuggled in as contraband) and, in 1680, was hauled before the Lords of the Treasury in London to explain discrepancies between the recorded and actual cargoes of recent voyages.[39] (Previously, the Council of Barbados demanded that he and a colleague account for a missing consignment of sugar and ginger.)[40] Before returning to England, Henry Drax – who now owned 705 acres and 327 enslaved people on the island – drew up detailed instructions for managing his plantations in his absence. Ranging over such topics as overseeing enslaved people and preventing the theft of estate produce, the document lays bare the horror and inhumanity of enslaved labour.[41] In it, Drax referred dispassionately to the annual mortality rate, instructing that ten to fifteen enslaved people should be purchased to replace those who died every year – unsurprisingly, given that their tasks included the deeply unhealthy and backbreaking work of 'dunging' to replenish the depleted soil. In times of contagion, meanwhile, the plantation manager should select about twenty 'Choyce Young Negroes Who will be fit for plant service'. (In a similar vein the plantation-owner Richard Ligon wrote, 'we breed both Negroes, Horses, and Cattle'.)[42] The calculations of these and other enslavers on Barbados during this period exposes their full knowledge that every cohort of 100 enslaved people would be worked to death within nineteen years.[43]

By 1690, plantation-owners on the island had reallocated most skilled roles – everything from bricklaying and carpentry to sugar boiling – from indentured servants to enslaved labourers.[44] Over time, as the system grew more complex, the experiences of enslaved people varied according to their seniority, gender and skin-colour. Indeed, the experience of colourism – allocating tasks according to skin shade – is integral to the history of Barbados, given the island's ever-decreasing population of African-born people and a corresponding rise in Creole and island-born enslaved people. Darker-skinned people – women as well as men – predominantly worked in the fields. Here, lines of people hoed, dug, manured, planted and weeded at speeds commensurate with their physical strength and endurance. Hoes rose and fell at timed intervals, and the lines advanced forward, commanded by overseers with whips in their hands.[45] Those with lighter skins, meanwhile, were considered by slave-owners to be more intelligent and less suited to field work or hard labour. They were allocated skilled work, and permitted some legal concessions, rewards and some freedoms during non-labouring hours.[46] Women with lighter skin tones were employed as housekeepers, were in unequal sexual relationships with White men, or became sex-workers, largely in the capital of Bridgetown. Enslaved domestic workers had children with White men, and these lighter-skinned children generally avoided field work as well.[47]

It was warm in the beer garden; around us, the fields stretched away. Louisa nodded at the surrounding landscape. Despite her love of nature, she said, as a person of mixed heritage who lives in the countryside, 'you more easily see racism, bigotry and poverty behind the veneer of these hills'. I recalled one of her poems – one of my favourites – in which, while working as a cleaner in a Lyme Regis hotel in Dorset, she reimagined herself as an African girl, brought back by 'my master, his mulatto child in fact'.[48] The poem formed in Louisa's mind as she cleaned the hotel guestrooms, thinking about the historical continuities between slavery and modern-day racism: 'Little has changed here, up at the big house,' the poem runs, 'pretending I was born for this; / smiling and dusting and cleaning white people's rooms.'

We set off again in the direction of Bere Regis, an ancient market town bounded by other old settlements: the Iron Age hillfort of Woodbury Hill to the east, Shitterton village to the west. Today, little remains of its antiquity, many of its older buildings having been swept away by fire over the centuries. But we admired the twelfth-century church of St John the Baptist, coveted the thatched cottages in the village centre and walked past the Drax Arms pub, its name an indication of the family's continued dominance in these parts.[49] We recalled how in 2021, 'BLM' (Black Lives Matter) and 'slaver' were graffitied on the pub's white outer walls. In response, the pub staff released a statement: 'We all believe in Black Lives Matter. We all think the slave trade is abhorrent. We cannot change the past, we can only learn from it.'

Leaving Bere Regis behind us, we continued west along the A35. Wareham Forest spread thickly to our left. The hedges were filled with wild flowers, yellow rosettes of cowslip and pink campions standing proud. At one point I managed to get us lost, Louisa following patiently as I steered us along an overgrown path on the wrong side of a ditch beside arable fields of sweetcorn. We continued onwards, passing through woods then climbing a low hill. There, in front of us, was Tolpuddle village.

An ancient watering place with an Iron Age earthwork, Tolpuddle takes its name from the nearby River Piddle. The main street is lined with cob-walled cottages covered in wisteria and resplendent with the thatched roofs typical of the region, topped with decorative pheasants. Several of the houses displayed Ukrainian flags.[50] The village was picture perfect. It was mid-afternoon, and school was out. Around us, children wandered home: headphones clamped to ears, they strolled the narrow pavements and ducked under the low eaves. We smiled: for them, the idyll they walked through was entirely normal.

On the way into Tolpuddle we'd seen a string of smart white vans pass by, offering services to heritage properties: thatching, carpentry and topiary. As we entered the village, a small private plane droned overhead. Where poverty once reigned, there was now money. Louisa and I walked along the main street to a thick-trunked sycamore, one of the most famous trees in the country: the Tolpuddle Martyrs' Tree. Knobbly and twisted, the tree – now 336 years old – leans towards the village green. We made our way to an empty bench on the green and, grateful for the rest, continued chatting. While her own story involves race, Louisa explained, it's also very much about class, given that she was raised in a single-parent household where money was scarce. And it is class that gave Tolpuddle its place on the historical stage, in the shape of six agricultural labourers who met at the Tolpuddle Martyrs' Tree, and whose story became a landmark in British union history.

During the early nineteenth century, Dorset, as elsewhere in southern England, had seen local disturbances. The trouble had begun at the end of the previous century, when the 1794 Enclosure Acts sold off the area's surrounding fields – including swathes of common land – to three separate owners, a development which was exacerbated by poor wages, fluctuations in grain prices and mechanization. In 1830, the region's labourers responded to the national mood, arranging local assemblies to discuss wage suppression by local landowners, who were notorious for paying poor wages. The average farmworker's weekly wage of somewhere between 7 and 9 shillings came nowhere near to covering the weekly rent and purchase of basics – tea and sugar, bread, potatoes, butter and cheese, candles, soap and wood – which typically came to around 13 shillings.[51] Across Dorset, people demonstrated, rioted, went on strike and participated in some arson and machine-breaking. Initially, the local gentry and authorities met these acts with concessions: the latest incumbent at Charborough Park, John Samuel Wanley Ellis Sawbridge Erle-Drax (he of the long wall), met his labourers with beer to head off trouble and temporarily offered small wage increases.

When these weekly increases were then reneged upon (in place of the promised 10 or 11 shillings, labourers found they were being paid only 8 shillings a week after all that), the unrest restarted – and the landowners proved uncompromising in their response. John Samuel Wanley Ellis Sawbridge Erle-Drax stopped offering beer and called out the Dorsetshire Yeomanry (of which he was captain). The Dorset authorities, meanwhile, put down rioters with imprisonment, transportation to British penal colonies and, in some cases, death.[52]

Alarmed by the riots, the local magistrate, James Frampton, kept a beady eye on the locals, because unionization threatened his interests as a landowner. Hoping to catch any agricultural worker who dared to form a union, he sent out spies, two Affpuddle labourers called John Lock and Edward Legg.[53] His infiltrators soon had something to report. Their information concerned George Loveless, a ploughman and Wesleyan preacher, and five Tolpuddle labourers: James Hammett, James Loveless (George's brother), his brother-in-law Thomas

Standfield, the latter's son John Standfield and James Brine. George Loveless, the leader of the Tolpuddle Six, was acutely aware of the injustice of depressed wages: it was, he said, 'hard to remain honest on a wage of eight shillings'.[54] In response to landowners' broken promises, he and his fellow labourers formed the Friendly Society of Agricultural Labourers. This was completely legal, as Loveless, well versed in the writings of social reformers, well knew: unions were then being formed across the nation. But, he added half-jokingly, joining a union was then regarded as something almost akin to 'witchcraft'.[55] In the upper room of Thomas Standfield's cottage, they looked at a picture of a skeleton – possibly strange to us today but typical of labour rituals at the time – and swore an oath of loyalty with their hands on a Bible. So the Tolpuddle Six formed their union and demanded a weekly wage of no less than 10 shillings, the pay rise they'd originally been offered.

Armed with information brought by his two spies, Frampton wrote to the home secretary, Lord Melbourne, to see if there was any way he could prosecute the Tolpuddle Six. After some deliberation, the home secretary advised him to test out an obscure naval law, the Seditious Meetings and Assemblies Act of 1817.[56] And so the Tolpuddle men were brought to trial.

As the Tolpuddle men would have been well aware, the trial was overseen by people with a vested interest in achieving a guilty verdict. Though he was a magistrate, Frampton, who openly stated that he wanted the trial to make an example of people who defied the authorities, sat on the jury. The presiding judge echoed Frampton's sentiments: 'The object of all legal punishment is not altogether with the view of operating on the offenders themselves, it is also for the sake of offering an example and a warning.'[57] Meanwhile, the foreman of the jury was the home secretary's brother-in-law, while Frampton's fellow jury members included his son, half-brother and other magistrates who had signed the original arrest warrant. Among the prosecution witnesses were Frampton's gardener and Frampton's two spies, John Lock and Edward Legg, all of whom likely calculated that displeasing Frampton would bring them worse consequences than testifying against their fellow workers. The trial testimony of Legg and Lock was vague. Both men swore they'd been present at the Tolpuddle workers' oath-taking ceremony, but had no idea who'd read the oath to them. To make things worse, Lock muddled up James Hammett's identity, confusing him with his brother. He said that he'd been asked by James Loveless and George Loveless to join the union and – quoting from his testimony – said, that they'd both been asked 'if we were ready to have our eyes blind-folded', which they agreed to, and 'a paper was read to us, but I do not recollect any of the words that were read'.[58] For all this, the jury and judge were eager to accept the prosecution argument that the union was seditious and handed down a verdict of high treason.[59] Five of the men were sentenced to be transported to New South Wales, where they would do seven years' hard labour in penal colonies; their leader, George Loveless, would be sent to Van Diemen's Land (modern-day Tasmania).[60]

A key episode in Britain's labour history, details of the trial also suggest how the slavery system was subtly embedded in trials like this one. An overlooked aspect of the Tolpuddle case concerns the figures involved in sentencing the men to transportation. One man who asked to be on the jury, and was granted his wish, was William Francis Spencer Ponsonby, whose family owned plantations in St Vincent. James Frampton, meanwhile, had married into a family with Antiguan plantations and also owned much of the land around Tolpuddle.[61] This was no tangential connection. Slave-owners rein-vested their profits in land; and landownership was a prerequisite for political and legal office.

After they had been sentenced, five of the Tolpuddle Six travelled to Portsmouth in a cart, shackled together. There, they were put on board the *York*, a 74-gun naval ship, formerly active in West Indies sea-battles; up the coast, they were then transferred to the *Surry*, which shipped them to New South Wales in Australia.[62] George Loveless, who had fallen ill in prison, followed a few weeks later on the *William Metcalfe*: he would remain separated from the other five men throughout his years of hard labour.

Loveless kept an account of his experience. Prison ships, he wrote, were regularly overcrowded. His own time on board the *William Metcalfe* was miserable and unsanitary, and there was insufficient room in his cramped berth for him to lie down for the entire voyage of some five months. He told of an incident on another transportation ship, the *George III*, which was wrecked off the Tasmanian coast. When convicted prisoners, trapped below the hatches of the sinking ship and waist-deep in seawater, tried to escape, they were pushed back below deck, shot and slashed with cutlasses.[63]

Loveless' depiction of the penal colony in Van Diemen's Land was a powerful indictment of the colonial system. Working on menial tasks during all daylight hours, convicts did so inadequately clothed, and often stripped to the waist. Punishments were severe, with fifty lashes for attempting to escape. Unsurprisingly, prisoners' health deteriorated; suicide attempts were common.[64]

The colony's governor, Sir George Arthur, was callous in the extreme: during his thirteen-year rule in Van Diemen's Land, he oversaw the execution of 260 convicts. Impressed by Loveless, however, Arthur sent him to work on his own farm.[65] Not that this improved matters. There, Loveless suffered from chronic overwork and ill treatment. There was no bed for him, and he developed health problems from lying on hard surfaces, mostly back and bone ache. He also narrowly escaped fifty lashes for supposedly neglecting a cattle herd when he'd simultaneously been allocated care of the sheep.[66]

Loveless learned of the governor's systematic displacement of Aboriginals (whom Arthur termed 'savages'), driving them off their traditional pasturelands onto inhospitable and isolated peninsulas; there, they were placed in internment camps, where many died of disease. Loveless wrote disapprovingly of the Aboriginal peoples' displacement. Though he called them 'uncivilized people' (a notion he didn't expand on, as it was then widespread), he wrote that they were left to die 'like rotten sheep'. Loveless also warned his fellow workers that they were unlikely to escape poverty by settling in the colonies. People were being fooled into thinking they could make money there, he wrote. But in reality the only people who could make money were those who already had it.[67]

Loveless and his fellow 'martyrs' were among 4,000 British political prisoners and social protesters who, between 1787 and 1868, were transported to penal colonies as punishment for fighting for their rights.

Comparisons between the position of British transportees and Aboriginals were both common and inevitable. One transported man, sent to the penal colonies for participating in the 1829 Barnsley weavers' strike, argued that – in Van Diemen's Land – colonial brutality was inflicted on convicts, free emigrants and Aboriginals alike. These, he argued, were expressions of an unjust class system and the unequal operation of repressive laws and social rules.[68] The reality was that Aboriginals fared far worse than convicts in the penal colonies. Aboriginals resisted the occupation of lands which had, for generations, provided them with water and hunting grounds, and they fought back when the land was converted into sheep ranches. Their food supply was disrupted, their camps raided, and they were frequently shot and killed by the English.

Another member of the Tolpuddle Six was James Hammett, whose conviction was a case of mistaken identity. It was his brother John, not him, who had been present at the oath-taking. With John's wife pregnant with her first child, the 21-year-old James remained silent about the mistake and took the punishment.[69] Arriving in Australia in August, 1834, he was sent 150 miles south-west of Sydney to Queanbeyan in New South Wales – a distance he had to walk – to work for a sheep farmer called Edward John Eyre (there, he dug a well still known as 'Hammett's well'). An Englishman from Bedfordshire, Eyre had emigrated to Australia and established himself as a livestock drover, finding inland routes along river courses to the South – and, like many colonists, benefited from the penal transportation system which provided him with a ready labour supply. Later, he would become an infamous colonial administrator, recalled for the brutal repression of Jamaicans while he was governor.

Back in Britain, the blatantly unjust sentencing and transportation of the Tolpuddle Martyrs became a cause célèbre. On 24 March 1834, 10,000 people attended a Grand Meeting of the Working Classes in London, called by Robert Owen, the leader of the Grand Consolidated Trades Union. This inaugurated a campaign to secure a government pardon for the Tolpuddle Six. There followed a demonstration, in April that year, of some 100,000 people near Kings Cross in London, and twelve union men carried an 800,000-signature petition to the home secretary, Lord Melbourne, which demanded the men's release. Lord Melbourne refused to receive the petition. In parliament, the radical journalist William Cobbett – now a Member of Parliament – raised the issue repeatedly with his fellow MPs. Ten months after the Tolpuddle men had arrived in the penal colonies – and after protracted negotiation – their pardon was finally granted in March 1836.[70]

In Queanbeyan, James Hammett learned of the pardon from a newspaper that had been left lying about at his sheep station, some weeks after it had been granted. His fellow martyrs had returned to England ahead of him, their arrival celebrated with a dinner and procession in Plymouth (their point of arrival) in their honour. The voyage was long. George Loveless arrived back first, on 13 June 1837, followed by the others – bar James Hammett – on Saturday 17 March 1838, their ship having been delayed in New Zealand for some weeks. In Plymouth, they were toasted by the MP Thomas Wakley, who had campaigned on their behalf. In his speech, the MP expressed hopes that the Tolpuddle Six should no longer be labourers but farmers of independent financial means, a small irony given their clashes with landowners and their struggle for better wages for all. He called upon people to donate money to them.[71] George Loveless, too, was one of many prominent Chartists – campaigners for parliamentary reform – and he was among many leading union figures who considered penal colonies to be sadistic dystopias which laid bare the consequences of unchecked abuses of power by the authorities back home in Britain. Until there was proper parliamentary representation, they argued, working-class demands would continue to be met with injustice and brutality on British as well as colonized soil.[72]

James Hammett finally arrived back in London in August 1839, where he was met by his wife Harriet; reunited, the pair returned to Tolpuddle. Back home, he left agriculture behind and took up the building trade.[73] A photograph of Hammett in old age shows him straight-backed with Victorian whiskers and a watch chain. There are deep lines around his mouth. Hammett went blind in old age and, not wanting his family to have to support him, he went to the Dorchester workhouse, despite his status as a national hero among union members. It is said that his special status earned him good treatment in the workhouse, however. He died there in 1891.[74]

Reluctantly, we got up from the comfortable bench on Tolpuddle green and made the short walk along the main street towards the medieval parish church of St John's, with its squat, crenelated tower, copper-green roof and mullioned windows. Here, in the kempt churchyard, Hammett is buried. His grave remains a site of secular pilgrimage: every year, during the Tolpuddle Martyrs' Festival, people come to pay homage to him, in a tradition which has been followed since the trial's first centenary in 1933. Louisa and I stood by Hammett's graveside in the mossy churchyard, the grass springy beneath our feet, and read the grave's inscription, 'James Hammett, Tolpuddle Martyr, Pioneer of Trades Unionism, Champion of Freedom. Born 11 September 1811, Died 21 November 1891'. I turned to Louisa. 'I think you've something in common with him,' I said. 'You've used your bad experiences to benefit and protect other people.' Louisa smiled. We walked back around the church and onto the main street.

I wanted to visit nearby Affpuddle, home to the magistrate Frampton's two spies, Legg and Lock, as well as James Brine, one of the Tolpuddle Six. 'It all must have felt very personal,' Louisa said, 'with your neighbours spying on you.' I nodded: 'And your landowner prosecuting you, then filling the jury with his relatives!' Despite her cold, Louisa was nonetheless keen to press on:

'The weather's too nice not to, and Affpuddle's bound to be pretty,' she said.

It was about four o'clock in the afternoon and, with the sun still warm on our backs, we set off along the lane. We were glad we did. Affpuddle is even lovelier than Tolpuddle, surrounded by water meadows full of watercress and buttercups and virtually traffic-free. The only vehicle we saw was a passing Land Rover, driven by a farmer who stopped in the lane, his sheepdog bolt upright in the passenger seat beside him. The farmer had spotted me taking photos of his period barn and told me it belonged to him. He knew it looked picturesque, he told us with a smile, but the roof was hell to maintain, and the tiles were expensive. He drove off with a good-natured wave.

Sleepy Affpuddle was peaceful with its millrace and medieval church. Like so much of rural England, the enclosed fields around the village had belonged to wealthy landowners for centuries. The present-day church was given its land by a Saxon man called Affrith, or Alfrith, in the Middle Ages, from which the village gets its name. The church once owned all the land hereabouts. After the dissolution of the monasteries, the land belonged to a family called Lawrence, who later married into the Washingtons (of George Washington fame). Then, the village passed into the hands of the Framptons, including James Frampton, the magistrate who pursued charges against the Tolpuddle men.

We walked into the village past bird-filled hedgerows. Its two rows of thatched dwellings stood on either side of the lane, with some larger houses set further back. Many cottage walls were washed with an earthy colour, whilst others were painted white. Their thick thatch made it easy to imagine the place in distant Saxon times, and we commented that its appearance was not so dissimilar to how it had been in the eleventh century, when the village was listed in the Domesday Book as 'Affapidela.' 'Thatch used to be a mark of poverty,' Louisa observed. 'Nowadays it's rustic chic,' I replied. (Until the nineteenth century, nearly all rural houses were thatched with straw: slate roofing didn't arrive until the Welsh stone could be transported by canals and railways during the Industrial Revolution.) Some were decorated with plastic Union Jacks, which flapped in the breeze. These flags made me think of my bed-and-breakfast stay the night before, where the nearby village of Milborne St Andrew had been similarly decorated. I told Louisa about it, talking above a mixed chorus of robins, wrens and sparrows: 'The owner of the guesthouse greeted me like an old friend, and we ended up having this wide-ranging, philosophical conversation all evening. Then, at breakfast the next morning this news item came on about Black Lives Matter and the proprietor said that racism doesn't exist any more.' Louisa asked how I responded. 'I mainly stuck to the evidence,' I said. Much of the previous night's conversation with the guesthouse owner had been about health, so I'd mentioned the different birth outcomes for Black and White mothers in the UK, then we discussed the statistics on police stop and searches. 'I listened carefully to everything she said,' I told Louisa, 'so I could understand what her ideas were based on. She listened closely too.' The proprietor had waved me off with such warmth and respect that I wished all such conversations could be so open-spirited.

We passed Affpuddle's parish church, St Laurence's, with its grand fifteenth-century tower of mellow grey stone and flint complete with stone buttresses and pinnacles. Like so many rural churches, it was closed, so we couldn't visit – a shame, as the interior reveals an even older history, with its thirteenth-century nave, fourteenth-century porch and Norman font. We walked on, following a bend in the road, and there found the footpath through the fields back to Tolpuddle. We thought of that short walk between the villages, on the day that Legg and Lock had accompanied James Hammett (according to the charge) and James Brine to Thomas Standfield's house to swear that fateful oath.

Apart from the farmer in the Land Rover, we didn't see a soul the whole time we were in Affpuddle: the soundscape was all birdsong and the trickling chalk stream. 'Hard to believe that 400 people live in this tiny place today,' I said. At the far end of the village we stopped to gawp at another cottage by the old mill. Standing beside the River Piddle and an old sluice gate, its lawn fell away into the clear chalk stream, which was lined with lush vegetation. We gazed at some garden chairs as though wishing ourselves into them, then ran our eyes over the cottage nooks and blue paintwork. 'I want this cottage,' I said. So, it turned out, did Louisa: we joked that we'd have to fight each other for it. Spotting another thatched cottage some way back from the road, I decided I could plump for that instead: 'In another life, maybe.'

On the path back, I told Louisa what happened to the colonial administrator Edward John Eyre, for whom James Hammett had worked in New South Wales. After an expedition across Australia in 1840–41, he was invited by Australia's colonial governor to become Protector of Aborigines in south-eastern Australia. His job – so it says in the preface to Eyre's exploration account – was to 'undertake the task of re-establishing peace and amicable relations with numerous native tribes of the Murray River . . . whose daring and successful outrages in 1841, had caused very great losses to, and created serious apprehensions among the Colonists'.[75] (Such commentary, of course, testified to Aboriginals' acts of resistance against colonial incursion and mistreatment.) Eyre's methods of re-establishing peace were not based on any sort of respect for Australia's indigenous peoples; quite the opposite. His proposed solution of 'managing' them saw the removal of Aboriginals into designated lands governed by colonial officials under orders from a missionary or protector. The protector would have the power to restrict people's movement to and from reserves, give permission to marry or to limit social activity among Aboriginals. He also advocated that these figures had the power to separate children from elders to reduce the influence of what he called 'the savage hordes', implementing a policy which left a traumatic and enduring legacy. With elders deprived of free movement, their children were placed in English-speaking schools, from which they graduated into menial apprenticeships as shepherds and stock-keepers.[76] Eyre's policies appeared to reduce violent conflict with Aboriginals by acknowledging their prior claims to land, then compensating them only with food and shelter (Britain took the land). Eyre's reputation in Australia helped him into his subsequent roles as governor of New Zealand, a position he held between 1846 and 1853, then of the Caribbean island of St Vincent, which he governed until 1860.

From there, after temporarily governing the Leeward Islands, in 1864 Eyre became governor of Jamaica.[77] By this time slavery was formally at an end, but its legacies were everywhere to be found in the form of mass poverty and the continued dominance of White landowners. Sugar plantations, meanwhile, were by then commonly worked by indentured labourers from India and formerly enslaved people. In 1865, Eyre imposed martial law in response to a demonstration about these ongoing injustices in Morant Bay. On his watch, a thousand Jamaican captives were tortured, sentenced without trial or made to watch executions before burying the dead.[78] Unapologetic and self-justificatory, Eyre's official report on the Jamaican Affair, as it became known, contradicted the stories of brutality which had already circulated widely because his troops had been writing home light-heartedly about their own atrocities.[79]

Eyre was recalled to Britain. Though he escaped prosecution, the episode brought the plight of Jamaicans into focus: through their petitions, speeches and pamphlets, routinely quoted in British newspapers due to the enormity of these events, they presented equality and self-determination not as a tentative moral question but as a legal right and moral imperative.[80]

Back in Tolpuddle, we popped into the one-roomed museum. Formerly a library, the museum forms part of a commemorative row of 1930s Tolpuddle Martyrs Memorial cottages. Inside, the story is told with information banners and two long glass cases containing copies of documents connected with the trial. 'This place is tiny!' Louisa said, as I pointed out a pitchfork hung up overhead. Tolpuddle Martyrs Museum may be small, but it is visited by people from all over the world who want to learn more about union history. We left the museum and stood outside on the grassy bank.

Louisa and I parted as the low sun slanted through the leaves of nearby trees. Hugging Louisa goodbye, I reflected that while James Hammett may have suffered in life, history has done him justice: remembered now as the man who took his brother's punishment, his graveyard is visited by thousands of people each year. The historical verdict on Governor Eyre is muddy. He is still remembered primarily as an explorer and depicted as having respected Aboriginal peoples despite the traumatizing policies he enacted.

All of which took my thoughts back to the Draxes. Charborough Park's official website gives a history of the estate and the family. It notes the estate's entry in the Domesday Book and the deeds of Richard Drax's parliamentarian forebears in the Civil War, as well as the house's rich architectural heritage. But there's no mention of the Drax family's sizeable profits from Barbados, or the connection between slavery compensation money and the building of the house's stunning east wing and 2 million-brick estate wall. Yet, as the history is uncovered, so the discussions over Drax Hall continue. A few years ago, the interconnected worlds Louisa and I had explored on our walk came momentarily together, when Black Lives Matter campaigners joined with Tolpuddle Festival-goers to march around Charborough's long wall to highlight the call by CARICOM for Drax Hall to be returned to the people of Barbados.[81]

Powerful historical figures will always have their monuments, but the stories of the Tolpuddle Martyrs continue to inspire. On the bank outside the museum, George Loveless has been hewn from Portland stone: he sits, head thrown back, awaiting transportation. Beside him are five empty seats, one for each of his fellow martyrs: we're invited to sit beside him. For Jamaicans, meanwhile, the Morant Bay events remain significant: they paved the way for greater economic and legal equalities on the island.[82] Some years ago the Jamaican attorney Bert Samuels wrote a play, a courtroom drama called *The Trial of Governor Eyre*. Using witness statements, defence and prosecution lawyers, this fictional trial revived the voices of Eyre's victims.[83] One hundred and fifty years after the event, Governor Eyre was found guilty.

The epic, intertwined tale of Tolpuddle, Australia and Jamaica has one final chapter. Back in England, Edward Eyre started drawing his – moderately reduced – colonial governor's pension in 1874. He moved to Walreddon Manor at the edge of Whitchurch village in West Devonshire, where he lived in peace and comfort until his death in 1901. The manor's walled gardens and woodland banks were far removed from the Dorchester workhouse where James Hammett had breathed his last a decade earlier. So, too, did Eyre's serene Devonshire property stand thousands of miles from the places where he had enacted his brutal policies.

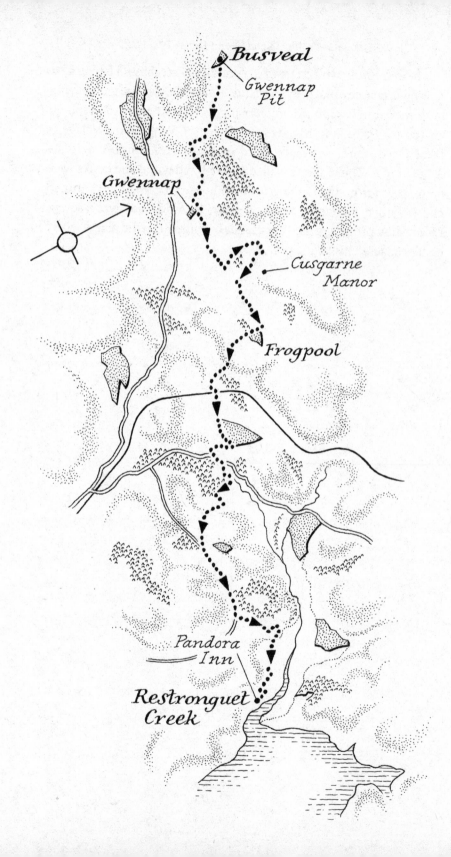

Busveal

Gwennap
Pit

Gwennap

Cusgarne
Manor

Frogpool

Pandora
Inn

Restronguet
Creek

10

The Copper Walk: Cornwall, West Africa and the Americas

Surrounded on three sides by sea, the peninsula of Cornwall is England's most south-westerly county: sailing west from here, your next stop would be Newfoundland. Today, Cornwall is a prime destination for surfers, gourmands and wealthy second-home-owners, who enjoy its mild, Gulf Stream climate and dramatic coastlines.

Cornwall has always felt, and feels itself, to be a land apart. The Cornish have their own language, and their own flag – a horizontal white cross with a black background – flies from buildings everywhere. The county's past is steeped in legend, including stories of King Arthur and his knights at Tintagel Castle. The area's more recent smuggling history also lends Cornwall an air of mystique. Back in the eighteenth and nineteenth centuries, its fishing boats and mail ships brought in contraband tobacco, cloth, wine and spirits, making a significant informal contribution to the region's economy. Cornwall's smuggling past sits alongside its significant maritime history; back in those days, it was a hub for shipping, global trade and communications.

Further inland, the remains of Cornwall's rich tin- and copper-mining history remain a defining feature of its landscape, with spoil heaps, brick chimneys and old engine houses across the countryside. The first Cornish mines were dug in the Elizabethan period and were worked intensively from the 1680s onwards. By 1800, the copper industry employed more than a third of Cornwall's workforce.[1] Copper has special properties. It conducts heat easily, is malleable and can be combined with alloys to make brass (using zinc) and bronze (using tin, which Cornwall also possessed in abundance). All of which made it ubiquitous in the eighteenth and nineteenth centuries: visit any antiques fair today and you will find an abundance of Victorian copper jugs, pans, kettles and coal scuttles. Yet copper was not merely destined for domestic markets. A major export, it was used widely across the British Atlantic world. The gleaming orange metal was sold by European slave-traders along the West African coast and beaten into vast containers to boil West Indian sugar. Copper sheeting also sheathed colonial battleships and slave-ships, preventing their wooden hulls from deteriorating in tropical waters. The applications for this versatile metal did not stop there. The challenge of pumping water from the bowels of Cornish copper mines inspired advances in steam technology. Initially invented for copper mines, steam engines subsequently powered the nation's factories in the second half of the Industrial Revolution. These steam-powered factories eventually brought about Britain's cotton boom.[2]

I made this Cornish excursion alone. By now I had completed ten walks – starting with Basildon Park and recently ending with Tolpuddle – and my companions' perspectives on these historical landscapes had expanded and deepened my relationship with the countryside. Cornwall presented a new challenge to my understanding of the relationship between urban and rural places. As I had grown up in the old industrial heartlands of the English Midlands, the Industrial Revolution was all iron, steam and canals to me. Until recently, I'd had no idea of copper's galvanizing role at the dawn of industrialization. I wanted to learn about copper mines, what mining conditions were like, what kind of livelihoods they produced, and I wanted to know more about copper's role in transatlantic slavery. In order to find out, I set out for Gwennap parish in central south Cornwall, once known as the richest square mile on Earth.

From Gwennap, my route would lead through an evocative and derelict industrial landscape to the coastal hamlet of Restronguet Creek, a waterside hamlet from which copper was once exported to Welsh smelting works and onwards to the Atlantic world.

*

It was a damp May morning with sunny intervals, the sort of day when the clouds gather, dance then disperse. The previous night, I'd stayed near the old mining village of Busveal; now, I headed to the former copper mine called Gwennap pit, which lies at the village's heart. Sculpted from the deep shaft of Cathedral mine, its terraces – which serve as grassy seats – were created by miners in 1806.[3] The air was fresh, and the hedgerows teemed with birdlife: I saw solitary robins, then flocks of yellow-winged goldfinches with their blushing faces. Looking across meadows and mature trees, it was hard to believe that this square mile was once crammed with mines and scoured of vegetation, the air thick with toxic vapours.

I passed Busveal's whitewashed chapel, a reminder of how pervasive the Methodist faith once was in Cornwall. The celebrated preacher and founder of Methodism, John Wesley, first visited the village in 1762. Wesley returned many times, preaching until he was eighty-six. This is how the old Cathedral pit became a preaching place which seated hundreds of people.

Wesley's habit of outdoor preaching suited Cornwall, bringing together people from isolated rural settlements. Locals also appreciated Methodists' efforts to combat illiteracy and ill-health, as well as their message of salvation for miners and seafarers whose occupations were dangerous.[4] Wesley wrote how, travelling to Gwennap, he was met a couple of miles east of the village at 'Three-cornered Down (so called)' by a reception committee of a few hundred miners, who accompanied him on his way. There, a crowd of 500 listened to his sermon. It proved so popular that Wesley returned to Gwennap a few weeks later to preach again. That September evening, he found 10,000 people waiting for him, the surrounding countryside covered with crowds. He preached until it got dark – 'we could scarcely see one another' – but nobody left. 'And there was on all sides the deepest attention; none speaking, stirring, or scarcely looking aside.'[5]

A sign near the chapel pointed the way to the pit, where I climbed some steps and found myself in a great grassy amphitheatre dotted with dandelions. Softened by grass, this chiselled pit is far more attractive than it would have been when Wesley encountered it. Its swirling form is hypnotic, like a whirlpool, with thirteen concentric circles that widen towards the top. The houses of Busveal cluster round the pit.

The amphitheatre's velvety surface conceals the mine's grim accident record. Long ago, when the pit was still being mined, a shaft flooded and drowned eight people whose felt hats were discovered during a recent excavation. Below my feet, a labyrinth of fume-filled tunnels hid similar tales of misery: hard to reconcile with the brightness and birdsong around me.

Leaving Busveal, I headed out of the village past beech, elm and oak trees. About a mile on stood one of Gwennap's old mines, Wheal Damsel. During the mid-nineteenth century, this mine yielded tens of thousands of pounds of copper. Now all that remains is a pile of stones by the roadside where an engine house once stood, amidst a profusion of cornflowers, foxgloves and ferns. I skirted the edge of Carharrack, which in Gwennap's boom years was a crowded village filled with miners' cottages. Now this residential area has retained its Wesleyan chapel and is surrounded by new housing developments and abandoned engine houses.[6]

Surveying the surrounding fields as I walked, I thought about the miners who lived in small settlements scattered across the countryside, their homes typically low-beamed cottages with small windows and two rooms upstairs and down. Men, women and children once made their way from these hamlets and villages to work in the nearby mines. As copper production boomed in the late eighteenth and early nineteenth centuries, new villages sprang up across Gwennap parish and local towns expanded to accommodate more mineworkers.[7]

One such was Gwennap village, a mile or so on from Carharrack. A buzzard perched on a gatepost and extended its wings in the midday sun. The village itself is tiny: an uneven row of lime-rendered miners' cottages dominated by the wide old church of St Wenappa. There's a reason the church needed to be so roomy:

during the nineteenth century, St Wenappa served up to 10,000 parishioners from the surrounding mining community.[8]

I welcomed the church's cool interior after my humid walk from Busveal. Inside, I scanned the walls for memorials. Passing between the wooden pews I came across a commemorative plaque to a young lieutenant from the parish called William Williams, who served in the 1842 Siege of Jalalabad, the sole victory in an otherwise disastrous (for the British) First Anglo-Afghan War: during the retreat from Kabul of the same year, some 16,000 British and Indian soldiers, families and servants were massacred or died of exposure. Thinking back on my ten walks, I realized that not a single church I'd visited was untouched by empire.

Emerging from the church, I continued into the village and wandered between the houses. Heavy rose-heads lolled against their white cob walls. At the end of the village, I climbed a stile to follow the way through some long grass. There, a fox lingered in the sunlight, and I stood watching him until the spell broke and his amber eyes met mine. He whipped round and zig-zagged along the hedgerow to find an exit, leaving me alone amidst the clover, ragwort and yarrow. Bees droned in the heat.

I wondered at these remote villages, located so close to the pits. The investors and shareholders, who actually got rich from copper, lived further east and enjoyed polite society in the prosperous city of Truro, with its elegant townhouses. (Much of Truro's conversation would have centred on the value of copper mine shares.) A few miles to the west of Gwennap, meanwhile, lies the town of Redruth, the beating heart of the copper business where smelters bid for ore and people talked about its weight, quality and price.[9] The ore bought by smelters was mostly shipped round the coast to Wales, which unlike Cornwall had plentiful coal.[10] The sea between Cornwall and Swansea – the Atlantic Ocean – could be rough: Welsh smelters sailed their cargoes on calm days and so stockpiled the copper to maintain a constant supply of ore.[11] Cornwall's copper was mostly smelted in Welsh places like Greenfield works to the north, which made 2-foot copper rods. In the 1750s, a Swedish traveller noted that these pliable rods, called 'Negroes', were used as ornaments for winding around arms and legs, and were accepted as currency in exchange for enslaved people.[12] Similarly used as currency were copper manillas, or bracelets, made at the Welsh White Rock works in Swansea, which had a building called Manilla House. Parys Mountain works, on the Welsh island of Anglesey, was run by the industrialist Thomas Williams, whose extraction of shallow-lying Welsh copper ore, from the 1770s, threatened Cornish mine production. He manufactured metals – in his own words – 'entirely for the African market.'[13]

By the 1770s, with the Gwennap mining business booming, almost 8,000 people were paid to sink shafts, excavate lodes and haul copper ore to the surface. The proliferating mines – 'wheals' in Cornish – were given distinctive names like West Wheal Virgin, Wheal Lovelace, Wheal Fortune, Wheal Cupboard and Ale and Cakes – and, of course, Wheal Damsel, which I had passed earlier that morning.[14] And the mines were astonishingly productive. In 1785, the workers of Huel-Virgin mine alone excavated a staggering 1,400 tons of copper in a single month.[15]

By 1824, Gwennap parish was producing over a third of the world's copper: a great success story for investors, far less so for those who worked in the mines. Labour conditions were terrible. Having been worked for over a century, the old mines were so deep that only young men were physically capable of reaching the ore. About half the miners were aged between fifteen and twenty-five. Until the 1840s, when cages were lowered by waterwheel, men descended a series of ladders leading from one level to another: it could take an hour and a half for a miner to reach the pitch he had been allocated.

Miners were required to purchase their equipment at inflated prices from the mine proprietor. They gathered their candles, ropes, hole-borers, pickaxes, drills and gunpowder then descended into the dark. On reaching their part of the mine, they bored at the hard rock and placed gunpowder into the hole, withdrawing during the explosion then collecting the fallen ore. It was skilled work: miners needed to know where the ore lay, and how to use explosives safely. Food was taken into the mine. The Cornish pasty, containing potatoes with mutton or pork, was conveniently designed for underground eating; hobbans, savoury cakes made with potato, were also popular. Once work ended, miners might spend two hours, often in wet clothes, climbing back up again. Ladders were often placed at odd angles; the rungs, if intact, were sometimes a foot apart, requiring real exertion.[16] With long, laborious days like this, it is no wonder that miners and their families – also vital to the mining process – wanted to live as close to the mine as possible. Ore was hauled to the surface, where women and girls 'dressed' it: breaking it up, sifting it, washing it free of debris and impurities,[17] then breaking the ore into pebbles and powder, ready for smelting.[18]

Over time, Cornish copper production became increasingly organized and specialized.[19] Mine captains supervised work and kept discipline. Tunnellers would be paid according to the distance and difficulty of the mine section they were working on. The productive parts of the mine were split into pitches, to be worked by two or more men for a rate set by the mine. A poor pitch was better paid because it took longer to extract ore from it and yielded less profit for the miners.[20] The men received a proportion of the ore they excavated, minus deductions for candles, tools and blasting equipment. All sorts of services sprang up around the mines: candle and rope-making, mules and horses, legal services, steam engines and engineers, as well as tramways and railways to transport ore to the docks and bring coal for steam engines.[21]

Mine accidents were frequent, and local newspapers reported weekly deaths and injuries. Blinding was common during rock blasts, and storing gunpowder was an obvious risk. Three miles north of Gwennap, at Poldice mine, two men smoked in the engine room and accidentally set alight some gunpowder barrels. Both were killed in the blast. In 1841 alone there were seventy-five fatalities in Gwennap Parish: five died in a boiler explosion, three men got entangled with machinery, eight died during blasting operations, twenty-five fell from ladders, and twenty-six were crushed by roof collapses while eight died of unspecified causes.[22] For obvious reasons medical services were vital in the mines, and doctors' fees were deducted from miners' wages.[23] The main cause of death, however, came not from accidents but lung disease: down the pit, the air was thin, hot and filled with fumes and dust.[24]

Thankful to be above ground, the only ugliness I could see was a row of giant electricity pylons standing astride the path as I picked my way onwards through flower-filled meadows. It was an effort of imagination to imagine how different this landscape looked 200 or more years ago. Then, the Gwennap mines left an indelible impression on visitors. Visiting in 1787, the novelist William Beckford described a vision of hell: cinder-heaps, flaming chimneys and bellowing steam engines; ragged miners crawling out of the earth with their pickaxes. Beckford, though, didn't express much concern for the exhausted human forms which emerged from the mines. He seemed more disturbed by the treatment of mules, 'poor brutes' whom child workers flogged 'without respite'.[25] His apparent indifference to the human suffering he so evocatively described was unsurprising, given that his own vast wealth proceeded directly from enslaved labour on Jamaican sugar plantations. Just three years after his visit to Gwennap, he began spending his Jamaican wealth on Fonthill Abbey, an extravagant neo-Gothic residence on his Wiltshire country estate. Beneath its soaring towers, he would write his novels and – in his words – 'sing hymns to the power of the heaven from their summits'.[26] Badly and hastily built, Fonthill Abbey later collapsed.

I turned into a narrow lane with soft verges, where forest rot and the smell of leaf mould lingered. I entered a tunnel of beech trees, illuminated by sunshine. I passed an empty campsite, and soon the lane opened out onto fields, enclosed by square hedges and stone walls, which gave way to fences and the treeline thinned as, to my right, I saw the sea. Along the way I passed miners' cottages, neatly restored as holiday homes or lets.

A minority of mineworkers did gain a degree of financial stability. By the late eighteenth century, roughly a fifth of miners – very likely the most highly skilled portion of the workforce – could afford to buy or lease plots of land to build their own homes. This skilled minority kept neat, well-maintained houses and, with their wages far higher than those of agricultural labourers, were able to put money away. But for the majority of workers and their families, living conditions were poor. Whenever Redruth's water supply dwindled during a summer drought, the town's mining families resorted to taking their water from adits – mining drainage channels – with predictably adverse health impacts. With privies shared by many households, conditions were insanitary.[27] Today, many of these old cottages are desirable, characterful homes; back then, they were damp and overcrowded, and fuel from nearby woods had to be gathered for fires to cook and keep warm by. The commonest working diet consisted of barley bread, pilchards or salt fish and tea, without milk. For the poorest-paid, sugar – boiled in Cornish copper vats on West Indian plantations – was unaffordable.[28] The fact was that mining profits were concentrated in the hands of men whose incomes most Cornish people could only dream of. The real financial beneficiaries were the mine-owners, investors and the proprietors of smelting works.

Yet the story of copper reached far beyond these Cornish landscapes, and my thoughts turned to another category of beneficiary: the copper trader. Copper was integral to the British transatlantic slavery system.[29] By the late 1720s, global demand was such that over half of Britain's brass and copper was exported. During the first half of the eighteenth century, copper commodities were shipped from England's Atlantic ports to the Bight of Biafra, which was fast becoming a major slave-trading centre.[30] By the following decade, copper exports to West Africa amounted to 20 tons annually, shipped by the Royal African Company as well as by private slave-traders. By 1800, English trade in copper and brass with Africa had soared to 3,000 tons.[31] Copper and brass (composed of copper and zinc) was prized on Africa's west coast and traded for human beings.

Meanwhile, West Indian sugar plantations were also using vast quantities of Cornish and Welsh copper. Sugar cane was part-processed on the plantation to stop it spoiling and, as early as 1700, about 100 tons of copper was used annually to make brass rods for crushing canes.[32] Sugar was also boiled in copper cauldrons and the hot liquid transferred to copper coolers using copper utensils. Plantations' copper consumption was about 1,123 tons in 1700.[33] In 1732, a single estate in St Kitts needed £1,000 worth of copper equipment, by no means an untypical figure. This equipment was made by London coppersmiths, using Cornish copper. By the mid-eighteenth century, mass demand for sugar required ever-larger boiling vessels: one sugar plantation worked by 300 enslaved people needed more than 5 tons of copper vessels.[34] The demand for sugar was reflected in Britain's domestic market also: by 1770, fifty-six 'sugar bakers' used copper boilers to refine sugar so that they could cater to the nation's burgeoning sweet tooth.[35]

Cornish copper was also required by ships that transported sailors, enslaved people and luxury cargo produced by slave labour. The copper was rolled into thin sheets for covering ships' hulls, a process known as copper sheathing. This sheathing prevented infestations of shipworm, milk-white molluscs found in African and Caribbean waters that burrowed into timber and ate it, like aquatic woodworms.[36] For centuries, hulls had been coated with tar to ward off these attacks, but this was an inadequate remedy. Iron was tried, while a second layer of wood was commonly attached to ships' hulls, but these also proved ineffective solutions. Copper sheathing worked. It also deterred seaweed and crustaceans like barnacles, which increased friction, slowing ships down and making them hard to manoeuvre. Once copper sheathing proved successful, in 1779 the Royal Navy sheathed its entire fleet in the metal. At about £1 a ton, copper sheathing was then more expensive than wood. In 1792, the navy's copper usage averaged 358 tons and, during the French Revolutionary Wars, this trebled to 1,047 tons.[37]

On slave-ships, copper sheathing shortened voyage times, correspondingly reducing deaths on the Middle Passage because it decreased the risk of provision shortages, mutiny and sickness, a fact testified to in parliament by one copper industrialist.[38] Slavers accepted the innovation wholesale: by 1781, 75 per cent of slave-ships were coppered, and the sheathing was replaced every four to four-and-a-half years.[39] Historians have compared a sample of fifty-four unsheathed slave-ships with a sample of sixty-five sheathed slave-ships and found that unsheathed ships lasted about five-and-a-half years, with coppered ships' hulls lasting about eight.[40] Accounting for variables such as sea currents and routes, they calculated that copper sheathing made slave-ships 16 per cent faster, cutting ten to eleven days off the voyage time. Middle Passage fatalities declined in the second half of the eighteenth century and, taking into account seasonal, geographical and legislative factors – 1788 and 1799 Acts requiring more space on board for each trafficked person – copper sheathing seems to have reduced deaths by around half. In cynical business terms, then, sheathing slave-ships made economic sense. From a slaver's perspective, focused on profit not souls, a reduction of ten to fifteen deaths per voyage meant that copper sheathing paid for itself in a single Atlantic crossing.[41]

From Gwennap a tree-lined lane led uphill to thick woods. Through the woods, and past two farms with barking dogs, the hill fell away steeply: fleetingly, I had the impression of what it might be like to fly over the landscape, the jagged fields below resembling mossy crazy paving in browns and greens. Now, I was aiming for Cusgarne, another sleepy, ordered village which had once been a key staging post in the connection between Gwennap copper mining, steam power and the manufacture of slave-produced cotton.

Passing a sprawling farm shop and a foraging flock of brown hens on the village outskirts, I climbed a stone stile and made for Cusgarne Manor at the lower end of the village. Here, in the last two decades of the eighteenth century, lived one of the great engineers of the Industrial Revolution, James Watt, his wife Ann and their family. What brought James Watt hundreds of miles south to Cornwall from his native Scotland and his base in the English

Midlands were Cornwall's copper mines. In the late eighteenth century, engineers were racing to find a way of removing the water that flooded deep mineshafts, and in 1769 Watt had patented his steam-driven beam engine which, he believed, would do the trick. This technological innovation transformed Gwennap's fortunes, its landscape and Britain as a whole, helping to bring about our factories and railways.

Today, Cusgarne Manor is still privately owned. It has retained its nineteenth-century appearance and has lost none of its old elegance. From the road, I contemplated the house: pleasingly proportioned, giving a sense of symmetry at its south-facing front, which, along with the wide sash windows, must have made it feel light and airy. Imposing chimneys stand at its side walls and gable ends. There is an unspoilt stone courtyard at the rear.

The manor is now a bed-and-breakfast with 'boutique' added to its name. I looked up the prices: £211 for a 'king room with a garden view'. The house still fits a description of it written by the campaigner and author Samuel Smiles in 1865: 'an old-fashioned, roomy mansion, with a good-sized garden full of fruit trees, prettily situated at Cosgarne'.[42] Smiles was right, I thought.

Born in 1730, James Watt grew up in the Atlantic-facing port of Greenock, west of Glasgow, where his father handled tobacco and other slave-produced goods, also trading wine for West Indian sugar[43] and later shipping enslaved people from South Carolina to Antigua, and on to Jamaica. As the Scottish historian Stephen Mullen has shown, the slavery business was foundational to James Watt's career (even though his mercantile roots were later downplayed by his pro-abolition son). As noted by the historian Eric Williams, profits from the West Indies underpinned Watt's advancement,[44] his father's wealth financing Watt's expensive London education as a mathematical instrument-maker.[45]

James Watt's younger brother John was far more directly involved in slavery but drowned in Jamaica in 1762.[46] Following his brother's death, James himself was directly drawn into transatlantic slavery, helping to traffic a boy, named Frederick, to

Scotland. He wrote to the boy's new enslavers, the Brodie family of Spynie, to apologize for Frederick's late arrival. In the letter, he enclosed an inventory of Frederick's clothes: a blue waistcoat, coat and breeches, stockings, shoes, checked shirts, a pocket handkerchief and a cap.[47] The boy later escaped from the Brodies, and it is not known what happened to him after that.[48] James Watt also managed his father's tobacco accounts and invested in Glasgow's Delftfield Pottery, which exported to plantation-owners (receiving twenty times his original investment in the process). In 1772, he was commissioned by the slave-owner John Robertson to estimate the value of cotton production and enslaved people on the Grenadian island of Carriacou, a prime destination for Scots at the time. His findings were designed to provide an evidence basis for the slave-owner to decide whether or not to develop his Carriacou estates.[49] But Watt is, of course, best known for his steam engine.

Watt first became involved with steam engines in his late twenties. He was then untutored in steam technology but he set about experimenting with it because he knew of the demand for more powerful engines to manage the longstanding mine flooding. Initially a failure, Watt's experiments inspired him to learn everything he could about them. He obtained a model of an earlier steam engine invented by Thomas Newcomen in 1712 and began experimenting in earnest at the Soho Manufactory, which he ran with his business partner, Matthew Boulton.[50] They aimed to come up with an engine that produced enough power without consuming too much coal. When Watt made his key invention, a separate steam condenser that made steam engines fitted with it three times more efficient, he kept the plans as secret as possible for fear that someone else would steal his idea.[51] His steam engine was patented on 5 January 1769. The invention came at the perfect time for Gwennap's mines. The discovery of shallow-lying copper at Parys Mountain in Wales in the previous year had focused the minds of Cornish mine-owners, who were alarmed at the obvious competitive advantage that this would provide, since Wales had plentiful coal and nearby smelting works. Cornish mines were far too deep to be pumped out with the Newcomen engine: Poldice, North Downs, Ting Tang and Wheal Virgin mines in Gwennap parish all needed something more powerful. Combining power with efficiency, Watt's new engine was a godsend. I had seen one of these massive engines at work in the London Museum of Water and Steam, with its giant pistons and 15-ton beam. The engine shoots out steam like a whale spouting seawater through its blowhole.

In 1776, the first of Watt's Soho-made engines was installed in Gwennap, at Ting Tang mine. The results were spectacular.[52] Within four years, Cornish mines had ordered forty of Watt's engines, the benefits of this newly patented technology far outweighing the expense.[53] It was during this period that Watt relocated to Cusgarne.

I could see why Watt's wife Ann loved the place. It was spacious, and she enjoyed its walled garden and fruit trees. Her letters express fondness for the garden's peaches, plums and vines. She appreciated the elm trees around the house, and its location in a sheltered valley. For her, the only disadvantage of her new home was poor roads – but she found the local store convenient enough.[54]

She was, however, troubled by her husband's bad temper. His moods were notorious; when steam engines broke down, Gwennap's mine captains hoped that Watt's popular chief engineer, William Murdoch, would come to fix them rather than the inventor himself.[55] Watt got frustrated when his engines were, as he saw it, mistreated. But what stressed him most were escalating quarrels over the patent for his unique condenser technology. Mine-owners had to pay Watt to use the machines and resented paying ongoing dues for machinery that they'd long since bought, some going so far as to withhold their dues pending ineffectual legal challenges.[56] Still worse, as far as they were concerned, no alternative engine design was available. Whenever Cornish engineers designed other engines using the patented separate condenser from Soho Manufactory, Watt would take out injunctions against them being built or sold.[57] Because of all this, there was no love lost between Soho Manufactory and the owners of Cornish mines. After living in Cusgarne for a while, Watt's business partner, Matthew Boulton, called Wheal Virgin's investors 'a mean, dirty pack'.[58]

The exasperated Watt left Cornwall in 1779. His engine had transformed Cornish copper production. Old mines were brought back to life, and new mines were opened, allowing Cornish mines to compete with Welsh copper producers.[59] But the associated pollution and noise helped transform Gwennap into the hellscape commented on by so many visitors to the region. In 1795, a traveller to the region found Redruth so smoky that he couldn't eat breakfast, while another visitor compared the sound of steam engines to the crashes and thuds of Cyclops working inside Mount Etna.[60] Not that this noise and pollution had much bothered Watt and family during their time in the secluded village of Cusgarne: as Samuel Smiles put it some decades later, 'not an engine chimney was to be seen from the house'.[61]

Watt's machine subsequently changed the nation. Steam power had many applications for factories and locomotion: soon it was in widespread use. Steam engines propelled Britain into a fossil-fuelled industrial era as it left behind the logistical constraints of water and wind power.

His steam engine also fuelled plantation slavery. Boulton and Watt had been aware of this from the start, when they first applied for the 1769 steam engine patent. Handwritten annotations on patent lists in the Boulton and Watt archive – drawn up by a factory employee – show that both men had an eye on colonial applications for their steam technology.[62] The Imperial Patent system then operated across the British Atlantic World so that English and Welsh inventors could add a clause to extend their patents to British colonies and plantations, where European consumer demand required intensive processing of goods like coffee, sugar and rum. It was not hard to see the financial advantages of extending the patent, which incentivized inventors and investors to increase their profits from colonial markets and the slave-worked plantation system.[63] Using the engine meant that more sugar could be extracted from the cane, and at far greater speeds.[64] Across the Caribbean, 119 Boulton and Watt engines were ordered, 90 of which were installed within Watt's lifetime. Watt's steam engine was adopted by plantations with large-scale production, which made the engine, and its associated costs, affordable. Not only was steam power more reliable than windmills, but sugar was more quickly and more finely ground. Costs were reduced: no longer did plantation-owners need to buy mules and cattle to drive their sugar mills. They also needed fewer enslaved people. (The owners of Cane Garden estate in Nevis claimed that, whereas 100 enslaved people processed the plantation's sugar without steam power, 75 enslaved workers could do it if they had a machine. In their minds, this further reduced the 'need' to buy human beings at a time when they saw threats to slavery's continuance in the British Atlantic world.)[65] What was more, the engine could also be deployed for land drainage, irrigation pumping and even drawing carts to and from the wharf from which processed sugar was transported to portside warehouses.[66]

While initial drafts stipulated that Watt should enjoy the 'sole privilege and advantage of making and selling these engines' in England and Wales, a later draft extended this to 'his Majesty's Colonies and Plantations'. The patent covered all these territories when it was issued.[67] We don't know who made this alteration, and on whose initiative it was done: perhaps a lawyer, Boulton, or Watt or a combination of all involved. Watt, of course, had long experience of the colonial trade; the business-brained Boulton later wrote that 'we have a natural claim' to patent the technology 'in all countries'.[68]

Steamboats provided yet another commercially viable application for the Watt engine. In America, steamboats were used for passengers and for shipping goods along navigable rivers. Once again, Soho Manufactory spearheaded technological innovation by buying a boat specifically to act as a floating laboratory where ideas could be tried out, like installing twin engines. Boulton and Watt did not initially devote their attention to their steam engine's commercial application in shipping, although they did sell an engine to Robert Fulton, for the first-ever passenger steamboat, the *Claremont*, in 1807.[69] Watt advised Fulton on where the condenser should go, the effects of saltwater on the boiler and, finally, how to get a patent.[70] Fulton's ship the *New Orleans* was, between 1811 and 1812, the first ever to sail 1,800 miles along the Ohio to Mississippi Rivers, heralding a new era in commercial passenger services. Steamboats subsequently made New Orleans into America's second-biggest port after New York, carrying passengers and slave-produced cotton under billowing smoke.[71]

Copper and cotton, then, lie at opposite ends of slavery's steam-powered continuum: from the 1780s, Watt's engine extracted copper for plantation use and later gave them steam-power. By 1816, his steam engines propelled enslaved people and slave-grown cotton to and from Louisiana ports.

Yet Watt's personal attitude to slavery was complicated. He made ongoing profits from it but opposed it when publicly confronted with the principle of anti-slavery. A few years before Soho Manufactory had supplied a steam engine to Cuban and British plantations, Watt wrote to a French company in the slaving port of Nantes about the Haitian Revolution. In the light of the revolution, he noted, Soho Manufactory was postponing its delivery of Watt engines. Though he sympathized with plantation-owners' predicament in Haiti, he wrote that slavery was 'disgraceful' and ought to be abolished. More generally, Watt believed that slavery should be ended through 'prudent and progressive measures'. In other words, he advocated gradual, not immediate abolition, and was not in fact in favour of it being stopped there and then.[72]

Watt died in 1819, just a decade later than his business partner Matthew Boulton. Their sons managed Soho Manufactory between them. Given the Watt family's connection with the slavery business, it is unsurprising that three leading West Indies plantation-owners successfully campaigned for James Watt's statue to be erected in Glasgow. It's still there today, in George Square.[73]

Beyond Cusgarne, the lowering sun bronzed the ploughed soil. For twenty minutes, I followed peaceful lanes to Frogpool village, named – literally enough – after a nearby pond that teemed with frogs. Like many old Methodist mining villages, Frogpool is dominated by the Wesleyan chapel, a square, utilitarian building with a bottle-green door and covered with pebbledash, and presenting a stern challenge to the whitewashed village pub, the Cornish Arms, down the same lane. A few years after the chapel was built, its publican organized a wrestling match on the Sabbath. Members of the Methodist congregation dissuaded the wrestlers and organized a prayer meeting instead. That was the end of Sunday wrestling matches in Frogpool village.[74] Tempted though I was to stop there, I had some way to walk and so pressed on, noticing that the chapel was built in the same year that John Wesley first preached at Gwennap pit, in 1843. Its schoolroom was added much later.

Cornish people spread Methodism far and wide after their copper industry finally went into decline because copper was discovered in Brazil and Cuba in the mid-nineteenth century. But all was not lost for miners from tight-knit communities in places like Busveal, Gwennap and Frogpool: as hard-rock specialists, their skills were in global demand. Chasing guarantees of work and promises of decent wages, Cornish miners emigrated on a massive scale. Their mining know-how became a major export: as many as a quarter of a million miners would emigrate between 1861 and the early twentieth century.

Cornish miners had long emigrated to mines in other parts of the world, though in far smaller numbers. They were sought out by colonial mine developers as early as 1721, when groups of mineworkers set out from Falmouth – within easy distance of Gwennap parish – bound for the West African Gold Coast in modern-day Ghana. This early venture proved disastrous: when the *Oslow* set out that year, it was raided by pirates. A second vessel, again setting out from Falmouth but this time bound for the Gambia, was lost at sea. In 1723, a third group finally landed on Kunta Kinteh, then James Island, in the Gambia River but, there, the miners were ravaged by sickness and death, leading the Royal African Company to send ships to fetch Cornish replacements.[75]

The exodus of Cornish miners began in earnest when London financiers backed the 1824 Imperial Brazilian Mining Association, established in London to mine the Minas Gerais goldfield in south-eastern Brazil. A mine captain called William Tregoning was enticed there along with other Cornish mining experts. Cornish miners also left the region bound for Rio de Janeiro to work for St John d'El Rey Mining Company in 1830. On arrival, they found that both mines used large enslaved labour forces, which they were told to work alongside.[76]

In the 1840s, Cornish miners were wanted in Cuba, where copper had become big business. Pascoe Grenfell, Member of Parliament for the Cornish borough of Penryn, up the coast from Falmouth, was the chair of the Cobre Company, which became the Company of the Proprietors of the Royal Copper Mines of Cobre, then valued at a massive £480,000.[77] Michael Williams, the owner of Welsh smelting works, attached himself to a rival company, the Royal Santiago Mining Company.[78] The shares were sold to the public at £40 each, raising vast sums to prepare the mines for extraction and export on a global scale. The mines' unskilled labour force came from Cuba. Technical expertise and equipment came from Cornwall. A Cornish workforce was easily recruited: both Pascoe Grenfell and Williams had Cornish roots, in St Just and Redruth. These Cornish recruits embarked at Portreath or Hayle and sailed to Swansea. From there, they were transported to Cuba. There were miners, senior pitmen, mine carpenters and engineers, all recruited in exchange for wages, travel, board and lodging.[79] Meanwhile, the Santiago Company had recruited thirty-eight Cornish miners, a head blacksmith and head carpenters. These men went out on fixed-term contracts, but many died of tropical diseases, especially yellow fever. The death rate in Cuba caused an understandable recruitment problem, and mine-owners signed up poverty-stricken Welsh miners instead. Welsh miners were cheaper because they couldn't match the Cornish miners for hard-rock expertise but – given the decline of their own local industry – these men were desperate for work as Wales entered an economic depression.[80]

In the 1840s, one of the Cornish recruits at the El Cobre mines in Cuba was James Whitburn. His job was to operate and maintain the steam engines for raising water from the mineshafts. As a Wesleyan, Whitburn looked askance at Cuban Catholicism. But what really disturbed him was the treatment of enslaved people at the mines. By this time, slavery was officially outlawed in most British colonial territories, but companies like El Cobre exploited a loophole in anti-slavery laws, because the practice was not outlawed in Cuba itself. In working alongside enslaved people, Whitburn saw up close the horrors of their treatment, writing in his diary that the 'flogging of the Negroes in this country is most cruel', and he described in detail other punishments and terrible injuries on the bodies of enslaved workers.[81] The company tried to keep its use of slavery quiet – company information referred simply and coyly to 'labourers' – but word got out. The testimony of men like Whitburn brought the matter to the attention of the British and Foreign Anti-Slavery Society, and their revelations about the extent and nature of slavery in Cuba led to an 1843 Act being passed in parliament for the more effectual Suppression of the Slave Trade, banning British subjects from using slave labour in any country regardless of the local legislation. Yet the El Cobre and Santiago Companies continued to bypass this new legislation. They persuaded parliament that the new legislation should not apply to enslaved people the companies currently held captive; and also to let them hire enslaved people who were owned by others. Accordingly, El Cobre mines registered their enslaved workers in the name of their Cuban employees, who leased them back to the mine.[82]

By 1841, a combination of Cornish expertise and slave labour had already extracted 25,000 tons of copper from El Cobre, delivering massive profits for the Cuban mines and their shareholders.[83]

British-registered and British-run, Cuban mines were technologically advanced and financially pioneering. Endorsed by social dignitaries, from Members of Parliament to bankers and lord mayors, the discovery of slavery's role exposed a joint-stock system which disguised the human suffering behind its glittering edifice.[84]

I descended a lane that wound steeply towards the coast from which Cornish miners had departed for foreign shores. On the way, it bridged a railway line. Standing on the bridge, I peered down at the line, which was fringed with pink willowherb. This industrial heritage was powered by Cornwall's steam-driven copper industry. Now, overhead wires hissed as a train whizzed by, though it was easy to imagine thunderous clouds of smoke in the age of steam. I walked on, descending to Perran Wharf, an old iron foundry which manufactured mining equipment and precision parts for steam engines. The foundry was financed by the Fox family of Falmouth, Quakers with substantial copper, shipping and landowning interests who also paid for Poldice tramway, which linked Gwennap mines to the ports.[85] Derelict for many years, the complex was recently converted into townhouses.[86]

Continuing along the road, I entered the shade of another tree tunnel, I climbed again and, at the crest of the hill, paused to drink water. From where I was, the coast was obscured by woodland. Soon, a soft footpath relieved my feet, weary from road-walking. The path neared Restronguet Creek, an inlet in the Fal estuary. Across the estuary, I could make out the faint outline of Devoran Quays, where the Redruth and Chasewater railway brought copper ore from Gwennap mines to the coast for export, returning with coal along the nine-mile narrow-gauge track.[87]

Pink daisies lined the lane to Pandora Inn, a pub with a wobbly thatched roof which stands at the water's edge. Originally built in the seventeenth century with parts added in subsequent years, the inn has painted rubble walls, wooden lintels and a squat chimney at its gable end. Inside, it is all low beams and flagstone floors. Situated on the old post road between Falmouth and Truro, it gave a good view of the estuary, from which copper and tin were exported, a fitting historical location to end to my Cornish walk, and indeed all of the walks.

I left the pub and walked along a pier which protrudes from England's western tip and points towards the American continent far beyond. Droves of miners departed these shores, little knowing what horrors would confront them in the Atlantic world of slavery.

The weather was so warm that I went for a swim near a rocky outcrop beside the pub, from which a Cornish flag flapped. Treading water, I could see across to Devoran and, turning around, the wooded hills I had descended from earlier. I reflected on copper's connections to the Gold Coast, to Jamaica, Trinidad, Cuba and Mississippi paddle steamers. A fish tickled my foot, and I swam back to the shingle beach.

Global copper demands drove Cornish miners ever deeper into the perilous mineshafts beneath Gwennap's fields and meadows. But it was not just Cornish miners whose lives were for ever changed by the copper industry. Having initially created his steam engine for Cornish mines, James Watt adapted it for cotton manufacture. His engine kick-started the factory system, the history of which I had encountered in the Lancastrian town of Darwen 360 miles north of here. It was hard to imagine which was worse: the sulphurous air of a copper mine or the fluff-filled heat of a cotton factory. Either way, Cornish copper – Gwennap copper – helped develop Britain's colonial trade and drove its northern cotton boom.[88]

Conclusion: Facing Our Colonial Past

The novelist Jane Austen lived out her final days in the Hampshire village of Chawton. Just 4 miles from Sir Thomas Baring's residence at Stratton Park, Chawton is a manorial village like East Stratton. In the 1740s, the surrounding lands were enclosed by the dominant Knight family, who adopted Jane Austen's brother Edward and made him the legal heir of Chawton House.[1] When this Elizabethan manor came into Edward's hands, in 1809, Jane moved into a roomy cottage on the estate. Living there with her mother and sister, Jane wrote and revised her six major novels.

Today, the cottage and manor house are the ultimate destination for Austenophiles from all over the world. Chawton itself is a cluster of houses with climbing roses and elegant gardens surrounded by chalk streams and pastureland. Still a tiny village, it is dominated by the manor house, a church and a library. The cottage, which still houses the tiny desk at which Jane wrote, is now the Jane Austen's House Museum, a square building of mellow red-brick fitted with elegant white sash windows, surrounded by modest lawns and deep-filled flowerbeds: a study in rural Englishness. From here, Jane and her sister Cassandra would take daily walks, following footpaths through the surrounding fields and woodlands. It was a quiet life, punctuated by the occasional gathering at their brother's house nearby.

A short walk from the cottage, St Nicholas church is set amidst hedgerows on the estate's lush parklands. This is where Jane and her sisters worshipped (though it doesn't look quite as it did in Jane's time: later in the nineteenth century it was devastated by fire, then rebuilt in classic Victorian style). At the churchyard entrance you meet a statue of Jane clutching a book, her expression quizzical, challenging (appropriately enough: she didn't suffer fools gladly). In the churchyard itself, two simple tombstones stand side by side, marking the graves of Jane's mother and sister. Jane herself was interred in Winchester Cathedral, in the city some 15 miles to the south-west, where she died at the age of forty-one, possibly from Addison's disease, Hodgkin's lymphoma or lupus.[2]

In 1993, around 176 years after Austen's death, the academic and intellectual Edward W. Said wrote a landmark essay called 'Jane Austen and Empire' about her novel *Mansfield Park*.[3] Said's piece sparked what remains an ongoing debate about Austen's attitude to slavery. Said believed that *Mansfield Park* failed to take an ethical position on the links between sugar plantations and the handsome houses and splendid grounds of English country estates. He argued that the novel's protagonist, Fanny Price, ultimately embraced the worldview of her uncle Sir Thomas, whose Antiguan plantations funded his rural retreat. Some disagree with Said's view, pointing to Austen's abolitionist sentiments and her partiality for William Cowper, who wrote anti-slavery poems. Others feel that Said underestimated Austen's aversion to polemical writing about the issue, and that he failed to grasp the widespread support for abolition among women of Austen's generation.[4] But perhaps the truth lies somewhere in between. For Austen and her family reflected Britons' variable and inconsistent responses to slavery at the time: silence and complicity on the one hand, and anti-slavery sentiment and action on the other.[5]

Yet Said's essay was a game-changer. Its forensic attention to the colonial world in which Austen was immersed forced Austen-lovers, however reluctantly, to acknowledge the deep-rooted presence of colonialism and slavery throughout Regency England. It was woven into the fabric of everyday life. And this was true for Jane Austen's family, as well as for so many others.

You barely have to scrape the surface of Austen's family to reveal these colonial associations. Jane Austen's father, the Reverend George Austen, was close friends with James Langford Nibbs, the owner of an Antiguan plantation. The reverend was named by Gibbs as a co-trustee of his plantations, meaning that he shared with other trustees a legal responsibility to ensure that the plantation – and enslaved peoples – were inherited by Nibbs' heirs when the time came.[6] Neither was this tangential to Jane's world: scholars have pointed out that this family connection was the inspiration for her portrayal of Sir Thomas' Antiguan plantation wealth in *Mansfield Park*.

Austen's sailor brothers, meanwhile, fought colonial battles, including in the Caribbean; her novels contain many references to their ships.[7] After the 1807 abolition of the slave trade, as part of their naval duties, Francis and Charles Austen also patrolled the seas to stop the newly illegal trafficking of people. In his unpublished diary, Francis Austen wrote emphatic anti-slavery statements: in his view, slavery in all forms was wrong, and he objected to its continued existence in 'modified' form in various British colonies.[8] Meanwhile Jane's favourite brother, Henry Thomas Austen, was directly involved in the anti-slavery movement, representing Colchester at the 1840 World Anti-Slavery Convention, which sought an end to global slavery. The conference was addressed by Thomas Clarkson, another figure whom Jane Austen admired.[9] None of this can confirm Jane Austen's personal views on slavery, but her father's legal association with Antiguan plantations and the brothers' anti-slavery activities remind us that the issue of slavery was a constant during the period. The shift in attitudes, moreover, was generational: while Jane's father was involved in the slavery business, her brother Francis believed that slavery was 'to be regretted'.[10]

The British-based Afro-Guyanese poet John Agard drew on Said's essay in his poem 'Mansfield Park Revisited' (which features in his 2006 collection *We Brits*). The poem jokes that slavery history is unfit for 'polite conversation', echoing the line in *Mansfield Park* which depicts 'a dead silence' in response to a question about slavery in Antigua.[11] Agard encapsulates the dilemma of heritage sites – from country houses to literary museums – whose incomes are at least partly premised on an escape to the rural idyll: who dares to interrupt this 'polite conversation'?

Yet in the intervening years since Agard's poem, things are starting to change – in the teeth of some entrenched opposition. In 2021, Chawton's Jane Austen's House Museum announced that staff would be incorporating colonial history into its displays. It would focus on the material culture around Jane Austen herself – muslin, cotton, tea and sugar – and would use these as a prism through which to explore wider issues, from her father's plantation trusteeship to her brothers' colonial sea battles. At the time, the museum's plan met with outrage in the mass media.[12] Claire Fox, now Baroness Fox of Buckley, tweeted 'No, no, no', adding, 'this guilt-ridden revisionism linking her [Austen] to slavery feels like barrel-scraping. PS. Ignore. Just read her novels.'[13]

Yet, as we've seen, readers of Austen's novels will immediately come across allusions to slavery; many more would have been picked up by Austen's contemporary readers. Dislikeable characters share their names with slave-traders: the spiteful Mrs Norris in *Mansfield Park* has the same surname as the brutal slave-captain John Norris, who was condemned by Austen's admired anti-slavery campaigner Thomas Clarkson. (In the same novel, the fickle Maria Bertram moves into the former home of the slave-owning Lascelles family.)[14] In *Emma*, Mrs Hawkins shares a surname with the slaver John Hawkins; her maiden name is Elton, another slaving family from Bristol. The novel also hints at Mrs Hawkins' father being a slave-trader.[15] A mixed-heritage character called Miss Lambe in Austen's unfinished *Sanditon* resembles Dido Belle, the daughter of an enslaved woman whose father was a British naval officer. Austen knew Dido Belle's cousin and possibly met Dido herself, who was brought up in Kenwood House.[16]

In the face of vociferous opposition and historical denial, Jane Austen's House Museum has given Austen fans the chance to explore slavery's relevance to the author's intellectual life and social world – and, in so doing, to gain a considerably fuller picture of both. It is not alone. In the last few years, British institutions and heritage organizations – which hitherto largely avoided exploring their colonial histories – have started to acknowledge the crucial importance of addressing them. There still is a long way to go, but some of these have shown responsibility and courage in doing so, the National Trust among them.

As we've seen throughout this book, colonialism's influence in Britain was not limited to ports and cities. It permeated country houses, islands, coastal hamlets, wool-making villages, mill towns, copper-mining settlements, countryside landownership and electoral boroughs. The British Empire had major impacts on the rural history of England, Scotland and Wales. Now, as we refamiliarize ourselves with our shared history in this postcolonial age, we are faced with a choice. We can either address the colonial history of the British Isles or we can deny and dismiss it.

When I found myself in the midst of the international media story about the National Trust report, I came across a book of Martin Luther King Jr's old sermons. Reading them reminded me that the culture war, as it is now known, is nothing new, but was present in the American Civil Rights struggle to throw off centuries of enslavement and its associated thinking. King's sermons diagnosed the challenge as proceeding from 'soft-minded' thinking. Whereas, he said, the 'tough-minded person always examines the facts before he reaches conclusions', the soft-minded person 'reaches a conclusion before he has examined the first fact; in short, he prejudges and is prejudiced'. King concluded that a lack of independent critical thinking makes people vulnerable to political manipulation, and correspondingly liable to commit all kinds of misdeeds in the name of patriotism or defending the nation. This cohort is easily misled by fiery rhetoric, misrepresentation or smears.[17] Meanwhile, those who stir up fear and division – many of them politicians and opinion-leaders – are, in King's words, 'cold and arrogant men whose hearts were hardened by the long winter of traditionalism'. In the face of these threats, King suggested that fighting fire with fire is ineffective: it only serves to stoke the flames of mutual suspicion and prejudice. For this reason, he advised, the civil rights movement should meet violence and aggression with courage and critical independence of mind, but that this should also be paired with compassion and altruism. In the terrifying circumstances in which he operated, King's approach required exceptional bravery, using emotional as well as political and intellectual astuteness.[18] Such qualities abound in each of my walking companions throughout this book.

All my life I have walked through the countryside, just as Jane Austen did, without any sense of being out of place. But the same cannot be said for my walking companions, who have consistently and courageously raised the issue of rural racism, both blatant and subtle. It is, or should be, everyone's birthright to enjoy the countryside without their presence being questioned. My fellow walkers bear witness to the fact that this is not the case.

Things may be shifting, however. In 2022, 400 Black and Asian Britons participated in Kinder in Colour, a commemoration of the 1932 Kinder Scout Trespass. Back in the 1930s, this act of mass civil disobedience highlighted the issue of ownership and access to land. The trespassers were met by gamekeepers. Arrests were made, but an outpouring of public sympathy eventually led to the 1949 National Parks and Access to the Countryside Act. With their resonant symbol of trespass, the 2022 Kinder in Colour event made history; it was the largest-ever gathering of people of colour in the British countryside. I hope that this book will inspire and resource many more countryside walks across and beyond Britain's final frontier of belonging.

Notes

Preface

1 English and Scottish activity before the 1707 Act of Union.
2 Nick Draper, 2017, 'A Black Presence in the Isle of Wight', lbsatucl. wordpress.com/2017/11/28/a-black-presence-in-the-isle-of-wight/; and Cumbria Records Office information sheet about the African and Indian presence in eighteenth-century Whitehaven.
3 Neil Chakraborti and Neil Garland (eds.), 2012, *Rural Racism* (London: Routledge).
4 Faima Bakar, ' "The English Countryside Was Shaped by Colonialism." Why Rural Britain Is Unwelcoming for People of Colour', *Metro*, 21 September 2021.
5 Jill Robinson, 'BBC Hit by 572 Complaints Over "Inaccurate" Countryfile Report on BAME People Living in the Countryside', *Sun*, 10 July 2020.
6 Fariha Karim, 'Countryfile Presenter Digs in Over "Gardening Racism" ', *The Times*, 19 December 2020.

Introduction: A Colonial History of the British Countryside

1 Charles Pugh and Tracey Avery, 2002, *Basildon Park, Berkshire, National Trust Guidebook*.
2 Richard Benyon was governor of Fort St George, now Madras. Warren Hastings resided at Purley Hall throughout his corruption trial in the 1780s. See Official List entry for Basildon Park, Historic England, https://historicengland.org.uk/listing/the-list/list-entry/1000581? section=official-list-entry.

3 Sathnam Sanghera, 2021, *Empireland: How Imperialism Has Shaped Modern Britain* (London: Viking).

4 William Dalrymple, 2019, *The Anarchy: The Relentless Rise of the East India Company* (London: Bloomsbury), pp. 135–44.

5 Sir John Sykes, in Margot Finn and Kate Smith (eds.), 2018, *The East India Company at Home, 1757–1857* (London: UCL Press), p. 417.

6 Ibid., p. 417.

7 Tillman W. Nechtman, 2006, 'Nabobs Revisited: A Cultural History of British Imperialism and the Indian Question in Late-Eighteenth-Century Britain', *History Compass*, 4(4), pp. 645–67, p. 646.

8 *Journal of the British Association for Cemeteries in South Asia*, https://www.britishempire.co.uk/library/nabob.htm.

9 Sykes, 2018, pp. 412–28.

10 David Olusoga, ' "Cancel Culture" Is Not Just the Preserve of the Left. Just Ask Our Historians', *Observer*, 3 January 2021.

11 Harry Howard, 'They've Taken a Political Decision That the British Empire Was Wicked', *Daily Mail*, 12 March 2021.

12 Lauren Smith, 'The National Trust Is at War With the Past', *Spiked Online*, 5 November 2022, https://www.spiked-online.com/2022/11/05/the-national-trust-is-at-war-with-the-past/.

13 The adaptation was broadcast in 2005 and starred Colin Firth and Jennifer Ehle.

14 W. G. Hoskins, 2015 [1955], *The Making of the English Landscape* (Beaminster: Little Toller), p. 13.

15 The Common Sense Group, 'Common Sense: Conservative Thinking for a Post-Liberal Age', www.marcolonghi.org.uk/sites/www.marcolonghi.org.uk/files/2021-05/Common-Sense.pdf.

16 Sophie Yeo, 2021, 'Futureland: Corinne Fowler on Colonialism's Impact on the Countryside', *Inkcap*, 10 March 2021, https://www.inkcapjournal.co.uk/corinne-fowler/.

17 Gabriella Swerling, ' "Woke" National Trust Academic Tasked With Reviewing Colonial Past "Intimidated" by Critics', *Daily Telegraph*, 20 December 2020, https://www.telegraph.co.uk/news/2020/12/20/woke-national-trust-academic-tasked-reviewing-colonial-past/.

18 Stephen Delahunty, 'Regulator Received Just Three Complaints About National Trust Slavery Links Report', *The Third Sector*, 23 November 2020, https://www.thirdsector.co.uk/regulator-received-just-three-complaints-national-trust-slavery-links-report/governance/article/1700842.

19 Sam Knight, 'Britain's Idyllic Country Houses Reveal a Darker History', *The New Yorker*, 16 August 2021.

20 Week six of the online course by Colonial Countryside, 2021, 'Country Houses and the British Empire', Massive Open Online Course on FutureLearn.

21 David Olusoga, 10 November 2020, at the launch of Being Human Festival 2020, https://www.youtube.com/watch?v=75hB4Ud99FE.

22 Peter Linebaugh and Marcus Rediker, 2022, *The Many-Headed Hydra* (Boston: Beacon Books), pp. 25–7.

23 Margot Finn and Kate Smith (eds.), 2018, *The East India Company at Home, 1757–1857* (London: UCL Press), p. 1; Dalrymple, 2019; Jac Weller, 2013, *Wellington in India* (Barnsley: Frontline Books).

24 Sathnam Sanghera, 'Was the British Empire All Bad?', *The Times*, 23 March 2022.

25 Miranda Kaufmann blog, 2021, 'Black History Matters: Changing What Happens in Our Classrooms', http://www.mirandakaufmann.com/blog/black-history-matters-changing-what-happens-in-our-classrooms-part-1.

26 I was first introduced to this concept by Professor Catherine Hall when she led the Legacies of British Slavery project at University College London.

27 Salman Rushdie, 1992, 'The New Empire in Britain' (first published 1982), in *Imaginary Homelands: Essays and Criticism, 1981–1991* (London: Granta), p. 22.

28 Finn and Smith, 2018.

29 Kate Smith, 2018, 'Armorial Porcelain Case Study: The Basildon Park Service', *East India Company at Home, 1757–1857*, https://blogs.ucl.ac.uk/eicah/armorial-porcelain/armorial-porcelain-case-study-the-basildon-park-service/.

30 Martin Luther King Jr, 'I Have a Dream' speech, delivered during the March on Washington for Jobs and Freedom, 28 August 1963.

31 Sykes, 2018, p. 414.

32 One of the earliest uses of this phrase can be found in the *Daily Mail*. See Kate Feehan, 'Every Reason the Woke National Trust Placed 100 Properties on BLM-Inspired List of Shame Including Homes of Winston Churchill, Rudyard Kipling and William Wordsworth', 22 September 2022, *Daily Mail Online*, https://www.dailymail.co.uk/news/article-8759219/National-Trust-accused-rewriting-history-property-list-shame-colonial-links.html.

33 I am grateful to the history teacher Nick Dennis for explaining this to me.

34 See Official List entry for Basildon Park, Historic England.

35 Margot Finn, 2018, 'Swallowfield Park, Berkshire: From Royalist Bastion to Empire Home', in Finn and Smith, 2018, p. 207 and p. 219.

36 Elizabeth Sykes married Richard Benyon de Beauvoir (1770–1854) in 1797.

37 Shashi Tharoor, 2017, *Inglorious Empire: What The British Did to India* (London: Penguin), p. 13.

38 Sykes, 2018, pp. 412–28.

39 The volunteer was Sarah Spink, a genealogist and historian. See also Sally-Anne Huxtable, Corinne Fowler, Christo Kefalus and Emma Slocombe (eds.), 2020, 'Interim Report on the Connections Between Colonialism and Properties Now in the Care of the National Trust, Including Links with Historical Slavery', https://nt.global.ssl.fastly.net/binaries/content/assets/website/national/pdf/colonialism-and-historic-slavery-report.pdf.

40 Catherine Hall, Nicholas Draper, Keith McClelland, Katie Donington and Rachel Lang, 2014, *Legacies of British Slave-Ownership: Colonial Slavery and the Formation of Victorian Britain* (Cambridge: Cambridge University Press).

41 Chris Evans, 2010, *Slave Wales: The Welsh and Atlantic Slavery 1660–1850* (Cardiff: University of Wales Press), p. 126.

42 Priyamvada Gopal, 2020, *Insurgent Empire: Anticolonial Resistance and British Dissent* (London: Verso). See also Linebaugh and Rediker, 2000.

43 E. P. Thompson, 1982 [1963], *The Making of the English Working Class* (London: Penguin), p. 730.

44 Ronald Blythe, 1969, *Akenfield* (London: Penguin), p. 29.

45 Thompson, 1982, p. 583.

46 William Cobbett, 1822, *Rural Rides* (London: The Political Register), p. 72.

47 Thompson, 1982, p. 362 and p. 364.

1. *The Sugar Walk: Jura and Islay*

1 'Campbell, Daniel, of Saltmarket, Glasgow; Shawfield, Lanark; and Ardentinny, Argyll (*c*.1642–1753)', in D. W. Hayton, E. Cruickshanks and S. Hanley (eds.), *The History of Parliament: The House of Commons 1690–1715* (London: Boydell and Brewer). Daniel Campbell bought both Jura and Islay for £12,000.

2 Peter Edwards, 2019, *Jura, Islay and Colonsay: 23 Wild Walks in the Southern Hebrides* (Kendal: Cicerone), p. 14.

3 Entry for Campbell, Rivers & Co., Legacies of British Slavery database, https://www.ucl.ac.uk/lbs/firm/view/-641488528. See also Stephen Mullen, 2015, 'The Great Glasgow West India House of John Campbell, Senior and Co', in T. M. Devine (ed.), *Recovering Scotland's Slavery Past* (Edinburgh: Edinburgh University Press), p. 128; and 'Glasgow's Benefactors. Captain Campbell of Jura', https://glasgowbenefactors.com/2017/10/24/captain-campbell-of-jura/comment-page-1/#_ednref5.

4 Kris Manjapra, 2022, *Black Ghost of Empire: The Long Death of Slavery and the Failure of Emancipation* (London: Allen Lane), p. xv.

5 Jasmine Taylor-Coleman, 2016, 'How Do You Trace Ancestors Who Were Slaves?', *BBC News*, 11 September 2016, www.bbc.co.uk/news/magazine-37291230.

6 Emma Ranston-Young specializes in tracing Jamaican ancestry across multiple records.

7 Stephen Mullen, 2022, 'Glasgow, Slavery and Atlantic Commerce: An Audit of Historic Connections and Modern Legacies' (Glasgow:

University of Glasgow), https://www.glasgow.gov.uk/CHttpHan dler.ashx?id=56499&p=0.

8 Rosalind Mitchison, et al., 2002, *A History of Scotland* (London: Rout-ledge), p. 252.

9 Christopher A. Whatley, 1989, 'Economic Causes and Consequences of the Union in 1707: A Survey', *The Scottish Historical Review*, 68(186), pp. 150–81, p. 178.

10 Mullen, 2022, p. 21. The City Council issued its formal apology on 31 March 2022.

11 Corinne Fowler, 2020, *Green Unpleasant Land: Creative Responses to Rural England's Colonial Connections* (Leeds: Peepal Tree Press).

12 Dirk Robertson, 1998, *Highland T'ing* (London: The X Press).

13 Letter of Columbus on the Fourth Voyage to Queen Isabella and King Ferdinand, https://content.wisconsinhistory.org/digital/collec tion/aj/id/4414.

14 Catherine Hall, 1993, 'White Visions, Black Lives: The Free Villages of Jamaica', *History Workshop*, 36, pp. 100–113.

15 The first castle was built in 1450 and it became the main seat of the Campbell clan chiefs by 1650. See Historic Environment Scot-land portal at http://portal.historicenvironment.scot/designa tion/GDL00223.

16 Inveraray Castle, 2023, 'Addressing our Connections with Historic Slavery', https://www.inveraray-castle.com/images/Slavery_and_ the_Argylls.pdf.

17 Stephen Mullen, 2018, 'John Lamont of Benmore: A Highland Planter Who Died "in Harness" in Trinidad', *Northern Scotland*, 9(1), pp. 44–66, p. 47.

18 See Stephen Mullen, 2013, 'A Glasgow-West India Merchant House and the Imperial Dividend, 1779–1867', *Journal of Scottish Historical Studies*, 33(2), pp. 196–233, p. 199; and Mark Quintanilla, 2003, 'The World of Alexander Campbell: An Eighteenth-Century Grenadian Planter', *Albion*, 35(2), p. 235.

19 Individual person entry for Col. John Campbell of Black River (1673–1740), Legacies of British Slavery database, www.ucl.ac.uk/lbs/ person/view/2146637757. See also Alastair Campbell, 2004, *A History*

of Clan Campbell, vol. 3: *From the Restoration to the Present Day* (Edinburgh: Edinburgh University Press), pp. 214–16.

20 Individual person entry for Duncan Campbell of St Martin in the Fields (died 1803), Legacies of British Slavery database entry, www.ucl.ac.uk/lbs/person/view/2146633087.

21 David Kent and Norma Townsend, 2002, *The Convicts of the Eleanor: Protest in Rural England, New Lives in Australia* (London: The Merlin Press). See also Anna McKay, 'Floating Hell', *BBC History Magazine*, October 2022, https://www.historyextra.com/period/victorian/prison-hulks-britain-conditions-escapes-transportation-social-reform-charles-dickens/.

22 David Alston, *Slaves and Highlanders: Silenced Histories of Scotland and the Caribbean* (Edinburgh: Edinburgh University Press): Captain Farquhar Campbell (1819–82). See also individual person entry for Farquhard Campbell (1760–1829), Legacies of British Slavery database, www.ucl.ac.uk/lbs/person/view/2146630873. The concept of slavery's 'demographic legacy' is used by the Liverpool-based historian Laurence Westgaph.

23 Andrew MacKillop, 2021, *Human Capital and Empire. Scotland, Ireland, Wales and British Imperialism in Asia, c.1690–c.1820* (Manchester: Manchester University Press), p. 242.

24 William Dalrymple, 2019, *The Anarchy: The Relentless Rise of the East India Company* (London: Bloomsbury), p. 250.

25 MacKillop, 2021, p. 74.

26 Francis Groome (ed.), 2019, 'Historical Perspective for Campbeltown', drawn from the *Ordnance Gazetteer of Scotland: A Survey of Scottish Topography, Statistical, Biographical and Historical*, originally published by Thomas C. Jack, Grange Publishing Works, Edinburgh (1882–5). In the eighteenth century the deep port allowed large vessels to dock with their cargoes. By 1880, local exports were worth just over 1 per cent of colonial and foreign imports, which were valued at £65,609.

27 MacKillop, 2021, p. 275.

28 Ibid., p. 222.

29 Ibid., p. 233.

30 Ibid., p. 225.

31 Ibid., p. 233.

32 Iain MacKinnon and Andrew MacKillop, 2020, 'Plantation Slavery and Landownership in the West Highlands and Islands: Legacies and Lessons. A Discussion Paper', www.communitylandscotland.org.uk/wp-content/uploads/2020/11/Plantation-slavery-and-landownership-in-the-west-Highlands-and-Islands-legacies-and-lessons.pdf.

33 'Campbell, Daniel (*c*.1672–1753), of Saltmarket, Glasgow; Shawfield, Lanark; and Ardentinny, Argyll'; and J. M. Simpson, 'Campbell, Daniel (1672–1753), of Shawfield, Lanark, and Ardentinny and Islay, Argyll', in R. Sedgwick (ed.), *The History of Parliament: The House of Commons 1715–1754* (London: Boydell and Brewer, 1970).

34 Colen Campbell, *c*.1722, *Vitruvius Britannicus . . .* , vol. 2 (London), p. 52; and Anthony Lewis, 2016, 'The Shawfield Mansion', *How Glasgow Flourished* (Edinburgh: Royal Society of Edinburgh).

35 'Campbell, Daniel (1672–1753), of Shawfield, Lanark, and Ardentinny and Islay, Argyll', in Sedgwick, 1970.

36 Daniel Campbell and York-Buildings Company, 1765, *Information for the governor and company of undertakers for raising Thames water in York-Buildings, for themselves, and in behalf of their creditors, and also for the trustees of their annuitants, defenders; against Daniel Campbell of Shawfield, Esq; pursuer* (Edinburgh).

37 British Parliament, 1716, 'An Act for the continuing the duty of two pennies Scots, or one sixth of a penny sterling, on every pint of ale and beer that shall be vended or sold within the city of Glasgow and privileges thereof, for the benefit of the said city' (London: John Baskett).

38 Mitchison, et al., 2002, p. 252.

39 Sedgwick, 1970.

40 Gentleman in Glasgow, 1725, *A letter from a gentleman in Glasgow, to his friend in the country, concerning the late tumults which happened in that city. Containing a true account of the plundering of Daniel Campbell of Shawfield's House, the murder of the inhabitants by Capt. Bushell* (Glasgow).

41 'Campbell, John (1664–1739), of Edinburgh', *History of Parliament: The House of Commons* (London: Boydell and Brewer).

42 Daniel Defoe, 1746, *A Tour Thro' that part of Great Britain* . . . (Dublin: George Faulkener), p. 124.

43 'Campbell, John (1664–1739), of Edinburgh'. Daniel Campbell bought Jura from John Campbell of Calder.

44 'Islay House', Historic Environment Scotland, list entry GDL00228.

45 John Senex, 1721, *A new general atlas, containing a geographical and historical account of all the empires* . . . (Temple Bar: Daniel Brown), p. 5; John Dart, 1723, *Westmonasterium. Or the history and antiquities of the Abbey Church of St. Peters Westminster* (London: Cole and Company), p. 49; Andrew Johnston, 1724, *Notitia Anglicana* (Printed for Andrew Johnston, London); David Scott, 1727, *The History of Scotland* (Westminster: J. Cluer and A. Campbell), p. 10; Daniel Defoe, John Harris, John Senex and Henry Wilson, 1728, *Atlas maritimus and commercialis* (London); and Colin Maclaurin, 1748, *An account of Sir Isaac Newton's philosophical discoveries, in four books* (London).

46 Judith V. Grabiner, 1998, ' "Some Disputes of Consequence". Maclaurin Among the Molasses Barrels', *Social Studies of Science*, 28(1), pp. 139–68.

47 'Islay House', Historic Environment Scotland.

48 Grace Nichols' 1996 poem 'Hurricane Hits England' begins 'It took a hurricane to bring her closer / To the landscape': in *Sunris* (London: Virago).

49 https://glasgowmuseumsslavery.co.uk/2021/01/25/robert-burns -and-jamaica/.

50 Glasgow Museums, 25 January, 2021, glasgowmuseumsslavery. co.uk/2021/01/25/robert-burns-and-jamaica/.

51 Lines 4–8. For further information see ibid.

52 Shara McCallum, 2021, *No Ruined Stone* (Leeds: Peepal Tree Press).

53 J. Mercer, 1974, *Hebridean Islands: Colonsay, Gigha, Jura* (Glasgow: Blackie), p. 94.

54 Editorial, *John O'Groat Journal*, 8 August 1851, 769, p. 2.

55 See Mathilde Blind's 1886 poem, discussed by Catherine D. Ostdiek in her essay 'The Highland Clearances and the "Trappings of

Nationality" in the British Isles', in *The Journal of the Midwest Modern Language Association*, Fall 2018, pp. 137–68.

56 Keith Tribe, 1995, 'Professors Malthus and Jones: Political Economy at the East India Company College 1806–1858', *European Journal of the History of Economic Thought*, 2(2), pp. 327–54, https://www.tandfon line.com/action/showCitFormats?doi=10.1080%2F09672569 508538573.

57 Eric Richards and Annie Tindley, 2012, 'After the Clearances: Evander McIver and the "Highland Question", 1835–73', *Rural History*, 23(1), pp. 41–57.

58 Tom Devine, 2011, *To the Ends of the Earth: Scotland's Global Diaspora 1750–2010* (London: Allen Lane), pp. 107–8.

59 Preface to the 1892 edition of *Gloomy Memories*, discussed in Charles J. W. Withers, 2005, 'Landscape, Memory, History: *Gloomy Memories* and the Nineteenth-Century Scottish Highlands', *Scottish Geographical Journal*, 121(1), pp. 29–44.

60 Donald McCloud, 1857, *Gloomy Memories in the Highlands of Scotland Versus Mrs. Harriet Beecher Stowe's Sunny Memories, in England (A Foreign Land): Or A Faithful Picture of the Extirpation of the Celtic Race from The Highlands of Scotland* (Glasgow: Sinclair).

61 Individual person entry for Donald Davidson, Legacies of British Slavery database, www.ucl.ac.uk/lbs/person/view/2146641915.

62 Richards and Tindley, 'After the Clearances', p. 48.

63 Ibid., p. 45.

64 John Prebble, 1968, *Glencoe: The Story of the Massacre* (London: Penguin), p. 3.

65 MacKinnon and MacKillop, 2020, p. 9 and p. 11.

66 Ibid.

67 Ibid., p. 20.

68 Individual person entry for James Evan Baillie (1781–1863), Legacies of British Slavery database, www.ucl.ac.uk/lbs/person/view/8570.

69 MacKinnon and MacKillop, 2020, p. 4 and p. 23.

70 Ibid., p.15.

71 Individual person entry for James Evan Baillie (1781–1863), Legacies of British Slavery database, www.ucl.ac.uk/lbs/person/view/8570. See also MacKinnon and MacKillop, 2020.

72 Jim McPherson, 'Badenoch and Slavery', *Strathey News*, 20 August 2020. See also Inverness-shire Ordnance Survey Name Book, 1876–1878, National Records of Scotland, OS1/17/7/40, https://scotlandsplaces.gov.uk/digital-volumes/ordnance-survey-name-books/inverness-shire-os-name-books-1876-1878/inverness-shire-mainland-volume-07/40. Thanks to Dr Kieran Hazzard for this reference.

73 MacKinnon and MacKillop, 2020, p. 15.

74 Individual person entry for James Evan Baillie (1781–1863), Legacies of British Slavery database, archived at: www.ucl.ac.uk/lbs/person/view/8570.

75 McPherson, 'Badenoch and Slavery'.

76 McBarnet and Rainy were criticized for their treatment of tenants. James Forsyth of Mull and Lord Cranstoun at Arisaig also moved many people off their lands.

77 James A. Stewart, Jr, 1998–9, 'The Jaws of Sheep: The 1851 Hebridean Clearances of Gordon of Cluny', *Proceedings of the Harvard Celtic Colloquium, 1998/1999*, vol. 18/19 (1998/1999), pp. 205–26, p. 205. See also David V. Taylor, 2014, 'A Society in Transition: Badenoch 1750–1800', PhD thesis, University of the Highlands and Islands, https://pureadmin.uhi.ac.uk/ws/portalfiles/portal/3078042/David_Taylor_PhD_Thesis_full_text.pdf.

78 'Gordon, John, of Cluny, Aberdeen; 4 St. Andrew Street, Edinburgh and 25 Jermyn Street, Mdx', in D. R. Fisher, 2009, *History of Parliament: House of Commons, 1820–1849* (Cambridge: Cambridge University Press).

79 MacKinnon and MacKillop, 2020, p.15.

80 Manjapra, 2022, p. xv.

81 Finlaggan Visitor Centre details this information on site, but it is also archived at: www.islayinfo.com/islay_finlaggan_lords_of_the_isles.html.

2. The East India Company Walk:
Wordsworth and the Lake District

1 'Welcome to the Lake District World Heritage Site', http://lakes-worldheritage.co.uk/.

2 Ingrid Pollard, 2005, *Postcards Home* (London: Chris Boot).

3 These images can also be found at www.ingridpollard.com.

4 Sarah Whittingham, 2014, ' "An eminently beautiful object is fern": The Romantics and the Victorian Fern Craze', blog post for Wordsworth Grasmere, wordsworth.org.uk.

5 Felicity James, 2020, 'Romantic Home', in Kate Kennedy and Hermione Lee (eds.), *Lives of Houses* (Princeton: Princeton University Press), p. 49.

6 Sarah Prescott, 2003, 'Making a Living: Booksellers, Patronage and Subscription', in *Women, Authorship and Literary Culture, 1690–1740* (London: Palgrave), p. 103.

7 Sally-Anne Huxtable, Corinne Fowler, Christo Kefalus and Emma Slocombe (eds.), 2020, 'Interim Report on the Connections Between Colonialism and Properties Now in the Care of the National Trust, Including Links with Historical Slavery', https://nt.global.ssl.fastly.net/binaries/content/assets/website/national/pdf/colonialism-and-historic-slavery-report.pdf.

8 Charlie Parker, 2020, 'Wordsworth's Home Linked to Slavery? It's Nuts, Says Descendent', *The Times*, 26 September 2020, https://www.thetimes.co.uk/article/wordsworths-home-linked-to-slavery-its-nuts-says-descendant-22017q07c#:~:text=A%20descendant%20of%20William%20Wordsworth,a%20slavery%20and%20colonialism%20report.

9 Dominic Sandbrook, 'How Dare the National Trust Link Wordsworth to Slavery Because His Brother Sailed a Ship to China?', *Daily Mail*, 23 September 2020, https://www.dailymail.co.uk/news/article-8762205/DOMINIC-SANDBROOK-dare-National-Trust-link-Wordsworth-slavery.html.

10 Richard Matlak, 2000, 'Captain John Wordsworth's Death at Sea', *The Wordsworth Circle*, 31(3), pp. 127–33, p. 127; and Kenneth R. Johnston,

2005, 'Review of Richard E. Matlak, *Deep Distresses. William Words-worth, John Wordsworth, Sir George Beaumont, 1800–1808*', *Studies in Romanticism*, 44(2), pp. 283–8, p. 284.

11 Entry on 3rd Viscount of Lonsdale in *The Oxford Dictionary of National Biography* (Oxford: Oxford University Press), 1992 edn. For general information about the South Sea Bubble see also Royal Museums Greenwich, 'What Was the South Sea Bubble? Discover What Led to the Collapse of the South Sea Company in 1720', https://tinyurl.com/4x4s7xan.

12 Joanne Dann, 1980, 'Some Notes on the Relationship Between the Wordsworth and the Lowther Families', *The Wordsworth Circle*, 11(2), pp. 80–82, p. 80; Dr Charles Littleton, 'A Trojan Horse in the House of Lords?', The History of Parliament, https://thehistoryofparliament.wordpress.com/2020/01/09/a-trojan-horse-in-the-house-of-lords-the-south-sea-company-and-the-peerage/.

13 'Lowther, Sir James, 5th Bt. (1736–1802), of Lowther, nr. Penrith, Westmld', The History of Parliament, https://historyofparliamentonline.org/volume/1754-1790/member/lowther-sir-james-1736-1802.

14 The Lowther role in tobacco imports and Whitehaven's transatlantic slavery business is explored in Chapter 3. Robert Lowther was the governor of Barbados between 1711 and 1720. V. Beckett, 1977, 'English Landownership in the Later Seventeenth and Eighteenth Centuries: The Debate and the Problems', *The Economic History Review*, 30(4), pp. 567–81.

15 Hilary Beckles, 1985, 'The Slave-Drivers' War: Bussa and the 1816 Barbados Slave Rebellion', *Boletín de Estudios Latinoamericanos y del Caribe*, 39, pp. 85–110, p. 96.

16 Dann, 1980, p. 82.

17 Ibid., p. 80.

18 Anon., 1783, *The American and British Chronicle of war and politics; being an accurate and comprehensive register of the most memorable occur-rences in the last ten years of his Majesty's reign: From May 10, 1773 to July 16, 1783* (Printed for the author, London), https://archive.org/details/bim_eighteenth-century_the-american-and-british_e-i-s_1783, p. 100.

19 Dorothy Wordsworth in Alethea Hayter, 2002, *The Wreck of the Abergavenny: The Wordsworths and Catastrophe* (London: Pan Macmillan), pp. 6–8.

20 Letter from John Wordsworth to Richard Wordsworth, in Ed Cumming, 2016, 'John Wordsworth and the Wreck of the Earl of Abergavenny', Nautical Archaeology Society, https://www.nauticalarchaeologysociety.org/john-wordsworth-and-the-earl-of-abergavenny p. 25.

21 United Nations Office on Drugs and Crime (UNODC), 'A Century of International Drug Control', Chapter 2 of *World Drug Report*, 2008, www.unodc.org/documents/data-and-analysis/Studies/100_Years_of_Drug_Control.pdf, p. 173.

22 Peter Kitson, 2012, 'The Wordsworths, Opium, and China', *The Wordsworth Circle*, 43(1), pp. 2–12, p. 4.

23 UNODC 'A Century of International Drug Control', p. 173.

24 Letter from John Wordsworth to his uncle, 8 August 1804, in Cumming, 2016, p. 37.

25 Hayter, 2002, p. 8.

26 Wordsworth wrote that he had 'lately been living upon air and the essence of carrots cabbages turnips and other esculent vegetables, not excluding parsley the produce of my garden', quoted in Matthew Bevis, 2015, 'Review of John Worthen *The Life of William Wordsworth*', *The Review of English Studies*, 66(274), pp. 388–9, pp. 27–8, https://doi.org/10.1093/res/hgu094.

27 James, 2020, p. 65.

28 William Wordsworth letter to Samuel Taylor Coleridge, 24 December 1799, in *Home at Grasmere: Extracts from the Diary of Dorothy Wordsworth*, written between 1800 and 1803 (London: Penguin Classics), p. 17.

29 Dorothy Wordsworth's diary in ibid., pp. 40–41.

30 Ibid., pp. 53–4, p. 60 and p. 64.

31 Ibid., p. 65 and p. 85.

32 He saw John as 'one of you' and 'a man ... deep in feeling, with subtle tact, a swift instinct of truth, and beauty'. See letter from Samuel Taylor Coleridge in Cumming, 2016, p. 47.

33 Dorothy Wordsworth's diary, in *Home at Grasmere*, p. 62.

34 Robert Morrison, 2007, 'A Biography of Thomas De Quincey', https://web.archive.org/web/20070503185933/http://www.queensu.ca/english/tdq/bio.html.

35 Cumming, 2016, p. 28.

36 Dorothy Wordsworth's diary, in *Home at Grasmere*, p. 71; and Hayter, 2002, p. 8.

37 This poem is reprinted in *Home at Grasmere*, p. 71; and Hayter, 2002, p. 48.

38 Andrew Hazucha, 2002, 'Neither Deep nor Shallow but National: Eco-Nationalism in Wordsworth's *Guide to the Lakes*', *Interdisciplinary Studies in Literature and Environment*, 9(2), pp. 61–73, p. 64.

39 Lindsey Porter, [n.d.], *In the Lakeland Footsteps of William Wordsworth* (Oxford: Guidelines Books and Sales), p. 32.

40 *Annual Register, Or a View of History, Politics, and Literature for the Year, 1794. The Second Edition* (London: R. Wilks), vol. 36.

41 Cumming, 2016, p. 28.

42 Dorothy Wordsworth's diary, in *Home at Grasmere*, p. 85.

43 Dorothy Wordsworth, in *Home at Grasmere*, p. 148.

44 David Dabydeen (ed.), 1983, *The Black Presence in English Literature* (Manchester: Manchester University Press), p. 43.

45 Ronald Tetreault, 1977, 'Wordsworth on Enthusiasm: A New Letter to Thomas Clarkson on the Slavery Question', *Modern Philology*, 75(1), pp. 53–8, p. 54.

46 The Guinea voyage was recounted in the following terms: 'His last voyage was to the coast of Guinea. He had been on board a slave ship . . . He said he would rather be in hell than be pressed [press-ganged]', and all these excerpts are from Dorothy Wordsworth's diary in *Home at Grasmere*: see p. 111, p. 125, p. 179 and p. 247.

47 John Wordsworth, letter to Mary Hutchinson, 19 May 1801, in Cumming, 2016, p. 19 and p. 20.

48 Ibid., p. 48.

49 In his 2017 thesis, Francis Nicolas Rossi observes that Captain Charles Luff died in Mauritius, after the former French colony was taken by the British; Dorothy Wordsworth's diary, in *Home at Grasmere*, pp. 259–60.

50 C. E. J. Simons, 2009, 'Alms and the Man: Wordsworth's Later Patronage', in Richard Gravil (ed.), *Grasmere 2009: Selected Papers from the Wordsworth Summer Conference*, Humanities-Ebooks, p. 177.

51 Cumming, 2016, p. 48.

52 Ibid., p.31.

53 Kitson, 2012, p. 4.

54 Letter from John Wordsworth to Dorothy Wordsworth, 2–9 April, 1802, in Cumming, 2016, p. 30.

55 William Wordsworth, 2012, 'To Touissant L'Ouverture', in *Poems by William Wordsworth*, vol. 2 (London: General Books), p. 206. The poem originally appeared in *Poems, Volume II*, published in 1815. The poem was first written in 1802.

56 John Agard, 2006, *Alternative Anthem: Selected Poems* (Tarset: Bloodaxe).

57 Dorothy Wordsworth's diary, in *Home at Grasmere*, p. 192.

58 Kitson, 2012, p. 5; and Simons, 2009, p. 177.

59 UNODC 'A Century of International Drug Control', p. 174; Johnston, 2005, p. 286.

60 Kitson, 2012, p. 3.

61 Johnston, 2005, p. 286.

62 Cumming, 2016, p. 21.

63 Letter from John Wordsworth to his uncle, 16 February 1802, in Cumming, 2016, p. 29.

64 Johnston, 2005, p. 286.

65 Kitson, 2012, p. 2.

66 Wallace W. Douglas, 1948, 'Wordsworth as Business Man', *PMLA*, 63(2), pp. 625–41, p. 631.

67 Cumming, 2016, p. 39, p. 4 and p. 21.

68 Jonathan Roberts, 2001, 'Shared Grief in the Elegies on John Wordsworth: "Farewell the Heart that lives alone" ', *The Wordsworth Circle*, 32(3), pp. 155–61, p. 158.

69 Richard Matlak, 2000, 'Captain John Wordsworth's Death at Sea', *The Wordsworth Circle*, 31(3), pp. 127–33.

70 Cumming, 2016, p. 21.

71 Ibid., pp. 16–21.

72 John Wordsworth, letter to William Wordsworth, in ibid., p. 19 and p. 20.

73 Cumming, 2016, p. 56.

74 Ibid., p. 23 and p. 42.

75 Ibid., p. 41.

76 John Wordsworth, letter on 31 January 1805, and Thomas Gilpin, letter to William Wordsworth, in ibid., p. 61 and p. 42; *An Authentic Narrative of the Loss of the Earl of Abergavenny, East-Indiaman, off Portland on the Night of the 5th February, 1805. Corrected from the Official Return of the East-India House* (London: Blacks and Parry), February 1805.

77 Ibid., p. 8 and p. 9.

78 Cumming, 2016, p. 55.

79 'Narrative of the Dreadful Loss of the Earl of Abergavenny, Indiaman – Wrecked February 5, 1805, on the Shingles [Shambles]', printed for J. Scales, in Cumming, 2016, p. 62.

80 *An Authentic Narrative*, p. 10.

81 Ibid., p. 11.

82 Cumming, 2016, p. 49.

83 Ibid., p. 125.

84 *An Authentic Narrative*, p. 11.

85 Johnston, 2005, pp. 283–4, citing Canto 36 of 'Don Juan', published fourteen years after the sinking, in 1819.

86 *An Authentic Narrative*, p. 17.

87 Cumming, 2016, p. 55 and p. 47.

88 Ibid., p. 15.

89 Letter from Captain Clarke to India House, in ibid., p. 125.

90 *An Authentic Narrative*, p. 6.

91 This information comes from Portland Museum in the UK. See Nick Hartland, 'Museum to Tell Story of Tragic 1805 Earl of Abergavenny Sinking', *Abergavenny Chronicle*, 14 February 2022.

92 *An Authentic Narrative*, p. 46.

93 Cumming, 2016, p. 62.

94 *An Authentic Narrative*, p. 47.

95 Richard Wordsworth letter to William Wordsworth, 7 February 1805, in Cumming, 2016, p.49.

96 William Wordsworth letter to Richard Wordsworth, 7 February 1805, in ibid., p. 50.

97 Dorothy Wordsworth letter to Jane Marshall, 17 March 1805, in ibid., p. 50.

98 Account by Dalmeida in Roberts, 2001, p. 157. See also Cumming, 2016, p. 55.

99 Lamb in Simons, 2009, p. 189.

100 Simons, 2009, p. 192.

101 Peter Swaab, 2014, 'Wordsworth's Elegies for John Wordsworth', *The Wordsworth Circle*, 45(1), pp. 30–38, p. 31.

102 Cumming, 2016, p. 50.

103 Ibid., p. 66 and p. 67.

104 Ibid., p. 66.

105 William Wordsworth letter to James Losh, 16 March 1805, in ibid., p. 52.

106 William Wordsworth, 1805, 'I Only Look'd for Pain and Grief' was written in the summer after his brother's February death that year. The lines quoted here are 26 and 27, 58–60 and 79–80.

107 William Wordsworth, 1805, 'Distressful Gift' was written in the summer after his brother's death in February that year. The lines quoted here are 3–5, 7 and 30.

108 Kitson, 2012, p. 5.

109 Ibid., p. 4 and p. 5.

110 Swaab, 2014, p. 31.

111 Johnston, 2005, pp. 283–4.

112 William Wordsworth, 1805, 'To the Daisy', lines 8–14.

113 Ibid., line 16 and line 20.

114 Kitson, 2012, p. 4 and p. 5.

115 William Wordsworth letter to James Losh, 16 March 1805 in Cummings, 2016, p. 52. See also Johnston, 2005, pp. 283–4.

116 Ibid., pp. 283–4.

117 See also Eric C. Walker, 1990, 'Wordsworth, Warriors and Naming', *Studies in Romanticism*, 29(2), pp. 223–40.

118 William Wordsworth, 1806, 'The Character of the Happy Warrior', lines 1, 3, 4 and 6.

119 Swaab, 2014, p. 31 and p. 32.

120 Dorothy Wordsworth, in Roberts, 2001, p. 158.

121 Dorothy Wordsworth, journal entry for 31 January 1801, in William Knight (ed.), 1897, *Journals of Dorothy Wordsworth*, vol. 1 (London and New York: Macmillan), p. 84.

122 John Edwin Wells, 1940, 'Wordsworth's Political Writings', *PMLA*, 55(4), pp. 1080–128, p. 1112.

123 Simons, 2009, p. 181, p. 183 and p. 192.

124 Ibid., pp. 197–8.

125 Crabbe wrote: 'Wordsworth will now be independent of the world, and may devote himself to poetry without any of the cares and anxieties of penury.' Douglas, 1948, p. 637.

126 Tim Burke, 2005, 'Lord Lonsdale and His Protégés: William Wordsworth and John Hardie', *Criticism*, 47(4), pp. 515–29, p. 512.

127 Simons, 2009, p. 187.

128 William Wordsworth wrote: 'You cannot but be aware that the populace of this town of Kendal were exasperated against the present Members [of Parliament], from a false notion that, by giving their voices for the Corn Bill, they had contributed to increase the price of grain, and thereby aggravating the distresses of the poor.' Quoted in Wells, 1940, p. 1086.

129 Editor of the *Chronicle* in ibid., p. 1081.

130 Wells, 1940, p. 1113.

131 'It is the natural and reasonable consequence of a long-continued possession of large property – furnishing, with the judicious Nobleman at its head, an obvious support, defence, and *instrument* for the intelligent patriotism of the County.' William Wordsworth, 'Two Addresses to the Freeholders of Westmorland, 1818', 24 February 1818, www.poetrysoup.com/short_stories/prose_of_william_wordsworth_i.aspx.

132 'Mr. Henry Brougham,' he wrote of Sir William's rival, 'has been writing to Mr. Clarkson, who has promised, I doubt not, to exert his influence for him among the Westmorland Quakers.' Quoted in Wells, 1940, p. 1221, p. 1223 and p. 1225.

133 Dann, 1980, p. 81.

134 'Nobody at Ambleside appeared in the least interested in the question; and really, anxiously as I desire to see the condition of the Negroes

improved, and slavery abolished . . . [t]he Petitions you are so desirous of obtaining may be of use in giving Ministers courage to act up to their own wishes; but is it not possible that those very petitions may make the Negroes impatient under their present condition; and excite them to disturbance.' William Wordsworth letter to Thomas Clarkson, 10 March 1824, in Ronald Tetreault, 1977, 'Wordsworth on Enthusiasm: A New Letter to Thomas Clarkson on the Slavery Question', *Modern Philology* 75(1), pp. 53–8, p. 54. William Wordsworth letter to Benjamin Dockray, *c.*1840, in ibid., p. 53.

135 'It is my honest opinion that well-intentioned Enthusiasts, (like my Friend Mr C.) with much talent and little discernment, are of all men living the persons who are most likely to do mischief when they meddle with legislation or Politics.' William Wordsworth letter to Sir William Lowther, in ibid., p. 53.

136 William Wordsworth, in ibid., p. 57.

137 Dorothy Wordsworth's diary, in *Home at Grasmere*, p. 87; and William Wordsworth, 1805, *The Prelude*, Book 7, line 68.

138 Douglas, 1948, p. 641; Johnston, 2005, pp. 283–4.

139 Buford Rowland, 1935, 'William Wordsworth and Mississippi Bonds', *The Journal of Southern History*, 1(4), pp. 501–7, p. 503.

140 https://mississippiencyclopedia.org/entries/banking/.

141 William Wordsworth's letters to his American agent, Reed, in Buford Rowland, 1935, pp. 504–6.

142 Wordsworth, 1805, Book 10, line 207. This poem was originally written in 1805.

143 William Wordsworth's letters to his American agent, Reed, in Buford Rowland, 1935, p. 506.

144 George Frere, 1768, *A short history of Barbados, from its first discovery and settlement to this present time* (London: J. Dodsley), p. 122.

145 Dorothy Wordsworth's diary, in *Home at Grasmere*, p. 297.

146 John Mariani and Gail Bellamy, 1998, 'Ginger', *Restaurant Hospitality*, 82(10), p. 86.

147 Dorothy Wordsworth's diary, in *Home at Grasmere*, p. 148, p. 224 and p. 254.

3. The Tobacco Walk: Whitehaven Coast

1 Sir John Lowther's ownership of mines, the relatively small returns from landownership and the significance of all this to local families is discussed in J. V. Beckett, 1981, *Coal and Tobacco: The Lowthers and the Economic Development of West Cumberland 1660–1760* (Cambridge: Cambridge University Press), p. 21.

2 Sir John Lowther made this point himself. See ibid., p. 20.

3 Oliver Wood, 1988, *West Cumberland Coal: 1600–1982/3*, Cumberland and Westmorland Antiquarian and Archaeological Society XXIV (Kendal: Titus Wilson).

4 Beckett, 1981, p. ii.

5 The church was built in 1768. *A description of England and Wales. Containing a particular account of each county . . . Embellished with two hundred and forty copper plates, of palaces, castles, cathedrals, 1769–1770* (London: Newbery and Carnan), p. 8.

6 Lynne Pearce, Corinne Fowler and Robert Crawshaw, 2013, *Postcolonial Manchester: Diaspora Space and the Devolution of Literary Culture* (Manchester: Manchester University Press).

7 Peter Kalu, in ibid., p. 23.

8 Peter Kalu, 2012, 'Old Radicals', in *Out of Bounds: British Black and Asian Poets* (Tarset: Bloodaxe).

9 The Loyalist Collection, Materials Relating to the West Indies from the Senhouse Papers: 1762–1831, HIL-MICL FC LFR.S4J6P3.

10 Peter Kalu, 'Whitehaven. The Keeper of Books', in Jenn Ashworth (ed.), 2018, *Seaside Special: Postcards from the Edge* (Hebden Bridge: Bluemoose Books), p. 29.

11 J. E. Williams, 1956, 'Whitehaven in the Eighteenth Century', *The Economic History Review*, 8(3), pp. 393–404, p. 394.

12 Charles Burlington, David Llewellyn Rees and Alexander Murray, 1779, *The modern universal British traveller; or, a new, complete and accurate tour through England, Wales, Scotland and the neighbouring islands.* (London: J. Cooke), p. 485. Enslaved labourers were available towards the end of the eighteenth century. See Brendan Wolfe, 'Indentured Servants in

Colonial Virginia' (7 December 2020). In *Encyclopedia Virginia*, https://
encyclopediavirginia.org/entries/indentured-servants-in-colonial-
virginia.

13 Eric Burns, 2006, *The Smoke of the Gods: A Social History of Tobacco*
(Philadelphia: Temple University Press), p. 83.

14 'Sir John Lowther (1642–1706), Second Baronet of Whitehaven, Cumberland', The History of Parliament, https://www.historyofparlia
mentonline.org/volume/1690-1715/member/lowther-sir-john-
1642-1706.

15 Beckett, 1981, p. 14.

16 Wood, 1988.

17 W. Jackson, 1888, *Some Account of Sir John Lowther, Baronet, from Original Sources*, Transactions of the Cumberland and Westmorland
Antiquarian and Archaeological Society, p. 334 and p. 348.

18 'Sir John Lowther (1642–1706), Second Baronet of Whitehaven,
Cumberland'.

19 Beckett, 1981, p. 159.

20 Ibid. p. 30.

21 Richard Newman, 2013, 'Port Development and Town Planning in
North West England', *Maritime Architecture*, 8, pp. 293–309, p. 293.

22 Nigel Tattersfield, 1991, *The Forgotten Trade: Comprising the Log of the
Daniel and Henry of 1700 and Accounts of the Slave Trade from the Minor
Ports of England, 1698–1725* (London: Random House), p. 61.

23 Thanks to Christopher Donaldson for drawing my attention to documents which show that members of the family began exploring
opportunities to invest in the RAC as early as the 1660s: D LONS/
L1/1/15, Carlisle Archive Centre. On Sir John's RAC membership see
Percy Ford, 1929, 'Tobacco and Coal: A Note on the Economic History of Whitehaven', *Economica*, 26, pp. 192–6, p. 193; and 'Sir John
Lowther (1642–1706), Second Baronet of Whitehaven, Cumberland'.

24 Katherine Julie Saville-Smith, 2016, 'Cumbria's Encounter with the
East Indies c.1680–1829: Gentry and Middling Provincial Families
Seeking Success', PhD thesis, University of Lancaster, p. 18.

25 Toni Morrison, 1983, *Playing in the Dark: Whiteness and the Literary
Imagination* (London and New York: Vintage), p. xiv.

26 Zak Cheney-Rice, 'Why White People Won't See "Black Movies"', *MIC* magazine, 20 November 2014.

27 Burns, 2006, p. 74.

28 Beckett, 1981, p. 105.

29 Ibid., p. 146 and p. 153.

30 Burns, 2006, p. 5, p. 10, pp. 29–30.

31 Ibid., p. 67.

32 Ibid., pp. 67–86. In 1773 a hogshead was being hoisted overhead just as an elderly man was passing by. The slings broke, and he was crushed to death. Eustace Budgell, 1733, 'The bee: or, universal weekly pamphlet. Containing something to hit every man's taste and principles . . .' (London: W. Burton), vol. 3, p. 1410.

33 Thomas Bluett, 1734. *Some Memoirs of the Life of Job, the Son of Solomon, the High Priest of Boonda in Africa; Who was a Slave About Two Years in Maryland; and Afterwards Being Brought to England, was Set Free, and Sent to His Native Land in the Year 1734* (London: Thomas Bluett).

34 Beckett, 1981, p. 108.

35 Ibid., p. 169.

36 Ibid., p. 205. Whitehaven's largest tobacco importers by far were Peter How – a wealthy magistrate and tobacco merchant with additional interests in coal and iron-ore – and Captain Richard Kelsick, with whom he established How and Kelsick Merchants of London. Other tobacco traders included Thomas and William Gilpin, the son and grandson of Lowther's former steward.

37 Ibid., p. 195 and p. 197.

38 Huw David, 2018, *Trade, Politics, and Revolution: South Carolina and Britain's Atlantic Commerce, 1730–1790* (Columbia: University of South Carolina Press), p. 55 and p. 56. David's stated 1747 date is an estimate.

39 Raquel Fleskes, et al., 2021, 'Ancestry, Health, and Lived Experiences of Enslaved Africans in 18th Century Charleston: An Osteobiographical Analysis', *American Journal of Physical Anthropology*, 175, pp. 3–24, p. 20.

40 Individual person entry for William Senhouse (1741–1800), Legacies of British Slavery database, http://wwwdepts-live.ucl.ac.uk/lbs/person/view/2146645567.

41 Jerome S. Handler, 1997, 'Escaping Slavery in a Caribbean Plantation Society: Marronage in Barbados, 1650s to 1830s', *New West Indian Guide*, 71(3/4), pp. 183–225, p. 206.

42 Tattersfield, 1991, p. 3.

43 This was his new overseer, John Spedding. See ibid., p. 74.

44 Ibid., p. 64.

45 Ibid., p. 66 and p. 74.

46 Ibid., pp. 65–9.

47 Ibid., p. 60 and p. 71.

48 The ship was captained by John Kennedy, also an investor; the vessel was owned by John and Thomas Hartley, John Hall, Edward Fletcher, R. Gale, T. Waken, William Peper, Joseph White, Elizabeth Frower and the captain himself. David Richardson and M. M. Schofield, 2022, 'Whitehaven and the Eighteenth-Century British Slave-Trade', in Jeremy Black (ed.), *The Atlantic Slave Trade*, vol. 3: *Eighteenth Century* (London: Routledge) p. 186.

49 Tattersfield, 1991, p. 64.

50 Trans-Atlantic Slave Trade database, voyage references 24904, 27066 and 24919, https://www.slavevoyages.org/voyage/database; and Tattersfield, ibid., 1991, p. 64.

51 Ibid., p. 188.

52 The first theory is held by Nigel Tattersfield, ibid. The second theory is advanced by Richardson and Schofield, 2022.

53 Robert G. David, 2010, 'Whitehaven and the Northern Whale Fishery', *Northern History*, 47(1), pp. 117–34.

54 This figure, which is necessarily incomplete, was calculated using the records of available voyages, which are each confirmed by at least two reliable sources, on the Slave Voyages database. In her 2007 bicentennial commemoration of the abolition of the slave-trade, the artist Lubaina Himid bought and painted crockery from Whitehaven as well as Lancaster. In an exhibition called *Swallow Hard: The Lancaster Dinner Service*, she displayed 100 pieces of repainted crockery at the Judge's Lodgings. She painted maps, slave-ships, account-book pages, elegant houses and West African patterns: https://lubaina himid.uk/portfolio/swallow-hard/.

55 The original lighthouse was built by Walter Lutwidge, another example of tobacco investment in local buildings.

56 'Sir John Lowther (1642–1706), Second Baronet of Whitehaven, Cumberland'.

57 J. V. Beckett, 1980, 'Illness and Amputation in the Eighteenth Century: The Case of Sir James Lowther (1673–1755)', *Medical History*, 24(1), pp. 88–92.

58 His first investment in the South Sea Company was £3,562. The Company's official name was then 'The Governor and Company of the merchants of Great Britain, trading to the South Seas and other parts of America, and for the encouragement of the Fishery'.

59 Beckett, 1981, p. 211 and p. 215.

60 Tattersfield, 1991, p. 63 and p. 64.

61 Percy Ford, 1929, 'Tobacco and Coal: A Note on the Economic History of Whitehaven', *Economica*, 26, p. 195.

62 Institute of Historical Research, 1998, 'False Friends, Spiteful Enemies: A Community at Law in Early Modern England', *Historical Research*, 71(174), pp. 52–74, p. 63. As a counter-tactic he introduced separate prices for summer and winter coal deliveries, to deter tobacco ships engaging in summer trade. Beckett, 1981, p. 51.

63 Will of William Hicks of Whitehaven, available at the National Archive, Prob. 11/117/279.

64 Tattersfield, 1991, p. 60.

65 Beckett, 1981, p. 7, pp. 22–4, p. 114, p. 119, pp. 130–31, pp. 138–40 and p. 154.

66 Ibid., p. 146.

67 Burns, 2006, p. 5, p. 10, pp. 119–21.

68 One owned a fleet of ships which served the company, another had a son who worked for the company, one was a former company mariner, and the other was the brother-in-law of an East Indiaman ship's commander. Saville-Smith, 2016, p. 163.

69 Mrs Littledale had family links to the Bengal army, Mrs Dixon to Madras-based soldiers and company civil servants, Mrs Milham Hartley's husband was a slave-trader, Mrs Steele and Mrs P. Hodgson were both from East India families, as was Mrs M. Spedding. It is not yet clear whether Mrs Steele was also related to Captain Steele of

Workington, a slave-trader. The advertisement appeared in the *Cumberland Pacquet and Ware's Whitehaven Advertiser*, 12 March 1805, and the names have been cross-checked with other sources mentioned earlier in the chapter and lists in the appendix of Saville-Smith, 2016.

70 Beckett, 1981, p. 196.

71 Ibid., p. 216, p. 217 and p. 219.

72 Ibid., p. 212 and p. 111. Richard Kelsick also branched out into slave-trading. English Heritage listing for Dodington House, Gloucestershire, https://historicengland.org.uk/listing/the-list/list-entry/1000566?section=official-listing. Following the 1833 Slavery Abolition Act, compensation money was used to transform the estate grounds. See Legacies of British Slavery database, https://www.ucl.ac.uk/lbs/physical/view/1995967865.

73 Beckett, 1981, p. 19.

74 Ibid., p. 195 and p. 197.

75 Ibid., p. 173. The database on Slave Voyages shows that Thomas Hartley part-funded at least three slaving voyages. John Kelsick part-owned four slaving vessels. Information about the Lutwidges is included in this chapter and taken from several sources.

76 Beckett, 1981, p. 173.

77 Tattersfield, 1991, p. 64 and p. 65.

78 Beckett, 1981, pp. 212–14.

79 The plan can be seen at http://www.whitehavenandwesternlakeland.co.uk/people/walterlutwidge.htm.

80 Beckett, 1981, p. 168.

81 Jonathan Swift, 1729, 'A Modest Proposal. For preventing the children of poor people in Ireland, from being a burden on their parents or country, and for making them beneficial to the publick', https://extra.shu.ac.uk/emls/iemls/resour/mirrors/rbear/modest.html.

82 Brian Parnaby, 2005, *The Jefferson's of Whitehaven* (Ullock: Travail Press).

83 This longstanding plantation-ownership is evidenced on the individual person entry for Henry Jefferson (1800–1877), the Legacies of British Slavery database at https://www.ucl.ac.uk/lbs/person/view/40823, and the 1832 ledger account book is quoted by Bucknell University, https://sugarmills.blogs.bucknell.edu/yeamons/.

84 Frederick H. Smith, 2005, *Caribbean Rum: A Social and Economic History* (Gainesville: University of Florida Press), p. 42 and p. 43.

85 Ibid., pp. 81–5, pp. 102–6, p. 117.

86 Ibid., p. 17, p. 19, p. 24, p. 27 and p. 35.

87 Ibid., pp. 81–5, pp. 102–6, p. 117.

88 Ibid., p. 64 and p. 65.

89 This sugarhouse had been set up in 1731.

90 Advertisement in the *Cumberland Pacquet and Ware's Whitehaven Advertiser*, 23 July 1816, p. 17.

91 Joseph Senhouse, 1794, 'A song, on the 27th of November 1794, being the birth day of his nephew Humphrey Senhouse Junior of Netherhall, when he attained to the Age of twenty one years' (London: S.N.).

92 Cumbria County records information sheet 'Slavery: Its Cumbrian Connections. Trading in People'. Based on research by Susan Dench.

93 Thanks to Christopher Donaldson for this reference.

94 Register of baptisms, marriages and burials, 1743–1794, St Bees Parish, YPR 42/4, Whitehaven Archive and Local Studies Centre.

95 Margaret Williamson, 2019, 'Slave Names and Naming in the Anglophone Atlantic', Oxford Bibliographies, https://www.oxfordbiblio graphies.com/display/document/obo-9780199730414/obo-9780199 730414-0291.xml. The burial of 'Othello' is marked in parish documents held by the Cumbria County records office and published in 'Slavery: Its Cumbrian Connections'.

96 Ibid.

97 Ibid.

98 Cato was also the name of a Lancaster slave-ship belonging to Richard Millerson, which had sailed throughout the 1760s.

99 'Slavery: Its Cumbrian Connections'.

100 Ibid.

101 Entry for Locust estate, Legacies of British Slavery database, www.ucl.ac.uk/lbs/estate/view/638.

102 Entry for Hartleys and Co., Legacies of British Slavery database, https://www.oxfordbibliographies.com/display/document/obo-9780199730414/obo-9780199730414-0291.xml.

4. The Cotton Walk: East Lancashire

1 S. A. Nichols, 1893, *Darwen and the Cotton Famine, 1862–1864: Thirty Years Ago. By the Honorable Secretary of the Local Relief Committee* (London: J. J. Riley), p. 2.

2 Virinder S. Kalra, 2000, *From Textile Mills to Taxi Ranks: Experiences of Migration, Labour and Social Change* (London: Routledge), p. 75.

3 The line 'I have seen hell and it is white, snow white' is spoken by the novel's hero Margaret Hale in an adaptation of *North and South* produced by the BBC in 2004.

4 *Khadi* was installed at Blackburn Art Gallery and Museum in 2021. Images of the exhibition are archived at https://britishtextilebiennial.co.uk/programme/bharti-parmar-re-thinking-khadi/.

5 Bharti Parmar, 2021, *Khadi: Cotton, Colonialism and Resistance*, https://vimeo.com/608353260/94e66cfe72.

6 Pam Blackwell and David Barrowclough, National Mills Conference papers, 13 May 1992.

7 Albert Forrest, 1990, *Old Blackburn and Darwen* (Preston: Carnegie Publishing), pp. 1–5.

8 Kalra, 2000, p. 77 and p. 80.

9 This has been attributed to Edward Bainz, in 1835.

10 Jonathan E. Eacott, 2012, 'Making an Imperial Compromise: The Calico Acts, the Atlantic Colonies and the Structure of the British Empire', *William and Mary Quarterly*, 69(4), p. 732.

11 Ibid., p. 753.

12 Zach Sell, 2021, *Trouble of the World: Slavery and Empire in the Age of Capital* (Chapel Hill: University of North Carolina Press), p. 72.

13 Eacott, 2012, p. 731.

14 This was Samuel Crompton's 1779 spinning mule. Historic England, *The Textile Mills of Lancashire: The Legacy* (Glasgow: Historic England), available at https://historicengland.org.uk/images-books/publications/textile-mills-lancashire-legacy/textile-mills-lancashire-legacy/.

15 Stephen Broadberry and Bishnupriya Gupta, 2005, 'Cotton Textiles and the Great Divergence: Lancashire, India and Shifting

Competitive Advantage, 1600–1850', (Birmingham: University of Birmingham), p. 2.

16 Kalra, 2000, p. 78.

17 National Museums Liverpool, 2023, 'A City Built on Cotton', https://www.liverpoolmuseums.org.uk/city-built-cotton.

18 Terry Wyke, 2007, 'Manchester, Cotton and Anti-Slavery', *Revealing Histories* (Manchester: Manchester City Gallery).

19 Sven Beckert, 2004, 'Emancipation and Empire: Reconstructing the Worldwide Web of Cotton Production in the Age of the American Civil War', *The American Historical Review*, 109(5), pp. 1405–38, p. 1415 and p. 1425.

20 'Darwen Tower' entry, *Cotton Town: Blackburn With Darwen*, https://web.archive.org/web/20110614175908/http://www.cottontown.org/page.cfm?pageid=755&language=eng.

21 Sell, 2021, p. 72.

22 David Olusoga, 2016, *Black and British: A Forgotten History* (London: Macmillan), p. 348 and p. 354.

23 Ibid., p. 342 and p. 346. So too, as Olusoga points out, did Liverpool switch from sugar to cotton after the 1833 Slavery Abolition Act, continuing its economic dependence on slave-produced goods.

24 Ibid., p. 348.

25 Ibid., p. 354.

26 Ibid., p. 342.

27 Kris Manjapra, 2022, *Black Ghost of Empire: The Long Death of Slavery and the Failure of Emancipation* (London: Allen Lane), p. 122. The phrase 'bid for freedom' is taken from Simon Newman's 2022 book *Freedom Seekers: Escaping from Slavery in Restoration London* (London: University of London Press).

28 Rosalind Hall (2003) 'A Poor Cotton Weyver: Poverty and the Cotton Famine in Clitheroe', *Social History*, 28(2), pp. 227–50, p. 227. This came straight after accidental overproduction during a market glut, adding to mills' problems.

29 Tarasankar Banerjee, 1969, 'Cotton Diplomacy in American Civil War Vis-à-vis Cotton Experiments in India', *Proceedings of the Indian History Congress*, 31, pp. 486–93, p. 486.

30 Onesimus Secundus, 1863, *The True Interpretation of the American Civil War and of England's Cotton Difficulty, Or Slavery from a Different Point of View Shewing the Relative Responsibilities of America and Great Britain* (London: Trubner and Co.), p. 41.

31 Olusoga, 2016, p. 147 and p. 348.

32 The Emancipation Proclamation of 1 January 1863, is held in the National Archives in Washington, DC.

33 Manjapra, 2022, p. 126. As an Illinois senator he had once even proposed a bill that fugitives found in DC should be returned to their enslavers (p. 127).

34 *Encyclopedia Britannica*, 'American Civil War: Causes, Definition, Dates, History, and Facts', https://www.britannica.com/event/American-Civil-War.

35 Hall, 2003, pp. 227–50, p. 227 and p. 241; and Olusoga, 2016, p. 351.

36 Edwin Waugh, 1862, *Home-Life of the Lancashire Factory Folk During the Cotton Famine* (Manchester: Manchester Examiner and Times), p. 5.

37 Letter to *The Times*, 14 April 1862, in Norman Longmate, 1978, *The Hungry Mills: The Story of the Lancashire Cotton Famine, 1861–5* (London: Maurice Temple Smith), p. 7.

38 Longmate, 1978, p. 133.

39 Nichols, 1893, p. 64.

40 The study, conducted between 1862 and 1863, was of thirty-three single millworkers. D. J. Oddy, 1983, 'Urban Famine in Nineteenth-Century Britain: The Effect of the Lancashire Cotton Famine on Working-Class Diet and Health', *The Economic History Review*, 36(1), pp. 68–86, p. 66 and p. 67.

41 Ibid., p. 76.

42 Nichols, 1893, p. 82.

43 Hall, 2003, p. 22 and p. 241; and Olusoga, 2016, p. 351.

44 Nichols, 1893, p. 74.

45 4 October 1862, entry no. 127, in the diary of George Burnett, 1862–3, https://www.cottontown.org/The%20Cotton%20Industry/Cotton%20Famine/Pages/George-Burnett%27s-Diary-1862-1863.aspx.

46 21 November 1862, entry no. 238, in ibid.

47 16 August 1862, entry no. 38, in ibid. See also reference to the *Blackburn Evening Standard* in the introduction.

48 24 March 1863, entry no. 268, in ibid. See also reference to the *Blackburn Evening Standard* in the introduction.

49 Nichols, 1893, p. 83.

50 Olusoga, 2016, p. 352 and p. 353; Oddy, 1983, p. 75.

51 Waugh, 1862, p. 7.

52 Nichols, 1893, p. 77.

53 4 March 1863, entry no. 238, in the diary of George Burnett, 1862–3.

54 Rooley Moor Neighbourhood Forum, 'Cotton Famine Road', https://www.rmnf.org.uk/area/cotton-famine-road/.

55 Forrest, 1990, p. 19. This movement was founded when weavers opened a shop in 1844.

56 Speeches were given by Richard Cobden, the manufacturer, and John Bright, the radical millowner.

57 Douglas Maynard, 1961, 'Civil War "Care": The Mission of the George Griswold, *New England Quarterly*, 34(3), pp. 291–310, p. 292 and p. 310.

58 Ibid., p. 305.

59 Ibid., pp. 303–4.

60 Simon Rennie, 2020, 'This "Merikay War": Poetic Responses in Lancashire to the American Civil War', *Journal of Victorian Culture*, 25(1), pp. 126–43, p. 139.

61 Washington Alcott, 2007, 'Rochdale and Cotton Production: Cotton Production and the Canals', *Revealing Histories: Remembering Slavery*, http://www.revealinghistories.org.uk/who-resisted-and-campaigned-for-abolition/articles/rochdale-and-cotton-production.html.

62 Olusoga, 2016, p. 365. Lincoln's 'Letter to the Working-Men of Manchester, England', 19 January 1963, American Civil War Society, https://acws.co.uk/archives-misc-lincoln_letter.

63 Maynard, 1961, p. 308.

64 Rennie, 2020, p. 126.

65 Ibid., p. 137.

66 Olusoga, 2016, p. 358.

67 Ibid., p. 373 and p. 374.

68 21 March 1863, entry no. 52, the diary of George Burnett, 1862–3.

69 Beckert, 2004, pp. 1405–38, p. 1414; and Banerjee, 1969, p. 492.

70 Hall, 2003, p. 241 and p. 243.

71 Waugh, 1862, p. 164; and Rennie, 2020, p. 134.

72 Beckert, 2004, p. 1433.

73 Ibid., p. 1432.

74 Ibid., p. 1425.

75 Ibid., pp. 1425–35.

76 Ibid., pp. 1425–7.

77 Sell, 2021, p. 66.

78 'Boycott of Foreign Clothes' notice in the *Bombay Chronicle*, 20 July 1921, p. 13.

79 Lisa N. Trivedi, 2003, 'Mapping the "Nation": Swadeshi Politics in Nationalist India, 1920–1930', *The Journal of Asian Studies*, 62(1), pp. 11–41, pp. 11–17; and Kalra, 2000, p. 79.

80 'Cotton Crisis. State of Trade with India and Unemployment: Resolution to Be Submitted at Mass Meeting April 28th, 1931', Amalgamated Weaver's Association: Cotton Crisis Papers, TU/WEAVERS/8/18, held at the Working Class Movement Library.

81 *Mahatma Gandhi Arrives in UK (1931)*, Pathé films, https://www.youtube.com/watch?v=P6njRwz_dMw.

82 This is the theory of local historian Harold Heys: see 'When Gandhi Met Darwen's Mill Workers', *BBC News*, 23 September 2017, https://www.bbc.co.uk/news/uk-england-lancashire-15020097.

83 'Mr. Gandhi in Darwen. What He Saw, What He Said', *Darwen News*, 3 September 1931 and 26 September 1931; and Mr Duxbury was interviewed for the *Darwen Advertiser*, 30 September 1981.

84 Charles Haworth, 1931, 'Mr. Gandhi. The Man and His Policy', *Darwen Advertiser*, Saturday 3 October 1931.

85 'My Impressions of Mr. Gandhi', *Northern Daily Telegraph*; Mohandas Karamchand, 'Visit to Darwen by Gandhi', *Northern Daily Telegraph*; both undated newspaper articles in bound and uncatalogued copies of newspaper clippings entitled *Immigration Covering the Period from 1958 to 1987*, Blackburn Library.

86 Haworth, 1931.

87 Ibid.

88 'Mr. Gandhi in Darwen. What He Saw, What He Said', p. 8. In 1969, an exhibition was held in the town to commemorate the visit on the centenary of Gandhi's birth. Photographs were displayed of his visit. The exhibition was organized by a Quaker resident of Garden Village, a Mrs Ward. Gandhi's stay in her house had inspired a lifelong interest in his words and strategy. The co-organizer was a Mr Goswani, the founder of Blackburn and District Indian League. See *Darwen Advertiser*, 7 February 1969.

89 Haworth, 1931.

90 'Mr. Gandhi in Darwen. What He Saw, What He Said'.

91 Haworth, 1931.

92 Ibid.

93 Ibid.

94 Articles about Oswald Mosley were found in the *Darwen Advertiser* by my researcher Elisabeth Grass, working in Blackburn Archive. The articles were printed on 7 January 1935 and 9 January 1935, including an article by R. H. Whittle about the fascist leaflet.

95 J. W. Daniels and J. Jewkes, 1928, 'The Post-War Depression in the Lancashire Cotton Industry', *Journal of the Royal Statistical Society*, 91(2), pp. 153–206.

96 Kalra, 2000, p. 76 and p. 80.

97 Ibid., p. 92 and p. 95.

98 Ibid., p. 105.

99 Ibid., p. 111–19.

100 Ibid., p. 102.

101 Ibid.

102 Ibid., p. 139–41.

103 Ibid., p. 161–3.

104 Ibid., p. 168.

5. *The Wool Walk: Dolgellau and the Americas*

1 Welsh Assembly Government, 2009, 'Dolgellau, Understanding Urban Development' (Cadw: Welsh Assembly, Cardiff), pp. 11–14.

2 Gwynedd Archaeological Trust, 'Historic Landscape Characterisation–Dolgellau Historical Themes', http://www.heneb.co.uk/hlc/dolgel lauthemes.html#:~:text=The%20Dolgellau%20area%20was%20 first,(DRO%20CQ7%2F76).

3 Rita Singer, 2021, '"The Devil May Take Snowdon", or: Inscribing Touristic Disappointment in Victorian Visitors' Books', *Studies in Travel Writing*, 25(3), pp. 334–59, p. 335.

4 Gwynedd Archaeological Trust, 'Historic Landscape Characterisation'.

5 Ibid.

6 Ibid.

7 Chris Evans, 2010, *Slave Wales: The Welsh and Atlantic Slavery 1660–1850* (Cardiff: University of Wales Press), p. 48.

8 Adam N. Coward, 2021, 'Welsh Wool, Slavery and the Built Environment', Royal Commission on the Ancient and Historical Monuments of Wales.

9 Marian Gwyn, 2020, 'Merioneth and the Atlantic Slave Trade', *Journal of the Merioneth Historical and Record Society*, 18(3), pp. 284–98, p. 292. This figure, as Gwyn points out, does not include the considerable market for Welsh plains in South America.

10 Charlotte Williams, 2002, *Sugar and Slate* (Cardiff: Planet Books), p. 2 and p. 26.

11 Ibid., p. 3 and p. 8.

12 Ibid., p. 39.

13 Ibid., p. 28.

14 Ibid., p. 89.

15 Evans, 2010, p. 46.

16 Williams, 2002, p. 50.

17 Ibid., p. 1.

18 H. V. Bowen (ed.), 2011, *Wales and the British Overseas Empire: Interactions and Influences, 1650–1830* (Manchester: Manchester University Press), p. 1 and p. 6.

19 Ibid., p. 6.

20 'Vaughan, Sir Robert Williames, 2nd bt. (1768–1843), of Nannau Hall, nr. Dolgellau, Merion', in D. R. Fisher (ed.), 2009, *The History of*

Parliament: The House of Commons 1820–1832 (Cambridge: Cambridge University Press).

21 Thomas Richards, 1960, 'Nanney (Nannau) family, of Nannau, Merionedd', *Dictionary of Welsh Biography* (Cardiff: Honourable Society of Cymmrodorion).

22 Philip Sidney, 'An Ancient Welsh Industry', *Welsh Gazette and West Wales Advertiser*, 14 December 1899. The family later produced their Meyrick Jones tweed for a family friend, the poet Alfred Lord Tennyson. Tennyson tweed was so named because of the poet's connection with the Meyricks.

23 M. J. Jones, [n.d.] 'Merioneth Woollen Industry. From 1750 to 1820', The National Library of Wales, https://journals.library.wales/view/1386666/1411229/204#?xywh=-1028%2C212%2C4476%2C2872, p. 188.

24 Nannau Estate entries on Sir Robert Vaughan, 2nd Bart., and Sir Robert Williames Vaughan, 3rd Bart., NannauWales.com. Gwynedd Archaeological Trust, 'Historic Landscape Characterisation'.

25 Gaynor Legall, Roiyah Saltus, Robert Moore, David Anderson, Marian Gwyn, Naomi Alleyne, Olivette Otele and Chris Evans, November 2020, 'The Slave Trade and the British Empire: An Audit of Commemoration in Wales', p. 48, https://www.gov.wales/sites/default/files/publications/2021-12/the-slave-trade-and-the-british-empire-an-audit-of-commemoration-in-wales.pdf.

26 'Vaughan, Robert Williames (1768–1843), of Nannau Hall, nr. Dolgellau, Merion', The History of Parliament, https://www.historyofparliamentonline.org/volume/1790-1820/member/vaughan-robert-williames-1768-1843.

27 Legall, et al., 2020, p. 48.

28 Welsh Government Report on Welsh Wool, Slavery and the Built Environment, Royal Commission on the Ancient and Historical Monuments of Wales, p. 2, https://rcahmw.gov.uk/welsh-wool-slavery-and-the-built-environment/.

29 'Vaughan, Robert Williames (1768–1843), of Nannau Hall, nr. Dolgellau, Merion'.

30 'Merioneth', The History of Parliament, https://www.historyofpar
liamentonline.org/volume/1820-1832/constituencies/merioneth1
820-1832.

31 Evans, 2010, p. 46.

32 This phrase is used by Simon Newman in his 2021 book *Freedom Seekers: Escaping from Slavery in Restoration London* (London: University of
London Press).

33 Douglas B. Chambers, 2016, 'African Runaway Slaves in the Anglo-
American Atlantic World, *Atlantic World*, vol. 1, 'North America',
pp. 1–31, p. 14.

34 Ibid., p. 13.

35 Evans, 2010, p. 49.

36 Gwyn, 2020, p. 290.

37 Evans, 2010, p. 50; Gwyn, 2020, p. 291.

38 Ibid., p. 290.

39 Evans, 2010, p. 972.

40 Philip Sidney, 'An Ancient Welsh Industry', *Welsh Gazette and West
Wales Advertiser,* 14 December 1899.

41 Evans, 2010, p. 54.

42 Ibid., p. 44.

43 With thanks to Gwynedd Archive Services and Rebecca Wragg Sykes
for retrieving this information from the Dolgellau Parish Minute
Books, Z/PE/33/6 at Merioneth Record Office. See also Gwyn,
2020, p. 285.

44 In the nineteenth century, shearers' command of the labour market
was threatened by the arrival of shearing machines, invented in the
1860s. These came twenty years too late for Dolgellau's woollen
industry, which declined after 1840. Woollen manufacturers elsewhere
in the country had received sinister handwritten notes from shearers,
threatening to destroy factories if the new machines were not
removed within a specified period. See E .P. Thompson, 1982 [1963],
The Making of the English Working Class (London: Penguin), p. 571.

45 Gwyn, 2020, p. 285.

46 'People's Collection Wales', https://www.peoplescollection.wales/
items/1367051.

47 Thompson, 1982, p. 274.

48 Jones, [n.d.], p. 188.

49 Gwyn, 2020, p. 285.

50 Jones, [n.d.].

51 George Eliot, 1861, *Silas Marner* (Delhi: Kindle edition).

52 Thompson, 1982, p. 324.

53 Ibid., p. 324.

54 Ibid., p. 211.

55 Fisher, 2009, p. 433.

56 Jones, [n.d], p. 187.

57 Adam N. Coward, 2021, 'Welsh Wool, Slavery and the Built Environment', Royal Commission on the Ancient and Historical Monuments of Wales.

58 Jones, [n.d], p. 187.

59 Thompson, 1982, p. 319.

60 Gwyn, 2020, p. 286.

61 Evans, 2010, p. 47.

62 Ibid., p. 52.

63 Gwyn, 2020, p. 285.

64 Ibid., p. 293.

65 The 1833 Act still required formerly enslaved people to work for up to eight years following the law's implementation in 1834.

66 Ibid., p. 54.

67 With thanks to Gwynedd Archive Services and Rebecca Wragg Sykes for retrieving this information from the Guardians' Minute Book Z/G/3/1 and 15/17/11.5, Merioneth Record Office.

68 Catalogue of Quarter Sessions documents Z/QS/43, 34, 44–6, 107 and 108, 109, 141 and 142. With thanks to Gwynedd Archive Services and Rebecca Wragg Sykes for retrieving this information from Merioneth Record Office.

69 The key historians of Welsh wool and slavery have been Chris Evans and Marian Gwyn.

70 Williams, 2002, p. 94.

71 Coleridge-Taylor, quoted in Legall, et al., 2020, p. 52.

72 Williams, 2002, p. 48.

73 Ibid., p. 87.

74 Chris Evans, 2011, 'Wales, Munster and the English South West: Contrasting Articulations with the Atlantic World', in Bowen, 2011, p. 126.

75 Williams, 2002, p. 91.

76 The National Trust, 'Penrhyn Castle and the Great Penrhyn Quarry Strike, 1900–03', https://www.nationaltrust.org.uk/visit/wales/penrhyn-castle-and-garden/the-great-penrhyn-quarry-strike.

77 Williams, 2002, p. 13 and p. 29.

6. An Indian Walk in the Cotswolds

1 'Sezincote Case Study: The Cockerell Family', East India Company at Home, 1757–1857, https://blogs.ucl.ac.uk/eicah/sezincote-gloucestershire/sezincote-case-study-the-cockerell-family/.

2 Jan Sibthorpe, 'Sezincote Case Study: Sezincote, Gloucestershire', East India Company at Home, 1757–1857, https://blogs.ucl.ac.uk/eicah/sezincote-gloucestershire/. This case study shows that Humphry Repton, whose designs for Sezincote were never used, was responsible for the Prince Regent visiting the Cockerell house and perceiving it as a model for the Indian architectural style of Brighton Pavilion.

3 Mark Edmonds, 'Does This Look Unpleasant?' *Daily Mail*, 15 January 2021, https://www.dailymail.co.uk/news/article-9153499/Academic-says-GARDENING-roots-racial-injustice.html.

4 E. P. Thompson, 1982 [1963], *The Making of the English Working Class* (London: Penguin); and Brian Manning, 1976, *The English People and the English Revolution* (London: Heinemann).

5 'Sezincote Case Study: The Cockerell Family'.

6 Ibid.

7 William Dalrymple, 2019, *The Anarchy: The Relentless Rise of the East India Company* (London: Bloomsbury), p. 209.

8 Steven Neill, 2019, 'The East India Company and Parliament's "Fateful Decision" of 1767', *Journal of the American Revolution*, 26 September 2019.

9 Kieran Hazzard, 2018, 'What Was the East India Company?' An Oxford Partnership Trusted Source article for the National Trust, https://www.nationaltrust.org.uk/discover/history/what-was-the-east-india-company.

10 Dalrymple, 2019, p. 210 and 219.

11 Raymond Head, 1982, 'Sezincote: A Paradigm of the Indian Style', unpublished thesis at the Royal College of Art, p. 12. The source cited by Head is the *East India Military Calendar* of 1823.

12 Letters from John Cockerell to Charles Cockerell 17/6/1779–7/12/1792, 13 April 1790, Papers relating to the Cockerell (later Rushout) and Grieve families held at Bodleian Archives and Manuscripts in Oxford, p. 29(r). Thanks to Elisabeth Grass for researching and analysing letters between the Cockerell brothers.

13 'Sezincote Case Study: The Cockerell Family'.

14 Hazzard, 2018.

15 Dalrymple, 2019, p. 215 and p. 216. The Englishman was James Grant.

16 Neil Sen, 1997, 'Warren Hastings and British Sovereign Authority in Bengal, 1774–80', *The Journal of Imperial and Commonwealth History*, 25(1), pp. 59–81, p. 60.

17 The Indian farmers' protest was against three farm acts which were passed in the Indian parliament in 2020.

18 A fuller explanation of the details of the Permanent Settlement can be found in the *Encyclopedia Britannica* entry for Cornwallis Code, https://www.britannica.com/topic/Cornwallis-Code.

19 See Bernard S. Cohn, 1960, 'The Initial British Impact on India: A Case Study of the Benares Region', *The Journal of Asian Studies*, 19(4), pp. 418–31.

20 Raymond Head, 1982, 'Sezincote: A Paradigm of the Indian Style', unpublished thesis at the Royal College of Art, p. 37.

21 Hyder Ali, in Dalrymple, 2019, p. 318.

22 See Letters from John Cockerell to Charles Cockerell 17/6/1779–7/12/1792, Dep.C.855.

23 See Letters from John Cockerell to Charles Cockerell 17/6/1779–7/12/1792, 13 April 1790, p. 29(r).

24 National Army Museum, collections item 1971-02-33-367-1 ('The Marquis of Cornwallis receiving the Hostage princes, sons of Tipoo Sultan, 1792' by D. Orm).

25 Head, 1982, p. 32. His source is a 1798 letter to Samuel Pepys Cockerell.

26 Transcribed by Peter Bailey for Families in British India Society from Calcutta's South Park Street Cemetery, p. 83.

27 Tony Webster, 2005, 'An Early Global Business in a Colonial Context: The Strategies, Management, and Failure of John Palmer and Company of Calcutta, 1780–1830', *Enterprise and Society*, March 2005, pp. 98–133, p. 99.

28 Webster, 2005, pp. 100–108.

29 Head, 1982, p. 12.

30 Letter from John Cockerell to Charles Cockerell from Hyde Park Corner, 27 June 1794, Bodleian Archives and Manuscripts in Oxford, p. 10(v).

31 Ibid. Letters from John Cockerell to Charles Cockerell 17/6/1779–7/12/1792, 13 April 1790, Bodleian Archives and Manuscripts in Oxford. p. 29(r).

32 Letter from John Cockerell to Charles Cockerell from Hyde Park Corner, 27 June 1794, Bodleian Archives and Manuscripts in Oxford, p. 10(v).

33 Head, 1982, p. 133.

34 Letter from John Cockerell to Charles Cockerell from Hyde Park Corner, 18 May 1795, Bodleian Archives and Manuscripts in Oxford, p. 49.

35 Letter from John Cockerell to Charles Cockerell from Hyde Park Corner, 5 December 1795, Bodleian Archives and Manuscripts in Oxford, p. 87(v).

36 This theory is also advanced by Head, 1982.

37 Ibid., p. 133.

38 In Finbarr Barry Flood, 2006, 'Correct Delineations and Promiscuous Outlines: Envisioning India at the Trial of Warren Hastings', *Arts History* 29(1), pp. 47–78, p. 66.

39 Letter to Charles Cockerell from John Cockerell from Hyde Park Corner, 27 June 1794, Bodleian Archives and Manuscripts in Oxford

p. 10(v). Letters from John Cockerell to Charles Cockerell 17/6/1779–7/12/1792, 13 April 1790, p. 29(r).

40 Kenelm Digby in Tillman W. Nechtman, 2006, 'Nabobs Revisited: A Cultural History of British Imperialism and the Indian Question in Late-Eighteenth-Century Britain', *History Compass* 4(4), pp. 645–67, p. 652.

41 Letter from John Cockerell to Charles Cockerell from Bath, 15 January 1795, Bodleian Archives and Manuscripts in Oxford, p. 30(v). Letters from John Cockerell to Charles Cockerell 17/6/1779–7/12/1792, 13 April 1790, p. 29(r).

42 With thanks to Elisabeth Grass, who researched these letters at Bodleian Libraries and reached this conclusion in relation to both Cockerell brothers.

43 Head, 1982, p. 56 and p. 58.

44 Allen Firth, 2005, *The Book of Bourton-on-the-Hill, Batsford and Sezincote* (Tiverton: Halsgrove House), p. 111.

45 An Act for Inclosing, and Exonerating from Tithes, Lands in the Parish or Parishes of Bourton-on-the-Hill and Moreton-in-Marsh in the County of Gloucester', 28 May 1821, UK Parliamentary Papers, https://parlipapers-proquest-com.ezproxy4.lib.le.ac.uk/parlipapers/docview/t70.d75.pa-000605?accountid=7420.

46 Firth 2005, p. 127 and p.159.

47 Letter from John Cockerell to Charles Cockerell from Hyde Park Corner, Bodleian Archives and Manuscripts in Oxford, 11 April 1795, p. 43(r).

48 Letter from John Cockerell to Charles Cockerell from Saville Row, Bodleian Archives and Manuscripts in Oxford, 26 February 1795, p. 43(r).

49 Letter from John Cockerell to Charles Cockerell, 11 April 1795, Bodleian Archives and Manuscripts in Oxford, p. 39(v).

50 Ibid., p. 43(r). Letters from John Cockerell to Charles Cockerell from Hyde Park Corner, 11 April 1795, Bodleian Archives and Manuscripts in Oxford, p. 43(r) and p. 46(v), and 18 May 1795, p. 49(v).

51 Dalrymple, 2019, p. 327.

52 Mithi Mukherjee, 2005, 'Justice, War and the Imperium: India and Britain in Edmund Burke's Prosecutorial Speeches in the Impeachment Trial of Warren Hastings', *Law and History Review*, 23(3), pp. 589–630.

53 Robert W. Jones, 2020, 'Review of Chiara Rolli's book *The Trial of Warren Hastings: Classical Oratory and Reception in Eighteenth-Century England*', *Eighteenth-Century Studies*, 53(2), pp. 316–18.

54 Sen, 1997, p. 61.

55 Dalrymple, 2019, p. 238. Ultimately, Hastings' trial allowed parliamentarians to regulate a company which had set Indian rulers against the British by interfering in their affairs and waging costly wars. Through military conquest and for financial gain, the company had accrued massive power which exceeded the authority of the British government. The 1783 India Bill and the 1784 India Act sought to curb this by establishing a new, legal order in India – under British authority – with treaties to promote non-aggression, judicial reforms and better-defined property rights. See Jones, 2020, p. 316.

56 Sen, 1997, p. 60.

57 Letter from John Cockerell to Charles Cockerell from Hyde Park Corner, 8 May 1795, Bodleian Archives and Manuscripts in Oxford.

58 Letter from John Cockerell to Charles Cockerell from Hyde Park Corner, 18 May 1795, Bodleian Archives and Manuscripts in Oxford, p. 49(v).

59 Nechtman, 2006, p. 654.

60 Ibid., p. 648.

61 First curry powder advert, archived at British Library, https://www.bl.uk/learning/timeline/item104061.html; and Nechtman, 2006, p. 655.

62 Transcribed by Peter Schofield for the Families in British India Society database.

63 'Sezincote Case Study: The Cockerell family' (ucl.ac.uk).

64 This point is made in relation to a very different aspect of colonial history – the slave-trade – in the walking tours of the historian Laurence Westgaph, a historian in residence at Liverpool Museums.

65 Dalrymple, 2019, p. 344.

66 Ibid., p. 344.

67 Ibid., p. 317.

68 Ibid., p. 347.

69 The Families in British India Society database, https://www.family historyfederation.com/societies-the-families-in-british-india-society#:~:text=FIBIS%20has%20no%20established%20 offices,photographs%2C%20newspapers%20and%20other%20 publications.

70 Mushirul Hasan (ed.), 2013, *Westward Bound: Travels of Mirza Abu Taleb* (Oxford: Oxford University Press), pp. 3–69.

71 Ibid., p. 65.

72 Cockerell held the seats consecutively until 1807.

73 Letter from John Cockerell to Charles Cockerell from Hyde Park Corner, 5 December 1795, p. 89(v).

74 'Sezincote Case Study: The Cockerell Family'.

75 Hasan, 2013, p. 65.

76 Ibid., p. 68.

77 Meike Fellinger, 2010, ' "All Man's Pollution Does the Sea Cleanse": Revisiting the Nabobs in Britain, 1785–1837', unpublished thesis, University of Warwick, p. 64.

78 Margot Finn and Kate Smith, 2018, 'Introduction', in *The East India Company at Home, 1757–1857* (London: UCL Press), p. 81. The newspaper in question was *The Morning Post and Fashionable World*, 6 October 1795.

79 Hasan, 2013, p. 69.

80 James Graham, 2014, 'Echoes of the Raj: What Britain Brought Home from Colonial India', *British Heritage*, July 2014, p. 36.

81 'Sezincote Case Study: The Cockerell Family'.

82 Finbarr Barry Flood, 'Correct Delineations and Promiscuous Outlines: Envisioning India at the Trial of Warren Hastings', *Arts History*, 8 February 2006, pp. 47–78, p. 49. Hastings also commissioned the German portraitist Johann Zoffany.

83 John Mcaleer, 'A Global Gaze: British Artists, Landscape Spaces, and the Wider World in the Late 18th Century', archived at British Library, https://www.bl.uk/picturing-places/articles/a-global-gaze-british-artists-landscape-spaces-and-the-wider-world-in-the-late-18th-century.

84 This collection of aquatints by William Hodges was published between 1786 and 1788.

85 Flood, 2006, p. 65. Hodges was apprenticed to the Romantic land-scape painter Richard Wilson (*c*.1713–82).

86 Nechtman, 2006, p. 656; Mcaleer, 'A Global Gaze'.

87 Flood, 2006, p. 66.

88 'Sezincote Case Study: Building Sezincote: Building a Reputation', East India Company at Home, 1757–1857, https://blogs.ucl.ac.uk/eicah/sezincote-gloucestershire/sezincote-case-study-building-sezincote-building-a-reputation/.

89 Fellinger, 2010, p. 64.

90 Tony Webster, 2005, 'An Early Global Business in a Colonial Context: The Strategies, Management, and Failure of John Palmer and Company of Calcutta, 1780–1830', *Enterprise and Society*, March 2005, pp. 98–133, p. 102.

91 Ibid.

92 Individual person entry for Sir Charles Cockerell, Legacies of British Slavery database, https://www.ucl.ac.uk/lbs/person/view/2146011675.

93 University of Leeds, 'Striking Women: Indentured Labour from South Asia (1834–1917)', https://www.striking-women.org/module/map-major-south-asian-migration-flows/indentured-labour-south-asia-1834-1917.

94 Sudhansu Bimal Mookherji, 1959, 'Indians in Mauritius, 1842–1870', *India Quarterly*, 15(4), pp. 367–81.

95 Announcement in *Gentleman's Magazine* 1837, p. 317.

96 This was the house where, in 2022, the prime minister Boris Johnson had his wedding party to celebrate his marriage to Carrie Symonds.

7. The Enclosure Walk: Norfolk and Jamaica

1 This chapter's database and record office searches were conducted by Kate Bernstock.

2 W. G. Hoskins, 2015 [1955], *The Making of the English Landscape* (Beaminster: Little Toller), pp. 92–9.

3 Carole Rawcliffe (ed.), 2005, *Norwich Since 1550* (London: Hambledon Continuum).

4   E. P. Thompson, 1982 [1963], *The Making of the English Working Class* (London: Penguin).

5   P. M. Zall, 2014, 'John Reeves: The Perils of Public Service', *The Wordsworth Circle*, 4(3), pp. 315–27.

6   Thompson, 1982.

7   Professor Christine Kinealy, 'Benjamin Benson Online Talk', 14 October 2021, https://www.youtube.com/watch?v=c-mOwIrUAPQ.

8   Victoria Horth, 2007, 'Slavery and Abolition: The Norfolk Connections', www.bbc.co.uk/norfolk/content/articles/2007/02/27/abolition_norfolk_overview_20070227_feature.shtml.

9   Norfolk Record Office, 2007, 'Norfolk and the Abolition of Slavery'.

10 Horth, 2007. Smith's story is connected to influential women in the county. His sister-in-law was the prison reformer and anti-slavery figure Elizabeth Fry, and the women in his family wrote some of his parliamentary speeches.

11 Zakia Sewell, 2020, *My Albion*, a four-part series for BBC Radio 4.

12 The route is loosely based on a local walk but makes a detour to Earsham Hall. The walk is archived here: https://bungay-suffolk.co.uk/wp-content/uploads/2020/08/waveney-valley-walks-full-guide.pdf.

13 Individual person entry for Thomas Walpole (1727–1823), Legacies of British Slavery database, https://www.ucl.ac.uk/lbs/person/view/2146645271.

14 The firm was Alexander and Sons.

15 The bank sold these on to James Baillie. See the Bank of England's 2022 exhibition, *Slavery and the Bank of England*. Part of the exhibition can be accessed online at: www.bankofengland.co.uk/museum/whats-on/slavery-and-the-bank. The bank's 2021 statement said that: 'The Bank of England was never itself directly involved in the slave trade but is aware of some inexcusable connections involving former Governors and Directors and apologises for them.'

16 Bank of England, 'Statement in Relation to the Bank's Role in the Slave-Trade', 19 June 2020, https://www.bankofengland.co.uk/news/2020/june/statement-in-relation-to-the-banks-historical-links-to-the-slave-trade.

17 *Slavery and the Bank of England* exhibition, 2022.

18 Individual person entry for William Tooke Harwood (1767–1824), Legacies of British Slavery database, www.ucl.ac.uk/lbs/person/view/2146645249.

19 Zakia Sewell and her mother created a podcast about this illness and their relationship which was broadcast on BBC Radio 4 on 12 March 2020 called *My Amey and Me*, by Falling Tree Productions.

20 Ravi Ghosh, 'Zakia Sewell: Can Albion Ever Truly Belong to Someone Like Me?', *Elephant*, 26 April 2021, https://elephant.art/zakia-sewell-can-albion-ever-truly-belong-to-someone-like-me-26042021/.

21 Jonathan Spain, 2004, 'Dalling, Sir John, first baronet', *Oxford Dictionary of National Biography*, summarized online at individual person entry for Sir John Dalling (1731–98), Legacies of British Slavery database, https://www.ucl.ac.uk/lbs/person/view/2146649321.

22 'Copy of a letter from Major General Dalling, Governor of the Isle of Jamaica, to Lord George Germain, one of His Majesty's Principal Secretaries of State, received by His Majesty's sloop Alert, Captain Vasbon', *The Westminster Magazine*, 9 January 1781, p. 36.

23 The overseer was called William Burdett.

24 William Burdett, 1800, *Life and exploits of Mansong, commonly called Three-Finger'd Jack, the terror of Jamaica in the years 1780 and 1781* (London: A. Neil), pp. 16–46.

25 Siva Michael, 'After the Treaties: A Social, Economic and Demographic History of Maroon Society in Jamaica, 1739–1842', PhD thesis, Southampton University, 2018, pp. 109–10.

26 Having once held the positions of governor and land forces commander concurrently, Dalling was used to making autonomous decisions.

27 Robert J. Bennett, 2015, 'Collective Action When Needed: The Kingston Chamber of Commerce in Jamaica, 1778–85', *The Journal of Imperial and Commonwealth History*, 43(2), pp. 165–88, pp. 169–72.

28 A Country Gentleman, 1792, *A Country Gentleman's Reasons for Voting Against Mr. Wilberforce's Motion for a Bill to Prohibit the Importation of African Negroes into the Colonies* (London: J. Debrett).

29 Sir William Windham Dalling (1775–1864).

30 Norfolk Record Office, 2007, 'Notes on the Bicentenary of the Abolition of the Slave-Trade'.

31 Frank Meeres, 2007, 'Earsham Hall Built on Slavery', Norfolk Records Office. Note that the Legacies of British Slavery database makes clear that the hall itself is not funded by slavery.

32 Individual person entry for Sir William Windham Dalling (1775–1864), Legacies of British Slavery database, www.ucl.ac.uk/lbs/person/view/12672. See also 'Court Circular', *The Times*, 16 April 1831, p. 5.

33 Individual person entry for Sir William Windham Dalling, Legacies of British Slavery database.

34 Church of England, 'The Church and the Legacy of Slavery', 19 June 2020, www.churchofengland.org/news-and-media/news-and-statements/church-and-legacy-slavery.

35 Rachel Hall, 2023, 'Exhibition Lays Bare Church of England's Links to Slave Trade', *Guardian*, 31 January 2023.

36 Individual person entry for Rev. George Sandby (1769–1852), Legacies of British Slavery database, http://wwwdepts-live.ucl.ac.uk/lbs/person/view/45931; 'Jamaica Hanover 56A-H (Tryall Estate)', Legacies of British Slavery database, http://wwwdepts-live.ucl.ac.uk/lbs/claim/view/15039.

37 Ibid. Circumstantial evidence suggests he is the same man because in the claim details for Jamaica Hanover (Tryall Estate), https://www.ucl.ac.uk/lbs/claim/view/15039, it is noted that Oliver Leblanc acted as agent for both Sandby and Day for the collection of compensation, suggesting a relationship or local connection. With thanks to Dr Kieran Hazzard for this detail.

38 Norfolk Record Office, MEA 7/8, 660X9.

39 Individual person entry for Thomas Hoseason (1765–1835), Legacies of British Slavery database, www.ucl.ac.uk/lbs/person/view/1692359697.

40 Norfolk Records Office, Norfolk Heritage Centre Display.

41 Hoskins, 2015, p. 231 and p. 234.

42 Four slave-owners invested money in the Diss–Colchester line and junction. One of these men invested a further £3,420 in the Norfolk extension. Two other slave-owning investors donated to the

London–Norwich line, which linked the region to commercial trading centres. Another helped fund the Wells and Dereham railway's Norfolk route. He was a banker and trustee for many West Indies estates. These investments were by George Bowley Medley and Netlam Tory, listed as commercial legacies entries in the Legacies of British Slavery project, www.ucl.ac.uk/lbs/person/view/21518 and www.ucl.ac.uk/lbs/person/view/11953, and individual person entry for William Borradaile (1787–1844), Legacies of British Slavery database, www.ucl.ac.uk/lbs/person/view/27656. Individual person entry for Charles William Bigge (1809–74), Legacies of British Slavery database, www.ucl.ac.uk/lbs/person/view/18565; individual person entry for John Ross of Berbice (1782–1849), Legacies of British Slavery database, www.ucl.ac.uk/lbs/person/view/8694; individual person entry for William Matthew Coulthurst (1797–1877), Legacies of British Slavery database, www.ucl.ac.uk/lbs/person/view/46462.

43 Tom Williamson, 2000, 'Understanding Enclosure', *Landscapes*, 1(1), pp. 56–79, p. 56.

44 Roger J. P. Kain, John Chapman and Richard Oliver, 2004, *The Enclosure Maps of England and Wales, 1595–1918* (Cambridge: Cambridge University Press), pp. 3–5; and James Boyce, 2021, *Imperial Mud: The Fight for the Fens* (London: Bloomsbury), pp. 127–8.

45 Williamson, 2000, p. 59.

46 See www.fadensmapofnorfolk.co.uk/.

47 Williamson, 2000, pp. 56–79.

48 Boyce, 2021, pp. 127–8.

49 Thompson, 1982, p. 262.

50 Williamson, 2000, p. 72. In 2023, university researchers found that 62 per cent of gypsies or travellers have experienced a physical assault. See Nissa Finney, James Nazroo, Laia Becares, Dhami Kapadia and Natalie Schlomo (eds.), 2023, *Racism and Ethnic Equality in a Time of Crisis: Findings from the Evidence for Equality National Survey* (London: Policy Press).

51 Letter to Sir William Windham Dalling from the Duke of Norfolk's agent, 11 July 1812, Norfolk Records Office, MEA 7/22, 661Xi. The 1812 Act for Inclosing Lands in the Parishes of Earsham,

Ditchingham, and Hedenham, in the County of Norfolk, Norfolk Records Office, 1,814X2.

52 Ibid.

53 Ibid.

54 Letter from J. Bedingfeld to the Reverend Womack, June 1738, MC44/27a 500X1, Norfolk Records Office.

55 Public meeting notice: 'Earsham, Ditchingham and Hedenham Enclosure', Norfolk Records Office, MEA 7/21, 661X1, p. 24.

56 Letter from the Duke of Norfolk's agent to Sir William Windham Dalling, October 1812, Norfolk Records Office, MEA 3/588.

57 'An Act for Enclosing the Lands in the Parishes of Earsham, Ditchingham and Debenham. Copy of the Act of Parliament Passed 20th Day of March, 1812', https://api.parliament.uk/historic-hansard/index.html.

58 Ibid.

59 Ibid.

60 'Enclosure Maps from the late 1700s to the mid-1800s', Norfolk Record Office. File MEA 7/33, 661X2 – Printed Copy of Inclosure Act for Bungay and Mettingham.

61 'Case for the opinion of Mr. Shepherd, 1803', Norfolk Record Office, MEA 7/8, 66 oX9. Letters from Revd George Day and agreements to pay tithes, Norfolk Record Office, MEA 7/8, 660X9. Also see letters to Sir W. W. Dalling from Kingsbury, Margitson, Robert Meade and George Day, rector of Earsham concerning suit for tithes, Norfolk Record Office, MEA 3/593, 659X3.

62 Susanne Seymour, Stephen Daniels and Charles Watkins, 1998, 'Estate and Empire: Sir George Cornewall's Management of Moccas, Hertfordshire, and La Taste, Grenada, 1771–1819', *Journal of Historical Geography*, 24(3), pp. 313–51, p. 320.

63 Ibid., p. 330.

64 Williamson, 2000, p. 66.

65 Individual person page for Thomas Coke (1754–1842), Legacies of British Slavery database, www.ucl.ac.uk/lbs/person/view/1297234974.

66 Norfolk government record no. 50893.

67 Williamson, 2000, p. 72.

68 Print and coloured line engraving held in the National Trust collection at Felbrigg Hall, entitled 'Felbrigg Hall, Norfolk', by J. Hawkesworth.

69 W. S. Crowell, 1846, *The History and Antiquities of the County of Suffolk*, vol. 1 (Ipswich: W. S. Crowell), pp. 119–61.

70 Paul Muskett, 1984, 'The East Anglian Riots of 1822', *The Agricultural History Review*, 32(1), pp. 1–13, p. 3.

71 Ibid., pp. 5–7.

72 Ibid., p. 1.

73 Ibid., pp. 1–13, p. 9 and p. 10.

74 Richard C. Maguire, 2014, 'Presenting the History of Africans in Provincial Britain: Norfolk as a Case Study', *History* (London: John Wiley), p. 879.

75 Thomas Salmon, 1739, *Modern History . . .*, vol.3 (London: Bettesworth and Hitch).

76 Ibid.

77 Individual person page for Crispin Molineux (1730–92), Legacies of British Slavery database, www.ucl.ac.uk/lbs/person/view/2146645503.

78 Richard C. Maguire, 2021, *Africans in East Anglia, 1467–1833* (Woodbridge: Boydell Press).

79 Maguire, 2014, p. 836.

80 Maguire, 2014, pp. 827–33. See also Maguire, 2021.

81 Roger Deakin, 2014 [1999], *Waterlog: A Swimmer's Journey Through Britain* (London: Vintage); and Nick Hayes, 2020, *The Book of Trespass: Crossing the Lines That Divide Us* (London: Bloomsbury).

82 Corinne Fowler, 2022, 'Landscape and Empire: Colonial Contexts and Legacies', in *Radical Landscapes: Art, Identity and Activism* (Liverpool: Tate), pp. 44–52.

83 Individual person entry for Thomas Daniell (?–1806), Legacies of British Slavery database, www.ucl.ac.uk/lbs/person/view/2146643847. Thomas Daniell's son, Edward Thomas Daniell, was born in 1804 and died in 1842.

84 Edward Thomas Daniell (1804–42), *Back River, Norwich (View at Hellesdon)*, Oxford Grove Art, 2003; 'Daniell, Edward Thomas', *Oxford Dictionary of National Biography*, https://www.oxforddnb.com/.

85 James Watts, 2022, 'Land Reform, Henry Rider Haggard, and the Politics of Imperial Settlement, 1900–1920', *The Historical Journal*, 65, pp. 415–35, pp. 417–18.

86 Elleke Boehmer, 1998, *Empire Writing: An Anthology of Colonial Literature 1870–1918* (Oxford: Oxford University Press), p. 86.

87 Watts, 2022, pp. 417–18.

88 Henry Rider Haggard, 1905, *The Poor and the Land: Being a Report on the Salvation Army Colonies in the United States and at Hadleigh, England, with a Scheme of National Land Settlement and an Introduction* (London), pp. xxix–xxx, in Watts, 2022, pp. 417–19, p. 428.

89 Watts, 2022, pp. 417–19, p. 424.

90 Ibid.

8. The Bankers' Walk: Hampshire and Louisiana

1 Baring Archive, Northbrook MSS, A21. Not all of Repton's designs were followed by Sir Francis.

2 Rudolph Ackermann, *Stratton Park, the Seat of Mr. Thomas Baring*, c.1820,https://www.prints-online.com/new-images-august-2021/stratton-park-winchester-seat-sir-thomas-baring-23389048.html.

3 Alexander Baring, 1st Baron Ashburton (1774–1848).

4 This saying has been attributed to the Duc de Richelieu, but there is no reliable source to confirm this.

5 Laurence Brown, 2010, 'The Slavery Connections of Northington Grange', English Heritage, p. 59, historicengland.org.uk/images-books/publications/slavery-connections-northington-grange/slavery-connections-northington-grange/.

6 Clint Smith, 2021, 'The Whitney Plantation', in *How the Word Is Passed: A Reckoning With the History of Slavery in America* (New York: Little, Brown), p. 82.

7 Sarah Lentz, 2013, 'David Parish, Alexander Baring and the US Loan of 1813: The Role of Nationality and Patriotism in the Transatlantic Mercantile Community in Times of War', *London Journal of Canadian Studies*, 28(1), pp. 68–89, p. 79.

8 Brown, 2010, p. 53.

9 Alexander Baring to John William Hope Esquire, sent from Boston on 8 December 1795, Baring Archive, DEP85.3.1. Retrieved by my researcher Kate Bernstock.

10 These had recently been ceded to France by Spain. France was eager to sell, having then failed to suppress the revolution in former Saint-Domingue.

11 Ibrahima Seck, 2014, *Bouki fait Gombo: A History of the Slave Community of Habitation Haydel (Whitney Plantation), Louisiana, 1750–1860* (New Orleans: University of New Orleans Press), p. 75.

12 *The Louisiana Purchase*, Exhibition at the Baring Archive, London, https://baringarchive.org.uk/exhibition/the-louisiana-purchase/.

13 Brown, 2010, p. 61.

14 Sven Beckert, 2015, *Empire of Cotton: A New History of Global Capitalism* (London: Vintage), p. 106.

15 Vincent Nolte, 1934, *The Memoirs of Vincent Nolte: Reminiscences in the Period of Anthony Adverse or Fifty Years in Both Hemispheres*, translated by Burton Rascoe (New York: G. H. Watt).

16 Letters to Barings from Thomas Baring, written on tours of business in the USA and Europe, 7, 27 and 31 November 1828, Baring Archive, 1.20.3. With thanks to Kate Bernstock who researched this archive for the book.

17 Beckert, 2015, p. 206; and Brown, 2010, p. 61.

18 Ibid., p. 60.

19 Account books of Francis Baring, Baring Archive, DEP193.40. Retrieved and interpreted by Kate Bernstock.

20 Slow Food in the UK, 'Traditionally Grown Hampshire Watercress', https://www.slowfood.org.uk/ark-product/traditionally-grown-hampshire-watercress-nasturtium-officianale/.

21 Smith, 2021, pp. 93–5.

22 Seck, 2014, p. 17 and p. 18.

23 Ibid., p. 29, p. 32, p. 59 and p. 60.

24 The plantation was then known as Heydel plantation.

25 Seck, 2014, pp. 66–70.

26 This temple design was a legacy of Henry Drummond, its previous owner, who wanted to outdo the Greek portico at East Stratton. See Brown, 2010, p. 53.

27 Baring's purchase of the Grange meant it had been consecutively owned by three families with transatlantic slavery connections: the Henleys, the Drummonds and the Barings. At the turn of the nineteenth century, the Grange had also been rented by James Lowther, the owner of a Barbadian plantation, whose story features in Chapter 2 of this book. See Brown, 2010, p. 22. 'Baring, Alexander (1773–1848), of the Grange, near Alresford, Hants, and 82 Piccadilly, Mdx', The History of Parliament, https://www.historyofparliamentonline.org/volume/1820-1832/member/baring-alexander-1773-1848. Between 1826 and 1831 he was MP for Callington and then, briefly, for Thetford, followed by Essex North, between 1832 and 1835.

28 Brown, 2010, p. 14.

29 Ibid., p. 15 and p. 16.

30 Ibid., p. 53.

31 House correspondence, Baring Archive, HC.5.5.1, HC5.5.5.1.27, HC5.5.5.1.30, HC5.5.5.1.32-7 and 201795.1. Retrieved and interpreted by my researcher Kate Bernstock.

32 William Cobbett, [1830], *Rural Rides in the Southern, Western and Eastern Counties of England*, vol. 1 (London: Dent Everyman Library), p. 99.

33 Ibid., p. 104.

34 Lost Heritage, 'Stratton Park', http://www.lostheritage.org.uk/houses/lh_hampshire_strattonpark.html.

35 Cobbett, 1830, p. 52.

36 Corinne Fowler, 2020, *Green Unpleasant Land: Creative Responses to Rural England's Colonial Connections* (Leeds: Peepal Tree Press), p. 361.

37 Trowbridge H. Ford, 1986, 'The Constitutional Association: Private Prosecutions in Reaction to Peterloo', *Journal of Legal History*, 293, pp. 293–314.

38 William Cobbett, 1822, 'To Sir Thomas Baring', *Cobbett's Weekly Register*, 21 September 1822.

39 William Cobbett, 1820, 'Cobbett's Letter to Alexander Baring', in *Cobbett's Political Register*, vols. 68–70, 2C2.

40 Hampshire History, 2020, 'The Swing Riots in Hampshire', https://www.hampshire-history.com/the-swing-riots/.

41 Ibid.

42 'Baring, Alexander (1773–1848), of the Grange, near Alresford, Hants, and 82 Piccadilly, Mdx'.

43 Brown, 2010, p. 61.

44 Daniel Deluna, 'The Economics of Cotton', Santa Ana Community College, California, https://courses.lumenlearning.com/sacushistory1/chapter/the-economics-of-cotton/.

45 Seck, 2014, pp. 98–102.

46 Sir Alexander Baring retired on 31 December 1830.

47 Solomon Northup, 2013 [1853], *Twelve Years a Slave* (London: Hesperus Press), p. 13.

48 Seck, 2014, p. 29.

49 Northup, 2013, p.39.

50 Ibid., p. 47 and p. 48.

51 'St John the Evangelist, Northington. A Visitor's Guide', leaflet published in 2020, available from the church, p. 8.

52 This memorial was transferred from the original church building.

53 Information about the church building is from 'St John the Evangelist, Northington. A Visitor's Guide'.

54 Nicholas Denbow, 2013, 'Alresford Articles', *Alresford Historical and Literary Society Journal*, vol. 2.

55 Smith, 2021, p. 126.

56 Seck, 2014, p.104; and Smith, 2021, p. 80.

57 Ibid., pp. 77–80.

58 Seck, 2014, p. 99.

59 Ibid., p. 11 and p. 12.

60 Ibid., p. 99 and p. 100.

61 Lentz, 'David Parish, Alexander Baring and the US Loan of 1813', pp. 68–89.

62 Brown, 2010, p. 59.

63 Beckert, 2015, pp. 212–14.

64 Ibid., p. 215.

65 Letter from Trinidad, 2 November 1824, Baring Archive, HC5.6.1335. Retrieved by my researcher Kate Bernstock.

66 Alexander Baring, parliamentary speech on immediate abolition, quoted in Brown, 2010, p. 59.

67 'Baring, Alexander (1773–1848), of the Grange, near Alresford, Hants, and 82 Piccadilly, Mdx'.

68 Parliamentary debate on 15 May 1823. See ibid.

69 Brown, 2010, p. 60.

70 Compensation claims found at 'St Kitts 206 (Priddies Morne (?))', Legacies of British Slavery database, www.ucl.ac.uk/lbs/claim/view/25677; and 'St Kitts 336 (Spooners)', Legacies of British Slavery database, www.ucl.ac.uk/lbs/claim/view/23754.

71 Individual person entry for Francis Baring (1800–1868), Legacies of British Slavery database, www.ucl.ac.uk/lbs/person/view/1299741814.

72 Individual person entry for Alexander Baring (1774–1848), Legacies of British Slavery database, www.ucl.ac.uk/lbs/person/view/-1411131717.

73 Land register of St Croix, 1865–1966, The Danish West Indies, Rigsarkivet, https://cs.rigsarkivet.dk/picture/view-values/158537?selectedTab=11&locale=en.

74 Letters from Charles Baring, from Runcombe, North Carolina, 13 July 1834, Baring Archive, HC1.24.1. Retrieved by my researcher Kate Bernstock.

75 Seck, 2014, p. 120.

76 Ibid., pp. 112–15.

77 Ibid., pp. 116–20.

78 Harriet Mary Baring (1805–57) and Bingham Baring (1799–1864).

79 David Olusoga, 2016, *Black and British: A Forgotten History* (London: Macmillan), p. 24.

80 Brown, 2010, p. 11 and p. 12.

81 Jane Geddes, 1983, 'The Grange, Northington', *Architectural History*, 26, pp. 35–48, p. 43.

82 William Cobbett, cited in 'East Stratton. History of the Church and Chapel', https://www.eaststratton.com/history-of-the-church.

83 Ibid.

9. The Labourers' Walk: Tolpuddle and British Penal Colonies

1 Mary Wills with Madge Dresser, 2020, 'The Transatlantic Slave Economy and England's Built Environment: A Research Audit Commissioned by Historic England', https://historicengland.org.uk/research/results/reports/8203/TheTransatlanticSlaveEconomyand England'sBuiltEnvironment_AResearchAudit#:~:text=Put%20 simply%2C%20the%20report%20considers,economy%20and%20 England%27s%20built%20environment.

2 David Robert Michel, who had Jamaican plantations, lived in Dewlish. See individual person entry for David Robert Michel (1735–1805), Legacies of British Slavery, www.ucl.ac.uk/lbs/person/view/21466 32303. Fonthill Abbey was a gigantic Gothic fortress built by the Jamaican plantation-owning Beckford dynasty. Julines Beckford owned 8,197 acres of Jamaica. In Dorset he created pleasure grounds at Iwerne Stepleton. See Wills with Dresser, 2020, p. 73. Kingston Lacy belonged to the husband of Frances Woodley, an heiress to Leeward Island plantations, where her father was governor. See individual person entry for William John Bankes (1786–1855), Legacies of British Slavery, www.ucl.ac.uk/lbs/person/view/2146645443. Merley House was built by a slave-owner in St Kitts. See individual person entry for Ralph Willett (1719–95), Legacies of British Slavery, www.ucl.ac.uk/lbs/person/view/2146639903.

3 David W. Galenson, 1984, 'The Rise and Fall of Indentured Servitude in the Americas: An Economic Analysis', *The Journal of Economic History*, 44(1), pp. 1–26, p. 4.

4 Louisa Adjoa Parker, 2007, *Dorset's Hidden Histories: Beginning to Explore Four Hundred Years of the Presence of Black People in Dorset* (Ferndown: Deed Publishers).

5 Eric L. Jones, 2018, *Landed Estates and Rural Inequality in English History: From the Mid-Seventeenth Century to the Present* (London: Palgrave), p. 51; Official List Entry for Charborough Park, Historic England, https://historicengland.org.uk/listing/the-list/list-entry/1000713?section=official-list-entry.

6 Individual person entry for John Samuel Wanley Sawbridge Erle-Drax (1800–1887), Legacies of British Slavery, www.ucl.ac.uk/lbs/person/view/2246.

7 Ibid. See also Official List Entry for Charborough Park, Historic England.

8 United Nations declaration on Crimes Against Humanity, 2019, Paragraph 13.

9 Joshua Nevett, 'Richard Drax: Jamaica Eyes Slavery Reparations from Tory MP', *BBC News*, 30 November 2022.

10 Paul Lashmar, 2021, 'Protesters Demand Wealthy MP Pays Up for Family's Slave Trade Past', *Observer*, 18 July 2021, https://www.theguardian.com/world/2021/jul/18/protesters-demand-wealthy-mp-pays-up-for-familys-slave-trade-past.

11 This is discussed in a short news feature by Channel 4, available at: www.channel4.com/news/calls-for-drax-hall-to-be-opened-to-public-as-barbados-becomes-a-republic.

12 Hilary McD. Beckles and Andrew Downes, 1987, 'The Economics of Transition to the Black Labor System in Barbados, 1630–1680', *The Journal of Interdisciplinary History*, 18(2), pp. 225–47, p. 226.

13 James Drax (1609–62).

14 Peter Thompson, 2009, 'Henry Drax's Instructions on the Management of a Seventeenth-Century Barbadian Sugar Plantation', *The William and Mary Quarterly*, 66(3), pp. 565–604, p. 573; and Richard B. Sheridan, 1989, 'Changing Sugar Technology and the Labour Nexus in the British Caribbean, 1750–1900', *Nieuwe West-Indische Gids / New West Indian Guide*, 63(1), pp. 59–93, p. 61.

15 Thompson, 2009, p. 572.

16 Ibid., pp. 568–9.

17 Hilary Beckles, 1985, 'Plantation Production and White "Proto-Slavery": White Indentured Servants and the Colonisation of the

English West Indies, 1624–1645', *The Americas*, 41(3), pp. 21–45, pp. 25–9.

18 This claim was made by fellow plantation-owner Richard Ligon in his 1647 account called *A True and Exact History of the Island of Barbadoes*.

19 David W. Galenson, 1984, 'The Rise and Fall of Indentured Servitude in the Americas: An Economic Analysis', *The Journal of Economic History*, 44(1), pp. 1–26, p. 9 and p. 10.

20 Beckles and Downes, 1987, p. 226.

21 Galenson, 1984, p. 11.

22 Beckles, 1985, p. 33; Beckles and Downes, 1987, p. 243.

23 Beckles, 1985, p. 23.

24 Dorset History Centre, DC-LR/M/9/17/.

25 Beckles and Downes, 1987, p. 227 and p. 232; Beckles, 1985, pp. 21–45, pp. 30–32.

26 Aubrey Gwynn, 1930, 'Indentured Servants and Negro Slaves in Barbados (1642–1650)', *An Irish Quarterly Review*, 19(74), pp. 279–94, p. 284 and p. 285.

27 Hilary McD. Beckles, 1990, 'A "riotous and unruly lot": Irish Indentured Servants and Freemen in the English West Indies, 1644–1713', *The William and Mary Quarterly*, 47(4), pp. 503–22, p. 504; and 'Governor Sir Jonathan Atkins to the Lords of Trade and Plantations. Barbadoes', *The Calendar of State Papers, Colonial: North America and the West Indies 1574–1739*, vol. 10, 26 March 1680.

28 Beckles and Downes, 1987, p. 230.

29 Beckles, 1985, p. 33 and p. 34; Beckles and Downes, 1987, p. 240.

30 Jerome S. Handler and Matthew C. Reilly, 2017, 'Contesting "White Slavery" in the Caribbean: Enslaved Africans and European Indentured Servants in Seventeenth-Century Barbados', *New West Indian Guide* 91(1/2), pp. 30–55, pp. 40–44.

31 Gwynn, 1930, p. 289.

32 Handler and Reilly, 2017, pp. 34–41.

33 Ibid.

34 Beckles and Downes, 1987, p. 246.

35 Journal of the Council of Barbados, 1677, *The Calendar of State Papers, Colonial: North America and the West Indies 1574–1739*, vol. 10, 15 March 1677.

36 Thompson, 2009, p. 577.

37 Ibid., p. 570 and p. 577.

38 Extracts from letters to the Royal African Company from their factors in Barbados, *The Calendar of State Papers, Colonial: North America and the West Indies 1574–1739*, vol. 11, 29 November 1681.

39 Journal of Lords of Trade and Plantations, *The Calendar of State Papers, Colonial, North America and the West Indies 1574–1739*, vol. 10, 10 June 1680.

40 Minutes of the Council of Barbados, 1683, *The Calendar of State Papers, Colonial: North America and the West Indies 1574–1739*, vol. 11, 7 November 1683; Thompson, 2009, p. 569.

41 Henry Drax, 1679, 'Instructions for the Management of a Plantation in Barbadoes and for the Treatment of Negroes'.

42 Thompson, 2009, p. 577.

43 Ibid., p. 578.

44 Beckles and Downes, 1987, p. 228.

45 Sheridan, 1989, p. 60 and p. 61.

46 Hilary McD. Beckles, 1998, 'Creolisation in Action: The Slave Labour Élite and Anti-Slavery in Barbados', *Caribbean Quarterly*, 44(1/2), pp. 108–28, p. 108 and p. 115.

47 Gertrude J. Fraser, 1993, 'Review of *Natural Rebels: A Social History of Enslaved Black Women in Barbados* by Hilary McD Beckles', *New West Indian Guide*, 67, pp. 302–5, p. 303 and p. 304.

48 The merchant was called Richard Hammett.

49 Tomas Malloy, 2021, 'Staff "Devastated" as Pub Targeted by Vandals with "BLM" and "Slaver" Graffiti', SomersetLive, 16 April 2021, www.somersetlive.co.uk/news/local-news/staff-devastated-pub-targeted-vandals-5305952.

50 Andrew Norman, 2008, *The Story of George Loveless and the Tolpuddle Martyrs* (Tiverton: Halsgrove), p. 84 and p. 85.

51 *Caledonian Mercury*, 29 March 1834. Tolpuddle Museum has a detailed list of weekly costs and rations.

52 Individual person entry for John Samuel Wanley Ellis Sawbridge-Erle-Drax, Legacies of British Slavery; Tom Scriven, 2016, 'The Dorchester Labourers and Swing's Aftermath in Dorset, 1830–8', *History Workshop Journal*, 82, pp. 3–23, p.3.

53 Norman, 2008, p. 38.

54 George Loveless, 2020 [1837], *Victims of Whiggery* (Dorchester: Tolpuddle Museum), p. 11.

55 Ibid., p. 20.

56 Norman, 2008, p. 38. The home secretary was then Lord Melbourne, the future prime minister who pursued the Opium Wars.

57 Tolpuddle Martyrs Museum, 'The Story', https://www.tolpuddlemartyrs.org.uk/story.

58 The testimony of John Lock and James Brine appears in *The Annals of Crime and New Newgate Calendar*, issues 1–53, pp. 289–90.

59 The Chartists, 'Tolpuddle Martyrs: The Trial', http://thechartists.org/assets/tolpuddle-martyrs-3-the-trial.pdf.

60 Ralph Dickson, 1986, 'The Tolpuddle Martyrs: Guilty or Not Guilty?', *The Journal of Legal History*, 7(2), pp. 178–87, p. 179.

61 'Moreton House', British History Online, https://www.british-history.ac.uk/rchme/dorset/vol2/pp173-178; individual person entry for Phillis Frampton formerly Wollaston (née Byam) (?–1829), Legacies of British Slavery, www.ucl.ac.uk/lbs/person/view/2146665521/#addresses.

62 Royal Museums Greenwich, 'Prison Ship York in Portsmouth Harbour', www.rmg.co.uk/collections/objects/rmgc-object-136960. The *Surry* was a copper-bottomed prison ship designed for tropical waters which had originally served as a West Indiaman vessel which made regular voyages to Jamaica.

63 Loveless, 2020, p. 32.

64 Ibid., pp. 32–4.

65 Governor George Arthur.

66 Loveless, 2020, p. 23.

67 Ibid., p. 41 and p. 43.

68 Kirsty Reid, 2008, 'The Horrors of Convict Life', *Cultural and Social History*, 5(4), pp. 481–95, pp. 480–86.

69 Norman, 2008, p. 138.

70 Ibid., p. 137.

71 Ibid., p. 140.

72 Reid, 2008, pp. 480–86.

73 Tolpuddle Martyrs Museum, 'Homecoming', https://www.tolpud dlemartyrs.org.uk/story/homecoming.

74 Norman, 2008, p.140.

75 Edward John Eyre, 1845 [1811] *Journals of Expeditions of Discovery into Central Australia, and Overland from Adelaide to King George's Sound, in the Years 1840–1* (Cambridge: Cambridge University Press), p. v.

76 Ian Henderson, 2014, 'Planetary Lives: Edward Warrulan, Edward John Eyre, and Queen Victoria', *English Studies in Africa*, 57(1), pp. 66–80, p. 71.

77 Julie Evans, 2002, 'Re-reading Edward Eyre: Race, Resistance and Repression in Australia and the Caribbean', *Australian Historical Studies*, 33(118), pp. 175–98, pp. 180–91.

78 Priyamvada Gopal, 2020 [2019], *Insurgent Empire: Anticolonial Resistance and British Dissent* (London: Verso), pp. 521–42.

79 Ibid., p. 62, p. 93 and p. 94.

80 Ibid., pp. 86–8 and pp. 101–4.

81 Lashmar, 2021. The marchers were also conscious that Drax received considerable wealth from the profits of slavery, owning more than 22 square miles of Dorset and 125 properties.

82 Stephen C. Russell, 2022, ' "Slavery Dies Hard": A Radical Perspective on the Morant Bay Rebellion in Jamaica', *Slavery and Abolition*, 43(1), pp. 185–204, p. 189.

83 Jason Allen-Paisant, 2019, 'Raising the Ghosts of Justice: Staging Time and the Memory of Empire in the Trial of Governor Eyre', *Cultural Dynamics*, 31(3), pp. 245–59, p. 248, p. 249 and p. 251.

10. *The Copper Walk:*
Cornwall, West Africa and the Americas

1 Nuala Zahedieh, 2013, 'Colonies, Copper, and the Market for Inventive Activity in England and Wales, 1680 to 1730', *Economic History Review*, 66(3), pp. 805–25, p. 805 and p. 801; and Nuala Zahedieh, 2021, 'Eric Williams and William Forbes: Copper, Colonial Markets, and Commercial Capitalism', *Economic History Review*, 74(3), pp. 784–808, p. 783 and p. 785.

2 Daniel Cunha, 2020, 'Coppering the Industrial Revolution. History, Materiality and Culture in the Making of an Ecological Regime', *Journal of World-Systems Research*, 26(1), pp. 40–69, p. 59 and p. 62.

3 C. C. James, [n.d.], *A History of the Parish of Gwennap in Cornwall* (Penzance: Burford), p. 55.

4 'John Wesley and Methodism', *Cornwall Guide*, https://www.corn walls.co.uk/history/people/john_wesley.htm.

5 Royal Institution of Cornwall, 1990, *A History of Gwennap Pit and Indian Queens Pit and St. Newlyn East Pit* (St Columb: Harvenna Books), p. 1 and p. 2.

6 D. B. Barton, 1968, *A History of Copper Mining in Cornwall and Devon* (Truro: D. Bradford Barton), p .51 and p. 52. In 1818, the nearby mine of Ting Tang employed 180 people, and Wheal Unity and Poldice had 1,200 people working at them.

7 Veronica Chesher and the Trevithick Society, 1978, *Industrial Housing in the Tin and Copper Mining Areas of Cornwall in the Later 18th and 19th Centuries* (Penzance: Headland Printers), pp. 3–11.

8 National Churches Trust, 'St Wenappa', https://www.nationalchur chestrust.org/church/st-wenappa-gwennap.

9 Bernard Deacon, 2021, *The Real World of Poldark: Cornwall 1783–1820* (Kindle e-book), p. 5.

10 Barton, 1968, pp. 11–12, pp. 25–6 and p. 94.

11 Ibid., p. 49.

12 The traveller was Reinhold Angerstein, who visited Wales in the 1750s, quoted in Chris Evans, 2010, *Slave Wales: The Welsh and Atlantic Slavery 1660–1850* (Cardiff: University of Wales Press), pp. 34–7.

13 Ibid. Evans points out that in reality less than half of his goods were exported for this purpose, despite this claim.

14 Collectively, these mines were known as Metal Works before becoming United Mines.

15 William George Maton, 1794 and 1796, *Observations relative chiefly to the natural history, picturesque scenery, and antiquities, of the western counties of England, made in the years 1794 and 1796. Illustrated by a mineralogical map, and sixteen views in aquantinta by Alken*, vol. 1 (London: J. Easton), p. 243.

16 Deacon, 2021, pp. 10–17.

17 Cunha, 2020, p. 54.

18 Deacon, 2021, p. 16.

19 Zahedieh, 'Eric Williams and William Forbes', pp. 784–808.

20 Deacon, 2021, p. 18.

21 Zahedieh, 2021, p. 794 and p. 797.

22 Barton, 1968, pp. 61–5 and p. 66; Deacon, 2021, p. 14.

23 From 1765 onwards.

24 Barton, 1968, pp. 61–5 and p. 66; Deacon, 2021, p. 14.

25 William Beckford, quoted in ibid., p. 9.

26 Letter from William Beckford to Lady Craven, cited in Amy Frost, 2018, 'The Beckford Era', in Caroline Dakers (ed.), *Fonthill Recovered: A Cultural History*, pp. 59–94, p. 74.

27 Chesher and the Trevithick Society, 1978, p. 12.

28 Deacon, 2021, p. 48.

29 Charles Dickens, 1882, 'At Gwennap Pit', *All The Year Around*, 29(707), pp. 415–17.

30 Evans, 2010, pp. 34–7.

31 Zahedieh, 2013, pp. 808–10.

32 Ibid., p. 809 and p. 811.

33 Cunha, 2020, p. 45; and Zahedieh, 2021, p. 791.

34 Ibid. By 1770 (by which time Welsh copper held sway over production and export) British plantations alone needed some 32,000 boiling cauldrons, the largest of which held 180 gallons.

35 Zahedieh, 2013, p. 808.

36 Peter M. Solar and Klas Ronnback, 2015, 'Copper Sheathing and the British Slave Trade', *Economic History Review*, 68(3), pp. 806–29; and Cunha, 2020, p. 47.

37 Solar and Ronnback, 2015; and Cunha, 2020, p. 47.

38 Thomas Williams, 1800 testimony for the *Report from the committee appointed to enquire into the state of the copper mines, and copper trade, of this kingdom* (London: House of Commons).

39 Solar and Ronnback, 2015, p. 807.

40 Ibid., p. 814 and p. 817.

41 Ibid., p. 822 and p. 824.

42 Samuel Smiles, 1865, *Lives of Boulton and Watt* (London: John Murray).

43 Stephen Mullen, 2020a, 'The Rise of James Watt: Enlightenment, Commerce, and Industry in a British Atlantic Merchant City, 1736–74', in Malcolm Dick and Caroline Archer-Parré, (eds.), 2020, *James Watt 1736–1819: Culture, Innovation and Enlightenment* (Liverpool: Liverpool University Press), p. 43.

44 Eric Williams, quoted in Joseph E. Inikori and Stanley L. Engerman (eds.), 1992, *The Atlantic Slave-Trade: Effects on Economies, Societies and Peoples in Africa, the Americas, and Europe* (Durham, NC: Duke University Press), p. 248, and alluded to by Stephen Mullen in his 2020b blog, 'James Watt and Slavery in Scotland', History Workshop, https://www.historyworkshop.org.uk/slavery/james-watt-and-slavery-in-scotland/.

45 Mullen, 2020a, p. 58.

46 Peter M. Jones, 2020, 'James Watt and the Steam Engine: A Calvinist Path to Enlightenment and Creativity', in Dick and Archer-Parré, 2020, pp. 11–38, p. 31.

47 Mullen, 2020a, p. 43 and p. 44; and the inventory is archived at: http://calmview.birmingham.gov.uk/CalmView/app_themes/customer/images/bah-source-Slavery%20in%20Archives%20of%20Soho.pdf.

48 Mullen, 2020b.

49 Mullen, 2020a, p. 55.

50 Smiles, 1865, p. 118.

51 'Patents for Steam Engines' MS3147/2/25/6, 7; 'List of Patents', MS3147/2/25/8; and 'Observations on Specifications' MS3147/2/25/6, 7; all at Wolfson Archives, Birmingham Central Library.

52 Barton, 1968, pp. 28–31.

53 Zahedieh, 2021, p. 795.

54 James, [n.d.], p. 144.

55 Barton, 1968, p. 34.

56 Ibid., pp. 34–40.

57 George Selgin and John L. Turner, 2011, 'Strong Steam, Weak Patents, or the Myth of Watt's Innovation-Blocking Monopoly Exploded', *Journal of Law and Economics*, 54(4), p. 841.

58 Barton, 1968, p. 33.

59 Solar and Ronnback, 2015, p. 812.

60 Deacon, 2021, p. 7.

61 Smiles, 1865, p. 262.

62 'Specifications of patents which may serve as examples', MS3147/2/25/6,7, Wolfson Archive Centre, Birmingham Central Library.

63 Aaron Graham, 2020, 'Patents and Invention in Jamaica and the British Atlantic Before 1857', *Economic History Review*, 73(4), pp. 940–63, p. 940.

64 Mullen, 2020a, p. 59.

65 David Small, 2021, 'Stationary Sugar Plantations in the Caribbean: Nevis 1816–1846', p. 7, https://seis.bristol.ac.uk/~emceee/steam.pdf.

66 Charlotte Goudge, 2019, 'Man vs. Machine: Betty's Hope and the Industrialisation of 19th-Century Caribbean Factories', *Industrial Archaeology Review*, 41(1), pp. 45–51, p. 48.

67 'An Abstract for an Act', MS3147/2/36/1-4, Wolfson Archive Centre, Birmingham Central Library.

68 Letter from Boulton to James Rumsey, 14 August 1788, reproduced in Jennifer Tann (ed.), *The Selected Papers of Boulton and Watt*, vol. 1 (London: Diploma Press), p. 97.

69 Jennifer Tann and Christine MacLeod, 2016, 'Empiricism Afloat – Testing Steamboat Efficiency: Boulton Watt & Co. 1804–1830', *The International Journal for the History of Engineering and Technology*, 86(2), pp. 228–43, p. 232.

70 Letter from Robert Fulton (Paris) to Boulton and Watt, 1 September 1803; letter from Fulton to Boulton Watt & Co., 13 July 1804; and letter from Fulton to Watt, 4 January 1812, MS 3147/3/496; Wolfson Archive Centre, Birmingham Central Library.

71 Ibrahima Seck, 2014, *Bouki Fait Gombo: A History of the Slave Community of Habitation Haydel (Whitney Plantation), Louisiana, 1750–1860* (New Orleans: University of New Orleans Press), p. 75.

72 Mullen, 2020a, p. 59; and Mullen, 2020b.

73 Mullen, 2020a, p. 39. The three men were Mungo Nutter Campbell, James Ewing and William Smith.

74 James, [n.d.], p. 143.

75 Charlotte MacKenzie, 2019, *Merchants and Smugglers in Eighteeenth-Century Cornwall* (Truro: Cornwall History), p. 109 and p. 114.

76 Chris Evans, 2013, 'Brazilian Gold, Cuban Copper and the Final Frontier of British Anti-Slavery', *Slavery and Abolition*, 34(1), pp. 118–34, p. 121.

77 Chris Evans, 2014, 'El Cobre: Cuban Ore and the Globalization of Swansea Copper, 1830–70', *Welsh History Review*, 27(1), pp. 112–31, p. 116.

78 Ibid., p. 117.

79 Ibid., p. 118.

80 Ibid., p. 120.

81 Ibid., pp. 119–27.

82 Evans, 2013, pp. 118–34.

83 Evans, 2014, p.124.

84 Evans, 2013.

85 Initially horse-drawn, the railway ran from the village of St Day and transported ore to Portreath port, on the west coast. Deacon, 2021, p. 25.

86 The Fox family also had their issues with Soho Manufactory; the mining investors Edward and Robert W. Fox wrote to Boulton and Watt in 1796, asking them to reduce the premium that they paid for machines in Polgooth and Hewas Mines.

87 Chesher and the Trevithick Society, 1978, p.11.

88 Cunha, 2020, p. 59 and p. 62.

Conclusion: Facing Our Colonial Past

1 George Rudé, 1964, *The Crowd in History: A Study of Popular Distur-bances in France and England, 1730-1748* (New York: John Wiley), p. 36.

2 Michael D. Sanders and Elizabeth M. Graham, 2021, ' "Black and white and every wrong colour": The Medical History of Jane Austen and the Possibility of Systemic Lupus Erythematosus', *Lupus* 30(4), pp. 549–53, p. 553.

3 Edward W. Said, 1993, 'Jane Austen and Empire', in *Culture and Imperialism* (London: Vintage).

4 Corinne Fowler, 2017, 'Revisiting Mansfield Park: The Critical and Literary Legacies of Edward W. Said's Essay, "Jane Austen and Empire" in *Culture and Imperialism* (1993)', *The Cambridge Journal of Postcolonial Literary Enquiry*, 4(3), pp. 362–81.

5 Devoney Looser, 2021, 'Breaking the Silence: Exploring the Austen Family's Complex Entanglements With Slavery', *The Times Literary Supplement*, 21 May 2021.

6 Ibid. See also individual person entry for James Langford Nibbs, Snr (1738–95), Legacies of British Slavery database, www.ucl.ac.uk/lbs/person/view/2146639585.

7 Margaret Doody, 2015, *Jane Austen's Place Names: Riddles, Persons, Places* (Chicago: Chicago University Press), p. 307.

8 Looser, 2021.

9 Ibid.

10 Ibid.

11 John Agard, 2006, *We Brits* (Tarset: Bloodaxe), p. 45.

12 See especially Craig Simpson, 'Jane Austen's Tea Drinking Will Face "Historical Interrogation" Over Slavery Links', *Telegraph*, 18 April 2021; and Nick Ferrari's show on LBC radio, 19 April 2021.

13 Claire Fox on Twitter, 19 April 2021.

14 Doody, 2016.

15 Fowler, 2017; and Doody, 2016.

16 Paula Byrne, 2014, *Belle: The True Story of Dido Belle* (London: William Collins).

17 Martin Luther King Jr, 2012, *A Gift of Love: Sermons from* Strength to
    Love *and Other Preachings* (London: Penguin).

18 Martin Luther King Jr, 2012, 'A Tough Mind and a Tender Heart', in
    ibid., p. 4 and p. 5.

Acknowledgements

Books are a collective effort. My agent at Madeleine Milburn, Emma Bal, offers pure quality and I'm grateful for her encouragement, experience and vision. Kathy Belden (Scribner) and Tom Penn (Penguin Allen Lane) are the brilliant editors of this book, providing astute and patient guidance from beginning to end. I can't thank them enough. Thanks are also due to the fine team at Scribner, especially Rebekah Jett and Madison Thân, the publisher Nan Graham, managing editor Annie Craig, art director Jaya Miceli, publicist Georgia Brainard, the marketer Ashley Gilliam, and Mark LaFlaur, the production editor.

I dedicated this book to the ten inspirational walking companions because it would be nothing without them. With openness and good humour, they shared their stories and reflected on the historical landscapes that we hiked through, and it hardly rained at all.

Thanks to the eagle-eyed Kieran Hazzard for fact-checking and to Professor Alan Lester for reading through the manuscript. Emma Ranston-Young showed exceptional dedication and persistence as she researched Graham Campbell's elusive Jamaican family records, for chapter one. Elisabeth Grass researched newspaper archives at Blackburn Library and Mary Painter sent me a comprehensive list of other relevant material on local cotton history for chapter four. Becky Wragg-Sykes investigated documents held at Meirionnydd Record Office, where the archivist Elaine Roberts kindly advised about further relevant papers in relation to chapter five. Edward Peake generously shared his knowledge about Sezincote Manor while Elisabeth Grass examined the Bodleian library's Papers Relating to the Cockerell (later Rushout) and Grieve Families in Oxford for chapter six. Kate Bernstock explored enclosure records and other papers at the Norfolk Records Office in Norwich, also conducting database searches for chapter seven. She also investigated and advised on the Baring Archive in London for chapter eight. Thanks, too, to archivists at Birmingham Library, where I looked at papers relating to the Soho Manufactory while researching chapter ten. I also received formative advice about this book from Steve Baron, Jeff Cowton, Christopher Donaldson, Katie Donington, Marian Gwyn, Felicity James, Miranda Kaufmann, Alan Lester, Raj Pal, Chris Powici, Tony Russell and Phil Shaw. An additional thank you to my events manager, Binny Sabharwal, for keeping me on track.

I have learned a lot from audience members, social media users, letter writers and emailers of all ages, heritages and persuasions. Most are keen to know more about British colonial history, others chide me for researching the topic at all. This book responds to challenges from all directions and is intended as an antidote to divisive forms of public debate. Meanwhile, to those colleagues, family and close friends who help me to survive Britain's culture wars: you know who you are and I'm there for you too.

Index

Page references in *italics* indicate images.